THE
ALPINE JOURNAL

1989/90

1. *Everest – Kangshung face 1988. Paul Teare climbing fixed ropes on the lower buttress.* (p 1)

THE
ALPINE JOURNAL
1989/90

Incorporating the Journal of the Ladies' Alpine Club & Alpine
Climbing

A record of mountain adventure and scientific observation

Volume 94 No 338

Edited by Ernst Sondheimer

Assistant Editors:
Johanna Merz, A V Saunders and Geoffrey Templeman
assisted by Marian Elmes

FREDERICK MULLER
in association with
The Alpine Club, London

IN ASSOCIATION WITH THE ALPINE CLUB

Volume 94 No 338
THE ALPINE JOURNAL 1989/90

Address all editorial communications to the Hon Editor direct at:
51 Cholmeley Crescent
London N6 5EX

Address all sales and distribution communications to
Mike Wicks
Century Hutchinson
Brookmount House
62–65 Chandos Place
London WC2N 4NW

Back numbers:
apply to the Alpine Club or, for 1969 to date, to
Cordee, 3a De Montfort Street, Leicester LE1 7HD

First published in 1989 by Frederick Muller in association with the Alpine Club
Frederick Muller is an imprint of Century Hutchinson Ltd,
 Brookmount House, 62–65 Chandos Place, London WC2N 4NW

Century Hutchinson Publishing Group (Australia) Pty Ltd
89–91 Albion Street, Surry Hills, NSW 2010, Australia

Century Hutchinson Group (NZ) Ltd
PO Box 40–086, 32–34 View Road, Glenfield, Auckland 10

Century Hutchinson (SA) Pty Ltd
PO Box 337, Bergvlei 2012, South Africa

The Alpine Club, 74 South Audley Street, London W1Y 5FF

Photoset by Deltatype Limited, Ellesmere Port

Printed and bound in Great Britain by
Butler & Tanner Ltd, Frome and London

British Library Cataloguing in Publication Data

The Alpine Journal.
  1. Mountaineering
  796.522
  ISBN 0–09–173659–5

Contents

Illustrations

Appearing in colour between pages 150 and 151

Everest Kangshung Face – First Ascent of the Neverest Buttress

STEPHEN VENABLES

(Plates 1–5, 56)

At 6.30pm on Tuesday, 10 May 1988, Robert Anderson, Paul Teare, Ed Webster and I broke through a cornice at the top of the Kangshung face and stepped out on to the world's most desolate mountain pass. We were the first people ever to reach the South Col from Tibet. Two days later I stood on the summit of Everest. Seven days later – after a protracted, harrowing retreat which nearly cost us our lives – we were all safely down at Advanced Base on the Kangshung glacier.

If we had died on Everest, we would perhaps have been dismissed as irresponsible fools but, because we returned, both the public and the mountaineering world have been indulgent, brushing aside uncomfortable questions about some of the risks we took in their eagerness to praise. People like success and ours was a dramatic success. We made the second ascent of the notorious Kangshung face, by a completely new route, starting with some of the most sensational technical climbing ever achieved on the mountain. Our four-man team, climbing without any support and without supplementary oxygen, was the smallest ever to achieve a new route on Everest, and I was the first Briton to reach the summit without oxygen.

The genesis of 'Everest 88' was haphazard. In 1985 an American climber, Robert Anderson, spent eight days above 8000m on the West Ridge Direct, eventually being forced to retreat only 250m from the summit. He applied almost immediately for another attempt on Everest; the first available permit was for the Kangshung face in the spring of 1988. The W ridge attempt had been a huge overstaffed shambles, but this time Robert would be leader and the team would be small. He invited two of his companions from 1985, Ed Webster and Jay Smith, who recommended the Canadian Paul Teare. Then he employed Wendy Davis in New York to raise the money. The expedition became the '35th Anniversary Assault', with Peter Hillary also invited on the climbing team and Tenzing Norgay's son, Norbu, on the support team. The leader of the 1953 expedition, Lord Hunt, agreed to be 'honorary leader' of this anniversary attempt, on condition that a British climber was invited to join what was essentially an American venture. And so in the autumn of 1987, quite out of the blue, I was asked to join the team.

I felt honoured, flattered and very grateful to John Hunt, but I had to think hard before accepting. The only previous ascent of the E face of Everest, in 1983, had been the work of a large team using sophisticated ropework, complete with motorized winches, to tame a gigantic rock-buttress and gain access to the central glaciated spur. Robert proposed tackling the face with half the number of climbers, by a route further left which, although shorter and therefore more feasible, was possibly more threatened by the notorious Kangshung avalanches. If his plan worked and we did reach the South Col, there would be no possibility of carrying up oxygen for the remaining 850m to the summit. The risks of oxygenless climbing had been graphically illustrated on K2 in 1986 and, of the 20 people who had so far climbed Everest without oxygen, four had not returned.

Several leading American climbers, including John Roskelley, declined invitations. Jay Smith dropped out. Peter Hillary decided not to come after all. That left just four climbers – Robert, Paul, Ed and myself – for now, by Christmas, I had decided to accept. A visit to Tibet's Kama valley, the beautiful approach to the Kangshung face, was an opportunity not to be missed. And if we did actually set foot on the face . . . it was the biggest and most spectacular on the mountain, and it would be an interesting problem. With just four of us there would be no redundancy, for each person would be fully stretched, sharing equally in the drudgery of load-carrying and the excitement of leading. It had to be worth a try.

My hunch that this improbable expedition had a chance of working was reinforced in January 1988, when I met Robert and some of the support team in New York. Six weeks later I met the other two climbers, Ed Webster and Paul Teare, in Kathmandu. Now we were on our way to the mountain and, in the best tradition of the pre-war expeditions, it was to be a gentle leisurely approach. Instead of the usual modern rush, we had time to enjoy radiant mornings at the Swoyumbunath temple and to bicycle out to Bakhtepur, time to wait two days at the Chinese border without fretting, time at Xegar to climb up a 5000m hill and contemplate the great snow-plume streaming from the summit of Everest.

The walk-in from the roadhead at Kharta, which was supposed to take four days, took 23, because heavy snowfalls reinforced the Tibetan porters' traditional antipathy to the work ethic. But again, this gave us the chance to get to know each other, to unwind and acclimatize. Four times we broke trail up to the 5500m Langma La, and on every occasion the light was different as we enjoyed one of the finest mountain views in the world – Chomolonzo, Makalu, Pethangtse, Lhotse and Everest, encircling the meadows and glaciers of the Kama valley.

When we did eventually reach Base Camp on 29 March, we must have been one of the best-prepared teams ever to attempt the mountain. We were perfectly acclimatized and reasonably fit; but, more important, we were mentally prepared. There was a calmness and confidence which no amount of 'training' at home could have achieved. And now we knew each other, appreciating our complementary qualities. Paul, like me, was no great rock-climber – more an all-round mountaineer, with a streak of impatience. Our tastes and personalities were very different, but I and everyone else found him warm-hearted and funny, and it was mainly his banter which had kept the porters sweet during the approach. Ed was quieter, more contemplative, slower, perhaps more sensitive to the risks; but he had enormous reserves of

strength and experience and was certainly the most talented climber on the team
– our chief technician. Robert, as chairman, made the right decision to keep us
swapping partners – avoiding a destructive 'A Team'/'B Team' mentality – and
as instigator of the whole mad project he maintained an insuppressible
optimism that inspired us all.

We made an efficient four-man climbing team, but we needed relief from
each other at Base Camp. Mimi Zieman, our doctor, Joe Blackburn, the
photographer, Pasang Nurbu, the cook (whose first Everest expedition had
been under Angtharkay in 1962) and Kasang Tsering, his young assistant from
Kharta, brought our numbers up to eight. Without their company it would have
been a much duller expedition, and I doubt whether we could have climbed the
mountain. Our only disappointment was that the additional support team
never reached Base Camp because of the delayed approach. Wendy Davis,
helped by Miklos Pinther of the United Nations and Sandy Wylie from New
Zealand, had secured sponsorship from American Express, Burroughs
Wellcome, Kiehl Cosmetics, Lindblad Travel, Kodak, Petroconsultants, Rolex
and the Weaver Coat Company, thus making the expedition possible. Robert
Dorival had done a superb job in organizing the food. Norbu Tenzing had
organized all the travel, and it was a great shame that he never saw the E face of
the mountain about which he had heard so much from his father.

Base Camp was at about 5000m in a grassy ablation valley on the north
bank of the Kangshung glacier. We kept on 20 porters to do one carry to
Advanced Base so that we could install ourselves immediately, at 5450m, ready
to start work on 3 April.

Robert offered me first lead, so that on my very first day's climbing on
Everest I found myself exploring interesting ground – in this case an 80m wall of
banded granite and quartzite, smeared with enough ice to make it interesting –
probably Scottish Grade 4. We fixed nearly 400m of rope that day, and during
the following five days we continued to make steady progress up the initial
buttress. I tend to succumb too readily to superlatives, but I really think that
those six days were amongst the best I have ever spent in the mountains.
Contrary to popular myth, an Everest expedition can be enormous fun. The
actual climbing – technical, varied and demanding – would have been a delight
anywhere; but it was the surroundings – *la grande ambience*, as the French
guidebooks would have it – that made it so special. Our buttress projected from
the back of a huge amphitheatre, with the unclimbed 3000m NE face of Lhotse
on one side and the Americans' 1983 buttress on the right. It was a fantastic
world of huge striated rock-walls, exquisitely fragile snow-flutings and
improbable ice-towers, which soon acquired names like Big Al, the Greyhound
Bus, the Gargoyle and the Cauliflower Towers, prompted by familiarity tinged
with fear. Sections of the route, particularly the great seracs of the Cauliflower
Ridge, were a little dubious, but certainly no more dangerous than the Khumbu
ice-fall in an average year.

On Day 5 Ed climbed the gently overhanging ice of Webster's Wall at
6400m, and we thought that we had almost cracked the buttress. However, the
next day we were stopped dead by a huge crevasse spanning the entire slope, so
we all retired to Base Camp, very conscious that we were due for a rest. Sieging a

big route with only four climbers is hard work. During this and later weeks on the mountain we often spent three days in succession leading and load-carrying – and they were long days, with perhaps 12 hours spent on the route. In 1975, at the same altitude in the Khumbu ice-fall, the SW face sahibs tended to work only on alternate days, saving themselves for higher up. With our heavier work-load we had to be extremely careful to pace ourselves, so we now spent three days at Base Camp doing some serious eating.

The second phase on the mountain was much slower, hampered by bad weather. While Paul and I ferried loads up to Camp 1 on the Cauliflower Ridge, the other two slept there for three nights and dealt with the crevasse, abseiling into it so that Ed could aid his way on ice-screws up the 30m overhanging wall on the far side. It took another day to fix ropes across the gap, then Paul and I had a turn in front, marvelling at the Tyrolean over the Jaws of Doom, then stomping up deep snow above and fixing a final 100m length of rope through a dangerous jumble of seracs. Now we had finally broken through the lower lip of the hanging glacier and reached the easy undulations of the upper snow-slopes. At 6650m we had cracked the technical crux of the route and the way was open to the South Col.

The weather, however, was not good and every day the upper face was becoming more dangerously laden with new snow. So once again we retreated to Base Camp, where we waited a week before returning to the mountain.

There are many attractive reasons for going on expeditions. One is the opportunity during rest periods for unlimited sleep; another is the chance to get some uninterrupted reading done, usually on subjects that have nothing whatsoever to do with mountains. However, on this occasion we did have a small climbing library of Bill Murray's *Story of Everest*, Audrey Salkeld's Mallory book and *White Limbo*, the account of the 1984 Australian expedition. During the days of watching and waiting we were all acutely aware of our predecessors, particularly E H Norton and his solo push to 8600m in 1924. Surely, if he, Wager, Smythe and Wyn-Harris could get that high in the 1920s and 1930s without oxygen – surely we, with our vastly improved climbing gear and clothing, could reach a little higher now? But, of course, far more important than equipment was the huge psychological advantage of knowing that what Messner and Habeler had done 10 years earlier had been repeated by others.

The Australians' 1984 ascent of the N face without oxygen was the greatest inspiration because they, like all of us except Robert, had never been to 8000m before Everest. Also like us, they were a small team climbing a new route. Ours started lower, with much harder climbing, but theirs finished with Norton's insecure traverse out of the Great Couloir, whereas we would complete our ascent by the easier SE ridge. We were now approaching optimum fitness and acclimatization and wanted to make the big push before we started to deteriorate. Our original plan had been to complete the route to the South Col, leave a cache there and descend to rest before the final push. Now, however, we changed that plan – partly because of delays, partly because of the precedents on the N face. In 1984 the Australians only went once to about 7000m before leaving on the final push. Messner, during his 1980 solo, and

Troillet and Loretan in 1986, barely went higher than 6500m before dashing for the summit. The message was clear: get really fit and acclimatized between 6000 and 7000m, but don't waste energy burning yourself out at 8000m before the final push – particularly if, like all of us in 1988, you have no fat reserves. So the plan now was to reconnoitre only as far as Camp 2 – 7450m – and never to sleep above Camp 1 until the summit push.

It was a tense time with all these calculations, hopes and fears going through our minds, even on the beautiful day when Ed, Joe and I walked up towards Khartse, the snow pyramid which Mallory had called the loveliest peak in the world. It would have been fun to have taken Mimi and Joe climbing on some of the lower snow peaks, and to explore further in such magnificent walking country; but, like Mallory, we were compelled to concentrate on the job in hand. Everest, like no other mountain, is a place of history and tradition, and we had a chance to take our place in that tradition. It was very poignant to watch the evening clouds, backlit by great shafts of setting sunlight, swirling around the NE ridge, and to think of Mallory, Boardman and Tasker, and to ponder the problems of ambition. By all accounts, Mallory wanted desperately to finish the job in 1924 so that he would not have to come back again. Boardman and Tasker seem to have been similarly driven in 1982, as were Julie Tullis and Alan Rouse in 1986, on K2.

The third phase started on 28 April, when we returned to Advanced Base. The weather was now much better as Ed and I did two carries to Camp 1, while Robert and Paul started to break trail towards Camp 2. On 1 May all four of us carried loads to the Flying Wing – a huge roof of ice at 7450m which would provide total protection for Camp 2. This middle part of the Kangshung face, once one has surmounted the spectacular lower cliffs, lies back at a gentle angle – meandering hanging glacier terrain, similar to but less steep than the Lhotse face on the normal route. We had always been concerned about avalanche danger. Judging Himalayan snow-slopes is an extremely inexact science, but these particular slopes did seem quite safe, and we picked a careful route through the hummocks and crevasses, avoiding steep undercut slopes and staying close to the crest of the spur, well clear of the giant avalanche gullies on either side.

It took 11 hours to reach Camp 2, marking the route with wands. On the final stretch I slowed to two steps at a time, with three breaths per step, but I was pleased to discover that I had no headache when we reached the haven of the Wing. We left the supplies for Camp 2 there, then slid back down to Camp 1 in 1½ hours. Everything was now in place for the summit attempt, but we were frustrated for another week by changing weather before we could finally leave Advanced Base at 4am on 8 May.

The journey to the South Col was long and slow. On 8 May we rested, ate and drank at Camp 1, enjoying the familiar view down to the valley to Chomolonzo. On 9 May it took 14 hours to break a new trail to Camp 2. It snowed most of that day, but the 10th dawned clear; we left at 8am, carrying tents, stoves, gas, food and all our personal gear, and leaving just three gas cylinders and some scraps of food for the descent. In spite of the 20kg load on my back I was enjoying myself, feeling incredibly lucky to be up here on this beautiful morning, completing our new route on the E face of Everest. However, as the day wore on and it began to snow again, elation gave way to resigned drudgery, and in the end it took us 11 hours to reach the South Col.

We emerged into a blasting wind which continued all night, shaking and battering our tents, pressing the icy fabric against our faces and intensifying breathless claustrophobia. Pasang, who had been here in 1969, had advised us to rest only briefly at the Col before pressing on to the summit. But our plan was starting to disintegrate. Even though we had deliberately placed Camp 2 only 550m below the Col, it had taken us 11 exhausting hours to cover that final stage. We were too tired, and in any case the wind was too strong on 11 May for us to continue to the summit.

Paul was ill that morning, possibly developing oedema, and the only choice for him was to descend immediately. We uneasily accepted his decision to go down alone and he set off, bitterly disappointed, for Advanced Base, which he reached in just seven hours. That left three of us waiting and hoping at 8000m, eating some food, drinking lots of liquid and discovering that, contrary to received wisdom, it was possible to recuperate slightly at this altitude. By the evening, when the wind miraculously dropped, I felt much stronger.

We left the South Col at 11pm on 11 May, each carrying just one long ice axe, one prusik loop, camera, spare mittens, bar of chocolate and a litre of Rehydrate juice. Our only hope of completing the remaining 850m was to travel light like this, and we hoped to be on the summit, taking lovely photographs in the early light, by about 11 the next morning.

But at 11am on 12 May I was still below the South Summit. Robert and Ed were lower still and I was beginning seriously to doubt whether I was capable of reaching the top. However, after an hour's rest I decided to give it a try. One of the biggest problems, after four nights with little or no sleep, was staying awake, so I took two caffeine pills. They seemed to help and with a new determination I continued to the South Summit, reaching it at 1.30pm. Once again, in spite of chronic exhaustion, I was swept along by emotion and instinct, thrilled to be up there, looking down, down to the Western Cwm and Pumori, and across to the W ridge and the big traverse on the SW face and, just ahead of me, the final narrow crest of the SE ridge leading across to the Hillary Step. I continued, confident that I could reach the summit, turn round by 4pm and return to the South Col before darkness fell at 7pm.

For a while my instincts were correct. I found myself enjoying the rock scrambling beyond the South Summit. The Hillary Step sported the expected fixed ropes and I was able to safeguard myself with a Bachman Knot. Then, on the final 300m or so to the summit, I was thrilled to find the snow firmly crusted and at last, after all the hours of trail-breaking on loose slabby snow, I could walk on the surface, keeping well to the left of the big cornices and stopping every three or four steps to rest and cough, telling myself that it really was time to give up smoking. At 3.40pm, just ahead of my revised schedule, I stepped on to the crest of the W ridge, turned right and took the remaining three or four steps to the summit. Three empty oxygen cylinders left by the Asian Friendship Expedition on 5 May were adorned with prayer flags, the letters 'CNJ' for China-Nepal-Japan and some remains of television transmission equipment.

So far instinct had served me well, but when I started down at 3.50pm the clouds, which had been building up steadily, enveloped the summit ridge completely. Suddenly I was struggling for my life, terrified of re-enacting Mick Burke's sad fate in 1975, as my glasses froze over and I groped my way through the mist, collapsing several times from oxygen deficit, hyperventilating furiously to refill my lungs. I had always suspected that the problem would not be climbing Everest without oxygen, but getting down again, and now for the first time in my life I was having to draw on a whole new reserve of will and strength. I had grossly underestimated my level of exhaustion and the problems of orientation in the mist, so that when darkness fell I had still only just crossed back over the South Summit. Our tents on the South Col were far below and, even with my head-torch, I could not find the correct route.

The only safe thing to do was what we had tried so hard to avoid by leaving the South Col so early – settle down for a long lonely bivouac in the open at about 8600m. Luckily the afternoon storm had blown over and it was a fine night and, like most of the people who have spent a night out hereabouts, I survived.

At about 3.30 that afternoon Ed had reached the South Summit, frightened by hallucinations and the possibility of blacking out and, like me, very conscious of Mick Burke's fate. He had wisely decided to turn back, soon passing Robert, who later also reached the South Summit before retreating. The two of them had descended as far as an abandoned Japanese tent in the big couloir, where they spent the night sheltering without sleeping bags. In spite of the numbing effects of cold and hypoxia on my dulled brain, I felt incredibly moved when I rejoined them early the next morning and the three of us tied symbolically to one rope to descend the remaining 300m to the South Col.

After all that trail-breaking up the E face, all those sleepless nights, the ridiculously slow 16½-hour ascent to the summit and now another sleepless night, we were exhausted. We knew perfectly well that we should descend immediately, but we were so desperate to lie down, drink and sleep that we stayed another day and night at our Camp 3. On 14 May lethargy started to take over and when we finally left at 3.45pm we had been 93 hours above 8000m. We had broken the rules and we were to continue to break them – allowing heat, hunger and thirst to reinforce our lethargy as we delayed feebly, wasting another whole day at the Flying Wing, so that when we started down from 7450m on 16 May, we knew that this was our final chance to escape alive.

Lying in the snow on that final morning, taking one hour to find the strength to stand up, I thought with detachment that this was how they must have felt on the shoulder of K2 in 1986, and we did not even have the excuse of a major storm. We were luckier and we all returned safely, despite many questionable decisions – agreeing to Paul's solo descent, climbing unroped to the summit, allowing lethargy to get the better of us, delaying dangerously, fooling ourselves that it was a good idea to descend unroped so that we could glissade more easily, leaving Robert behind on the fixed ropes on the final night of the descent . . . However, in our defence I have to point out that, although we ate virtually no food for four days, we still had spare gas for melting snow at the Flying Wing and further reserves and tents at Camp 1. Tackling such a big problem with such a small team obviously has its risks, but we all knew what we were letting ourselves in for. Although people on the Nepalese side saw us above the South Col, we never saw them and we never seriously considered the possibility of outside help, preferring to rely on our own prepared line of retreat down the E face. Our descent to 6650m was marked, albeit sketchily, with wands and below that we had a safety line of meticulously fixed ropes. It took a whole night excavating and abseiling those final 1600m of descent, but it was rewarding to discover that one did still have the instinct and control to cope safely with all the changeovers at anchors.

We were too weak to help each other physically, yet I am convinced that during that harrowing retreat we were spurred on by an extraordinary, intangible bond. Afterwards all three of us admitted independently to a strong sensation that Paul had also been on the mountain, and I think that each of us, in his private struggle, was sustained by the close team-spirit that had made the whole climb possible. Down at Advanced Base Paul, Joe, Mimi, Pasang and Kasang took over, nursing us back to some semblance of health for the return to Kharta. Robert eventually lost half a big toe from frostbite. I lost 3½ toes. Ed lost parts of three toes and eight fingers. Many people would say that Ed paid too high a price. I cannot answer for him – only report the courage and humour he has shown throughout the trauma of operations, without the sustaining bonus of those final 80m to the main summit of the mountain. I was luckier and, although I am saddened by the loss of toes, it seems a price worth paying for an incomparable adventure with people who will always remain good friends.

The Boys and the White Stuff

The First Crossing of the Pinnacles on the NE Ridge of Everest

PAUL MOORES

It's a strange feeling, climbing with lads whom you've known for years but probably have never climbed with before. This summer a group of 16–20 of us assembled at the Rongbuk for an attempt on the NE Ridge of Everest. The group varied in numbers because doctors changed over in midstream, and also cameramen and TV presenters came and went as they pleased. The expedition was labelled by the climbing press as the 'Golden Oldies' Expedition', mainly because of the inclusion of Joe Brown, 57, Philip Horniblow, 60 and Mo Anthoine, aged 50+ (but with the mind of a 21-year-old). The team also included plenty of 40+'s, all quite experienced and still quite fit!

The expedition was full of hassles from the word go. It started when we had to take a rubber raft from Heathrow to Kathmandu – nothing to do with the expedition, we were just doing a favour for a rafting company based in Nepal. We spent several days delayed in Kathmandu because of the normal customs routine, and left on 5 June heading up the road to Lamosangu where we spent the night. We would have progressed further, but we had endless trouble at police checkpoints even though we had all the necessary permits and permission to use the military road up to the border with China. After a reluctant early rise the following day, we waited for several hours and were then told that the road was still closed to us because our permit was now out of date: it was valid for only one day, the day we departed Kathmandu. After several meetings with military personnel we were allowed to continue and arrived at the Chinese-Nepalese border at 6pm, only to find once again that the border was closed – and this time we were told that it was for three weeks!

Back in Kathmandu, a little poorer but wiser for the experience, we had to rethink our plans. Brummie Stokes, the expedition leader, busied himself visiting the Nepalese and Chinese Embassies and the British Military Attaché to try to find out the exact score on the border closure. Meanwhile the remainder of the team milled around Kathmandu, wondering what to do with our six tons of equipment and how to get to Base Camp.

Mo Anthoine had left Great Britain three weeks earlier, to take over a Base Camp cardboard hut from the Joint Services Everest Expedition. So he would be sitting at Base Camp, wondering when we were all going to arrive; this was causing us concern as the longer we took to reach him, the more likely he was to think that we weren't coming at all. He had also collected a lot of equipment which the expedition had left in Lhasa in 1986, after an attempt on the same route. All this gear had now been transported to Base Camp and was waiting on our arrival, along with Mo and one Sherpa, Lhakpa Dorje. Back in Kathmandu we decided that it was best for three of us to fly from there to Lhasa and to get to Base Camp as quickly as possible; not only would this put Mo and the rest of the expedition at ease, but we could also report back on the state of the road and the border situation on the Chinese side. Pete Long, Harry Taylor and I were 'volunteered' to form this advance party, and we got ourselves a flight to Lhasa on 11 June. There we were duly met by the Chinese Mountaineering Association representative and taken to the Lhasa Hotel. From there it was a jeep ride of two days to Base Camp where at last we met Mo, who was pretty glad to see us. Over the next few days he kept us amused by tales of his journey to Base Camp and of the Joint Services' efforts on Everest. He had done a fantastic job in setting up Base Camp, so there was very little for us to do when we arrived except to acclimatize. Harry and Pete made a couple of forays up to where Mo had left a tent which was to be an interim camp between Base and Advanced Base at approximately 5900m. After one week there was still no news of the remainder of the expedition, so we made tentative plans for a four-man assault and what to do about food if the others didn't turn up. As it turned out, we were down to one pint of petrol for cooking when (as if they had been listening) the others arrived with three trucks and a jeep, and the team was at last complete. They had all had to fly to Lhasa, as the border was still closed. We had masses of gear to organize and weigh out into loads for yaks to carry up to Advanced Base Camp, 22km away.

Before the expedition could be formally started in the eyes of the Sherpas we had to have a *puja*, a religious ceremony which ensures the safe return of all members. Shortly after the ceremony Pete Long left with the first load of yaks for the two-day walk to Advanced Base Camp; a day later I joined him. Our job was to organize and set up Advanced Base Camp and then to cross the glacier to the foot of the buttress – Bill's Buttress, named after Bill Barker from the 1986 attempt on the ridge. Over the next five or six days Pete and I made several journeys across the glacier and up the buttress, fixing new ropes and also finding ropes from our last attempt. We also found fixed rope from Doug Scott's expedition in the autumn of 1987. Harry and Russell Brice had joined us by this time at Advanced Base Camp, and we soon had Camp 1 established at 6400m on the ridge. The conditions on the hill were similar to those of two years previously, with deep unconsolidated snow above 6700m, but below that there was considerably less snow than before and it was much warmer.

Time is now pressing on, it's the beginning of July and the weather is extremely unsettled. Members are slowly drifting up to Advanced Base Camp, and we have a rota system of working in fours. Generally speaking this means doing a week's work as high on the mountain as one can get, along with the Sherpas, and then returning to Base Camp for a rest of about five days. So, at any one stage, there could be two groups up working from Advanced Base Camp, a third on the way up to Advanced Base and a fourth group resting at Base Camp. The mountain certainly seems to eat up all the numbers and quite often – depending on where you are – you might not see other members for two weeks.

When we tried this route in 1986 we had no Sherpas at all and found that the ferrying of loads was wearing members out, so much so that after four or five carries we virtually had to have a week off, and in the long term no one was sufficiently fit to get high enough to make an attempt on the pinnacles. This time we decided to have Sherpas along to help resolve the situation; we had 10 in all, two of whom were cooks, leaving eight working members on the mountain. Unfortunately several of the Sherpas became quite ill: two got pneumonia, one had very bad teeth and suffered extremely painful toothache, and another got a blood-clot in his leg; so our work-force was greatly reduced.

Our progress seemed to have ground to a standstill: first of all we were three weeks behind because of our late arrival; then we made good progress in getting Camp 1 established, but now Camp 2 seemed to be miles away because of the deep snow. Several teams have been working on the section between Camps 1 and 2 but progress is slow: there are many avalanches and high winds, making life very difficult. Eventually Harry and Russ reach Camp 2, having waded all day in chest-deep snow, with four of the Sherpas carrying loads behind. Camp 2 is established at last. Harry and Russ manage to fix some rope towards Camp 3, finding one of Chris Bonington's ropes from the first attempt on the ridge in 1982, with a team that included Pete Boardman, Joe Tasker and Dick Renshaw. Conditions aren't good, with very deep snow making progress extremely slow. Harry and Russ are pretty tired – they have been on the hill for five days now. Pete Long and I are going to have a go up front, to try to push the ropes out a little further.

We arrived at Camp 2 just after midday, just as Harry and Russ were departing for Advanced Base Camp. The following morning I was feeling pretty rough and was not able to accompany Pete up the fixed ropes towards Camp 3. Pete did a good day's work fixing rope almost to Camp 3, about 200m short of the proposed camp. The next day the weather was awful and we had no chance of returning to establish Camp 3; instead we waded chest-deep in snow down to Camp 1 and then onwards to Advanced Base Camp. The weather remained bad for some time and the majority of the team were confined to Base Camp; it was pointless to stay up at Advanced Base Camp, as one does not recover very well at that altitude. It was now nearly the end of July; Mo, Joe, Ian Nicolson and Davey Jones were all being hindered by the deep snow and finding it difficult to live at above 7000m – most of them find it difficult enough to live at sea-level! Time was getting short, and it looked as if we might have a repeat of our last unsuccessful attempt. Harry and Russ went up to relieve Mo and Joe's team on 30 July, in the belief that it would be our last attempt on the ridge. The efforts of Mo, Joe and Sam Roberts to reach and excavate Camp 2 had been thwarted by the bad weather and the poor conditions. Ang Lhakpa Dorje, who had previously accompanied Chris Bonington to the summit of Everest via the South Col on the Norwegian expedition, along with Rinsing Sherpa joined Harry and Russ later the same day. A comfortable night was spent at Camp 1, with clear skies which afforded magnificent views of Makalu and Kangchenjunga in the distance.

The next day saw the four at Camp 2, armed with shovels to dig out the tents which had been avalanched. Several hours later, the tents had been re-sited and anchored down. It was a comforting thought that, although covered by five feet of snow, Mo's box-tent withstood the onslaught and, if the camp had been manned, the occupants would have survived. An early start on the morning of 1 August enabled them to reach our previous high point at 7750m. The winds – which had been gusting all night – now roared along the ridge, blowing crystalline swords into their faces. Progress was difficult and painful, sense prevailed and they headed down to Camp 2. Spindrift had all but covered the tents and, after repeated attempts to clear the Snowdon Mouldings Limpet, Lhakpa announced that he and Rinsing would go down to Camp 1 for a comfortable night. On arrival at Camp 1 both Sherpas decided that the weather was too bad for them, and they descended to Advanced Base Camp. The wind abated in the night, and at 5am Harry and Russ left Camp 2 with small loads, re-ascended the ropes to the high point and then continued to fix a small amount of rope to 7900m, where they were able to establish Camp 3. They erected a lightweight tent and sat for a few hours brewing up, before heading down to Camp 2 in buoyant mood.

In effect a 'double six' had been thrown: the Pinnacles now appeared imminently close, the game could begin!

Lhakpa Gelo and Norbu Sherpa moved up to Camp 2 to assist Harry and Russ, and on the following day they moved up to Camp 3 carrying loads of food, gaz and oxygen. The afternoon was spent filming, interspersed with the usual non-stop brewing. They also managed to link up with Brummie in Hereford via the Racal radio and the Dymac satellite system, situated 20km away at Base Camp. Harry thought it quite perverse to be sitting at 8000m talking to someone thousands of miles away in his home, but it was none the less a welcome interlude.

They were off by 5.30 the following morning and 45 minutes of steady plodding took them to the start of the first Pinnacle. The familiar orange and blue rope that belonged to Chris Bonington's expedition was visible at the start, alongside several harnesses, cookers and gaz canisters belonging to either the Duff or the Scott/Allan attempts.

Harry tells the story: *I led off on relatively easy ground; the conditions were not good but certainly workable. After 100 metres the angle steepened as I then began to parallel the ridge proper. Snow conditions deteriorated and wading became the norm, something at which this team had become very adept! Progress was slow but methodical, and soon the 200m of 8mm polyprop was in situ. Russell jumared up with consummate ease, a quick chat, and off he led with the second drum of rope. From my airy stance I had a good view of the E (the so-called 'Fantasy') ridge which joined the NE ridge by our Camp 3 at 8000m.*

I decided that this route would have to be attempted by someone with a strong sense of humour! Near the top of the first Pinnacle the ridge started to sharpen, but Russell made good progress leaving his ice-axe behind to secure the descent. We arrived back at Camp 3 just after 5pm, after over 11 hours' climbing above 8000m. On the radio scheduled that night we spoke to Paul at Camp 1 and informed him of our progress and of the fact that we would go lightweight from now on in a bid through the Pinnacles along to the summit. When asked how the Pinnacles looked from the first one onwards,

Russell spoke the immortal words 'they're a piece of weasel piss!' We spent an almost sleepless night even though we were on oxygen, and the next morning it was 6am before we got away, laden with sacks weighing 30kg. We carried bivvy kit, no sleeping bags or tent, a small oxygen bottle each and masks for sleeping, and the Sony video along with the Racal radio. Our climbing gear was minimal, one length of 8mm polyprop to climb on, one ice-tool each and one deadman between us.

By 9am we were at our high point. Russell led off, and I filmed him. It was a testament to the route that the video never saw the light of day again until the following day on the N ridge. The ridge was truly knife-like, with cornices blown to either side and difficult mushrooms to negotiate. Progress was decidedly slow, but momentum was maintained by methodically knocking off the top 45cm of loose snow and virtually climbing heel-to-toe. It was a sobering experience, with the gullies sweeping down to our right, and steep flutings of the Kangshung face immediately to our left. After four hours of tightrope walking a 55° ramp led off right to the second Pinnacle. The snow conditions were now atrocious, with almost bottomless snow on the ramp which left us both gasping like old men. The weather was now also looking decidedly ominous, with thick cloud billowing up from the Kharta Valley.

The top of the ramp brought us behind the second Pinnacle: the Pinnacle itself is not en route and is indeed set forward to the north by some 30 metres. The difficulties remained constant for another two hours until a subsidiary ridge met us from the north. It was our first opportunity to sit down without having to cheval the route, and we took it gladly. A brew was made and I opened up on the radio, to be greeted by the enthusiastic voices of Davey Jones and then Paul. He and Bill Barker had moved up to Camp 3 as our back-up, with the intention of following us through the next day. We were now just short of the third Pinnacle and were clearly visible to Advanced Base Camp, even with the naked eye. Only two hours of daylight remained as we set off again. Just before the third Pinnacle we cut down into a gully, then on to a small arête where our bivvy would have to be. It was now dark and it began to snow. We hit rock after two feet of digging, so the scene was set for an uncomfortable night. We clambered into bivvy bags and had a brew and delved into our sacks for the oxygen gear. The regulator on my set had broken, so the night was spent passing the one set to and fro between us. Both of us slept with and without the comfort of oxygen. Our plan, to leave at midnight to push to the summit, was dashed when the snows began. Heavy flakes fell constantly throughout the night. We set off at 5am in a virtual whiteout, having once again gained the ridge. It took two hours to reach the last Pinnacle where we descended into a large gully at its foot and traversed around it to the north. Over 45cm of snow had fallen in the night, and we were constantly setting off slides and small avalanches. Visibility was still very poor, so we sat down for a much-needed brew and came up on the radio. Communications to Advanced Base Camp were only just workable, but Joe Brown came in loud and clear from Base Camp. He said that the weather there was clearing a little and suggested that we sit tight, in order to find our way down the N ridge. True to form, Joe was right and the clouds lifted and gave us a glimpse of the summit which appeared tantalizingly close. We were in fact below and to the left of the First Step. The time was now 11.30am.

Our only option was to descend the N ridge: the weather and conditions were atrocious, and our time had run out. The decision to forgo the summit was bitter for both of us: Russell had already been to 8000m on the W ridge when he and Paddy Freany made a bold alpine-style ascent in 1981, and this was my third attempt on Everest.

The descent was torture; both of us were extremely tired and we had to rest frequently. Mo Anthoine spotted our descent off the North Col; we took a line to the north which Mo described as a 'bum-slide'. In fact we front-pointed the whole 500m down. John English, Davey Jones and the Sherpas were there to greet us at the bottom, and all that remained was a walk back to Advanced Base Camp for that welcome brew!

After Harry and Russell's 'good day out' I decided to call off the expedition as the weather and conditions had continued to deteriorate. The expedition slowly made its way back to Kathmandu – not without incident.

Although we didn't reach the summit, we had reached the peak of effort and had shown to ourselves that it could be done. Despite missing the joy of the summit, we had experienced the pleasure of the climbing and had learnt many of the lessons which we had come to learn.

Parasite or Publicity

Climbing Everest with a film crew

LUKE HUGHES

(Plates 6–8)

'Sod all those alpine-style suicidal maniacs,' said Dougie Keelan, the expedition leader, as he poured another liberal shot of Scotch into a plastic beaker, 'I want this to be a solid, safe, old-fashioned expedition.' And so it was. With 36 servicemen, five Sherpas, assorted Nepalese cooks, a four-man camera crew from Granada, an expedition artist (à la *Illustrated London News*) and a dozen cases of Famous Grouse, there was not much to distinguish us from the pre-war expeditions to the Rongbuk glacier – an absence of tweed, perhaps, and an absence of the monastery for sure; but at least the Base Camp was in the same place.

We were not without gadgetry: solar panels for recharging radios, wind generators for recharging the neon light-strip at Base Camp, a 'mountain bike' (not that anyone could pedal very hard at 5200m), a computer to plan the logistics, a satcom telephone link, and the prodigious paraphernalia of the film crew. But we were ill-equipped compared with the tri-nation Base Camp. There a joint Chinese-Japanese-Nepalese expedition had gathered a 300-strong battalion which was split into two and set to climb Everest from both sides at once, to arrive at the summit on the same day, to shake hands on the top to foster good-neighbourliness, and to descend the way they hadn't come. They had separate eating facilities for each nation, heaters and telephones in their tents, a truck with a crane to off-load their supplies, a full TV broadcasting link and a transmitter set in a 20cm slab of concrete, not to mention five fax machines receiving daily updates of the weather predictions from Tokyo, Moscow, Washington, Paris and London – and even a metereologist to interpret them.

The Japanese metereologist never made a reliable local prediction. For our part, our computer buff constantly and insistently predicted that we would be climbing with gear weighing a maximum of 4 kilos, and would reach the summit on the specified day. As with all computers, if you put garbage in, you get garbage out; the computer is only as good as the operator. And yet man's folly is not in taking this kind of equipment to such inappropriate places, but in believing in it, deferring to it, being distracted by it. It is especially the kind of distraction that plagues large expeditions. Apart from all the difficulties of protocol (the Duke of Edinburgh had graciously consented to be the Patron), of inter-service etiquette (Dougie had pledged himself to try to get a sailor, a soldier, an airman and a marine on top together), and of the high profile that service authority attracts, there were two especially dynamic distractions.

The first was the satcom telephone, generously loaned by Marconi;

British Telecom donated £15,000-worth of calls. There was much diplomatic bartering with the Chinese about permission to operate the kit in Tibet, and it might be considered a *coup* to have them agree. The team members were not slow in using up the allotment with direct calls home; this facility led to the bizarre but not uncommon occurrence of climbers announcing, 'I think I'm going down to Base Camp today, I want to make a call.' The political opportunities were not lost on 10 Downing Street either, the Prime Minister clearly having recognized the media potential of talking to servicemen on top of Everest. Was it possible, asked the Cabinet Office, to relay the calls through the walkie-talkies? Over a period of a week we had three dress rehearsals with her secretaries, with a view to filming the reception of the news of the actual summit bid by Granada TV in London and at Base Camp. One is reminded of her appearance at the end of some of the James Bond films. When we failed, the Prime Minister was 'unavailable' and we had to make do with the Chief of the Imperial General Staff. Even so, the time and energy expended on that exercise were enormous.

The second distraction was the presence of the cameras. Granada Television were keen to make six half-hour documentaries to be screened on the opposing channel to 'East-Enders'. This was obviously attractive to sponsors, who would appreciate their logos featuring at prime-time viewing, but it had other ramifications. On the flight out to Kathmandu, Nick Plowright, the chief cameraman, was foolish enough to leave a postcard lying around the aircraft. I was rude enough to read it:

> Dear Mum and Dad,
>   Finally we're on our way, my first taste of military service has so far been OK . . . we always seem to end up hoping things will go wrong. For the first two weeks people will be walking, eating, and sleeping, albeit in picturesque countryside, but I hope there's some disasters. We hope to make two episodes out of it.

So it was true: all one's reservations might be justified. This realization highlighted two things. First, with the camera around no one wanted to be seen at the wrong end of any disaster, either as victim or as the man responsible. Second, however hard the camera crew might declare their intent to become integrated with the team, there would always be suspicion and reservation.

The first consideration distorted behaviour on the mountain. Military personnel are traditionally wary of the press. Experience in the Falklands or in Ulster justifies this caution and has taught them again and again that the mere presence of a camera can inflame, incite or inhibit the normal course of events. Many of the boys had had direct and unfortunate experiences.

To some extent this wariness was part of another syndrome: servicemen's anxiety about History. Official histories of service activities tend to glamorize *pour encourager les autres*. The VC citation of Colonel H Jones's performance at Goose Green, for example, bears little resemblance to what eyewitnesses can relate. In fact, service life is rarely 'active' these days and there is scant opportunity for immortality. Mess chat revolves around a mixture of gossip, myth and legend. Absolute truth should never be allowed to get in the way of a good story, so the adage goes. The Everest trip, with all the hype associated with the largest Joint Service Venture since the Falklands invasion, was just the kind of event from which official histories – not to mention the gossip, myth and legend – were likely to emanate. What came out of the cutting room might just tell a less massaged story. To Dougie's eternal credit, he forswore any editorial control of the final film.

The result of this was a tendency for everyone to appear utterly, boringly sensible. Rash actions and hot-headed decisions have little place on a mountain, but there are times when boldness is required; risks are involved and people must be found to take them. I am left with the lingering thought that we might have pushed the boat out further (especially on the three summit bids) had there not been the beady eye of Granada's lens recording every detail for the 'Great British Public', wise after the event, to judge from the comfort of their sitting-rooms whether the right decision had been made. Dougie, I suspect, was under far greater pressure in this respect than any of us appreciated at the time. There is a certain bitter-sweet satisfaction in knowing when to turn back. On this expedition we played safe, more fearful than usual of what might be said if one of us failed to return.

Another result was that we were all impressively loyal to one another when the camera was around. Four months of living together in aggressive conditions is bound to throw up tensions; sometimes these are aired explosively, and they would have made marvellous television. But there was no way the team members would start griping about each other with the knowledge that the arguments would be immortalized on celluloid. That said, if any of the climbers were using the little video camera at the higher camps in the privacy of the snow holes, indiscretion would have abounded. This might be considered to indicate that the loyalty was inspired less by the presence of the camera than by the presence of the film crew.

The effect of the second point might seem obvious. Media men are not naturally imbued with team spirit, whereas the services select people on the strength of it and are skilful at fostering it in training. Much camaraderie and team spirit is either based on hardship mutually experienced (a former Operation, or even a previous expedition) or on respect for another's similar adventures. As a climber, one will naturally find an affinity with a man who has been to the Himalaya four or five times before. The chances are that he knows what he is doing in that environment. The camera crew clearly did not. The daily pantomime of their putting up their tent on the trek; their self-pitying misery as victims of altitude sickness; their complaints about the non-existent weight of their rucksacks; their griping about the cold and the conditions; all these made the climbing team feel the need to behave like a benign host towards a parasite. Allowances clearly had to be made, but this was sometimes difficult. One evening over a game of Scrabble, details of their formidable earnings were revealed – in the region of £1,000 per week on top of their normal salary; it was felt that this more than compensated for any temporary discomforts. It has to be said that Base Camp was one of the most palatial I've ever occupied. Moreover it was clear that in making the programme their careers benefited hugely. Ludicrous pay, good prospects . . . what were they complaining about? Alan

Evans, the assistant cameraman, was the most at home, having a climbing background and a passion for fell-running. Nick turned out to be the comfort clown, complaining like a union convener about his rights and clearly missing the deep leather sofas of the Holiday Inn. Ian Hills, the sound man, seemed totally dazed most of the time and in the early stages had to be bullied to eat, drink or even take his boots off. 'I think the altitude is slowing down his thought process,' remarked Nick one evening at supper. 'Really?!' exclaimed Mark Anderson, himself surprisingly equable in the environment – though not, however, a man to get out of his sleeping bag one night to help rescue a mess tent blown away amidst a clatter of poles and frenzied cries for help.

Inertia ruled. When they did move to Camps 1 or 2, they were extremely unwilling to move again. At Camp 2, in the early stages, this caused particularly bad feeling amongst the climbing team who had been lugging the food themselves and were more than a little irritated to watch it being wolfed by those who did no carrying. They were also extremely slow. One morning they set off two hours ahead of the main party, thinking it appropriate to film the yaks crossing the East Rongbuk river. Yaks are slow, lumbering beasts and it is normal for walkers to move ahead and not wait. In the history of load-carrying, Granada are unique in being overtaken by the yaks; they didn't even have a chance to film. As they limped into camp late that evening, Mark said, 'Well, we may be slow, but at least we're rich.'

Now that the trip has long passed, the programmes have all been screened, the post-mortems have been held and it is possible to look more objectively at the reasons why we failed, I have to admit that the final film is terrific, especially if you have a chance to see it not in six parts but in one. There is some sensational footage of some memorable adventures. Most of the footage high on the mountain was obtained with 8mm Sony videos by the climbers; it has subsequently been enhanced and is of excellent quality. The film also records well the atmosphere of an extremely happy expedition. The evening when the last programme was first broadcast, I had dinner with Mark and his girl-friend Vicky Price, who was also the editor. They had been working non-stop in the cutting room for five months. Mark had thus spent nearly 10 months attached to the project – four and a half on the mountain. Vicky knew every detail of every character on the expedition and every occurrence rather better than if she had been there herself. While we had our mountain to climb, they surely had their stable to clean. We had very different goals.

And that, ultimately, seems to be the problem of old-fashioned Himalayan expeditions: there are too many distractions, too many interested parties with different objectives. It becomes too easy to dissipate energy on gadgetry and public profile, and to lose sight of actually getting up. In last year's *Alpine Journal*, in an article by Trevor Braham, there were revealing statistics about fatalities and successes in the Himalaya. I do not know of any statistical comparison between alpine-style climbing expeditions and the bigger, more conventional efforts, but my hunch is that the 'alpine-style maniacs' are not as suicidal as all that.

Summary

The British Service Everest Expedition 1988 set out to climb the W ridge of Everest by the northern approach. It was led by Lt Col Douglas Keelan OBE, RM, and comprised climbers from the Marines, the Royal Air Force, the Navy, the Army, and from their reserves. There were three summit attempts; Luke Hughes was on the second and third. The highest point was reached in the Hornbein Couloir by Dave Nicholls and Al Macleod (c8500m). The attempt was abandoned in blizzard conditions. Oxygen was used.

Cho Oyu 1988

The First British Ascent

DAVE WALSH

(Plates 9, 10)

I cannot recall when the idea for the trip was first seeded but, knowing that the incubation period (beyond the initial suggestion) tends to be lengthy, I maintained a low profile, at least until the job of organizing the food had been allocated.

The obvious choice for this task was Derek Price who, having spent the past 35 years eating what is probably best described as an 'uncomplicated' diet was less likely to eat into our already limited funds.

My experience of previous ventures is that the whole project gathers momentum at frightening speed, culminating in last-minute phone calls, followed by futile attempts to compress large amounts of gear into woefully small sacks with one useless arm hanging limply from the shoulder after having been injected (again at the last minute) with all kinds of microscopic nasties.

Our trip was going to be alpine-style. This is a phrase I never quite understand, but our own interpretation was that it should not cost more than an alpine holiday and should not involve half the population of Nepal. Fortunately, we had a leader whose attention to financial detail has a track record which would be the envy of many a household struggling to make ends meet. With his iron fist locked on to the purse-strings and a Gandhi-like outlook on our calorie intake, we were ready (to coin a phrase) to give it our best shot.

The choice of Cho Oyu as our objective was made for several reasons. The fact that it is an 8000m peak was obviously a major attraction, that it had had no British ascent was another, and also we considered it a suitable peak for making a ski descent: there is only one steep section that was unlikely to be skiable.

At the very outset our plans implied a degree of commitment about the trip. We would not use any porters above Base Camp – we had yet to agree if there was to be a Base Camp at all and, if so, where; there would be no doctor, and emergency oxygen was dismissed as being of limited use and too expensive anyway. Much local food was to supplement an already meagre diet, six old 9mm ropes were taken, tents borrowed and rucksacks received as gifts. It was with this miscellaneous assortment that we met at Heathrow to be greeted by the Scottish contingent, festooned in Highland fruit and oatcakes.

Permission to climb Cho Oyu had been granted in 1985; the route was to be via the W flank (climbed by Herbert Tichy in 1952). This approach to the mountain has been the accepted way via Nepal since the Tibetan borders were closed to Westerners many years ago. In 1987 these restrictions were lifted by the Chinese, and the approach through Tibet became the most logical.

But the approach has its drawbacks, not least in the greatly increased costs; also, much of the journey is by vehicle across a barren Tibetan plateau where bouncing about in the back of a dusty lorry soon loses its Eighth-Army-like appeal. Our much less hurried approach – taking six days, walking, eating and sharing accommodation with the local people – acclimatized our group gently into the nuances of the Himalaya.

Himalayan climbing has many bad moments, personal battles with health, fitness, personalities within the group and the many external happenings beyond the control of the expedition. Such factors have combined to ruin many a promising team's aspirations. We were little affected by these afflictions, however, which is quite surprising as several of us had never met before.

The team of Derek Price, Alan Hunt, Dave Walsh, Dave Morris, John Hall, Wes Sterritt and young Dorjee (listed in descending order of age, but not descending very far), along with its cake, arrived safely in Kathmandu on 21 March 1988. Our few days there were taken up with trying to track down the few remaining gas cylinders which had been overlooked by some multinational Everest circus that was being staged at the time. Our liaison officer was assigned, the necessary documentation obtained and we were all set for the flight to Lukla.

This was preceded by a final meal in town, followed by an embarrassing three hours spent by Derek and myself when we tried to follow Wes (on hired bikes) back to our flat on the outskirts of town. Having lost him after the first turn, our main concern focused on the vulnerability of exposed ankles to the numerous street dogs attracted to our flashing white flesh. Derek, having received the first instalment of his course of anti-rabies inoculations (before discovering the cost) ran the gauntlet of the dogs, steering an erratic course in the general direction of the North Star. My confidence in the law was confirmed when a policeman stepped out of the shadows to reprimand me for short-cutting a roundabout (it was midnight in a deserted suburb of Kathmandu!).

The airport resembled a farmyard auction as sacks of produce, assorted items of furniture and implements were entered on to the plane's manifest. We were once again too heavy for comfort, of course. Taking a back seat, while our agent caused rupees to materialize from the most unlikely places and to disappear with equal speed into the necessary pockets, was a clear lesson in Nepalese airport etiquette.

We boarded the Twin Otter with a quiet sense of relief after observing our baggage being loaded on to the same aircraft. I am pleased to report that our pilot, who was under instruction, made a very passable landing on a not very passable runway.

We had now been joined by Dorjee Lhatoo – and left by Dave Morris, who was to meet us again at Base Camp; a complicated plan, as we were undecided about its location. Dorjee, as organizer of local transport and food, was accompanied by a cook and his assistant who were later to be a great help with load-carrying. After a meal of Dal-Bat and deep-fried apple pie, we organized loads for collection by the yaks.

The walk to Namche Bazar was pleasant and uneventful. Yaks, who walk at a gentle pace and do not insist on a daily cigarette ration, allowed us plenty of time to reflect on the surroundings. We could afford to walk aimlessly along, drifting in and out of Chi shops along the way, taking in the sights and aroma of a foreign land.

The procession continued on its way to the junction of the Nangpa and Sumna glaciers where the yaks, having encountered several patches of soft snow, became – as it were – stuck in the mud. At this point someone described them as being yackered, a term we would soon attribute to ourselves after we had relieved them of their loads. Having waved a fond farewell (while secretly wishing the yaks were equipped with snow-shoes), we set about ferrying equipment to what appeared to be an idyllic camp-site on the Sumna glacier.

This Shangri La was surrounded by several large boulders on an otherwise flat expanse of ice. Tents were soon erected and the famed Sherpa tea arrived. The large boulders must have weighed between 300 and 400 tons apiece, just about enough to prevent them from being blown off the end of the glacier along with everything else that was left unattended. Our attempt to erect some form of wind-break was just taking shape when Derek, a builder by profession, downed tools at 5pm, mumbling something about the quality of the stone with which we were attempting to keep him supplied. We did not stay long!

Relations between Tibet and Nepal have been strained of late, resulting in a delicate border situation. Unfortunately for us, this change came about after our original request to climb the peak by the Tichy route had been granted, and it now placed us in the difficult position of having to gain the W flank by some circuitous route. We were aided in our choice by the map supplied at our interview at the ministry in Kathmandu on which a red line had been drawn, linking the head of the Sumna glacier with the summit of Cho Oyu; the gradient of the ground straddled by the line was seemingly of little concern. This ridge has yet to be climbed and, being entirely above 7000m, it would present a challenging approach to the mountain.

Having dismissed this approach as being beyond our resources, the alternative was brutally obvious. Two cols had to be crossed to gain access to the W flank. By now the cook-boys together with Dorjee had set off on the Nangpa glacier approach and were to meet us later. Dave had not yet caught up with us. This left five of us to ferry loads for the next two weeks, setting up an intermediate camp at each col. With load carrying you are confronted with a number of alternatives: one heavy load or two lighter ones? short or long carries? The terrain was not much help either, consisting of a rubble-laden glacier with steep mobile sides. On the second col we were confronted by a steep slope of hard ice, down which we lowered our heavy packs 200m to the glacier.

Much has been written about the tedium of expedition life, sporadically broken by bouts of exhilarating climbing or fear of some impending disaster. Between these bursts of mental and physical activity there are hours of inactivity, mostly spent lying in a tent filling time with cooking, reading in eye-straining light or just talking about all manner of things, usually not associated with the event that has brought us together. Most evenings I spent with a couple of batteries in my groin, trying to cajole some life into their chilled innards.

At this point in the expedition we were able to use skis for the first time to

2. *Everest Kangshung face. Ed Webster on the easy middle section starting for Camp II on 9 May. The spectacular 1983 buttress rises out of the clouds. Khartse, climbed by Mallory in 1921, is the obvious pyramid on the left horizon.* (p 1)

3.   *Everest Kangshung face. The 1983 buttress is at extreme R. The 1988 buttress is L of the huge central depression (Big Al Gully) and rises to the South Col. (p 1)*

4.   *Everest Kangshung face. Venables, Teare and Anderson leaving Camp II for the South Col on 10 May. Peak 38 is on the extreme R. In the centre is the skyline of Chomolonzo (L), Makalu II and Makalu. (p 1)*

5.   *The Kangshung face from the Langma La. A big plume blows from Lhotse on the L. Everest is on the R, with the 1988 route partially visible, rising to the South Col in the centre. (p 1)*

6. *W ridge of Everest, c7300m. Climber: Ted Atkins.* (p 15)

7. *Base Camp, c5000m, British Services Everest Expedition 1988 (as used by all pre-war British Everest expeditions).* (p 15)

8. *Looking W along the W ridge towards Pumori (centre) and Cho Oyu (right), c7500m. Climber: Nigel Williams.* (p 15)

9.   *Cho Oyu, W flank.* (p 20)

10. *Cho Oyu from Fusi La.* (p 20)

11. *Peak (c6350m) in Upper Menlung valley, Rolwaling of Tibet.* (p 34)

12.   *S face of Menlungtse from E peak of Gaurisankar.* (p 26)

13.   *Gaurisankar (7134m) from Base Camp.* (p 34)

14.   *Unclimbed peak (c6400m) above Fusi La.* (p 34)

speed up the load carrying. By now it was becoming increasingly obvious that our peak was not likely to become over-popular with the ski fraternity. The W ridge was visible in profile, and so was the summit cone; both seemed to be a mixture of bare ice and rock.

At last we assembled our belongings at the foot of the ice slope after spending the whole day coaxing reluctant overweight bags into sliding down our fixed ropes. The next section on to the Nangpa glacier looked easy, a gentle slope with not too many crevasses: we could sledge down! As soon as the suggestion had been made plans were submitted and passed and the prototypes began to take shape. Alan was first away, disappearing crablike off the end of the glacier, followed shortly by Wes and John who adopted a Shackleton approach; they too disappeared over the lip. Derek and I were more pragmatic and secured lashings of which Baden Powell would have been proud. Pull as we might, nothing moved; the bags had slipped between the skis and were firmly set in the snow. We arrived at the camp late, having hauled the bags over the snow, tempers and ropes frayed, to be greeted sympathetically by the others who were cocooned in down and clutching mugs of tea.

For the first time since leaving Kathmandu we were together as a team. Ahead lay a two-day haul up the moraine-choked Nangpa glacier to its junction with the Gyabrag glacier. The upper reaches of the Nangpa glacier become less steep and have many hidden crevasses; the skis were particularly useful here. The view from the head of the glacier gave us an opportunity to study the various sections of the route in some detail. First the Gyabrag glacier had to be crossed and a camp made at the foot of the infamous 500m scree slope. At this point we took stock of the remaining food: six days' supply at a rate which was already barely enough to sustain us. So far the weather had been fine, with only light winds and mostly clear skies.

The ascent of the scree was a pleasant change from the slipping and sliding amongst the moraine and bare ice of the glaciers; the mind could slip into an indifferent state, free to wander at will. Thoughts never strayed far from food: freshly baked bread with slabs of farmhouse cheese would drift across visions of family camping holidays spent in the Highlands. Three hours later, two tents were set on chiselled ledges overlooking Tibet. Wes and I whiled away the hours brewing tea and discussing the merits of free-falling from university buildings, something he had tried in his youth but didn't enjoy.

A decision had been taken to leave the skis at the bottom of the scree slope; in retrospect it was the right one. The next section of the ridge consisted of a series of ice steps which were covered in places with powder snow. Sections of the ridge had the remains of fixed ropes left by other teams; some of them were set into the ice and gave me a strange psychological boost, even though they were several inches below the surface. Fortunately a kindly group of Swiss was also on the ridge at the same time. Although moving more slowly, they had placed a number of fixed ropes on the steeper sections.

We were now at nearly 7000m and four of us were going reasonably well, helped along by the stable weather. At this point there is an ice-fall which forms the main technical section of the climb. Our camp here afforded tremendous views of the surrounding peaks, dominated by Everest to the SW only 30km away. Much closer to the south are the two unclimbed peaks of Nangpa Gosum 1 (7352m) and 2 (7296m), linked by a 3km-long ridge above 7000m. This same ridge continues for a further 5km to the summit of Cho Oyu.

The ice-fall gave a couple of pitches of what at a more sensible altitude would be enjoyable Grade 3 climbing. At this height, carrying around 20kg, with lungs fibrillating madly inside a skeletal representation of one's former self, this particular word was never further from my mind. We slumped in an untidy heap of ropes and ironmongery at the top of the ice-fall. Happily, the next 200m were set at a more reasonable angle. The evidence of old fixed rope belied the innocent appearance; the angle was fine, about 45 degrees, but the ice was green and hard. A sharp pair of crampons would have helped, but it is a long time since I owned a pair of those, so after commiserating with our calf muscles we shinned up the fixed ropes.

Others had selected the same spot for their camp in the past; the remains of a tent projected from the snow to serve as a reminder to future visitors of the impartiality of the climate. We expected that the siting of the next camp would put us within range of the summit. A seemingly endless slope ascended in a series of giant zig-zags, finally ending below the NE face at 7500m.

Four of us arrived at the site, hoping to attempt the summit the next day. Unfortunately, Dorjee was experiencing severe headaches and descended the same day. Feeling better, he returned the day after, only to suffer the same effects and to be forced down again.

The morning of our summit bid, we were awake at 5am. This did not induce an alpine-like frenzy of activity but rather a resigned, bleary-eyed view of the inch or so of ice crystals hanging precariously from the inside of the tent. A handful of these down the neck at this hour of the day is not to be recommended. I sat up carefully and set the stove on my lap, a hot drink being an essential catalyst to elevate mountaineers from the supine to the vertical plane. For the next two hours I sat, attempting to melt enough snow for three cups of tea.

Half a cup of warm tea was the long-awaited prize, just enough to wash down some fruit-cake and chocolate. The day looked set to be fine and I set off ahead of the others, anxious to get to grips with what we all hoped would be the final day. 200m on I stopped for a breather. Wes had turned back and Dave was moving very slowly, stopping frequently. He had walked at his own pace throughout the trip, and there seemed little point in waiting for him.

I knew that there were two rock-bands. The first looked like Stanage Edge, with the colour of Chamonix granite. At the highest point it was probably 50m high, tapering off to around 15m. I was making for the obvious weakness on the left side and, after an abortive attempt at a short cut, I emerged above the rock-band faced with a long diagonal traverse back right.

Broken ground and a short snow-slope were followed by the second rock-band. This one consisted of layered sandstone and was only 10m high; set at an easy angle, it was soon climbed. The remaining gentle slopes of rock and snow led to the summit plateau. It was 5pm on 30 April 1988.

It had taken eight hours from the camp; I was tired and conscious of the limited daylight left. I set off down almost straight away, only then realizing just how weak my legs were; frightened of a slip, I picked my way. The weather was beginning to change, the sky gradually clouding over and the wind picking up. In the distance I could see Dave just above the first rock-band, but off to one side. I detoured over to him.

He was preparing to spend the night there. I told him that I didn't think this a good idea at almost 7900m, but he said he felt too tired to go on and thought he could try again tomorrow. I gave him what spare clothes I had and continued down, reaching the tent at 7.30pm to a welcome cup of tea. Wes had developed a chest infection and had suffered severe bouts of coughing which were to prevent him from making any further attempt on the summit. He volunteered to stay at the camp to await the outcome of Dave's attempt the next day. About midday I left Wes, intending to make my way slowly down.

My reunion with John and Dorjee on the scree slope was an emotional one; they had started back up the mountain to assist where they could. As I expected Wes and Dave to appear the next day, we all returned to our camp below the scree slope.

The pair had not returned two days later, during which time there had been a period of bad weather. Dorjee went back up to do what he could and found them at one of the Swiss camps, in reasonable shape but not fully aware of the danger they were in. Dave had frostbitten hands and feet, and Wes had frostbite in his fingers.

We met Derek at a lower camp. He had kept a lonely vigil for a week, not knowing what was happening to the rest of us.

Stumbling back home in various states of repair, thoughts turned to the subject of food. With shrunken stomachs we attacked all that was put before us with vigour, and never mind the human cost!

Menlungtse

CHRIS BONINGTON

(Plate 12)

Cho Oyu, Gyachung Kang, Menlungtse, Everest, Lhotse, Makalu were all higher than us, but Menlungtse was the nearest and loveliest vision of all. A mighty white obelisk of snow and pale pink granite, whose shape matched that of the Matterhorn from the east.

Peter Boardman, describing the view from the summit of Gaurisankar.

I first saw Menlungtse in 1961 on my way back from climbing Nuptse. We had crossed the Tesi Laptsa pass and saw it quite close, steep, twin-summited, encased in grey granite and ice, desirable, yet unattainable for it was entirely in Tibet. I gazed at it subsequently from the slopes of the SW face of Everest, from where it appears as a sharp pyramid almost lost in the greater mass of Gaurisankar behind it. It was in 1984 that I wrote to the Chinese Mountaineering Association to ask for permission to climb Menlungtse; this was a long shot, since it was not on their list of peaks that were open to foreign climbers, and I was pleasantly surprised when they gave me their permission.

No one had made a serious attempt on Menlungtse, though I had heard rumours of an illicit effort across the border which had reached a height of around 6000m. We were also told by the local people that they had apprehended an expedition in the Menlung valley to the south of the mountain and had confiscated most of their gear before sending them on their way.

The Rongshar valley had been reached in 1921, from over the Fushi La, by Howard Bury and Heron as part of the Everest Reconnaissance Expedition and then again, at the end of the 1924 expedition, by Bruce, Hingston, Shebbeare, Odell and Norton after the loss of Mallory and Irvine. Their wanderings show, incidentally, the more leisured approach of those pre-war days, when expeditions meant being away from home for at least six months. There was none of the mad rush to get back by the first plane available. Each party descended the Rongshar Gorge until it became precipitous; then they crossed the Nepalese frontier, but were stopped by a fallen bridge.

It was in 1951 that the Menlung valley was first reached by Europeans, when Eric Shipton and Mike Ward, on the way back from that year's Everest Reconnaissance, crossed the Dingjung La (which is so named in the Schneider map, used for all place references in this article, though Shipton and Kogan referred to it as the Menlung La) and descended the Drogpa Nagtsang. They named the impressive peak on the north side of the valley Menlungtse, unaware that its local name was Jobo Garu. On the way down the valley, near its head, they saw the tracks and produced the photos that have become the classic yeti track picture. They went on down the Menlung Chhu to sneak past the Chua Gompa at night to descend the Rongshar Chhu into Nepal.

In the autumn of 1954 a Swiss expedition led by Raymond Lambert set out to climb Gaurisankar from Nepal. They decided that it was too difficult and turned their attention to Menlungtse, crossing the Menlung La. They explored the upper Menlung valley, thought that Menlungtse was also too difficult, so crossed the Dingjung La and tried Cho Oyu without success. It was certainly a remarkable journey.

In 1987 I invited to join my team Odd Eliassen and Bjorn Myrer-Lund, the two Norwegians who had accompanied me to the summit of Everest in 1985, and Jim Fotheringham, one of my regular climbing partners in the Lake District, with whom I had climbed Shivling in 1983. The team was completed by Helge Ringdal and Torger Fosse who were supporting us.

We crossed the Nepalese/Chinese frontier at the Friendship Bridge on 8 March and travelled by truck through Tingri to a frozen river about 24km north of the deserted village of Kyetrak, which is at the base of the Kyetrak glacier leading up to the Nangpa La. A road built by the Chinese crosses the Fushi La and drops down into the Rongshar Chhu to the village of Changbujiang, but this is only open to tractors for about two months in the year, during July and August. We used yaks brought from the villages around Tingri to cross the Fushi La. The journey took five days to Changbujiang, but should have taken only four; the official timing, for which we had to pay, was seven.

It is a gentle walk over the Fushi La, with magnificent views of Cho Oyu and of Cho Rapsam, the peak on the western side of the Kyetrak glacier. The pass itself is on the high rolling hills of the Tibetan plateau and the Rongshar valley begins almost imperceptibly, starting with open yak pastures before cutting down into the increasingly precipitous gorge of the Rongshar Chhu. This is on the southern side of the Himalayan divide, and the flora is similar to that of the Nepalese valleys of the Rolwaling. The village of Darzang at around 4200m is the highest village of the valley. It is built in the traditional Tibetan style with flat-roofed houses terraced into the hillside. About 16km further down the valley is the village of Changbujiang which is more like a Sherpa village, with eaved roofs of wooden shingles weighed down with rocks. This is the district headquarters with a compound housing the small administration just above the village. We had to change our yaks here for those of the local villages for the final stage of the journey into the Menlung Chhu. In 1987, however, there were no yaks and we had to use a certain number of porters as well, most of whom were women. But in 1988 there were enough yaks from Changbujiang alone to carry much more gear up to Base Camp. The reason for this was the timber boom that is certainly increasing the prosperity of the village but is threatening to denude the magnificent forests of the Rongshar Chhu and its side valleys; the timber is destined for construction work on the Tibetan plateau.

The Menlung Chhu comes into the Rongshar about eight kilometres below Changbujiang at the site of the Chua Gompa, a beautiful little monastery and temple which at first sight seems hardly damaged but, sadly, on closer inspection the damage is seen to be extensive. Today the building is derelict,

ROLWALING HIMAL

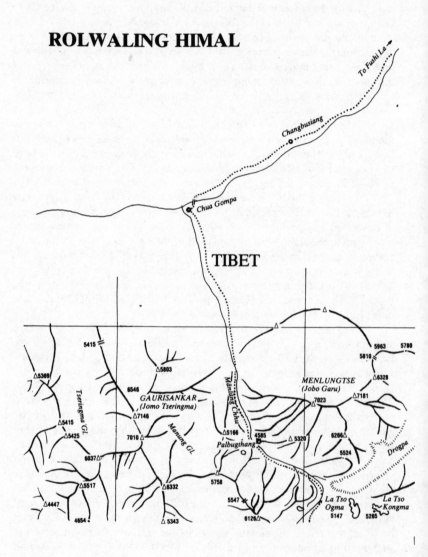

To Fushi La

Changbusiang

Chua Gompa

TIBET

5963   5780

5810

5415   △6328

△5369   △5803   MENLUNGTSE   △7181

                                   (Jobo Garu)

Tseringma Gl.   6546   △7023

                 GAURISANKAR

                 (Jomo Tseringma)

△5415   △7146   △5166   6266△

△5425   7010△   Manlung Chhu   4585   △5320   Drogpa

6037△   Palbugthang   5524

△5517   5758   La Tso   La Tso

△4447   5547   Ogma   Kongma

4654   △6332   6126△   5147   5265

△5343

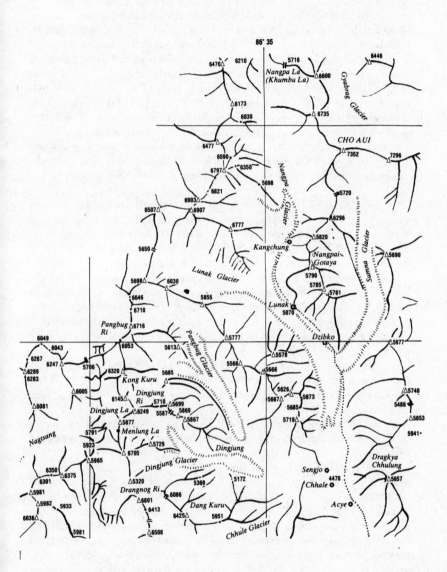

though it would be comparatively easy to renovate. The Menlung Chhu goes steeply through bamboo, rhododendron and conifer forest, between Gaurisankar and the outer peaks of the Menlung basin. It took us two days to reach our Base Camp beside a huge rock under which the famous sage Milarepa is said to have sheltered. The height was 4000m. We reached base on 24 March and immediately began to explore. There is a glaciated open valley to the north of Menlungtse with extensive high pastures, bounded on the north by two attractive peaks of around 5800m. The NW and N faces of the mountain are formidable, guarded by sheer granite walls, threatened by seracs. The S face, overlooking the Menlung Chhu, seemed to offer more hope. A series of buttresses and ridges reaches down from the twin summits which are about a mile apart. We established an Advanced Base Camp on 1 April, just above the summer yak-herders' camp of Palbugthang, and chose the SSW buttress for our attempt.

Having established a first camp at the bottom of the initial difficulties at 5450m, we started fixing ropes. For our first attempt we ran out about 600m of fixed rope up a broken granite ridge of frighteningly loose rock, before setting out on 6 April for our first alpine-style push. In three days we experienced exhilarating climbing up rock that improved in quality, with pitches about E1 Va in climbing standard. On reaching the intermediate snow section of the buttress, we were hit by a fierce storm that destroyed one tent and forced us to retreat. We made two further attempts but never managed to get higher, being hit by storms on each occasion. It was on one of the recces in the Menlung valley that we photographed tracks which seemed to have been made by a two-legged creature.

I returned in the spring of 1988 with a different team. I was joined by David Breashears and Steve Shea from the United States and Andy Fanshawe from Britain. Charles Clarke and Jess Stock were to be our support team, and in addition we had with us a film crew from the BBC Natural History Unit and a journalist and photographer from the *Mail on Sunday* with Alan Hinkes, a very competent mountaineer, acting as their mail-runner – all bent on hunting the yeti.

Since it had been very cold and windy in 1987, we set out slightly later, reaching Kathmandu on 31 March. We planned to cross the border at the Friendship Bridge on 5 April, only to receive a telex from the Chinese Mountaineering Association on the eve of departure to say that it was not convenient for us to climb Menlungtse. After a week of frantic telexes to Beijing we at last received the summons to cross the border. Later we discovered that we were pawns in a wrangle between the Chinese Mountaineering Association and the Tibetan authorities over who had the right to give permission for Menlungtse.

We finally crossed the border on 12 April to be met by Fan Xiachan, our very competent and friendly interpreter who told us that our Tibetan liaison officer had been forbidden to join us. Francis, as he asked us to call him, made up for this with his efficiency, taking on the role of liaison officer himself.

We reached the roadhead a few miles short of the Tibetan side of the Nangpa La on 16 April and set out on the 18th, with 89 yaks, for the Fushi La, the pass leading into the Rongshar valley. We arrived at the village and district headquarters of Changbujiang on 21 April and changed yaks there, to make Base Camp at 4585m at the yak-herders' camp of Palbugthang on 27 April. This was close to the site of our Advanced Base of 1987 and had the advantage of being higher than our previous Base Camp, on a flat grassy valley bottom, surrounded by superb peaks.

The most attractive route up the mountain seemed to be the E ridge which leads straight up to the main summit. On 28 April David Breashears, Steve Shea and I walked up the valley to a viewpoint from which we could examine this ridge. It looked formidable, very long, bristling with cornices and obviously steep on either side. We therefore decided to attempt the W ridge, which seemed more straightforward though it did entail crossing the W summit and making a high, but seemingly easy, traverse of a mile to the main top. On 1 May David Breashears, Andy Fanshawe, Steve Shea and I climbed Point 5753m to the immediate south of Base Camp topping the south retaining wall of the Menlung valley, in order to acclimatize and to get good views of the W ridge.

After fixing 180m of rope on mixed ground on the lower part of the ridge, we set out on 7 May to make our first attempt on the mountain. That day we reached 5800m, after climbing up a steep open ice-gully, with a covering of snow that barely gave support, to the crest of the W ridge. We found a good camp-site and, although very tired, we had a relaxed night.

The following morning, a long easy traverse across the hanging glacier that covers the centre of the W face took us to a wide scoop leading into the centre of the face. There was a pitch of good Grade 3, first led by Andy Fanshawe, and then some hard green ice leading into a wide, filled crevasse below a huge bergschrund that stretched across the face. This gave another good secure camp-site at 6250m.

That night I led out a single rope-length up 50-degree green ice, and the following morning we set off, hoping to reach and climb the head-wall. It was bitterly cold with a biting wind and, as the morning wore on, clouds built up over Nepal threatening to engulf us. A storm appeared to be coming and, since we had reached another bergschrund with a perfect camp-site, we decided to stop there at a height of 6600m. The threatening clouds stopped like a huge tide on the south retaining wall of the Menlung valley, but we enjoyed the afternoon's rest and David Breashears ran out our two ropes over towards the gully we had seen from below that appeared to lead through the head-wall.

We set out at 7am, just after dawn, the next morning (10 May). A diagonal traverse of five rope-lengths, at first on névé and then on green ice, took us to the foot of the head-wall. We reached it at midday, but it looked very much more formidable than from Base Camp. We were already short of rations and weighed down by our loads which included filming gear. It certainly didn't look as if we could get through that day. We were tired and not sufficiently acclimatized, and so we decided to retreat, getting back to Base Camp on the 19th.

After four days' rest we had another look at the E ridge, this time going round on to the glacier at its E flank, but this aspect appeared even worse than the view we had already seen. At this point, David and Steve felt that they didn't want to return to the W ridge. I was very tired still and so suggested to Andy, who was keen to have another go at the W ridge, that he ask Alan Hinkes, who had just returned from taking the *Mail on Sunday*'s story and film back to Kathmandu. Although he hadn't been over 5400m on this expedition, Alan was certainly extremely fit and had a very good track record, having made a new route on Xixabangma the previous year.

Alan had just been preparing to attempt, with Jess Stock, an unclimbed peak of 6301m on the south retaining wall of the Menlung La, so I agreed to take his place. This climb, in fact, proved to be a lot harder than it looked, and Jess and I were forced to turn back about 100m below the summit. Nonetheless, we had a great day's climbing lasting 20 hours and got some good views of Menlungtse.

Dave and Steve very gallantly carried gear for Andy and Alan up our fixed ropes on the W ridge on 18 May and, at 2am on the 19th, Andy and Alan set out from base to reach our first camp at 5800m that afternoon. They were very tired, however, and so decided to have a rest day. On the 21st they had a very long day, moving through to our third camp at 6500m. That night they were caught by a severe thunderstorm; their tent was tucked into a wide crevasse, but during the night it was nearly covered and they were forced not only to dig it out, but to shift it to a safer place. Next morning they discovered that their ropes had been buried and it took them four hours to dig these out. By that time it was too late to set off, so they had another rest day.

The morning of the 23rd dawned cloudy and threatening. They delayed setting out until they could see that the weather was settled, leaving at around 9am. They had decided to travel light, leaving behind their tent and sleeping-bags, but taking down-jackets and a stove in one rucksack so that the leader could climb unladen. Instead of traversing to the gully we had looked at on our first attempt, they climbed straight up towards the head-wall, reaching it around midday. The rock on the wall was both loose and difficult, giving mixed climbing on thin slabs alternating with icy runnels. Andy described much of the climbing as Scottish Grade V. The top provided the crux up a frighteningly loose overhanging chimney. It was Andy's turn to lead and for a moment he didn't think he was going to be able to make it, when Alan, the perfect supportive second, suggested: 'Take your sack off, take your crampons off and pretend you're doing a pitch on Stanage in the wet.'

It did the trick. Concentrating on the few feet in front of him, Andy struggled up the chimney and pulled out over the top. They had overcome the rock band.

But, once on the ridge, their troubles were not over. Powder snow covered smooth slabs for a further 40m and they had to pick their way precariously across before they reached firm snow. By this time it was nearly dark, but they kept going by the light of a head-torch to reach the summit at 10.30pm Beijing time. Before dark they had superb views of Cho Oyu, Gyachung Kang and the E summit of Menlungtse which was about a mile away across a broad easy saddle that led to the knife-edged summit ridge of green ice.

They had already been on the go for 13½ hours, so they decided to be satisfied with the W summit. After a precarious descent in the dark they got back to their camp in the bergschrund at two in the morning, to find that their tent had been holed by one of the rocks they had dislodged during their ascent of the rock head-wall. They returned to the bottom the following day to join the rest of the team who had already started the return march with their yaks and yak herders.

We had climbed the West Peak of Menlungtse, had found some more intriguing tracks around the base of the mountain and, most important of all, we had enjoyed a happy and cohesive expedition. It is a wonderful area, with the main prize still waiting to be won and a host of smaller peaks still unclimbed.

Summary

Area:

The Menlung valley on the Nepalese border of Central Tibet in China.

Ascents:

First ascent of W peak of Menlungtse (7023m) on 23 May, by Andy Fanshawe and Alan Hinkes.

First ascent of Point 5753 on the S wall of the Menlung valley on 1 May, by Chris Bonington, David Breashears, Andy Fanshawe and Steve Shea.

Attempt on Point 6301, reaching within 100m of the summit on 20 May, by Chris Bonington and Jess Stock.

Personnel:

Climbing team: Chris Bonington (leader), David Breashears (USA), Andy Fanshawe, and Steve Shea (USA).

In support: Charles Clarke (doctor and catering) and Jess Stock (base manager).

BBC Natural History film unit: John-Paul Davidson (director), Nigel Meakin (cameraman) and Arthur Chesterman (sound).

Mail on Sunday: Iain Walker (journalist), David O'Neil (photographer) and Alan Hinkes (courier).

Cook staff: Krishna Bahardur Rai and Nima Chotor Sherpa.

Chinese: Fan Xiachan (liaison officer and interpreter).

The Ascent of Menlungtse West

ANDY FANSHAWE

(Plates 11, 13, 14, 57, 58)

This expedition in the spring of 1988 had two clear objectives – to find the yeti and to make the first ascent of Menlungtse in the Rolwaling of Tibet. The BBC and *Mail on Sunday* thought the former an attractive prospect and sponsored the trip, with a little help from William Hill, Safeway, Berghaus, Wild Country and others. The team comprised Chris Bonington (leader), David Breashears, Steve Shea and myself as lead climbers, with Charlie Clarke and Jess Stock in support. BBC and *Mail on Sunday* delegates numbered six – including Alan Hinkes as the latter's dispatch runner.

Political hassle left us for 10 days in Kathmandu, slowly sinking into bureaucracy and dust. Menlungtse, it seemed, was suddenly off the permission list! The novelty value of the Annapurna Hotel pool and of the superb 'snack shacks' wore off quickly. Shea's commentary on Kathmandu moved from beautiful Buddhist monasteries and bargain carpets to the 'Kathmandu dogpie on my sneakers'. In case it isn't obvious, Shea is American, and like us all he was finding the waiting a little tedious . . .

'Change money.' A Hindu boy tugged at his shirt.

'Sure,' enthused Steve; 'I give you one rupee, you give me 28 dollars.'

The boy looked keen . . . then he didn't.

The Chinese Mountaineering Association was embarrassed. 'Perhaps you would like to climb Xixabangma?'

'Xixabangma,' remarked Shea, '. . . is as high as s--t can be stacked.' So we held on and were later rewarded with permission. So kind.

On 12 April we crossed Friendship Bridge into Tibet and here met Francis, our interpreter from the CMA. He had spent one whole week in Lhasa waiting on our political struggle, which can be a particularly boring experience for an atheist. Francis was, however, a lively character and it seemed that no amount of waiting or political nonsense could suppress him.

An absence of yaks at the roadhead sent Chris and Francis wandering in search. 'Keep out of sight of the Tibetans,' urged Francis. Their wandering grew more pronounced as the consumed quantity of village headmen's *chang* increased. Bonington eventually meandered into the compound with 90 yaks on tow, and we scrambled from our hideout to attention. It was time to start walking. Six days of that saw us 'sucking wind' at Base Camp on a meadow at 4600m beneath the E face of Gaurisankar and the W face of Menlungtse.

Menlungtse has two peaks, separated by a ridge about 2km long. The E (main) peak at 7181m had no realistic routes to its summit, other than a traverse from the W top (7023m). The W summit was pretty well guarded itself, but its 2000m W face immediately above Base Camp looked reasonable. Complicated but easy ground led to a long 55° ice-field and finally a 300m granite head-wall, right below the summit.

Our first attempt on the W face during five days in early May ended at 6700m just below the head-wall; we were defeated by fatigue and lack of calorific intake. Our commitment to filming left everybody with giant sacks full of BBC film cartridges (and for David a camera), leaving little room for 'peripheral luxuries' such as food. A combination of my restless fidgeting and Bonington's snoring and enthusiasm for diary-writing at two in the morning left Chris and myself with little sleep. Progress was slow, in descent also, and it was four weary climbers who eventually scrambled down the lower scree slopes to be met by welcome tea and puris.

Back at Base Camp, a recce to the desperate looking E ridge served to confirm our earlier suspicions. Dave and Steve decided that enough was exactly that and declared that they had found a superb place to go bouldering. This was tempting. Chris admitted that he had not fully recovered from our last attempt and also opted out of more climbing on Menlungtse. Meanwhile Alan Hinkes had returned from Kathmandu, completing his mail-runner duties; he agreed to join me on a last-ditch effort on the W face. Even carrying only four days' food and no film gear, our sacks were still painfully heavy.

19 May

2am. Pathetic stumbling and groping across the scree. At first light we reached the base of the fixed ropes left by the first attempt and quickly ascended these for 350m up the W ridge. Easy ground, no problem there. Next an abseil (this felt committing) into a couloir running to 5800m, and the start of the face proper. The couloir was bare at its top, rearing up to skirt a huge serac spilling off the face. Plenty of green ice, and screaming calves. We arrived at a site for the tent at 5800m in the middle of a burning afternoon. Al declared that tomorrow should be a rest day. 'It's often better to creep up a mountain and creep back down. It's a question of strategy.' He sounded convincing and I didn't argue; it made sense. Instead, I took a sleeping pill for the first time on the trip.

20 May

We enjoyed a long lie-in, then sat outside brewing and peering over the frontier ridge. There were big anvil clouds in Nepal, but we were enjoying fine windless weather here.

21 May

Route-finding was not a problem, despite the poor visibility at times, as I had previously been up and down this way. Al and I managed on this day to reach our highest bivouac of the previous attempt, at 6600m. Nothing too difficult about the climbing, except the monotony of repetition – pitch after pitch of 55° névé, green ice or occasionally deep unconsolidated snow. We had previously decided to leave our tent and its contents at this bivouac, whilst on a summit bid. There were around four pitches of steep snow and ice to the head-wall where we expected the hard climbing to begin. We pitched our tent here, within a crevasse below a tiny serac – primarily to protect us from stonefall. However, spindrift sloughs had been slowly burying us as they poured over the lip of the serac and eddied in towards the tent.

Avalanche! About 11pm, while we were still brewing, there was a low-pitched rumbling noise from above. Al bolted upright and his jaw dropped – he had the look of a man anticipating a horror about to begin, and helpless to prevent it. 'Sweet death take me now' – I lay quite still and listened to the approaching slide. If there was one thing that prevented my heart from stopping, it was the thought of that serac saving us from the full brunt of the snow. After about a minute all was peaceful again. Alan might have noticed that the walls of the tent were no longer flapping and were unusually depressed, but I did not. I opened the tent door and made the discovery myself – we were buried.

I left the tent and started to dig it out, but immediately the walls began to cave in. 'Like a scene from an Edgar Allan Poe novel,' Alan said. This was no time to be cultural. I remembered another scene – lying on a beach on the Riviera. Climbing really can be horrible.

22 May

In the morning we started to look for the ropes which we had left unattended and unattached. Four hours later we found them under two metres of snow! Another rest day. We ran out of food.

23 May

We set out lightweight for the top, at first in very poor visibility. Three long pitches (we had 60m ropes) of 60° ice took us to the base of the rock-wall. Al looked secure on his ice-screw and pointed me up a crack-line on the left, disappearing into a bay out of sight a little over 40m above. It felt strange to find myself suddenly doing some scratching, after so much snow and ice below, but the pitch passed easily enough. Alan followed through and led a pitch across a powder-covered slab and into a vertical crack-line in a rib, descending in about two long pitches from the final leaning wall.

The first pitch of 50m from Al's tiny hanging stance in a niche above the W face was the finest of the route, and one of the best mixed pitches I can remember. Stemming across an ice-choked crack, hooking on incuts and over solid granite blocks, I felt for the first time totally content with my lot. There could hardly have been a finer situation, and route-finding was pleasantly thought-provoking. Primarily this was why I had travelled to Tibet. Al enjoyed my euphoria and I enjoyed his encouragement. Another long pitch on a series of flakes in an incredible position allowed us to traverse leftward from the rib and up to a traverse line which would lead to the base of the fault-line. I perched myself amongst some small detached blocks. There was no ice and most of the flakes were expanding. The head-wall was vertical here.

I brought Al up for him to lead through, but my tied-off blade was, he pointed out, of more use as a runner than as a serious attempt at a belay, considering the gravity of our situation and the difficulty of the climbing. Al belayed on a good spike 6m below me and glanced at the chimney 20m distant. The 20m traverse across the vertical wall and the 20m of climbing through the chimney took close to three hours. I remember dislodging many huge blocks and being very, very gripped. I got my first runner, apart from the blade, 40m out from Al and hung my sack and crampons there. If I could not have seen the summit ridge above, I would never have managed those last few rewarding metres. I was in tears on the final scrambling moves to the ridge and upon my first view north and east to Cho Oyu and Gyachung Kang.

Al didn't waste time following the pitch and we quickly dumped one rope and most of our hardware and set off with only half an hour of light left. We knew that we would not make the E summit so we directed all that was left of our energies towards reaching the W top. We didn't need a discussion to come to this decision – it just happened.

Edging along the summit's clean edge from the head-wall's turret top, we were tiny intruders. We felt neither easy nor confident. There was no pleasure here; and if we did not go on, there would be no pleasure later. In failing light we could only see each other as silhouettes against vague shapes of rock and ice, cloud and sky. Above all difficulties and faces, with only an open broad slope to the summit, I started to count steps and breaths; many more of the latter. It was 10.30pm when the slope flattened . . .

We stood together on the summit, casting tiny pools of head-torch light on its snow. It was an unusually unhurried occasion tinged, for me, with a contentment I hadn't felt for a very long while. The perfect bulk of Menlungtse's main summit in the east was elegantly outlined against a pale moonlit sky. Such pleasure – such brevity.

We didn't linger, setting off down our tracks and abseiling the head-wall in the small hours of the 24th. At last we were descending, and it felt really good.

Bhutan – A Summary of Climbing and the Anglo-Indian Ascent of Jitchu Drake

DOUG SCOTT

(Plates 15, 16, 59)

A visit to Bhutan had been on the agenda since the mid-1960s when that great Himalayan explorer Augusto Gansser published photographs of unclimbed 7000m peaks in *Mountain World* (1964/65). The seed sown then lay dormant for 20 years, until news percolated through in 1983 of Japanese and Austrian visits to the mountains of Bhutan. My interest grew further as a result of a chance visit to the Darjeeling trekking conference in 1985. Nedup Dorje, representing the Bhutanese Tourism Corporation (BTC), gave a memorable discourse upon the underlying philosophy governing the future of tourism and mountaineering in Bhutan – the message was controlled development.

The Bhutanese government was in the advantageous position of being able to scrutinize closely the mass tourism which had taken place in Nepal, where the cultural heritage had been seriously eroded by an estimated 200,000 tourists visiting that country each year.

Bhutan had been virtually barred to foreigners until the Coronation of the present King, Jigme Singye Wangchuk, in 1974. During that year 287 foreign visitors were allowed into he country. That allocation has increased to 2500 per annum, but not all the places are taken up because of the high costs imposed by BTC – between $85 and $200 a day, depending upon whether the visitor is on a mountaineering expedition or a 'cultural' visit to the towns and temples.

The temptation to increase the Gross National Product was being resisted, for as the King once told the World Bank experts, he is not so interested in the GNP as in the Gross National Happiness of his people. Nedup Dorje managed to rekindle my interest in his country, but at the same time it seemed even less likely that I could ever raise the funds to become one of the fortunate two and a half thousand.

After the conference I and Mike Westmacott, the other Alpine Club representative, went on a short visit into Sikkim. Also on that visit was Maggie Payne, a Canadian who was running the Tiger Tops trekking operation in the Middle East. She too had been fired with curiosity to visit Bhutan and we discussed the idea of her arranging a 'support trek' to help fund an expedition to the highest mountain in Bhutan – Kankar Pünzum, one of the highest unclimbed mountains in the world. In fact I was already scheduled to go to that mountain with a group from Bristol. In the end Maggie took her support trekkers, but unfortunately I was not able to go on that expedition. She continued to visit the country, either as Trek Leader or as a guest of the government. During her sixth visit to Bhutan she told me that she had secured permission in the summer of 1987 for me to climb on Jitchu Drake and also to take in a trek (subsequently the Royal Geographical Society trek), and that she herself could take in a support trek on the actual expedition.

A month before my departure in March, our expedition had received generous donations of food and equipment necessary for the climb, but very little in the way of funds. I was on the point of cancelling the expedition when the *Guardian* newspaper let it be known that they would like to follow up their part sponsorship of our attempt on the NE ridge of Everest the previous autumn with full sponsorship of another climb. This gave us all the financial support we needed for Jitchu Drake.

In the meantime, I had been collecting information on all the climbing which had been achieved in Bhutan.

Chomolhari (7315m) was thought to be the highest peak in Bhutan at the time of its first ascent in 1937. The Himalayan chain east of Chomolhari was left a blank on the map, but penetration of this area had in fact been achieved by Claude White, the Political Officer for Sikkim, Tibet and Bhutan during 1905–07. (See Claude White, *Sikkim and Bhutan: twenty-one years on the NW Frontier*.) In 1933 the Political Officer for Sikkim at the time, Mr F Williamson, journeyed from Paro east to Bumtang, before striking north to cross the main Himalaya Divide near Kunla Kangri by way of the difficult glacier pass, Monlakarchung La, into Tibet. The naturalists Frank Ludlow, George Sherriff and Frank Kingdon-Ward added further to our knowledge of the area as a result of their various journeys in the 1930s.

It was not until Gansser's geological explorations in 1963 and the publication of his notes and topographical map that any accurate, all-embracing information became available. His visit was followed by those of Doctors Michael Ward and Frank Jackson, and then in the 1970s by school-teacher John Tyson. There is still great confusion over names for the peaks, some of them having as many as five alternatives depending on what map or text you happen to read. Jitchu Drake has been variously named Tshereim Kang, Shumkang, Jichu Dakketh or Tseringegang. There is also a great variation between official and actual heights of the peaks.

There is no confusion surrounding the name nor the height of Chomolhari. On the western border of Bhutan with Tibet, the north side of the mountain drops down to the Chumbi valley – a tongue of land jutting south from the Great Plateau of Tibet. Until the occupation of Tibet by the Chinese in the 1950s, this was the traditional route from India to Lhasa. Many travellers, missionaries, traders, surveyors, military personnel and climbing expeditions have journeyed through the valley during the last 250 years, all of them passing by the spectacular 3000m snow, ice and rock cliffs descending from the summit of Chomolhari. As a result of Younghusband's Tibet Mission of 1903–04 the surveyors Captains Ryder, Wood and Cowie – who were attached to this expeditionary force – surveyed the approaches to Lhasa from Sikkim, including the Chumbi valley.

Although many Everest climbers had considered an ascent of Chomolhari, the first to take up the challenge was Freddy Spencer Chapman, who with Charles Crawford and three Sherpas arrived in 1937. Chapman had secured permission from the King of Bhutan to tackle the mountain from the south. After the expedition had crossed into Bhutanese territory from the Chumbi valley, Chapman and Pasang Dawa Lama reached the summit by the SW ridge on 21 May. They had an epic four-day descent through cloud and blizzard, over difficult snow and broken glacier ice. Pasang slipped, pulling Chapman down with him for 100m until Chapman managed to arrest the fall. Unfortunately his camera was damaged in the fall and half his film ruined, which presumably accounts for the fact that he was unable to produce any photographs from the summit area, looking north-east on to such nearby peaks as Jitchu Drake. They were in a very exhausted state by the time they reached the shelter of a yak herder's hut.

This was an amazing effort by Chapman and Pasang Dawa Lama, considering Pasang's limited mountaineering experience. They had reached the summit only eight days out of Phari, in alpine style and without much prior reconnaissance of this 7300m peak.

Chapman, of course, became well-known to the public as an extraordinary adventurer, mainly through the books he wrote, one of them being required reading by every schoolboy of my generation: *The Jungle is Neutral* – an account of his three years' fighting in Burma during the last war.

The joint Indo-Bhutan expedition of 1970 to Chomolhari was only the second officially sponsored expedition to the country (apart from the officially sanctioned trek and climbs achieved by Ward and Jackson). Prem Chand, Dorje Lhatoo, Santosh Arora and Sherpa Thondup reached the summit on 23 April. Sadly, on the following day, Captains S L Kang and Dharam Pal disappeared whilst making the second attempt on the summit. Despite a determined effort by the leader, Colonel Narinder Kumar, to find the missing climbers, a search by helicopter on the Bhutanese side and search parties dispatched by the Chinese from Tibet, no trace of them could be found. This expedition had climbed by way of the 1937 route. It actually stopped a few feet short of the summit in deference to the religious feelings and sensibilities of the local inhabitants.

Chomolhari ('Goddess of the Holy Mountain') is one of the most sacred mountains in this part of the world. After the tragedy and because of pressure from the local villagers – who complained to the authorities that their cattle had suffered as a result of the climb – a complete ban upon climbing Chomolhari has been imposed ever since.

Five miles north-east from Chomolhari, along the main Himalaya Divide, beyond Chomolhari E peak, lies Jitchu Drake (6790m), a name which means either the angry bird or, more specifically, the angry swallow, depending on which local you consult. In 1983 the Bhutanese decided to open up their mountains systematically, albeit in a very limited way, to all comers, and Jitchu Drake was the first peak put out for tender. It was the Japanese (as usual) who had their ears closest to the ground, and the Japanese ladies' expedition – under the leadership of Everest summiter Junko Tabei – was the first in. They tackled the mountain by the E ridge *integrale*. After 10 days they had established three camps, but they abandoned the route at slightly over 5200m on 14 May, finding the climbing just too difficult and time-consuming. They left the area and trekked around to Shoda from where they climbed Sepchu Kang (5200m). On 20 and 21 May, nine Japanese and four Bhutanese reached the summit.

An Austrian expedition which followed closely on the heels of the Japanese decided to attempt Jitchu Drake by the SW ridge. After difficult rock and ice climbing and eight days above 6000m, Werner Sucher, Albert Egger, Alois Stuckler, Sepp Mayerl and Toni Ponholzer reached the S summit on 17 May. Shortage of time and incessant bad weather, especially in the afternoons, forced the Austrians to abandon an attempt at the higher N summit, but they had achieved a fine varied climb – in fact, one of the best lines on the mountain.

The following year a Himalayan Association of Japan Expedition arrived at the foot of the SE ridge and followed that to the S summit. They bypassed the lower gendarmes of the ridge, which had given the Japanese ladies so much trouble, by traversing around from the south to a col on the E ridge at 5300m. As with most expeditions from Japan to the Himalaya, this expedition fixed ropes, in this case from the scree to the actual S summit; possibly some 3000m of rope were employed before the summiters, Sudo, Hara, Deguchi, Shinmasu and Yagihara, arrived on the S summit on 20 May, three weeks after establishing Base Camp.

During the autumn of 1984 an Italian expedition attempted to repeat this elegant line, establishing Base Camp on 30 August at 4300m. According to their report (AAJ 27, 244–246, 1985), they fixed rope from Base Camp to 5900m. On 15 September the crest of the ridge broke away as Giorgio Corradini and Tiziano Nannuzzi were breaking camp and they were hurled down the E face; their bodies were never found despite an extensive search by the Italians, Bhutanese soldiers and a helicopter. There were no further attempts to climb Jitchu Drake.

Approximately 24km due east of Jitchu Drake and well south of the Himalayan Divide lies Kang Bum (c6500m). This was climbed in 1984 by eight Japanese and Bhutanese climbers (23 and 25 October) who approached the mountain from the south. A peak to the north in the Lunana region, called Namshila (5710m), was climbed by another large Japanese party. The summit was reached on 18 August by six Japanese and two Bhutanese, on the 19th by seven Japanese (including three women), and on the 20th by six more Japanese.

In 1985 there were two attempts, both in the autumn, to climb Kankar Pünzum (7541m), the highest mountain in Bhutan. The Himalayan Association of Japan Expedition of 10 arrived at Base Camp on 31 August. They attempted the central (S) ridge of the mountain, but temporarily gave up because of the difficulties and turned their attentions to the W ridge. This proving no easier, they returned to the south and reached a height of 6880m on 30 October. Next day one of the members succumbed to pulmonary oedema. All the others were needed to evacuate the sick climber, and they then decided to give up.

During this period the Explorers' Club of America launched an expedition to the mountain. They had great difficulty in actually reaching the base of Kankar Pünzum, finding it impossible to cross over from the Chamkar Chu approach valley designated by the BTC. The expedition consisted of some of America's most experienced high-altitude climbers such as John Roskelley, Rick Ridgeway and Phil Trimble, but they had to be content with a number of peaks below 6000m east of the Chamkar Chu glacier, climbed between 30 September and 5 October. It was a very disappointed and disgruntled team which arrived back in Thimpu.

A 16-man Japanese expedition was more successful further west on Massa Kang (c7200m). On 13 October, Yokoyama, Hitomi, Nakayama and Tsukihara climbed to the summit via the NE spur, 4½ weeks after arriving at Base Camp (4900m). On 14 October, four more climbers reached the summit, and another four on the 15th. Their altimeter put the summit at 6800m.

Sepp Mayerl returned to Bhutan in 1986 to lead an Austrian expedition, this time to try Kankar Pünzum. They too attempted the S ridge but failed 200m below the Japanese high point. They reported only two days out of 21 on the mountain when the weather was at all reasonable. Snowfall was at times 50cm.

A British (Bristol) expedition to Kankar Pünzum established Base Camp on 25 September. They found the climbing technically far more difficult than expected. Steve Findlay and Lydia Bradey (NZ) did most of the lead climbing, with the help of old Japanese and Austrian fixed ropes. Steve Monks and Geoff Jackson put in a fine final effort, but by then (20 October), although the skies were clear, the incessant winds which had plagued the expedition were causing frostbite, and so the attempt was abandoned by the leader Stephen Berry some 50m below the Japanese high point. The expedition was evacuated from Base Camp by helicopter. Since 1986 this mountain has been taken off the list of peaks available for climbing.

Last year (1987), Kunla Kangri over in Tibet was climbed by the Japanese and, in Bhutan, Reinhold Messner arrived with one companion, with permission to climb on Jitchu Drake. After a 10-day reconnaissance and an attempt at a peak to the east (Kung Phu, 6532m), he retired. According to our Bhutanese trekking staff, he said that climbing further in the area with the prevailing snow conditions would have been suicidal.

Bhutanese policy towards climbing and tourism in general vacillates. Certainly they are not allowing an increase in climbing activity. In fact for 1988, as far as we know, our expedition to Jitchu Drake was the only one allowed. The fees for 1989 are due for an upward hike at a time when the level of tourism appears to be dropping.

I was fortunate enough to enter Bhutan 2½ weeks ahead of the rest of our expedition and to come in from the Indian airport at Bagdogra, as leader of the RGS trek. We were met off the plane by Kandu Dorje, a guide from the BTC, who had arrived that morning with a Toyota bus and driver. They took us through the undulating Dooars, tea-growing areas, east to Bhutan. We spent our first night in the country at the frontier town of Phuntsholing before continuing by a good road, well surfaced, taking a fine line through the dense jungle and teak forests up to the conifers around Paro. It was not hard to imagine why Bhutan had remained so isolated all these years. Before the Indian Government began its road projects here and elsewhere in Bhutan, it was a very hard flog up to the central area where most of the inhabitants live, some 1500m or more above the plains of India.

Accommodation at Paro was in comfortable chalets scattered around our government hotel, in surroundings not unlike Uttarkashi in the Garhwal. The food at the hotel was excellent, as was the local whisky, Bhutanese Mist, produced by the Army Welfare Project. After visiting Paro Dzong and the national museum housed in a watchtower standing sentinel over the paddy-fields below, we left for the capital, Thimpu, only an hour away by bus. More sightseeing, archery competitions, the Sunday vegetable market, visits to the Tashichho Dzong – the seat of power in Bhutan, both temple and secular – and after visiting the shops and purchasing beautiful homespun fabrics, we took off for Gortey Gompa on the first of two fairly easy treks in the central part of Bhutan.

This was the first trek I had ever led. It proved to be a very pleasant and interesting experience, especially with this group with ages ranging from 24 to 78, all of them travellers but not all used to camping under canvas nor to trekking over rough terrain. I certainly enjoyed their company and it got me fit, for I had arrived in Bhutan somewhat under par, having completed a series of 70-odd lectures in an attempt to catch up on paying for my mountaineering pleasures over the years.

At the end of April our team began to assemble, just as the RGS group was preparing to depart. They came in with Maggie Payne and three of her support trekkers, Neil Lindsay, John Ryle and Harry Jenson. Maggie had met our team in Calcutta and boarded the Druk Air plane from Calcutta to Paro; then they had gone by road to Thimpu, Paro being the only airport in the country.

It was good to see again Sharu Prabhu, whom I had first met in Darjeeling in 1985, and with whom I had since climbed in Jordan and South India. She had climbed on our Everest NE ridge expedition the year before, up to 7600m. She had also been to 7300m on the Indian Women's Expedition in 1984, and had climbed half a dozen peaks in India. It was also good to see Lindsay Griffin loping around our Thimpu hotel, 1m 95, with one leg shorter than the other from a severe accident some 10 years earlier. Although I had never climbed with Lindsay, I knew of his numerous explorations into remote Himalayan and Karakoram valleys. David Rose had been sent along by the *Guardian* to cover the story; he started climbing four years ago and last year had climbed 17 routes in the Alps, obviously keen and strong, 1m 93, big and very enthusiastic. At the very last minute Robert Schauer from Austria had to turn down his chance to visit Bhutan as his second child had arrived a few months before expected, and now Lindsay told me that Jim Fotheringham's arrival was uncertain as his locum had had a heart attack and Jim might have to remain in his dental surgery.

In the meantime we talked of Bhutan. The newcomers were full of enthusiasm, having arrived on a clear early morning into Paro. From the flight they had fine views of the snow-capped mountains to the north. I bored them with my impressions of the country, which were basically that this country really works; it's bureaucratic like every other country, but not as bureaucratic as Britain, India or Pakistan. Here it's small enough to work, to have a human face to it. You can usually trace the line of decision-making and meet the people who will make the decisions. They are flexible, which they would need to be now and in the future, especially if Jim did not arrive. Each expedition (with the odd exception) is obliged to have a minimum number of seven members. We would also need flexibility as to which route to climb. In Nepal there is a problem – you have to state your route and stick to it, no matter what the snow conditions, avalanche danger or rock-fall danger; but here Jigme Tshutim, the Managing Director of the BTC, had already indicated that we could attempt any route on the mountain. We would also have some leeway in the numbers of actual climbers as we had Maggie's support trekkers to add on, which would count towards the required total. It is this sort of give-and-take which helps to get expeditions off to a good start.

My overwhelming impression of this country was already one of space. There are only 1.3 million people living in Bhutan, a country the size of Switzerland. I had dropped down through forested slopes to broad, wide valleys with only a few scattered chalets and hamlets dotted about. In Nepal, every square mile would have been terraced and heavily populated, with the forest cut back and the soil eroding. I felt privileged to be in Bhutan. We had not seen any other trekkers on our trails and only a few tourists in the hotels. It felt as if we had this wonderful land to ourselves.

The only children who had approached us had come to walk with us for a while, out of curiosity and occasionally to practise their English (the second language in all Bhutanese schools). None of them had asked for anything more. 90% of the people work on the land. That they had not lost their integrity as individuals in nature showed in their smiling faces and their general contentment with their lot. The only cloud on the horizon was the fact that in two weeks of trekking I had hardly seen the Himalaya. All through late March the mountains had been covered in cloud. Every evening and most nights we had rain or snow. At least the weather could only get better. I was just content to have had the chance to come to this country, to walk through its dense pine forests and thickets of rhododendron in full spring colour, to have spent time with the local people, supping Tibetan tea while sitting on the floor of their homes.

With two-thirds of the country heavily forested, Bhutan is not short of timber and they certainly use it to good effect in their homes, which resemble (as everyone has noticed) Swiss chalets. I would say that the level of carpentry is far higher and more interesting than in Switzerland.

On 2 May I saw my RGS group through customs and into the departure lounge and met Victor Saunders alighting from the Druk Air plane, fresh from Britain and Calcutta. There he stood on the hot tarmac in double boots and yeti gaiters, video cameras slung across his chest and heavy handbags in both hands. It was good to see him but sad to hear that Jim, unable to find another dentist to cover his absence, had made the decision to stay at home.

That afternoon we packed our loads for the ponies and yaks to take us up to Base Camp, four days due north of our Paro hotel. David was rushing round between typewriter and toilet as he had his first article to dispatch on impressions of the country so far, but he had also picked up a stomach bug *en route* from England.

On 3 May we motored up the Paro Chu valley to the roadhead, passing under the Taktseng (Tigers Nest) Monastery clinging to the granite hillside above us. We had made the visit – mandatory for anyone visiting Bhutan – the day before Victor's arrival. We had gone up with our guide for the expedition, Karma Tenzing, who told us that he expected, some time in the future, to spend three years, three months, three weeks and three days in a little cabin stuck in a gully just below the main monastery. He explained that the self-interned were only visited by relatives once a day, to push food through a trapdoor. Taktseng is really a shrine to the Guru Rimpochi (Padma Sambhava) who first brought Buddhism to Bhutan and Tibet in the eighth century; reputedly he arrived at the monastery on the back of a flying tiger.

It was one of the most spectacular sights I have seen in the Himalaya, the monastery perched on that precipice: actually the only good rock I had seen fit for climbing in the country, but here obviously out of bounds. We could not go inside because, after pressure from the Buddhist monks and lamas, all the occupied monasteries had been put out of bounds to tourists earlier in the year.

At the roadhead village, by the ruined Drugei Dzong which had been set ablaze after an earthquake in the early 1950s, we offloaded the gear from our bus and left Karma and his staff to arrange for the ponymen who were already waiting on us. In fact they had arrived the day before and were now claiming extra pay for waiting time. We took no part in the ensuing negotiations here or anywhere in Bhutan; the BTC staff deal with all such problems. Just below the old monastery there were stone-baths: a feature of many a Bhutanese village. They are filled with water, hot rocks are thrown in sizzling and the locals follow them into the hot water.

We were honoured to have Palden Dorje join us for this part of the trek. Palden is the son of Leni Dorje, who for a time was acting Prime Minister of Bhutan. He was armed with a pistol at his hip, to shoot marmots, he said; but he was on the lookout for blue sheep with the longest horn-span he could find, with a view to hunting them down later. It rained heavily all afternoon and night, and it rained most of the next day as we walked 22km in seven hours. We spent the night at Thangthanka at a yak herders' hut, occupied by a Japanese trekking group, with one lady groaning with mild oedema.

On 5 May we arrived at Thangothang, after a lovely walk through conifers and juniper forest. We could see the tip of Jitchu Drake above the clouds, shining white. We spent the evening bouldering and putting up camp by a stream below a ruined Dzong. Our camp obviously made a good base for exploring the western side of Jitchu Drake. Even though our mountain was only about 6800m we would still have to acclimatize during the next two weeks and that's what we did – first on the west, then on the east and finally on the south sides of the mountain.

Our explorations of the western side were hampered by almost continuous cloud-cover. The weather was usually clear in the mornings, but by the time we had reached any height the cloud was down, and it got thicker towards the evening. On one long day we walked along the true right-hand ablation valley and moraine of the S Jitchu Drake glacier, right up to where it merged with ice-fields coming down from the western side. We could only see two-thirds of the western ribs reaching up into the cloud. Although this reconnaissance had been inconclusive, we decided to move camp and check out the E side.

The day before departure, Victor managed to severely strain a tendon in his ankle. We were out bouldering; he jumped off only two feet but landed awkwardly and his ankle went over with a resounding snap. He hobbled to his tent with our help, but despite hot and cold water treatment the ankle blew up like a balloon.

This was serious: with the demise of Robert and Jim we were already very depleted on high-altitude climbing experience. Next day we set off following Victor who was riding a horse. Unfortunately Victor has a severe allergy to horses, so he rode with his Gortex salopette and anorak, balaclava, scarf wrapped round his face, yeti gaiters and boots, and also dosed himself with antihistamine. Unfortunately too the horse was more allergic to Victor than he to the horse, and it kept shying away with fits of sneezing.

We marched off and up through the hills, north of the usual track from here to Lingshi, taking a more direct route to a lake close to the E side of our mountain. We eventually set up camp that evening by this beautiful oval lake about one kilometre long and a little less across. We camped amongst willow thickets on the grassy alp and just across from yak herders in two cabins, surrounded by the yaks and guarded by two angry and forever barking dogs. Back in England we had been inspired by the photographs supplied to us by Sir Edward Peck to check out this E side. There seemed to be a rib of steep ice and snow heavily fluted in parts, like some Andean peak. Now our chances of climbing that route with our depleted party seemed very remote.

However, during the next week we went up and camped on the rocky ridge separating the two glaciers which come down from the E face of Jitchu Drake. During this period it snowed every afternoon, but from various vantage points on the rocks we could see the face. It did look steep viewed head-on, and it also looked highly dangerous, with huge mushrooms of snow barring the way at several places. Unless we went back to check out the W side more thoroughly, the only possibility seemed to be up the S face. After some debate we decided to go for that from our lakeside Base Camp, down at 4300m.

By now Maggie had returned home with Harry and John. Neil had decided to stay and help us establish an Advanced Base Camp beneath the S face. With the help of Neil, Karma and his three staff – Sonam Dorje (trekking assistant) and the two cooks Tshering Dorje and Pasang Gayta – we moved our tents, food, fuel and equipment up to a lovely lake nestling in the rocks at 4900m. While the rest of us were bringing up more supplies, Neil and Lindsay carried out a superb recce of the approaches to the S face and reached a point just below the plateau, most of the way through the ice-fall which comes tumbling down towards the S Jitchu Drake glacier. A few days later we established our Camp One at 5500m on the great snow-shelf. Then we retreated back down to Base Camp for a good rest before launching off on the actual climb.

On 24 May we left Base Camp for Advanced Base Camp. I had awoken that morning in the small hours thinking of the S face collapsing, ice cascading down from 800m. I thought of the strength of the party or rather the lack of it:

Victor hobbling about with his injured ankle, Lindsay with a torn shoulder-muscle, Sharu with stomach troubles, myself trying to combat old age, only David fit but on his first Himalayan expedition. Then there was the weather, the wind, deep snow, what to do about clothing, food, fuel, we were running out of time, children back home. Definitely the darkest hour is just before the dawn. Anyway, I got up at five to write a few more postcards to accompany David's *Guardian* article going down to Thimpu with Karma. Coffee and breakfast over, we were away around the lake with rhododendron in full bloom up here and bright patches of azalea and primrose amongst the grass.

Actually Sharu was now going much better and so was Victor, although he continued to carry a very light load. Neil left for home after leaving a huge load at ABC. After a good night at Advanced Base we set off next morning with Sharu breaking trail first, then myself followed by David.

On the 26th we awoke to an amazing morning of white mist-filled valleys, and the rising sun filling the sky with orange beyond Masang Kang and all the other Kangs to Kankar Pünzum. We were late getting off. At 11 am, just as the mist was rising, we broke trail in the sweltering heat, up to the base of the S face. From there David took over the awful work and traversed for about a mile in dense mist until we were lost — all of us with a different opinion as to which way to go; so we sat there and brewed up. As some of us were carrying huge sacks of 30kg, we could not risk making a false move at this point. From here on we had to have enough food and equipment to climb the mountain. After this attempt there would not be time for another.

As the mist did not clear, we decided to find a camp-site nearby. After a brief recce we picked a site below an ice-cliff with a chasm behind which, we reckoned, would catch any debris falling off the S face. In the middle of the night I was awakened by Victor, discussing the starry sky. The moon was out and I went out to find that we were right on course. We got up at 3am, but it was four hours before we had had breakfast and packed our gear. David had a bad stomach — all the excitement, he said — and Lindsay had had little sleep.

Victor and I broke trail up to the bergschrund. The important thing, he said, is to take it easy at this stage, so I slowed down and he rushed by! He was definitely on the mend. I climbed around the bergschrund with some difficulty, mainly on account of the very heavy sack. Sharu followed, then the others — Victor, Lindsay, nursing an injured shoulder, and David with a mammoth sack. It was soon obvious to all of us that, despite promising weather, we had left it far too late and that we had no hope of reaching the only likely bivouac sites some 600m higher, so we settled for leading out and leaving our four ropes for the morrow, Lindsay, Victor and myself taking turns at leading. Sure enough at 1pm, back in the tents, we were hammered by the afternoon storm.

Clearly, in Bhutan you have to reckon that 1 o'clock means the end of the story, just as surely as if night has fallen. The only way to accommodate the ever-present afternoon storm is to go off very, very early in the morning. We could now do this by the light of the moon, getting up at midnight, hopefully away by 2.30am and up to a bivvy site by early afternoon. So we spent the afternoon eating sardines, cheese, biscuits, tomato soup etc and drinking, trying to rehydrate. Victor had already discovered that he had left the tapes for the video camera back at Base Camp, and now David's tape-recorder had failed, so no film for TV and no tapes for Radio Four. Someone was telling us to keep it simple and to travel light. We spent the rest of the day whittling away at our food and gear, discarding everything superfluous.

We were able to sort out, take stock and contemplate the next day's 750m ice climb. This would be the first time Sharu had been on anything so continuously steep and icy. We discussed ways to conserve energy, not to hammer picks in too deep and to get into a rhythm of fast movement between natural ice-ledges.

On 28 May, I heard Victor's voice announcing that we had overslept; we had meant to wake at midnight, and it was now 2am. Never mind, we would just have to cope with the inevitable storm. We packed up in double time and were away by 4.30, moving rapidly up to the bergschrund. Sharu pulled up the rope hanging free over it; this took her some time with a heavy sack and Victor went up to offer advice and a foot-sling. She was soon up and over, and off we went in a rhythm of sorts up the four pitches we had completed the day before. The next pitch was steep and had me gasping and feeling a little sick, picking my way over a vertical step of hard green glacier ice. Victor, the smallest member, was carrying the lightest sack. It did not matter whether he was seconding or leading, his ankle still hurt, so he went into the lead and led off just as the afternoon storm came in. I placed myself in the centre to encourage the rearguard and to keep Victor supplied with rope and gear. He chose a good line in dense mist and swirling snow, and pitch followed pitch as the storm gathered momentum and strength.

At 1pm Victor expressed his doubts about continuing. I told him that we should take a diagonal line rightwards towards the SE ridge, for there we would be more likely to find a bivvy site. I suggested to Victor that we take stock at 2.30pm, when we would have our last chance to abseil off in the light. I knew that, if we did that, we would lose most of our ice-screws and thus the means to make another attempt. For once I felt remarkably confident that we should continue; I don't know where the feeling came from, but I had no hesitation in countering David's concern when he came up to me later. By the eighth pitch the storm was very violent and snow was pouring down the face in waves. It was hard for us to communicate or to see each other, 50m away. Tiny ice-ledges soon filled with soft snow and piled up on the hanging rucksacks attached to the ice-screws. The situation was getting serious and I asked Sharu what she thought of continuing. She had no hesitation in saying that, having come so far, we should keep going; she, too, could see that this was our last chance.

Lindsay at the rear was moving very slowly because of his shoulder. He and David were a long time passing up the ropes, the light was fading, we were still two pitches below the SE ridge and the storm was at its height. Even here, with only some 100m of face above us, the snow was cascading down. We thanked our lucky stars that we were not in the middle of the face, when in such conditions we might well have suffocated. Just as the sun was setting Victor reached the ridge, there were brief gaps in the cloud and we could look across to Chung Kang, covered in fresh snow.

I led off up the heavily corniced ridge for about 100m and stopped at a flat part of the cornice. I tied off the rope and began to hack the top off, hoping to produce a site for our two bivvy tents. First Sharu, then Victor came up to help and, much later, David and Lindsay. By then we had one tent erected.

Sharu, somewhat exhausted, was inside warming up and brewing cups of tea. We were all set to carry on, hacking at the snow and (now) ice to provide a platform for the second tent, when Lindsay found a huge grotto under the cornice, 3m above our tent. He, David and Victor settled down for the night in that icy cave. Next morning the sun shone wanly through the thin grey clouds. I woke Victor at 6am, and at 8am we both set off to find a better camp-site. We went up some 150m and found a snow-slope, protected by a steep bulge in the ridge above. Later that day we all moved up to occupy what was probably the site of the final Japanese camp.

On 30 May, I woke Victor for a timecheck at 0.30am. Both tents were creaking under the weight of spindrift. He came down to my tent at 1am and said that the other two were not very well and definitely did not want to go up that day. He himself had not slept so well in the storm because of the angle of their platform. We had brews and noodles and eventually Sharu and I set off at 6am to fix two ropes. It was a glorious morning with a sprinkling of light snow like icing sugar on all the lower hills. Rivers were shining silver threads, small lakes glinted in the sun, not a bad place to be! May as well be here as anywhere, I thought.

Eventually Victor arrived with a third rope. After fixing that, we descended back to the camp and rearranged it, hoping to provide for a better night's sleep. Lindsay was flat out in his tent; a 1m 95 man trying to fit into a 1m 83 tent hadn't helped, and he was very groggy. He said he had no symptoms other than sleeplessness, but why? I think that it was probably due to his severe accident the year before, when his partner had pulled him off a pitch in the Alps and he had damaged again the side injured 10 years before; perhaps his body was still recovering from that.

We sat by the tents in the calm afternoon; such a pity that we were not able to make the best of this weather. A huge black-and-yellow butterfly fluttered around Sharu's yellow javlin salopette.

Later that evening David signalled his dilemma. If he continued, he reasoned, we would have less chance of getting up, as four would be slower than three – it being assumed that Lindsay would not be going. From a journalistic point of view it was important that some of us reach the summit, and he would be satisfied with that even if he did not himself make it. After all, we had accomplished a new route up the S side of the mountain, as far as the ridge. He added that he knew that he was basically being guided, and he found it more satisfying to be out leading with his friends in the Alps, learning from his own mistakes.

Sharu's position came into the discussion. Although she was going to be slower than Victor or myself, I pointed out to David that it was thanks to her determination lower down that we were up here now. In the end it was decided that Victor, Sharu and I would head off early next morning with light daysacks for the summit. So ended my dream of all five of us reaching the summit. I knew that David was disappointed with this turn of events. He had set his heart on reaching his first Himalayan summit on this trip, but he could take comfort in the knowledge that he had contributed greatly to the expedition, taking on the burden of writing articles at high altitude, usually carrying the heaviest sack and doing a great deal of trail-breaking through the lower ice walks. His wit and repartee were always light-hearted and amusing, but the bottom line was really Lindsay. None of us wanted to leave him on his own, so David offered to stay and supply him with cups of tea while we climbed.

Sharu and Victor set about making breakfast at 0.30am. It was miserable up there, with the wind shaking the tent and blowing powder snow over frosty gear every time we opened the entrance. After three brews and a pan full of noodles, we were off by 2.30am, pulling the hanging ropes as we went and on up the ridge, in the bitter cold. Gradually the dawn colours appeared on the eastern horizon, but it was still very, very cold. We moved fast, with the second and third climbers climbing together as the leader took in both ropes. By the time the sun was up, it was time to stop. Occasionally our ice-axes poked through the cornice and we could look right down the E face. Between the E face and Chung Kang we could look across and down on to the Tibetan plateau which, in complete contrast, stretched brown and mauve north as far as the eye could see. From time to time we came across Japanese rope. It would have been churlish to ignore it, and occasionally we clipped on for protection, or as a belay additional to our ice-axes and deadmen. There was very little chance of getting in ice-screws, as the snow and ice were of a lacy texture for some 60cm down towards more solid ice.

Victor's lead took us to the S summit, and right on the summit we found the end of the Japanese fixed rope. It was good to be there, to sit on our sacks and to look around on that wonderful morning. Victor had done well to lead half the climb, considering his ankle, and so had Sharu. She had pulled out all the stops and had moved as fast as any of us. If Sharu had been tired she would have waited here at the S summit whilst Victor and I made the crossing down and up to the higher N summit, about 300m away. But she was raring to go and off we went, down 30m along the intervening cornice ridge, and up the steep but easy snow-slopes on the W side of Jitchu Drake's main summit.

By midday we were on the summit. We stayed for an hour, a couple of feet below the actual crest, not wanting to upset the gods that may reside up there. There can be few pastimes more satisfying than climbing mountains and seeing it through to the end. The summit not only marks the end of the route and the effort of getting there, but is also the place for immense satisfaction and elation. We all know that it's the journey and not the arrival that matters, but from the summit of Jitchu Drake we had that 360-degree panorama to which I for one always look forward.

We could see all the Tibetan plateau in this part of the world, a high-altitude desert stretching out northwards from the main Himalaya Divide. What a dramatic division of countries it is. The whole of the Tibetan plateau is higher than the forests of Bhutan.

Below us we could see the remarkable triangular peak of Chung Kang and the even more remarkable S face, and beyond that Kang Cheda, Massang Kang, Tsendakang, Table Mountain, Kankar Pünzum, Künlar Kangri and even the mountains of Arunachal Pradesh, about 300km away.

In the opposite direction we could clearly see Kangchenjunga, Jannu and Kabru on the borders of Nepal and Sikkim. We could also see Pauhunri and many smaller peaks on which Kellas had been active in the early part of the century. To the south-west, immediately below us, were Chomolhari II and Chomolhari itself. We could make out the long easy-angled SW ridge which Spencer Chapman and Pasang had taken in 1937 – easy-angled, but a long way and taking them to a point about 500m higher than ourselves – what an effort that must have been.

Not all the mountains of Bhutan lie on the edges. There are considerable peaks to the south and in the central part, poking up into the clouds which were now gathering. These clouds never looked threatening, they didn't strike fear into our hearts and so we were in no rush to leave the summit. There was time for a panorama of photographs and also photographs of ourselves, and then we were off back down to share the good news with the others, but we knew that we had to take care for this is when most accidents seem to happen. We made one awkward, often diagonal, abseil after another to arrive in Camp 4 just before dark.

The next day, after down-climbing two pitches and abseiling 12 full rope-lengths, we were back on the glacier to pack up our tent and the supplies left there, and then to carry our huge sacks down through the ice to the grass and flowers. The climb was over, and we had survived it.

In my tent at Advanced Base Camp, there was a message from Karma which told us that he had come up on the day of the storm and had prayed for better weather. The message read, 'I pray for the victory I want to see in your smiling faces. May God be victorious. Love and regards. Karma.'

After another beautiful morning the winds came in with a vengeance, and from then on there was always a mist and snow-plume blowing off our mountain as we walked out via Lingchi Dzong. We had climbed the mountain on the only day when there was no snow and cloud hanging over it. This is not to say that any of us are deterred from making another visit to the mountains and people of Bhutan. Whether or not we ever get that chance, we are grateful to have been there in 1988.

Unknown Spiti: The Middle Country

HARISH KAPADIA

(Plates 17–19)

Most of us have heard of Heinrich Harrer and Peter Aufschnaiter. Their escape, followed by their seven years in Tibet, is a legend. Like them, H Paidar and Ludwig Schmaderer had also escaped from a British internment camp during the war. They followed a year after Harrer, using much the same route to the frontier and into Tibet, but they returned to Spiti with tragic consequences:

> In July 1945 when still wandering aimlessly and not knowing that the war is over, L Schmaderer was brutally robbed and murdered at or near the little village of Tabo in Spiti. H Paidar returned to Poo on the Sutlej, and followed the river down to Sarahan where he gave himself up and made a full report to the police. The murderers were arrested.[1]

It was the first such crime reported in Spiti for over 40 years.[2] Perhaps this was the first time that the area was reported in such a bad light.

The earliest travellers here were the famous Gerard brothers, who explored 'Bashahr, Spiti and Kanawar' (Kinnaur) in 1817.[3] Since then, except for a mountaineering party, it has been cocooned in its own fold.

Spiti, which literally means 'middle country', lies between India and Tibet, across the main chain of the Himalaya. One of the routes from Kinnaur allows an easy route into Spiti; it is now motorable and is kept open for most of the year. The original six-week journey on foot is reduced to 24 hours, but is equally tiring with crowded buses, road-blocks and unmetalled roads. About 10km ahead of Puh, the Satluj river enters India, cutting through the Himalaya near the Shipki La. The Spiti river flows into the Satluj after its turbulent journey at Khab. The road climbs up a series of loops (the Kah loops) in 10km to enter the barren lands of the Hangrang valley. About 30km ahead of Chango one enters Spiti at Sumdo. A road branches east to Kaurik, at the bottom of which the Pare Chu river re-enters India. The Spiti river cuts the valley almost in the centre, with side-valleys joining it broadly from the east and west.

The Eastern Valleys

The road goes along the Spiti river, the valley-floor itself now above 3700m all along. Valleys open up on the east. The first eastern valley is the Giu nala, a short valley which leads to the Lingti valley in the north and also has an exit to Tibet. Ahead at the Lingti village, the river with the same name meets the Spiti

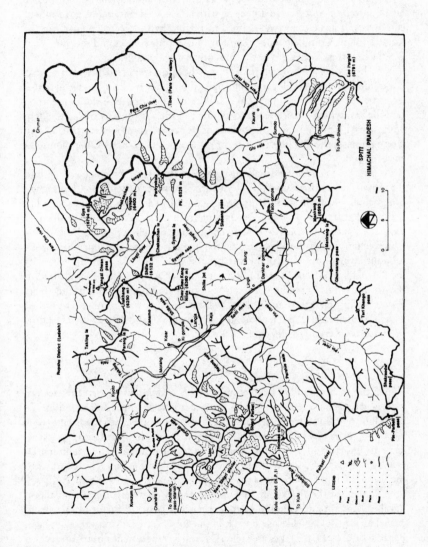

river. Lingti is one of the largest and longest valleys of Spiti; it is 60km long, and at its north-eastern head, on the Tibetan border, stands Gya (6794m), the highest peak in Himachal. (It is 3m higher than Leo Pargial.)

Further ahead one reaches Kaja (412km from Shimla), the administrative headquarter of Spiti. A small place with few locals but many government employees, it has electricity, supplied through a hydro-electric plant from the Ratang valley. Complete with video-parlours, eating houses and rest-houses, it is a far cry from earlier days and from other parts of Spiti.

Ahead of Kaja the main road crosses the Spiti river on to its western bank. But to the east are the valleys of Shilla nala (though the road does not lead to this legendary peak) and Parilungbi nala. This latter nala leads to the famous Parang La (5600m) which in turn leads to Chumar in the Rupshu district of Ladakh. Some early crossings of this pass by Europeans have been recorded.[4] An alternate pass, the Takling La (5500m) is easier and completes the picture of eastern Spiti.

All these valleys are small in size except the Lingti which goes deep into the mountains, taking a north-westerly turn at its junction with the Chaksachan Lungpa nala. At its head lies the pass of Yangzi Diwan (5890m) and across lies the peak Parilungbi (6166m). Descending from the pass on the other side one joins the Parang La route, the relay completing the circle. At the head of the Chaksachan Lungpa valley stands the majestic Gya, a stupendous rock monolith which offers one of the finest challenges. This peak is circumvented by the Pare Chu river. The Pare Chu starts at the foot of the Parang La and flows to the north-east. After about 30km it takes a huge turn to the south to enter Tibet for an 85km journey. It again takes a sharp westerly turn to re-enter India at Kaurik and meets the Spiti river at Sumdo. This peculiar course, with a fast flow of water at a very high elevation, is unique.

The Western Valleys

Whilst the eastern valleys have relations with Ladakh and Tibet, the western valleys are joined to Kinnaur and Kulu. After entering Spiti from Sumdo, the large Pin river flows from the south-west, exactly opposite to the Lingti river. This long valley gives major routes of access to Spiti. The Teri Khango (4865m) leads to the Pin valley from the Bhabha valley of Kinnaur. The Manirang La (5888m) allows access from the Ropa valley of Kinnaur to Pin. A little further to the west, the Pin-Parbati pass (5319m) leads to the Parbati valley and Kulu.

North of the Pin valley there lie three still relatively unknown valleys: Parahio, Ratang and Gyundi. Each is a narrow gorge, difficult of approach; each has a host of peaks, side-valleys and no easy passes on the Kulu side. Parahio bifurcates from the Pin valley. Gyundi has three major branches, each a valley by itself. It is proposed to declare the Gyundi valley a National Park; this will forbid all entry into the valley by locals, in order to preserve the flora and fauna. The difficult Ratang gorge now boasts a hydro-electric station right near the glacier. A 10km road has been blasted out in this gorge. Finally, at the northern end the road climbs up to the Kunzum La (4550m), the traditional western exit into Lahul (and Kulu over the Rohtang pass). This road leads to

15. *S face of Jitchu Drake.* (p 38)

16. *Looking E over the Himalayan Divide. Tibet L, Bhutan R.* (p 38)

17. *Gya (6794m), the highest peak in Himachal Pradesh (Spiti) SW face.* (p 52)

18. *Legendary Shilla (6132m) in Spiti. The true peak is L.* (p 52)

19.   *Chau Chau Kang Nilda (The Blue Moon in the Sky), rising above Langja.*
(p 52)

20. *Mike Harrop on Agyasol's E ridge with rock buttress immediately behind.
P5900m and Druid in background.* (p 63)

21. *Kalidahar Spire (5600m) L and Kalidahar Main Peak (5900m) R, from Dandagoporum Base Camp.* (p 63)

22. *Agyasol from summit of Tupendo 2. Rock buttress and E ridge in centre, Spear Peak to L.* (p 63)

23. *Chomochior from top bivouac on Kishtwar Shivling. The W ridge faces the camera L of the skyline.* (p 63)

24. *A better use of parapentes – Kunyang Kish Base Camp.* (p 76)

25.   *Kunyang Kish (7852m): NW spur leading up to N ridge.* (p 76)

26. *Julian Fisher descending from Camp 3 on Kunyang Kish. The N ridge is in sunlight behind.* (p 76)

27. *Yak pastures beside the Hispar glacier overlooked by the N face of Makrong Kish (6605m).* (p 76)

Manali (201km from Kaja) and is daily traversed by buses (in 10 hours) and trucks, for six months in the year.

Climbs and Explorations

Mountaineers have visited Spiti sporadically. The first climber in the area was J O M Roberts in 1939, who made the first ascent of Chau Chau Kang Nilda (CCKN) (6303m) (then known as Guan Nelda).[5] J de V Graaff and K Snelson recced the area in 1952. But some of the most admirable exploration was done by P F Holmes in 1955 and 1956. In the first trip, he entered the Ratang valley with T H Braham and made fine ascents. They briefly entered the Gyundi valley and made some detailed observations. CCKN was also climbed and the true height of Shilla clearly established.[6] On his return visit in 1956, Holmes was most energetic in climbing and exploring the Ratang and Parahio systems. He ultimately crossed two interesting passes, first from Ratang to Parahio and then into the Dibibokri nala to Kulu. It is to his credit that such a difficult and unknown area was so well recorded. To date no other party has ventured into these gorges, which remain a most inviting area.

Similarly, the Lingti valley had no visitors until 1983, when an Indian team led by Harish Kapadia went up the valley until stopped by the Tangmor gorge. They returned to Kaja and explored the approaches from Shilla jot, further to the north. In the outcome five peaks were climbed, but a full exploration of upper Lingti eluded them.[7] In 1987 they returned again, fortified by their earlier experience. The Lingti valley was penetrated to its head, the problem of locating Gya was solved and the peak was photographed. Crossing over the Yangzi Diwan pass (5890m), they crossed the watershed to Ladakh and climbed Parilungbi (6166m). Shilla was attempted from the north for the first time, and also from its eastern col. They returned via the Shilla jot, completing the full exploration and climbing various other peaks in the different side-valleys.

Other climbers visiting Spiti have mostly repeated the ascents of CCKN, Shilla and Kanamo, all near Langja village.

No account of Spiti would be complete without mention of many other facets. It has a unique store-house of shales and a unique geological collection. The positions of the Gompas (monasteries) are a sight to behold; religion here is a real guiding force. In the last few years Spiti has witnessed much better administration and has made progress by way of road-building, bus services and canals. The average Spitian is better off, even in the worst of winters. Of course some loss of cultural values is evident, but then all progress has its price.

In spite of the better access and means of communication, there has luckily been no excess of climbing activity. To a mountain-lover it is still an unknown and inviting proposition, with several trekking routes and hundreds of unclimbed peaks. To an outsider, even the area and the name Spiti, let alone the mountains, inspire awe. It is as forbidden as ever. After Schmaderer's murder, Paidar went back to the internment camp. Thank God he did not stay seven years and write about it!

A Note on Shilla

This small peak on the divide between Lingti and the Shilla nala became so famous that any mention of Spiti leads to the memory of Shilla and vice versa.

It was first reported to have been climbed in 1860 by an unnamed *khalasi* of the Survey of India, who erected a pole on the top. The peak appears as 'Parang La No 2 S' with a height of 23,064ft on SOI Sheet 64SW, published August 1874 (Gya is mentioned as 'GUA Snowy Peak', 22,309ft on the same sheet). Thus Shilla retained a dubious altitude record for 47 years, until Dr Longstaff climbed Trisul (23,360ft) in 1907.

The first visitors to Spiti had doubts about its height. In 1952 Snelson and de Graaff felt that it was a much smaller peak, and a high peak was observed to its NE (see a letter by de Graaff in *HJ40*). Holmes and Braham felt the same. A letter in *HJ26* p169 established its height as 20,050ft. Now on the latest maps, with modern methods of surveying, the height of Shilla is firmly established as 6132m (20,120ft) and that of Gya as 6794m (22,291ft). Thus Shilla has lost 2944ft while Gya has lost only 18ft!

In Spiti we found that Shilla is better known to the locals than any other peak. Almost every lama and villager, however far away, seems to know of it. They associate it with a place for the dead leading to heaven, and they still believe that it is the highest point in Spiti and Ladakh from which one can see heaven. It has a legendary air built around it. No one – the most elderly lama included – seems to be aware of the ascent by a *khalasi*, either to confirm or to deny it. And very few villagers in Langja knew about the route leading to it. Anyway, according to them it is still the highest and is virgin. The Shilla legend is here to stay.

REFERENCES

1   K Mason, *Abode of Snow*. Diadem Books, 1987, p286.
2   See *HJ15*, 69–74, 1949, for a full account by H Paidar.
3   K Mason, *loc cit*, p69.
4   *HJ1*, 79, 1929; *HJ8*, 118, 1936.
5   *HJ12*, 129, 1940.
6   P F Holmes, *Mountains and a Monastery*. London, 1958. Also *HJ20*, 78–86, 1957.
7   *HJ40*, 96–108, 1982–83.

A Return to Lingti, 1987

HARISH KAPADIA

Returning to an area of past exploits is like rekindling an old love affair. One has the knowledge and the experience, but is still unsure whether all the excitement and expectations of the first time will ever be repeated. However, this is all the excuse one needs to fall in love again with old memories, pictures, peaks and people.

Three of us, who ultimately made it, were old hands at Spiti. Muslim Contractor and I had climbed in the Lingti valley in 1983,[1] when the deep gorge and lack of proper logistic support stopped us at the halfway mark. Dhiren Toolsidas had missed the trip, though he had been part of the Spiti dream till the last. Now, with this return trip, his attraction for Spiti stood vindicated, just as ours was reconfirmed. Ravi Mariwala accompanied us during the initial trek and made every meal a healthy eating competition. Our four old Kumaoni porters were back too.

The bus journey to Kaja (3600m) was completed with the usual hardships, after the inner-line permits had been obtained at Shimla. We visited the Dankhar and Ki monasteries, and were immediately struck by the change. A lama passed by on a battered cycle, a great achievement for an area which had missed the wheel revolution until about 25 years ago (except for the prayer-wheel, of course). We inquired about the Rimpoche (head lama) from a meditating priest and he pointed a finger upwards. Looking at our solemn faces, about to offer condolences, he spat out some chewing gum which was helping him to concentrate and quickly stated: 'He has gone to Japan.' That was our re-introduction to Spiti: Japan was replacing heaven, there were buses and roads everywhere, electricity and supplies in plenty. Tons of wood stored in summer by the Commissioner is distributed in winter; solar energy is harvested for daily use, monasteries are well supplied, movie shows and travel have changed life-styles. The Ladarsa 'mela' has been revived. For many years a fair used to be held at Ladarsa (near Kibar), where traders from Rupshu and Kulu gathered to barter goods with the Spitians. Now the fair is there for buying modern goods from Kulu and traditional items from Spiti. Some of the old values remain. Village laws rule and religious ceremonies are a way of life – for how long, one wonders? There is talk of a helicopter service for tourists (Heaven forfend), and even some small industry. But as Spitians themselves would say: 'Flow with the river, don't try to swim. If you swim you get tired.'

Back to Lingti

Lingti is the unknown valley in eastern Spiti. As there are no known passes at its head, the locals don't venture beyond the Chaksachan La, which is the last

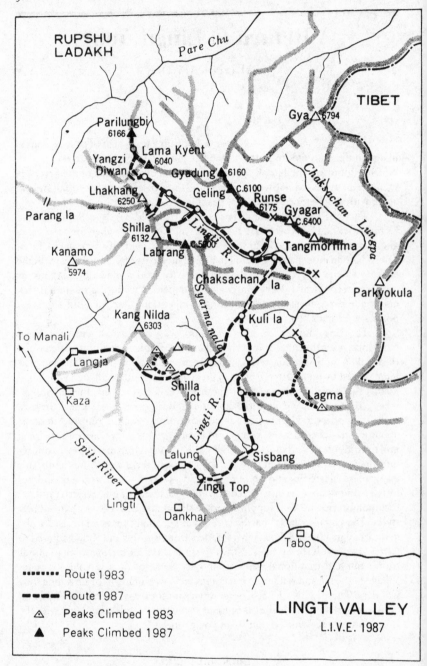

RUPSHU
LADAKH

Pare Chu

TIBET

Gya △ 6794

Parilungbi
6166 ▲

Yangzi   Lama Kyent
Diwan   ▲ 6040   Gyadung ▲ 6160   *Chakspchan*

Lhakhang   Geling   C.6100 Runse   *Lun gpa*
6250 △   6175 ▲ Gyagar
                                                  × C.6400
Parang la

Shilla   *Lingti R.*   Tangmorhma
6132 △
Kanamo   Labrang ▲ C.5800   ×
5974 △
                                                                          Parkyokula △
                        Chaksachan   la

                Kang Nilda   *Ssyarma nala*
                △ 6303   Kuli la

To Manali   ×
                                △ △
        Langja   △ △
        □
                    Shilla
        Kaza   Jot   Lagma
        □   △

                Spiti River   *Lingti R.*

                Lalung   Sisbang
                □
        Lingti □   Zingu Top □
        □   Dankhar □

                                        Tabo
                                        □

········· Route 1983
▬ ▬ ▬ Route 1987
△ Peaks Climbed 1983
▲ Peaks Climbed 1987

LINGTI VALLEY
L.I.V.E. 1987

grazing point. From Lalung the valley goes north-east to its junction with the Chaksachan Lungpa river. From here it takes a sharp turn to the north-west up to the watershed with Ladakh. A high pass ('Yangzi Diwan') leads across to Rupshu to join the trade route from the Parang La (5800m). In the distant past the Yangzi Diwan may have been in use, but no one seems to remember it, particularly as the Spitian is neither a trader nor a traveller, and the Parang La was always more popular. On the eastern rim of Lingti, the high peaks of the Parkyokula range rise up to 6526m, effectively blocking off Tibet (Pare Chu valley). Gya (6794m) is at the head of this valley, at the important triple junction of Spiti, Rupshu and Tibet. No one seems to know of Gya as the highest peak in Himachal Pradesh (or the highest between Nun-Kun and Satopanth). We intended to investigate the approaches to it, photograph it and establish the glory which is its due.

The upper Lingti has side valleys, each with many peaks. On the north the major valley is that of 'Gyagar'. On the south lies the Chaksachan La and the 'Labrang' and 'Lhakhang' nalas which pave the way to high areas.

We were back at Lalung village, our entrance to Lingti. This year the yakwalas charged us almost double the previous rates. We had a nine-day journey over a known route. They agreed to take us up to the Chaksachan La (5230m). They had no knowledge of anyone having gone beyond that, and they would not venture further. From 17 June we followed the route over the Sisbang pass to Sheru and down to Phiphuk, as we had done in 1983. We settled down to a routine, a late start after the yaks had been gathered, reined and loaded. It was instructive. This sturdy animal takes a long time to be gathered, shooed and pampered. But once the string attached to the nostril is caught, it resigns itself to its fate and carries for the day without any more trouble.

We went over rough terrain, admiring lovely scenery. From Phiphuk (4005m) our new venture started on 22 June. Initially the route went up in two days to Lakshitang (4560m), Shelatse (4800m) and over the Kuli La (4880m) to Shaktijung (4530m). On the final day the route climbed steeply to a high notch on a ridge which they call Chaksachan La. We were deposited here in front of a great view.

We surveyed the scene. 'Gyagar' (c6400m) with all the peaks on the high ridge was opposite. Below was the Lingti river. Since Phiphuk, where we had crossed the river, it had taken a sharp north-westerly turn. At this turn the Chaksachan Lungpa comes in from the north-east. It was evident that Gya (6794m) was very far from us, and the only way to it was to go down the Lingti to the junction with the Chaksachan Lungpa and then go up along the latter valley. This was our first objective. We had to ferry all our luggage 1000m down for three days into the valley and were camped on its bank. We called it 'the cantonment': a lovely glen with plenty of juniper. After a rest and a bath we were ready for our first failure. It was 29 June.

Going down the Lingti for four kilometres, we recognized the difficulties. We had to wade across four times and had to climb up the adjoining steep scree-slopes twice. At the end we ran into a gorge where, true to its name, the Lingti ('an instrument that cuts rocks') cuts through steep walls on both sides. It was possible to go ahead only in winter or early summer, but at that time the passes would be blocked lower down. This was the problem of the approach to Gya, which we had to leave for a team with a year in hand.

Returning to the cantonment, we decided that what could not go down should go up and for the next three days we went up the Lingti to its head, bordering on Ladakh. A most beautiful and difficult valley unfolded. The gorge was narrow, but luckily it always allowed us a passage. Crossings were frequent, and by now we had settled down to a routine for them. The spot was decided after observations, and then one of us would probe and go across with a rope tied to him. Once the rope was fixed, we went over in turns carrying light loads and making ferries to and fro. At some places where the river was too wide, it had to be done in batches, with belays from both sides moving up and down. It was not possible to cross after midday and, as the days passed by, each crossing required more time and expertise, the last one being almost disastrous. In the unknown Transhimalayan areas these river-crossings are a challenging aspect of the trip and assume as much importance as climbing a peak. We did about 15 major crossings and had to be very careful in order to remain unscathed.

Climbs in the upper valley

We established a camp at the junction of the Lhakhang nala on 3 July. Muslim left with Harsinh (jr) to climb Lhakhang (6250m), a shapely dome. In two days they were established at a 6000m col between the peak and Shilla. Next day, 6 July, as they went up the porter complained of headache and a frustrated Muslim had to return. After this we did not divide the group.

Dhiren and I had left with Balamsinh for the Yangzi Diwan on 4 July. We had to negotiate a minor glacier and ice-walls up to the high ridge at 6000m. 'Lama Kyent' (6040m) was next to the col and was climbed, offering a fine view. Many peaks stood on the same ridge, giving an appearance of a 'village' full of peaks (see the note at the end for an explanation of names). We crossed the watershed and descended to Rupshu, a high camp at 6000m above the pass. Parilungbi (6166m) was in front of us, separated from the Lama Kyent ridge by the Yangzi Diwan pass and standing aloof in Rupshu. At its foot the Parang La trade route passed by, and on its two sides the valleys dropped towards the trade route.

On 6 July we descended 250m to the pass and climbed unroped on the S ridge. It was very steep scree with gendarmes which we had to bypass. By 9.50am we were on the summit of Parilungbi – marked by a survey cairn and a pole. The survey party must have climbed to here from Rupshu, as it was standing on the trade route. It was called 'Parang La Station No 1', but we could not ascertain the year of ascent.

We spent a delightful hour on the top. The view extended right across the Rupshu plain, to the Tso Morari lake and Demchok in the north. Nearby, towards the north-west, were the Parang La and unnamed peaks of 6364m and 6343m. In the north-east were high peaks of 6623m and 6642m. We almost mistook one of them for the elusive Gya, which was in the distance. To the south, Lhakhang, Shilla and the Lingti completed the circle. The visual and intellectual delight in unravelling the panorama was just as great as the physical pleasure in climbing up to it. What a forbidding country lay across. We had spent hours studying the maps and dreaming about how it would look from up there. Almost like a dream of the poem 'Kubla Khan' fulfilled and confirming the topography.

Back to reality, and in the Lingti valley we were reunited with Muslim at the upper base on 7 July. We withdrew down one valley camp to enter the Labrang nala. Shilla (6132m) was our next aim; this famous peak had aroused attention to Spiti because of its inaccurately given height.[2] It was called 'Parang La Station No 2' and, with Parilungbi, played an important role in the survey. On its south lay the Syarma nala, but we were approaching it from the east through the Labrang nala. We quickly went up the valley in two days, to establish ourselves at the foot of the northern ridge on 10 July. It was corniced, and may possibly allow access only from a high point. The next day I staggered on the slopes because of a late dose of Valium. Muslim and Dhiren continued to within striking distance of the N col, but the ridge they saw ahead was sharp and certainly not easy. Our hope of trooping up the 20° slope with a flag-pole, like the unnamed *khalasi* in 1860, evaporated.

Next day (12 July) we decided to attempt the peak from the E col. In 1985 an Indian team had reached the summit via this route.[3] They had come up from the Syarma nala, whilst we climbed the slopes from the east. From the col we could see that the ridge was full of gendarmes and cornices. The true peak lay over a subsidiary hump. The time to climb Shilla most easily is after the disappearance of snow and on the summer scree. We proceeded to climb south to 'Labrang' (c5900m). It gave us a good ridge walk and an excellent view all around.

By this time Muslim had run short of tobacco for his pipe and he put his foot down for a refill in the true Shiptonian fashion. That was all the excuse we needed, and we were quickly down to the cantonment again on 13 July.

The Gyagar nala

By 16 July we were ready to move up the Gyagar nala for our last climbs in the valley. As we entered the valley we were faced with a gentle col of scree at 5840m to the north. We christened this 'Chaksachan La north', as it appeared to lead down to the foot of Gya. We studied it on the map and later confirmed it by observation from above. Our excitement to view the peak now mounted and in two days we were at the foot of the very steep névé coming from Runse. Climbing this was tricky, and our porters excelled here. We had to fix ropes and on 18 July we were on the Gyagar ridge at 5970m. And behold, across the valley in the north stood Gya. It was a majestic rock-monolith, rising steeply about 1200m from the valley bottom. A sharp conical top guarded the view to Tibet. It was awe-inspiring and this view was a fitting finale. It will defy the best rock-climbers and will require immense logistic arrangements to approach it.

The same evening, 18 July, we went up 'Runse' (6175m), now easily within our reach, in an hour. But ahead the ridge dropped to a col and to 'Goor' (c6160m). It was impossible to cross this peak to reach the final slopes of

Gyagar (c6400m), so we decided to go west from the camp next day. 'Geling' (6080m) was a rounded dome, while 'Gyadung' (6160m) was a sharp ridge top. Both were fairly good climbs. Again and again the views from the tops were exciting.

The cantonment was humming with activity on 21 July. We had ferried up the luggage and it was time for the final departure from Lingti. We quickly withdrew to Shelatse below the Kuli La, each stage being a hard repeat ferry for the luggage. No yaks would come up, as the Lingti lower down was unfordable in July. We took a different route to return, something that would complete a full investigation of the valley.

We climbed up to the Syarma La (5040m) and down the steep scree-slopes to the Syarma nala on 24 July. It was turbulent, and next day in cold cloudy weather Dhiren was almost swept away in the crossing. Wet and shivering we climbed up to the Shilla jot (5850m) to link up with our route of the 1983 trip. It was a long two-day march that led us through to Langja and Kaja – back to chhang, momoes and a rough bus journey to Manali.

For five years we had dreamed of Lingti and Gya and now the project was fulfilled, substantially if not in full measure. Working to fulfil a dream is satisfying. And it was important to pursue it: for if Samuel Taylor Coleridge's dream had been broken, 'Kubla Khan' would never have been written.

Nomenclature in the Lingti valley (refer also to *HJ40*, 106, 1982–83, for earlier names and explanations).

Gyagar:	Indian.
Runse:	A famous monastery.
Geling:	Piped instrument of lama.
Gyadung:	Long trumpet of lama-band.
Yangzi Diwan:	A new pass.
Lama Kyent:	Monk's village. (For many peaks on the ridge.)
Lhakhang:	God's house.
Labrang:	Lama's house. (Both near Shilla, 'the place of monastery'.)
Goor:	A disciple through whom a local deity manifests itself. (The peak leads to Gyagar.)

REFERENCES

1   *HJ40*, 96–108, 1982–83.
2   See the preceding article (p56) for the early history of Shilla.
3   *HJ42*, 190–191, 1984–85.

A Peak-Bagger's Guide to the Eastern Kishtwar

SIMON RICHARDSON

(Plates 20–23, 60, 61)

The first mountaineers to visit the eastern Kishtwar were probably two Austrians who, after making the first ascent of Mulkila in Lahul in 1939, were interned in India at the outbreak of war. Eight years later, in 1947, whilst waiting for their passages back home, Fritz Kolb and his friend visited the Kishtwar range. From a base at Machail they explored the eastern approaches to Sickle Moon (the highest peak in the range), and climbed two small peaks. They considered making an alpine-style ascent of Agyasol from the north, and it is interesting to speculate how the pair would have fared, for their plan was very much in the modern idiom. They decided to visit Zanskar instead, but their first attempt to cross the main Himalayan watershed failed when, much to their surprise, the difficult Muni La led to the Darlang Nullah. This not only confounded them, but has confused mapmakers ever since. They continued up the Darlang Nullah, crossed the remote Poat La into Zanskar and returned to the Kishtwar side over the Umasi La. Their time of three days for this arduous journey of nearly 100 miles was remarkable. Six days is now considered normal for trekking parties travelling from Machail to Padum over the Umasi La.

After a period of closure, the area was again open to foreigners in the early 1970s, and there was a rush to climb the obvious plums in the western region. In 1973 Nick Estcourt and Chris Bonington made a much publicized ascent of Brammah I (6416m), and two years later the Indian High Altitude Warfare School made the first ascent of the difficult Sickle Moon (6574m). Meanwhile, the peaks to the east were neglected until, in 1976 – nearly 30 years after Kolb's visit – a Japanese party attempted Barnaj II (6300m). They retreated low on the mountain, but climbed P5130m on the opposite side of the valley before leaving the area. The first peak in the eastern Kishtwar had been climbed. This focused attention on the Barnaj group for the next four years, and the following spring a larger Japanese expedition climbed the S ridge of Barnaj II to reach P6170m – the S summit. After being defeated by appalling weather in 1976, Paul Nunn returned in 1979 with John Yates and made an alpine-style repeat of the Japanese route on Barnaj II. In 1978 Lindsay Griffin and Phil Bartlett climbed Maguclonne (5750m), to the south of Barnaj III. Lindsay later visited the Chiring Nullah and soloed three small technical rock peaks of about 5600m. In 1980 another Japanese expedition repeated the 1977 route on Barnaj II, but failed to reach the central or main summits. It would appear that no expedition has visited the Barnaj group since, and, although there is some confusion as to the naming of the peaks, it seems certain that none of the main

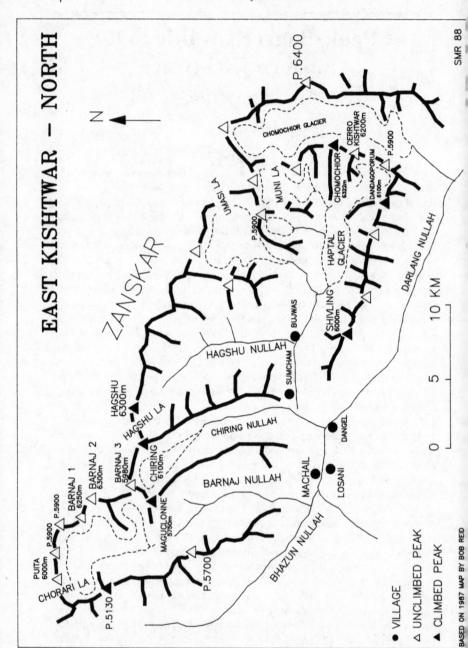

EAST KISHTWAR – NORTH

SMR 88

BASED ON 1987 MAP BY BOB REID

● VILLAGE

△ UNCLIMBED PEAK

▲ CLIMBED PEAK

summits of the Barnaj group has been climbed. (In 1988, whilst exploring the Hagshu glacier from the north, Nick Kekus noted a straightforward snow route to one of the main Barnaj summits, so an approach from Zanskar may prove to be the simplest way of attempting these fine mountains.)

It was early in 1980, while I was looking for a suitable objective for a first Himalayan trip the following year, that Phil Bartlett suggested the Kishtwar during an OUMC lecture. Following up the Oxford connections, an examination of Lindsay Griffin's slides and those of Steve Venables (who had been trekking in the Hagshu Nullah in 1979) pointed to two objectives – Agyasol (6200m) and Kishtwar Shivling (6000m). Lindsay was very taken by the north side of Agyasol – as Fritz Kolb had been, who described it in his book *Himalayan Venture* as 'a beautiful, really splendid mountain'. Steve, on the other hand, pointed out the N face of Shivling, remarking (with much foresight) that climbing it would lead to instant superstar status! It was with a certain naïvety and arrogance, therefore, that we decided to attempt both mountains, and the 1981 OU expedition to Kishtwar was born. 'We' consisted of three students – Mike Harrop, Nick Barrett and myself – but John Wilkinson and Roger Everett, together with his wife Dairena Gaffney, came along as well to balance our youthful enthusiasm with a little more experience.

It was something of a shock, later that year, to discover that a party from Kingston Polytechnic had attempted Agyasol that autumn, but had failed to cross the Darlang river. (This still puzzles me, since there is a bridge at Losani, directly under the mountain. I can only surmise that they did not travel far enough up the valley to find it.) Showing remarkable determination, they then moved their Base Camp to the virtually unknown Kaban Nullah on the S side of the mountain, where they found an approach on to the E ridge. Running out of time, they retreated at 5600m below a prominent 300m-high rock buttress. This was an enormous contribution to the exploration of the area, and I wonder whether we would have found the mountain at all, let alone been able to climb it the following year, without their reconnaissance. We had managed to leave our maps back in Britain and, having reached Athole, we were guided to the Kaban Nullah by the many locals, who told us that the Kingston party had gone that way the year before. We were not quite as incompetent as this sounds, for the valleys in Kishtwar are deep and steeply sided, so that it is impossible to see the mountains at all until one reaches the higher villages such as Machail.

Agyasol is a large and complicated mountain but, once found, the E ridge proved to be an excellent route. We established ourselves fairly quickly at the Kingston highpoint below the rock buttress, but the weather turned bad that night and it stormed for the next three days. During a lull John, Mike and I (who was suffering badly from the altitude) descended, leaving Roger and Nick to sit out the storm for another two days. They climbed the rock buttress (which turned out to be not quite as fierce as it looked) in perfect weather, to a bivouac at its top, and continued along the long corniced ridges to the E summit the following day. They found it difficult to tell whether the central summit was any higher; reaching it would have involved many hundreds of metres of ascent and re-ascent along a sharp and exposed ridge, so they decided to descend.

John unfortunately had run out of time and returned home with Roger,

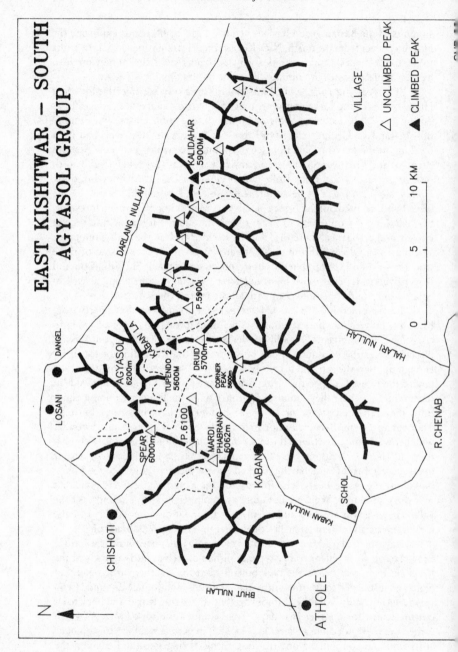

EAST KISHTWAR – SOUTH
AGYASOL GROUP

● VILLAGE
△ UNCLIMBED PEAK
▲ CLIMBED PEAK

0   5   10 KM

but Mike and I repeated the route after sitting out another five-day storm below the rock buttress. The weather in Kishtwar is variable, to say the least! After his first visit to Barnaj II in 1977, Paul Nunn described the weather as the worst he had encountered in 21 years' climbing, but other parties have experienced fine settled spells of up to two weeks. Most expeditions have climbed post-monsoon and have been well established on their mountains in early September, although the Japanese parties have tended to climb pre-monsoon. The Zanskar side of the range receives little precipitation, so it may be possible to climb on this side throughout the summer. However, any major weather system will affect the whole range, but the western and southern peaks appear to receive the bad weather first.

Mike and I reached the summit of Agyasol on a perfectly still clear day, and we had a superb view looking across to the mountains north of the Darlang Nullah. At that time they were virtually all unclimbed, but now many of the important peaks have had ascents. Almost directly opposite lay Kishtwar Shivling with its impressive S face. Steve Venables returned with Dick Renshaw in 1983 to climb the N face – a difficult seven-day climb up steep ice and rock. Together with the 1982 Polish routes on Arjuna (6230m), this is probably the most difficult climb, to date, in the range. Further to the east was a fine pyramidal peak which we called Kishtwar Weisshorn (6100m). It was climbed in 1986 by Bob Reid and Ed Farmer, who made a long and unseen approach directly up from the Darlang Nullah. Unacclimatized, they made a remarkably fast ascent of the icy SW face, taking only three days from the valley. Their liaison officer named their peak Dandagoporum – Hindi for 'Ivory Tower'.

Directly to the north, at the head of the Hagshu Nullah, lies Hagshu Peak (6300m). Steep on all sides, it is one of the most impressive mountains in the area. This peak was attempted several times from the Kishtwar side, until it was eventually climbed in 1988 with a northern approach from Zanskar via the Hagshu glacier. Chiring (6100m), just to the west across the Hagshu La (a difficult pass that is now only occasionally used), was almost climbed in 1980 by a British party, when Chris Lloyd fell from the summit ridge. They climbed a nearby peak (5638m), and named it Khagayu Dost (Hindi for 'Lost Friend') in memory of Lloyd. In 1987, after failing on the SW face of Hagshu, Andy Dunhill and Roger Brooks climbed the S ridge of Chiring to the S summit where they found an abseil sling. The Indian Mountaineering Foundation, however, was unaware that Chiring had been climbed, but had an ascent of Hagshu on its records. It is possible that a French party, who climbed a mountain they named La Shal (6135m) from the Hagshu Nullah in 1983, actually climbed Chiring, and that this was recorded by the IMF as an ascent of Hagshu.

It was the other peaks in the Agyasol group, however, which were to draw me back again in 1984. Before we went home in 1981, Nick and I spent a day and a half climbing a prominent aiguille above our Base Camp, which we called Spire Peak (5000m). It was really the first pinnacle on the long and complicated SE ridge of Mardi Phabrang (6062m), which is a very impressive mountain, and the most southerly of the Agyasol group. (This peak is marked as Gharol on many maps, but the local people from Kaban call a smaller rocky peak above their village Gharol. 'Gharol' was first climbed in 1980 by an Indian team, but it is unclear which mountain they climbed.) The NE pillar of Mardi Phabrang was the objective of the 1984 expedition which consisted of Mark Miller, Sean Smith, Tom Curtiss and myself. In marginal weather we established a tent at the top of the long icy couloir that led to the col at 5200m, between the pillar and P6100m to the north. The weather never let up and conditions were always too icy to attempt the 200m rock buttress which led up to steep mixed ground and a beautiful narrow 'S'-shaped summit ice-field. After it had snowed every day for three weeks we gave up our attempt. Ironically, once we had descended to Base Camp the weather turned fine. We reacted to our disappointment in different ways. The rest of the team wanted to return to Delhi as quickly as possible, whilst I was keen to explore the peaks at the head of the valley, so, after packing a rucksack, I set off alone up the Kaban Nullah.

On entering this valley one finds that the higher mountains are hidden; the most striking peak is Tupendo I (5700m), a fine rock spire with some resemblance to the Dru. It is also worshipped as a god from Kaban, which is why John coined the name 'Druid' for it in 1981. To its left is Tupendo II (5600m), a straightforward snow peak (something of a rarity in Kishtwar); it seemed a sensible mountain for a solo attempt. I crossed the Agyasol glacier and bivouacked at 4600m by a rock rognon. Rising early next morning, I climbed the glacier to the col between the two mountains, and then climbed the broad S ridge to the summit. The weather was excellent, and I had plenty of time to study the surrounding peaks.

The Druid was not quite as steep in profile, and an interesting rock route could be climbed on the front (west) face. Corner Peak (5600m), at the south end of the Agyasol glacier, has a gully line cutting up through the NE face that leads on to the E ridge, which would make a good training climb. Behind me was P5900m, with a beautiful curling N ridge that would give reasonable climbing in a very impressive position overlooking the imposing Eiger-like NW face. It could either be approached from the col between the Druid and Tupendo II (which has an easy descent on the east side), or, in a more leisurely fashion, up the Halari Nullah from the Chenab river. This valley is unexplored and would also provide access to the Kalidahar group from the south. The main Agyasol group to the west provided an impressive backcloth of 6000m peaks, with Mardi Phabrang standing proud at the western end of the chain. I still believe that the NE pillar is the finest prize in the area. It was attempted again by a British party in 1986, but, arriving in the middle of September, they had a similar experience to ourselves and, suffering from poor weather, they were unable to make any significant progress on the route. Given good conditions it would make an ideal objective for a strong two-man team. The two mountains to its north, P6100m (which Mark christened 'Big Red Gnarley Peak') and Spire Peak (6000m) are both steep and impressive, but unfortunately consist of very poor rock. It may be possible to climb their icy N faces from the Bhut Nullah, but access would be difficult. A good view of P6100m can be had from just above the bridge at Chishote, halfway between Athole and Machail. (The rock varies in quality throughout the range. The rock buttress on Agyasol is gneiss, which was very friendly and provided lots of holds. Dandagoporum is mica schist, whilst Kishtwar Shivling consists of good rock akin to granite.) The greatest mountaineering challenge in the group, however, is the traverse of the two Agyasol summits. This committing route would provide an exciting adventure for a strong team. The N face (which is similar in appearance to the Aiguille du Plan) can be reached from Dangel in the Darlang Nullah, and leads directly to the unclimbed central summit. Once the E summit is reached, the descent to Kaban and then Athole would take between two and three days.

It was a new experience to stand alone on an unclimbed summit, and it was tempting to stay longer, but I wanted to descend before the sun softened the snow. I retraced my footsteps to the Agyasol glacier, and then made the long haul to the site of the 1981 Agyasol Advanced Base at 4500m. I was intending to cross the Kaban La (a pass that is used frequently by shepherds in the summer) into the Darlang Nullah, and then, hopefully, to catch up with the others in Kishtwar. I started early next morning, and soon reached the glacier below the E ridge of Agyasol. On the north side it seemed remarkably snowy for a route supposed to be suitable for animals, but I put it down to the weeks of bad weather and continued on down. Several hours later, after I had gingerly picked my way through an extensive crevassed zone, the penny dropped, and I realized that I had missed the route. I should have traversed the slopes east from the ABC site to above a small glacier below the steep NW face of Tupendo II, which is cut by a superb gully that leads directly to the summit. I felt tired and, unsure of where exactly the Kaban La was, I was unwilling to retrace my steps in the knee-deep snow, and so I continued on down. It proved to be a big mistake. The crevasses became larger and I was forced to start abseiling, until suddenly I came out at the top of a huge vertical ice-wall. I sat down and thought. The easiest option was to abseil down the ice-wall and pray that two ice-screws were enough to reach the bottom. I set up the first abseil from an ice bollard, but after clipping my descendeur into the ropes, I couldn't bring myself to make the commitment. After a succession of bad decisions and poor judgements throughout the day, sense prevailed and I knew that I had to find another way. Eventually I summoned up enough energy to climb over a small rock peak, and then abseiled down a steep icy gully on its N side. When I ran out of gear, I downclimbed to reach another glacier system which led down into a tiny hanging valley. My worry now was whether it was possible to follow this down into the Darlang Nullah, but just as darkness fell I found a tiny deserted shepherd's shelter by a small pasture. Someone had been here before me! I was moved to tears. I reached Machail at 11am next morning, and just made Athole by nightfall. The following evening I caught up with the rest of the team in Kishtwar, and we all left for Jammu early next morning.

Roger Everett and I returned in autumn 1988 to climb Chomochior (6322m), at the head of the Haptal Nullah. Roger's account of our ascent is printed elsewhere in this volume (pp71–75). In contrast to my previous visits, the weather was poor on the summit, but we did get the occasional glimpse of the higher mountains. Agyasol, Sickle Moon, Barnaj and Hagshu dominated the skyline, while the nearer, shapely Dandagoporum just poked through the cloud. Across the Chomochior glacier to the east stood P6400m, a steep peak with no obvious route to the top. It is now the highest unclimbed summit in the range, and will be attempted by a Scottish party in autumn 1989. The nearest peak, however, was Cerro Kishtwar (6200m), a daunting rock spire that would not have been out of place in Patagonia. We spent a long time studying the W face from our Advanced Base Camp on the upper Haptal glacier, before we eventually spotted a line up a narrow ice couloir that led up, through its seemingly blank upper walls, to reach the S ridge. From the summit ridge of Chomochior, however, we saw a perhaps more climbable route on its tremendous 2000m NE face. A steep line of icy gullies and grooves leads all the way to the summit. Other worthwhile objectives from the Haptal Nullah include several small rock peaks between Dandagoporum and Kishtwar Shivling, and the SE pillar of Shivling itself, which would provide a magnificent rock climb.

Carl Schaschke and Jeff Knight met us on our return to the valley. They had just made the first ascent, by a good ice and mixed route up the E ridge, of Kalidahar Main Peak (5900m), which lies across the Darlang Nullah from Dandagoporum. The rest of their party was attempting the impressive Kalidahar Spire (5600m). We learnt later that Conran Anker and Kevin Green climbed the N ridge by a superb 15-pitch climb (5.10 and A2), but Geoff Hornby and Tom Norris were less fortunate when they were defeated after 22 pitches by expanding flakes at half height on the larger NW face.

It had been fascinating to explore the cirque of mountains around the Haptal glacier, but one thing still puzzled us. Where exactly had Kolb gone when he crossed the elusive Muni La in 1947? My initial thought was that the icy col below P5900m, on the right fork of the Haptal glacier, must be the pass, but Roger was not convinced. He rather shrewdly guessed that Kolb must have taken the valley to the east of the Umasi Nullah. After all, he reasoned, the Umasi La led into Zanskar, and it seemed logical that Kolb should have tried a parallel valley. From Chomochior we had noticed a sharp notch in the rock wall on the west side of the huge glacier basin below the N face. Was this Kolb's Muni La? After a day's rest at Base Camp it was time to put the theory into practice, so we packed four days' food and set off to repeat Kolb's journey. We were tired, and it took us two days to reach the tiny glacier at the head of the valley – a journey which must have taken Kolb half a day or so if he was to keep to his demanding three-day schedule. Unfortunately the weather closed in for the next two days, so we never crossed the notch, but it did look reasonable from its eastern side and we were certain that we had found the Muni La. Kolb's journey remains unrepeated, and is an excellent example of the exploratory trekking the area has to offer.

Twelve years after the ascent of the first peak, most of the higher summits have been climbed at least once, but often only by the most obvious route. There is plenty of scope left to satisfy those looking for a technical challenge with a hint of the unknown.

A Scramble in the Kishtwar Alps

ROGER EVERETT

The Kishtwar region of the Indian Himalaya is an ideal venue for the mountaineer who relishes unclimbed peaks of moderate altitude in an uncrowded environment. Lying between Kashmir to the west, Lahul to the east and Zanskar and Ladakh to the north, it is just to the south of the main watershed. Compared with these other well-known areas, Kishtwar is relatively unfrequented by tourists and trekkers, and has been less extensively explored by mountaineers than many of the other Indian Himalayan ranges. This is particularly true of the eastern part of the Kishtwar range, where the majority of the peaks remain unclimbed. Why this should be so is not clear. The valleys are strikingly beautiful, the people are friendly, the climate is relatively dry (the region being close to the deserts of Ladakh), and the mountains provide a wealth of objectives at all levels of difficulty and at amenable altitudes.

Simon Richardson and myself, together with our wives Christine and Dairena, were searching for an objective for a family expedition of the type I had often enjoyed before. Kishtwar seemed a suitable possibility with its unclimbed peaks and excellent trekking, and we were particularly attracted by a mountain photographed by Steve Venables from his highest bivouac on Kishtwar Shivling (which he climbed with Dick Renshaw in 1983). This prominent peak displayed a striking steep ridge line leading from a glacier to the summit snow ridge about 1400m above. As far as we could judge from the map, the peak lay close to the elusive Muni La; the only peak marked on the map in this region was unnamed and given as 5900m. Therefore officially our objective was UNP5900m, but since this height was clearly an underestimate, we renamed the mountain Chomochior (from the name of a glacier on one of our maps) and guessed the height, with surprising accuracy, as 6300m. Thus the British East Kishtwar Expedition 1988 was born.

We managed to escape the numbing heat of Delhi so rapidly that our liaison officer was unable to keep up. After the overnight train journey to Jammu we maintained the momentum with a taxi ride to Kishtwar and the bus the next day to Galhar. One of the advantages of small expeditions is their mobility. The walk to Base Camp was to take five days. The first two days took us up the Chenab gorge, which some years before had presented a really splendid walk through wild scenery, with the mule path sometimes built out from steep rock-walls with amazing exposure. Now a motorable road is being blasted straight through the cliffs; next year it may well be possible to take a bus all the way to Athole. This blasting almost caused a premature end to our trip when faulty communication nearly sent us – along with a sizeable mule train – on an aerial trip into the river. We reached Athole on the second day (where our liaison officer, much to our mutual surprise, caught up with us), and then turned north along the Bhut Nullah. The walking became more interesting and strenuous as the path meandered up and down steep wooded hillsides with occasional villages. We stopped for our third night at Kundail (2300m). Our fourth day saw a steady increase in altitude through some spectacular scenery. Cliffs reminiscent of Colorado's Eldorado Canyon rose above the torrent, while we wandered through pine-woods, crossed some huge avalanche debris and had the odd glimpse of 6000m peaks far above. After passing through Chisote we continued to Machail (2954m), the major town of the region, and camped a little further on. The last day of the walk-in was very exciting, as we gained height and left the main valley to reach the foot of the Haptal Nullah at Sumcham (3450m). There were superb views of Agyasol (which Simon and I had climbed in 1981) and Shivling, and then, for the first time, we saw our objective at the head of the valley. The view was encouraging: it didn't look totally impossible. We came to a halt at Bujwas (3480m), where our donkeys could not cross the river at the foot of the Hagshu Nullah, and found a delightful site for Base Camp.

Our intended route, the steep NW spur of Chomochior, rose from a glacier basin about 600m above the head of the main Haptal glacier. This basin was guarded by a substantial ice-fall; despite various explorations, we failed to find a way round it. Being married men, Simon and I took our responsibilities seriously and, making no attempt to overcome our fear of a direct assault, we decided to try elsewhere. It seemed that we could reach another glacier below the W ridge of the mountain by a circuitous route which skirted two smaller ice-falls to the south-west. We judged that, once under the W ridge, we could either cross some broken ground to reach our original objective or, failing that, make an attempt on the W ridge itself. This appeared to be a feasible line, although the final tower looked formidable. Our first problem was the huge distance between Base Camp and the mountain. Although an ideal sunny spot suitable for the LO, and for Dairena and Christine to start their traverse of the Umasi La, Base Camp was two days' walk from the foot of the serious climbing and almost 3000m below the summit. Our attempt was to be in alpine style, implying an ascent in a single push from Base Camp. Obviously, the length (and therefore in part the difficulty) of an ascent depends on where Base Camp is situated. Since ours was so low, it seemed reasonable to keep our ascent within the rules of alpine style by simply moving it progressively uphill.

Dairena carried a load for us to the site of our Advanced Base Camp, in a splendid ablation valley near the head of the Haptal glacier. This proved to be beside a shepherds' hut which was guarded by three aggressive dogs. Our regular battles with these beasts, at all times of the day and night, gradually changed from terrifying experiences to a bit of harmless fun. For all their threatening behaviour, we discovered that they would not actually attack us and, like 'Fido' on Brighton beach, they playfully chased the stones we hurled at them.

With ABC established it was time for Dairena and Christine to start their trek, leaving Simon and myself to climb. Since they would be returning to Britain via Padam, Kargil and Srinagar, we wouldn't be meeting again until after the end of the holiday; a poignant moment. During the next two days we carried all our food and equipment from ABC to a camp below the W ridge at 4900m. Our Base Camp had now become Super Advanced Base Camp. Reaching SABC involved a six-hour trip from ABC, first crossing the main glacier, then avoiding one ice-fall on moraine and skirting most of a second one near the bergschrund on its left bank. The second ice-fall had a frightening section, crossing steep serac walls above a collapsed area of deep holes. Above this the glacier was straightforward, with easy walking in a magnificent setting.

A short way above SABC an ice couloir led through the rock-walls below the W ridge. This was such an obvious line that we shelved the idea of traversing to the NW spur, which was still out of sight and a long way away. On 6 September we made a very early start, carrying five days' food, in order to be as high as possible before the sun could create a risk of stonefall. The couloir was easy at first, but it gradually steepened and turned to hard uncompromising water ice. Although never very steep, the ice made sufficient demands on arm and calf muscles to necessitate belaying. In any case, as we gained height, a rope-length's climbing was quite far enough without a rest! Higher up there were a couple of tricky sections where the ice was not continuous, but after climbing for six hours we gained easy ground leading to a col on the W ridge. Although it was still quite early, we decided to stop as the next possible tent site was clearly a long way above. We were rather surprised and pleased to find the altimeter reading 5600m; we had come quite a long way. An excellent tent platform was easily made on a ledge of broken rock, and then we settled down to a cooking marathon while gazing at the superb views.

Above us a snow ridge led to a band of slabs before mixed ground went up to a shoulder below the final tower. This still looked very hard; success was still in doubt. The weather continued excellent, but our rapid progress was causing acclimatization problems, so we had a rest day. That night an electric storm far to the south kept up a continuous illumination. Although we were under clear skies the storm was a little worrying. Would it come our way? Was this the start of some bad weather?

After the rest day we made a fairly early start and quickly climbed the snow to the foot of the slabs. A series of cracks and grooves gave enjoyable delicate climbing for a pitch, and then a short steep icy corner led to mixed ground on the crest of the ridge again. Whenever the ridge steepened we took the snow, ice or mixed slopes to its left. The climbing was never very hard but always interesting and well protected. Again we gained height quickly, only to slow down as the increased altitude made itself felt. After a six-hour shift we reached a shoulder in rapidly worsening weather. The totally unrealistic idea of making a dash for the summit was quickly discarded for the less adventurous but safer course of digging out a tent site. Once inside the tent we tried to imagine that it wasn't snowing, and we also tried to forget that we had earlier spent a whole day of perfect weather doing nothing. Had we lost our chance? We were at just over 6000m, so the summit could not be too far away. However, the final tower still looked extremely formidable, although there was just a hint that there might be a route round behind it. The evening was spent discussing theoretical mountain topography.

That night we slept (if that is the right word) probably higher than either of us had done before. (I had been higher once, but then I definitely didn't sleep.) We woke before dawn and started melting snow. The stove (an MSR Whisperlite International), which had been a complete disaster from the outset, produced its most stubborn performance yet, and after an hour we only had half a cup of cold chocolate each. Both of us felt rough, but as the weather was obviously threatening it was clearly important that we should make an immediate attempt on the summit, or the chance might be lost completely. In any case, neither of us contemplated another night at this height with any enthusiasm. We packed a day-sack and, sandwiched between layers of cloud above and cloud below, climbed mixed ground towards a rocky ridge leading to the final tower. Just below the ridge the rock reared up steep and smooth. Obviously suffering from lack of judgement induced by altitude, I threw myself at a difficult crack leading to a large overhang. As the time raced by and the clouds gathered, I vainly struggled upwards until what should have been obvious finally dawned on me: I couldn't climb it. But Simon had a moment of real inspiration and suggested a diagonal abseil to reach an easier line down to the left. At the cost of this point of aid we arrived on more mixed ground which brought us up to the ridge. The new view generated much excitement, for not only could we see into Zanskar for the first time, but it was clear that in the space of a few moments we had gone from a situation of likely failure to one of almost certain success. The tower was avoidable. Leaving the rucksack, we set off on the last stage to the summit. Moving freely, we kicked steps in good snow up to the summit ridge, and then wandered along through patches of mist (but with very atmospheric views of the nearby summits which still protruded from the cloud) towards the top. Just below a prominent mound I stopped so that we could reach the summit together, but it turned out to be a false top. So much for the emotional gesture! The ridge continued to curl away, until suddenly there was no more; the ground fell away steeply to the east. We had climbed the mountain.

After so much good weather it was frustrating to be peering through the mist for glimpses of the mountains which had been our neighbours for the previous week. Occasionally the highest summits (such as Agyasol) would break clear in the west, while the lower hills in Zanskar to the east were frequently clear, but a fine granite peak (Cerro Kishtwar) just across the glacier remained hidden. As we had looked forward to this trip for so long it seemed odd to start going down, but we were several days from the nearest village and, with the cloud all around us and snow beginning to fall, descent suddenly seemed a good idea.

We reversed the snow slopes, scrambled along the rock ridge to a position from which we could abseil to retrieve the gear abandoned in the difficult crack, and reached the tent in increasing cloud and snowfall. We hurriedly packed all the gear and then continued down. The tent site above the couloir eventually appeared through the gloom, and we settled down to a relaxed evening, battling with the stove and feeling quite pleased with ourselves. The weather remained poor throughout the night and it was still gently snowing in the morning. After abseiling down the couloir, we got back to SABC early in the afternoon; a combination of real tiredness, lethargy and the weather dictated that we should stop there for the night. The glacier, with its ice-falls, was no place to be wandering about exhausted in poor visibility, and we now had so much spare food that it seemed a good idea to eat some rather than carry it down.

We woke to a brilliant morning, rather wishing that we could go back and enjoy all those views which we had missed on our summit day. With regret, we packed all the spare gear and food into the heaviest sacks that we had yet carried, and struggled down through the new snow on the glacier. We arrived at the ice-fall zone; only a short trip through this, and all major difficulties and dangers would be behind us. But first, Simon had to climb down a steep wall to make an awkward step above a huge void. As he made the necessary pick placement, there was a resounding cracking noise followed by a chain reaction of frightening cracks, as the whole mass appeared to be rearranging itself. Somewhat shaken, we retreated and were confronted by the problem of finding an alternative route. This took another two hours as we climbed down steep ice walls, in and out of crevasses, and followed intricate, almost subterranean routes between rock and ice. Finally, a short abseil took us over the last of the major holes to the safety of the flat glacier below.

We were quite looking forward to the inevitable battle with the dogs at ABC, as a mark of our return to the world at large, but they had gone. Autumn was well established; in our short absence the grass had turned yellow and the annual plants were beginning to die back. The shepherd had obviously decided to begin his long journey to winter pastures, some 150km away. We were too late to follow him and had one more night at ABC.

The next day we followed the trail of destruction made by the large herd of sheep and goats as it descended what the Americans would call the fragile tundra. Our arrival back at Base Camp was marked by a superb chicken curry with chips; the chicken had been bought for 25 rupees in Sumcham (only about an hour away) by our enterprising cook, and he sold it to us for 75. We had arrived back in the real world.

Ups and Downs on Kunyang Kish

The Second Ascent, 11 July 1988

ANDY WINGFIELD

(Plates 24–27, 62)

The final week before departure for Pakistan, and the telephone was red hot. Preparations continued amidst the random heaps of gear and food which were rapidly filling both Mike Sheldrake's house and mine. Despite the cleverly designed bureaucratic assault course, it was beginning to look as if we might at least get there. Then a friend phoned . . .

'Have you seen the *Independent* today?' he ventured in a voice which didn't give much away. 'The Shias and Sunnis have started shooting each other and Gilgit is sealed off to the north and south. The army has been called in and no one knows when the area will reopen.'

I couldn't believe it. A year's preparation, trying to visualize every eventuality, anticipating illness, storms, and porter strikes, but never a civil war at the gateway to the Karakoram!

A week later and our team – comprising Ju Fisher, Mark Lowe, Keith Milne, Mike Sheldrake (Shell) and myself, together with four trekkers, Derek Brown, Maggie Boyd, Phil McHugh and Jane Worthington – had miraculously made it as far as Rawalpindi. Ju, the demon dentist who is periodically banished to the Antarctic to allow his patients to recover, had for once put his boyish charm to good use and managed to organize free champagne on the flight out. We arrived in a heatwave – even the locals were finding it too hot.

First priority was to get into some cooler clothing. The local shalwar camise looked practical, but how boring the colours seemed. Men never swayed from the greys, blues, khakis and whites although the shops were packed full of cloths in pinks, purples and yellows. The tailors measuring us up seemed highly amused by our choice of gaudy colours, but we thought nothing of it. People in the streets stared, but we thought this was simply because we were foreigners. Then we got chatting to a gentleman who spoke excellent English; he pointed out that only women wore such colours and if local men were seen in our clothes they would be considered insane and locked up!

We spent five days doing the usual rounds of government offices, cargo warehouses, bazaars and banks. On our second day in the capital we unexpectedly met our liaison officer while visiting the tourist office. At the age of 24, Captain Mahmood Khan was obviously expected to go places in the Pakistan Army. In keeping with every other government official we met, he didn't seem to understand the concepts of democracy or delegation. To him there was no point in discussing options, especially with mere team members. No, it had to be the leader whom he dealt with, and he had firm ideas on how everything should be done. From my point of view this was bad news. Many months before, in a rain-swept Otley, I had been 'chosen' as leader so that someone could attend the Mount Everest Foundation interview. Now I had suddenly become the figurehead which, as Derek pointed out, was only there to save the ship from hitting the pier.

For reasons of economy we had forsaken the alcohol licence at Flashman's Hotel and booked into the 'Pine'. This proved to be a mistake in more ways than one. A group of lean, mean Yugoslavs moved into the adjacent rooms. The girls swooned; this was their big chance to get their own back for all the times we had been caught staring past their ears in pubs at the leggy blonde in stilettos. They dashed our egos, staring across the courtyard every time a Yugoslav passed by. Talk was of K2 and not KK.

To celebrate our last night in Rawalpindi we gorged ourselves at the Pearl Continental's outdoor barbecue. Shell and I left early to arrange the morning pick-up with our bus driver. Sitting in the Pine Hotel's reception, we struck up a conversation with a Pakistani guest. 'How I admire your physiques and good equipment,' he said. We stared at one another, completely taken aback – was this to be taken as an innuendo or a case of mistaken identity? 'You must be very brave to climb so high,' he went on, smiling. 'Are you sure you mean us and not the Yugoslavs?' I ventured. Shell and I laughed at our in-joke, secretly surprised and I suppose relieved that someone appreciated our exploit. 'When do you leave for K2?' he added innocently. We managed a weak smile and tried to explain the attraction of climbing a mountain other than K2, but it was a lost cause.

The following morning we left the city bound for Aliabad, a village some two hours beyond Gilgit on the Karakoram Highway. The town of Chilas was reached by 10pm; it had been the centre of much of the recent fighting and according to local reports had seen several thousand deaths. The road from here to Gilgit had only just reopened following the hostilities and we were stopped at a number of 'security check-points'. These generally consisted of a solitary OAP armed with a musket guarding a large twig placed across the road.

Once in Aliabad we made the big mistake of assuming that the locals knew the extent of their road network. They seemed certain that a jeep track ran all the way from the KKH to Hispar village; this was great news, reducing our anticipated walk-in from six to three days. It was only by driving as far as we could, clearing minor landslides, failing to clear a rather more major slide and eventually walking, that we found the track ended several miles short of Hispar. The weather was bad and everyone was dispirited by this setback. Even the arrival of a group of nymphets, masquerading as Operation Raleigh, did little to raise morale. The following morning Mark, Keith, Phil and Derek joined the girls for a day's walk up to Rakaposhi Base Camp beneath the W face of the mountain. Early in the descent Phil twisted his knee badly; unable to walk, he managed to slide and hobble back to the road. This proved to be the end of the trip for him, all plans of trekking up the Hispar glacier with Jane, Maggie and Derek frustrated.

The next day, Thursday 9 June, saw us go our separate ways; Phil to England and a knee operation, the rest of us to Nagar and negotiations for porters. The Nagari men have acquired a reputation over the years for demanding high rates of pay, walking short stages, stealing and even the murder of clients. Two days earlier we had seen Piotr Młotecki's Polish Expedition leave Aliabad bound for Batura I. They seemed pretty experienced and by coincidence included Zygmunt Heinrich, one of the four men to reach the summit of Kunyang Kish back in 1971. We watched their porters strike several times in the course of leaving and wondered what the Nagars had in store for us.

Our negotiations were completed surprisingly quickly; always a bad sign. Within four hours, terms were agreed and porters picked. We knew that we were being ripped off financially but, going on all the information available from previous trips to the area, we were paying the typical Nagar rate for six stages. Unfortunately, the men were not prepared to reduce the walk-in to five stages by using tractors to the end of the track, and in any case there was the major landslide which we had reached previously, preventing us from driving to Hura. Nobody could say when the road-gang would get around to clearing the block and we knew damn well that it could wait longer than us.

Our first choice of cook, having read about him on Mick Fowler's and Tony Saunders's Spantik Expedition, had to be Rajab Ali. As the call went through the assembled crowd, a small gnarly character struggled to push his way to the front and climb on to the verandah. He proudly produced his photographs and reference from the previous year's trip and asked if we could supply him with some boots. His feet looked about size 6, but he seemed happy with Ju's size 10 American baseball boots, complete with multicoloured stars, declaring them a great fit. He shuffled off to gather his belongings together while trying his best to prevent the unlaced boots from falling off. The crowd erupted with laughter at this comic scene. Rajab was a real comedian and kept us cheerful throughout the trip.

Our 45 porters arrived early the following morning to be allocated their loads. It had stopped raining for the first time since our arrival in the mountains and everything appeared to be going smoothly. As each porter was given his load, he fixed up a harness and disappeared around the back of the building. It came as a surprise to discover them loading all the gear on to tractors and trailers. As soon as agreement had been reached the previous day, a gang had been sent out with dynamite to clear the landslip. The road was 'miraculously' clear again and they even had the gall to offer us a lift if we paid! I think it was more for reasons of pride than the desire to get fit that we chose to walk.

We quickly fell into a routine: Mahmood lining up all the porters for early morning parade, then marching at the head of the column while the Sirdar carried his sack, with everyone else ambling along at various speeds. Base Camp was set up on 15 June at Bularang, a grassy ablation valley above the Kunyang glacier at 4300m. Kunyang Kish itself lay on the opposite side of the glacier, its W summit hiding most of our chosen route, the N ridge, from view. It is always a bit difficult to find superlatives which make your objective sound special to prospective sponsors. Other people's quotes are especially useful, making the world's 33rd highest mountain grow in stature to: '... possibly the biggest single massif in the world, a peak which covers an area three or four times that occupied by K2 ...' (from an article by Stephen Venables, himself a would-be conqueror of KK on two previous occasions). To add spice, we were also planning a parapente descent of the mountain.

Kunyang Kish has been attempted many times, with little success. The peak's long S ridge was tried by the British in 1962 and the Japanese in 1965 before Zawada's Polish team triumphed in 1971. All three expeditions resulted in loss of life, giving the peak something of a reputation. Attention then turned to the N ridge, with Dave Wilkinson's expeditions of 1980 and 1981. Accompanied by Venables and Bartlett, he made the first serious recce of the NW side of the mountain, finding a relatively non-technical route up the NW spur which runs from the Kunyang glacier (c4700m) to its junction with the N ridge at 7100m. This meeting point, marked by what appears from a distance to be a mere pimple, grows into a sizeable problem on closer acquaintance and was aptly christened Sod's Law Peak by Wilkinson. It is so-named because there is no easy way of avoiding its summit in order to reach the N ridge. Wilkinson and Co were dogged by bad weather and heavy snowfall on both expeditions, failing to climb the final 750m of ridge above Sod's Law. On arrival in Hunza, we discovered that a Japanese expedition had also attempted the route in 1987, retreating after one member was killed in an avalanche at about 6700m.

The route from Base Camp to the climb lay in a 7km arc up the Kunyang glacier. This proved to be a particularly demoralizing start to the route, but Shell and Maggie found a route through the maze to establish Advanced Base Camp beneath a 400m rock pyramid which marked the foot of the spur. Derek, Jane and Mahmood helped us with gear carries up the glacier before leaving on their trek to Snow Lake via the Hispar La.

To reach the crest of the spur we planned to use a straightforward ice gully, so avoiding the difficulties of the pyramid by sneaking around the back. This had previously been named Garadh Gully because of the likeness to its namesake on Ben Nevis. The following morning, Wednesday 22 June, called for a 2.30am start. I was feeling a mixture of excitement, apprehension and gross overburden, not helped by 3kg of parapente. By 9am we were at 5500m on the ridge, gasping a bit and happy to leave the next narrow section of the ice arête until the following morning when it would be considerably easier; or so we thought. Sitting around all day in beautiful weather, admiring the surrounding chain of 7000ers, brewing up and chatting all seemed good value – perhaps this Greater Ranges lark was OK after all. But by midday we were being fried alive and the novelty was starting to wear thin.

Another 2am start, traversing the sharp arête with huge drops hidden by darkness. I set off shortly before the others so that I could take my time. The technicalities increased and I stopped to weigh up a course of action. Mark climbed around me and disappeared behind a rocky kink in the arête, coming to a halt below a blank section of rock. The rest of us sorted out a 7mm rope, but as I started running it out we came to the conclusion that things seemed wrong. If our predecessors had soloed their route, it certainly wasn't on this kind of ground. As we sat perched on a rock ledge waiting for dawn to arrive, a call drifted across from Mark out in the void: 'If I had a pair of rock-boots I think it would go!'

Daylight confirmed our suspicions; a series of difficult pinnacles lay ahead. With our puny resources and the size of the hill it seemed sensible to retreat to the top of Garadh Gully and climb a different gully to the ridge, so bypassing the pinnacles. Sure enough, an 800m ice slope led to a site for Camp 1, snuggled beneath a large ice cliff.

We started finding lengths of Japanese fixed lines, often running up vertical cliffs where we chose to walk round the side. Within three days of leaving ABC we had established Camps 1 and 2, Keith and Mark had dumped some food near a site for Camp 3 at 6630m, Shell had spent a solitary night in a snow-hole beside the dump, while Ju and I carried loads up to Camp 2. The following morning Shell descended to Camp 2 with a chest infection and a particularly virulent gut problem. Ju and I carried loads up to Camp 3, discovering at the lunchtime radio call that the others were returning to Base Camp for a few days' rest. Plans to make a further carry up to Camp 3 were thwarted by overnight snowfall and whiteout conditions the following morning. Not wanting to be trapped beneath a huge avalanche slope during a protracted storm while the others ate all the tinned fruit at Base, we followed our stomachs off the hill.

With the return of good weather Shell accompanied Maggie down to Gilgit, hoping to get back in time for a final attempt on the mountain. Mark and Keith set off for ABC, followed a day later by Ju and myself. They stayed a day ahead of us for the next three days, carrying food up to a dump just below the summit of SL Peak as we arrived at Camp 3. We all sat out a day of bad weather on 5 July, with wind and snow blasting the tents. Morning revealed mist, a fresh blanket of snow and an overnight drop of 90m in the barometer. Ju was struck down with an upset stomach, Mark felt it prudent to descend, while Keith and I were both fed up with going up and down – our next descent would be our last! So it was that Keith and Mark packed up their tent and personal kit, I shouldered food and gas for Ju's and my summit push and the three of us set off up the steepening slope towards the summit of SL Peak. Keith and I shared the trailbreaking through demoralizing deep powder. He was far stronger and did 70 per cent of the work; I kept on thinking that we were mad to go on in such conditions.

We reached the previous dump at 7000m but there was still no sign of Mark. I left my load and began descending tracks which were almost obliterated by fresh snow, meeting a rather unhappy Mark half-way down. He still thought that we should be descending, and had only set off because he had the tent and radio. On reaching the dump, they dug the tent in below a rock outcrop and prepared to sit out the bad weather. Ju and I did likewise at Camp 3, enlarging Shell's snow-hole to fit two of us. Another day of boredom followed, with Ju's condition worsening to the point where he couldn't eat or move from his sleeping-bag at all.

The cloud was starting to disperse by the following morning, so Keith and Mark set off upwards. Ju seemed worse, listless and groaning; I packed our kit and coaxed him into first gear. The descent rapidly steepened and I wished we had a rope. Ju slowly descended the line of pigeonholes, periodically slumping over his axes in a groaning heap, while I waited for him to peel off backwards. On reaching Camp 1 he offered to continue down alone, but it was too late to catch the others and I couldn't face that waist-deep snow again. I had been unable to carry my parapente above this point on the ascent, so as a consolation prize I decided to fly back down to ABC. Laying the canopy out on a creaking cornice in a flat calm I felt as nervous as on my first flight. It inflated perfectly but takeoff eluded me, as I struggled to run fast enough down incredibly lumpy wet ice with an oversize rucksack. I was fuming at having lugged my canopy up to 5850m, only to carry it down on my back in a hopelessly tangled mess. My depression reached new depths when Ju made a remarkable recovery, collecting his parapente from a lower cache and flying from the top of Garadh Gully down to ABC. If this was the highest British parapente flight to date, then mine was surely the highest crash!

Meanwhile Mark and Keith had pressed on over the top of SL Peak, dumped food at the base of the N ridge and returned to Camp 4. The following day they continued across the broad col and established Camp 5 a short way up the ridge. Deep snow often hampered progress and on the steeper sections they would probably have chosen to carry a rope, but the last decent length was fixed below the summit of Sod's Law. A final camp was made on 10 July and the following morning they set off carrying only day food and brewing kit. They couldn't believe it when the summit was reached at 1.30pm, with the altimeter indicating a further 600m to go and clear weather to boot!

During the following two days they safely descended avalanche-prone slopes to reach Base Camp, while Ju and Shell returned to clear Camp 1 and fly down to ABC. Shell had narrowly missed getting back in time for a summit attempt, following his mammoth one-day walk-in from the roadhead. The rest of us cleared ABC and Rajab proudly prepared a celebration feast. First Mark and later Keith ambled into camp, looking rather as if they had just left a five-day beach party.

Celebrations in the cook tent – a mixture of whisky and excessively rich air seemed to be affecting Keith: 'You see, that's the problem with walking downhill,' he explained in his lazy drawl. 'You forget to breathe.' So that's where I had been going wrong!

Central Tibet – Tanggula Shan

MICHAEL WARD

(Plate 28)

This range runs east–west across the central part of the Tibet plateau, but further east it curves to the south. It divides the Xizang Autonomous Region from Qinghai Province. The road from Lhasa to Golmud reaches its highest point as it crosses the range by the Tanggula Pass (5206m).

Close to the pass, to the west, is a peak 6022m, while to the east is a peak 6104m. Both have extensive snow-fields and rounded summits.

It is in this region that Tibetans are said to have mined 'quartz' for many months of the year, working at altitudes up to 6000m.

Further to the north and west is a group of peaks 6621m (Geladandong) and 6527m; from these the Tongtian river rises, one of the origins of the Yangtze Kiang. These peaks can be seen from the end of the track that leads from Wenguan station to the valley of the Tongtian river.

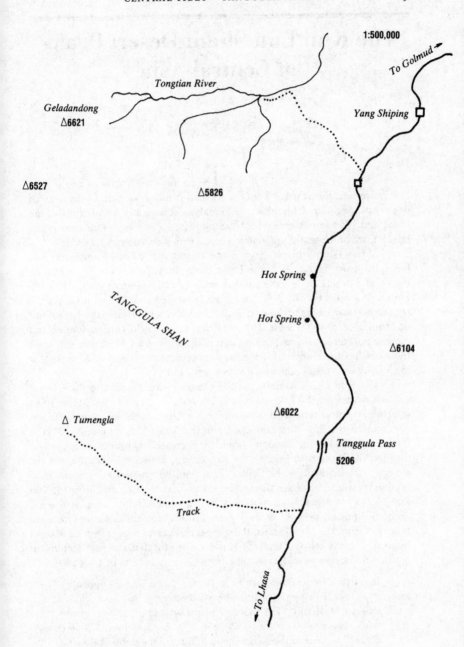

The Kun Lun Shan: Desert Peaks of Central Asia

MICHAEL WARD

(*Plates* 29, 30, 32)

The gaunt, bare backbone of the Kun Lun range runs for 2250km from the Russian Pamir to western China over 30 degrees of longitude. Older than the Himalaya, it separates the plateaux of the Pamir and Tibet from the deserts of Central Asia, and it is one of the longest and least known of the world's mountain ranges, with peaks up to 7700m.[4,8,17,22,51]

At its western end it is joined by the Tien Shan (Celestial Mountains) that forms the northern border of the Tarim Basin, in which lies the Takla Makan desert, and in this angle is the strategic oasis city of Kashgar (Kashi).[11,29,36,59] Here four arms of the Silk Route meet: one from the Indian sub-continent to the south, two from China to the east, by the north and south rims of the Tarim, and one from Europe to the west. The Silk Route is the world's oldest, longest and most important land-route, linking the civilizations of the Mediterranean with those of China and India, and for more than 5000 years it has been a conduit for ideas, religion, culture, disease, invasion and trade.[10]

The Kun Lun's western portion separates the Pamir and the Central Asian plateau from the Takla Makan desert and the Lop Nur.[61] At 80°E it splits into two, the northern portion becoming the Altyn Tagh, while the southern continues as the East Kun Lun, ending in the Amne Machin group. Between these two arms lies the Tsaidam Basin.[53] It is crossed by four main highways: through the West Kun Lun by the Gez Gorge, between Chakragil and the Kongur massif; through the Central Kun Lun, which continues as the road around the south rim of the Tibet plateau; through the East Kun Lun by the Kun Lun Pass (4772m); and by a route west of the Amne Machin group. It also has numerous passes. Because of their great altitude, and the constant stream of travellers from the Middle East, the steppes of Central Asia, Tibet, China and India which has crossed them, it is not surprising that the first account of mountain sickness should have come from Chinese sources in 37–32 BC:

> In the time of the Emperor Ching-Te (37–32 BC), Ke-Pin [possibly Afghanistan] again sent an envoy with offerings and an acknow-ledgement of guilt. The supreme board wished to send an envoy with a reply to escort the Ke-Pin envoy home. Tookim [a Chinese official] addressed the Generalissimo Wang Fung to the following effect ... 'From Pe-Shan [south-east of Yarkand] southwards there are four to five kingdoms not attached to China. The Chinese Commission will in such circumstances be left to starve among the hills and valleys. Again on passing the Great Headache Mountain,

the Little Headache Mountain, the Red Land, and the Fever Slope men's bodies become feverish, they lose colour, and are attacked with headache and vomiting. The asses and cattle being all in like condition.'[58]

A later Chinese traveller, Fa-Hsien (399–414 AD), gives a description of a companion who died after foaming at the mouth on a mountain pass in this region, quite possibly a case of high-altitude pulmonary oedema.[12] The identity and position of these mountains and passes is not known, though there has been speculation in medical journals. Joseph Needham, in his magisterial work *Science and Civilization in China*, suggests that the occurrence of mountain sickness and its complications may have been taken by the Chinese as a sign for them not to transgress their natural boundaries.

Of the early European travellers in the region, Aurel Stein probably knew the Kun Lun better than any other, and during three expeditions in 1900–01, 1906–08 and 1913–15 he made many of the original European maps and gave topographical descriptions which have served as a basis for knowledge of the area.[40,41,43] Other early travellers included Bonvalot,[3] Hedin,[14,15,16] Deasy,[6,7] Rawling,[31] Forsyth,[9] Littledale,[21] the Pandits,[1,52] Carey,[20] Dalgleish,[20] Prejevalsky[30] and Ney Elias.[26] It was in the Central Kun Lun, too, that in 1865 Johnson – an extremely able surveyor from the Survey of India – claimed, honestly but mistakenly, that he had ascended peak E61, 7300m, which at that time was thought to be the greatest altitude to have been achieved on a mountain on foot. The arguments against his having done so may be found in articles by Mason and Stein in the *Alpine Journal*.[23,42] The exact site of this peak is not clear, though it might have been Muztag (6710m).

Most recently, Chinese geological and topographical survey parties have visited all parts of the range. In particular, the Burhan Budai section of the East

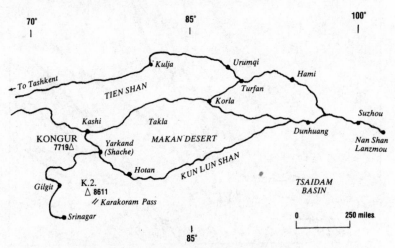

SINKIANG (CHINESE TURKESTAN) AND KUN LUN SHAN
SHOWING MAJOR SECTIONS OF THE EASTERN PART
OF THE SILK ROUTE

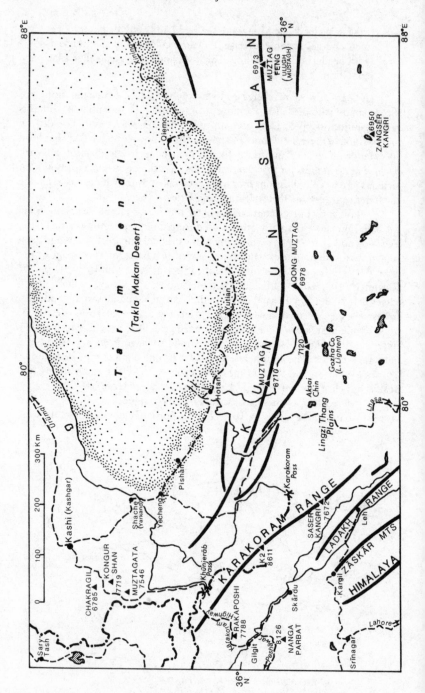

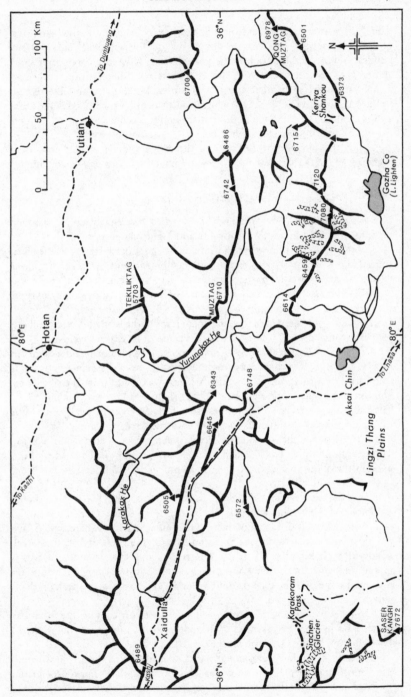

Kun Lun was visited by a Royal Society party in 1985[45] and extensive geological mapping was carried out, based on topographical surveys and Landsat Imagery. Mountaineering parties, too, have been exploring and climbing in the region for the last 100 years and some groups of peaks, particularly in the west, are relatively well known. Kongur (7719m), the highest peak, was climbed in 1981,[2,54,55] while Amne Machin was climbed in the early 1960s,[29] although the highest summit was only ascended in 1981.[48] Ulugh Muztagh (6987m) (Muztagh Feng) had its first ascent in 1985.[25]

For the purpose of description, the range will be divided into four portions: the West, Central and East Kun Lun, and the Amne Machin Shan.

West Kun Lun

This extends from 74°E to 78°E and includes the Chakragil group, the Kongur massif, Muztagh Ata, and the Shiwakte and Tigurman groups.

Lying close to the northern portion of the Karakoram Highway, the main route from Kashgar (Kashi) to the Indian sub-continent, this area has been visited by many people, particularly in the late 19th century, the era of the 'Great Game'. Initially, considerable confusion was caused by the inability of the early travellers to identify the highest peak, Kongur (7719m).[9,26,49,50,54,55]

It is the best-known of the three main parts of the Kun Lun, and climbing parties are increasingly visiting the area because of its ease of access.

The Chakragil peaks, 6700m and 6500m, lie to the north and west of the Gez Gorge, along which the Karakoram Highway passes. The glaciers of the N side form the Chikir Jilcha; an early attempt was made from the N side by Shipton and Tilman, and their route did not appear to be too difficult.[37,46,47] The S side of the group, with a number of small glaciers, can be clearly seen from the Bulun Kul valley, in which there are nomadic settlements.

The Kongur massif consists of two main peaks, Kongur and Kongur Tiube, both of which have been climbed. A full account of the history of the exploration of the area has been given in a number of books and journals listed in the references.[2,26,54,55]

There are several subsidiary peaks, notably the 'Gez Matterhorn' (c6000m) on the N side, which would be a good objective. Good lines can be seen on the N wall of the Kongur-Kongur Tiube ridge too; these would give excellent and serious routes of a high standard. On the S side of Kongur there is a considerable number of peaks up to 6500m which would be worth attempting, and some of the lower ones have already been climbed. Routes on the S and E faces of the massif could be made, and a subsidiary peak on the E side was climbed in 1980.

The Shiwakte and Tigurman groups lie east of Kongur; the area was visited and mapped by Skrine.[38,39] It appears to be most easily approached from the east by the Qaratash Gorge.

To the north the Tigurman group, with peaks up to 5500m, lies around the Tigurman glacier. It is possible that this glacier could be approached from the west, over a col at the head of the Qurghan glacier which drains the E face of Kongur and runs towards Gez Qaraul and the Gez Gorge.

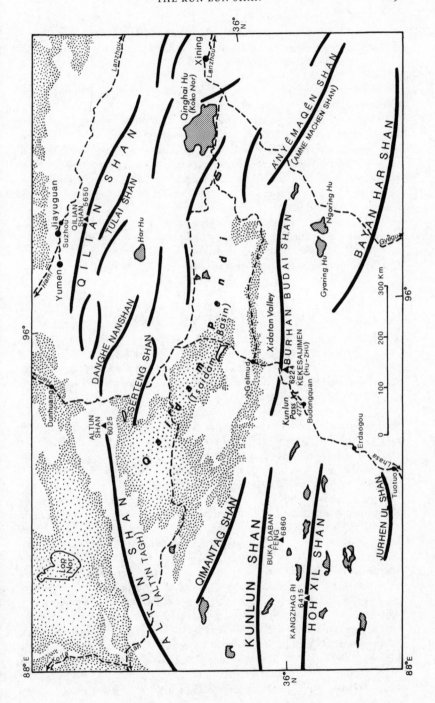

The Shiwakte group, with peaks up to 6000m, lies around the Kaying and Torbashi glaciers. From the head of the Kaying glacier, a pass can be crossed in a southerly direction which leads to the Chimghan Jilgha that joins the Qaratash river.

To the east of these two groups, and east of the Qaratash river, is the unknown Qhijag group of mountains.

Muztagh Ata (7433m) is an outstanding and much photographed cone-shaped mountain rising close to the Karakoram Highway, near the Karakul lakes which are considered to be one of the most beautiful viewpoints in Central Asia. The first attempt on the summit was made by the Swedish traveller Sven Hedin, who rode from the west up to about 5800m on a yak.[13,14] There have been a number of successful ascents since then, the first in 1956 by a Russian-Chinese party, and the N peak has been climbed.[2,18,19,54,55] A successful ski-descent has also been made.[5] The W side of this peak is well known, but there is great scope for routes on the other sides which remain unvisited. The peak, being so close to the Karakoram Highway, has become popular.

The mountains between Muztagh Ata and the first sizeable peak (6200m) in the Central Kun Lun, at 77°30'E, 36°30'N, rise to around 5800m.

Central Kun Lun (77°30' to 82°E)

The Central Kun Lun is divided into two parallel ranges by the river valleys of the Karakash (Karakax He) and Yurung Kash (Yurung Kax He). The northern portion continues in a north-easterly direction and changes its name to the Altyn Tagh, whilst the southern runs east and peters out in northern Tibet.

The Karakash river rises in the peaks of the Aksai Chin and initially runs west, being joined by the route from the Karakoram Pass (5500m). From near this junction Stein, on his 1906–08 expedition, climbed from the Karakash river up the southern side of what he described as the main range of the Kun Lun, reaching a snow col at 6000m. From here he was able to take a panoramic photograph, including peaks in all directions except to the east and north-east. All those peaks appeared to be heavily glaciated.[40,41]

The Karakash breaks through the northern more continuous line of the Kun Lun at Xaidulla (Saltula) and continues north and east to Khotan (Hotan).

The Yurung Kash river rises to the east of the Aksai Chin from a cirque of heavily glaciated peaks at 81°E 36°N. According to Stein, they were 'all clad with glaciers more extensive than any I had seen in the Kun Lun'. These glacier sources were visited by Stein in 1906–08 and, from a survey point at around 5300m, he was able to take a complete panorama of the peaks from which these glaciers rise.[40,41] There is one particularly large glacier, almost a mini ice-cap, which feeds the eastern headwaters of the Yurung Kash. Stein also observed that, whereas on the northern slopes of the main range the snowline descended to approximately 5300m, on the southern slopes it was 600m higher. This is the highest group of peaks in the Central Kun Lun and the highest, 7120m, is marked on the ONC map at 81°10'E, 35°22'N.

To the south of this group is Lake Lighten (Gozha Co), 5200m. Photographs of the peaks around this lake can be found in Sven Hedin's many-volume work on South Tibet.[16] To the east, again, is another group of peaks up to nearly 7000m.

The Yurung Kash runs west to start with, but then turns north to break through the main Kun Lun at 80°E, 36°N. It continues north to Khotan (Hotan), joins the Karakash river and traverses the Takla Makan desert to Aksu.

Where the Yurung Kash breaks through the Kun Lun, a peak (7200m) is marked on Stein's map. However, the ONC map gives a height of 6500m. A photo of this peak, K5, may be found in Stein's *Memoirs* and *Mountain Panoramas*,[40,43] and it is probably Muztag (6710m);.

The panoramic photographs which Stein took from six different stations show the northern aspects of a considerable number of peaks of 6000m and above. No doubt both the heights and the names that he gave them have now been revised by Chinese geographers.[40]

Between the valleys formed by the Yurung Kash and Karakash rivers, there is a group of peaks clustered around a glacier named Otrughul by Stein.[41] A recent Chinese map (1:2,000,000) of the glaciated regions of Central Asia confirms that this region of the Central Kun Lun is the most heavily glaciated of the whole range.

East Kun Lun

The East Kun Lun branches off the Altyn Tagh at 86°E. The northern limb – the Altyn Tagh – continues, dividing the deserts and swamps of the Lop Nur and Kansu corridor from the Tsaidam Basin.

The southern limb, the East Kun Lun, becomes a discontinuous range that runs due east. There is a group of peaks at about 87°E which include Ulugh Muztagh (6987m), Kangzhag Ri (6415m) and Buka Daban Feng and, at 89°E, Xinqing (6860m), the highest peak in Qinghai Province. On the southern, plateau side of this range there are numerous lakes between 88°E and 93°E.[27]

Ulugh Muztagh was climbed for the first time in 1985 by a Sino-American party, along its E ridge.[25] Its altitude was computed to within a few metres, and geological work extended that carried out on the Royal Society-Chinese Academy of Science's Tibet Geotraverse in the same year, 1985.[45] The conjecture that the mountain might be a volcano was disproved.

At 92°E the East Kun Lun becomes a continuous ridge with an altitude of about 5500m, plus an occasional higher bump, and at 94°E it is called the Burhan Budai Shan, or Angirtaksia in some of the older maps.[1]

The main highway between Xining and Lhasa, a centuries' old route traversed by the Jesuits, Pandits and others,[1,52,57] runs through the Kun Lun Pass (4772m) at the western end of the Burhan Budai. The most unusual feature of the range is the Xidatan valley, just to the north, which is about 5km wide and 100km long. Through its floor runs an earthquake fault, the Xidatan-Tuosuohu-Maqu fault. This has occurred because of the pressure exerted by the Indian sub-continent, which is travelling north and compressing, crushing and crumbling the earth's crust to such an extent that it is twice its normal thickness, forming the Tibetan plateau. This northward pressure has caused a split in the crust, the Xidatan fault, and the Burhan Budai range has been split off from the rest of the East Kun Lun and is moving east at about 2cm each year, causing earthquakes. Because of the remoteness of the area, these have caused little or no loss of life, but are of considerable size.

The break between the main range of the East Kun Lun and the Burhan Budai is a wide shallow pass some 30km west of the Kun Lun Pass. From this pass it would be easy to walk up the snow-covered corries to the crest of the main range and traverse along as far as desired. If the snowfall is adequate – and this must be problematic because of the dry climate – a ski-traverse would be possible.

The main peak of the Burhan Budai is Kekesaijimen (6179m or 5989m), just east of the Kun Lun Pass. (This peak was called Hu Zhu in my *Alpine Journal* article in 1986.[56])

It stands as a clear landmark, from north and south; and from both sides the glaciers, buttresses and couloirs are easily accessible from the road. The group of which this is the main peak has a number of summits of 5700m, and is bounded to the east by the Drovers' Route and on the west by the Kun Lun Pass.

The Drovers' Route starts from the Lhasa-Golmud Highway at the Surgang river, just by a cement works. It follows a circuitous route along valleys to the north of the Xidatan, and then through the Burhan Budai, with a peak (5548m) to the west, to gain access to the plateau. Herds of yaks, sheep, goats and camels take three to four days to travel from the Tsaidam to the plateau. It is a much-used route, just passable for lorries in dry conditions. There is a small, disused opencast coal-mine just before the route joins the Xidatan valley (here called the Dongdatan) from the north.

To the north of the Xidatan there is a maze of hills between 4800m and 5100m, many with rock-faces and ridges rising from dry valleys. Extensive and detailed geological maps were made of the Burhan Budai during the Royal Society-Chinese Academy of Science's Tibet Geotraverse, 1985.[45]

A series of roads passes through the range at 98°E, and the Amne Machin group starts at 100°E.

The Altyn Tagh (Nan Shan) range extends from 85°E and runs north-east. At this longitude there are a number of peaks around 6000m. The range then continues with lower peaks until the area south of Yumen-Suchow is reached, where there are ranges running south of east and more or less parallel to one another. These ranges are named the Qilian Shan, with a peak of 5650m, Tulai Shan, Serteng Shan, with a peak 5609m just north of the Ha La (Har) Hu (lake). East of this lake there is a peak 5650m.

The higher peaks in this region are snow-covered and the whole area is extremely dry, but forest growth towards the east indicates increased rainfall. Both Stein's[40,41,43] and Obrucheff's[28] books contain photographs of these ranges.

The **Amne Machin Shan** extends south and east of the Burhan Budai; it is enclosed on three sides (not the north-west) by the Hwang Ho (Hwang He), which rises from the Ngoring Hu on the Tibet plateau. It is possible that the first reference to these peaks in the European literature is to be found in Dutreuil de Rhin's book,[32] and the area was also visited by the Russian travellers

Roborovsky and Kozloff.[44] Roborovsky had a stroke in 1895 while crossing the Mangur Pass (4300m) in east Tibet, from which he recovered after eight days. This is the first recorded incidence in the literature of a vascular episode at high altitude, and it was due to a combination of dehydration and an increased number of red cells in the blood. The whole range was virtually unknown until the early 1930s.[34,60]

J F Rock made a number of journeys, particularly on the north and east side, and photographed the range, but he was not able to explore the mountains themselves.[33] Later, the range attained a degree of notoriety as it was thought that it might contain a peak as high as, or higher than, Everest. The highest peak is now called Magen Gangri (6268m) in Pin-Yin.[27] A Chinese party climbed the 'highest' point in 1960;[29] however, it was later shown that they had in fact climbed a point some way from the summit. Controversy remains over who made the first ascent in 1981. Many European parties have now visited the range.[35,48]

Acknowledgements

I thank Mr Ted Hatch of the Drawing Office, Royal Geographical Society, for drawing three of the maps in this paper. They are based on *The Mountains of Central Asia*, published by the Royal Geographical Society and Mount Everest Foundation. Additional information has been obtained from papers on The Royal Society-Chinese Academy of Science's Tibet Geotraverse in 1985, published by the Royal Society.

REFERENCES

1   A–K. *Report on the Explorations in Great Tibet and Mongolia made by A–K in 1879–82 in connection with the Trigonometrical Branch, Survey of India*. Prepared by J B N Hennessey, Dehra Dun, India, 1884.

2   C Bonington, *Kongur, China's Elusive Summit*. Hodder & Stoughton, 1982.

3   G Bonvalot, *Across Thibet*. Cassell, 1891.

4   S G Burrard, H H Hayden, *A Sketch of the Geography and Geology of the Himalaya Mountains and Tibet*. Superintendent Government Printing Office, Calcutta, 1907.

5   J Cleare, 'Ski-Mountaineering in China. The Ascent of Mustagh Ata'. *AJ*88, 29–36, 1983.

6   H H P Deasy, *In Tibet and Chinese Turkestan*. Fisher Unwin, 1901.

7   H H P Deasy, 'Journeys in Central Asia'. *Geographical Journal 16*, 141–163, 501–526, 1900.

8   P Fleming, *Travels in Tartary*. Cape, 1936.

9   T D Forsyth, *Report of a Mission to Yarkund in 1873*. Foreign Department Press, Calcutta, 1875.

10   I M Franck, D M Brownstone, *The Silk Road. A History*. Facts on File, New York, 1986.

11   M A Gerard, T H Holditch, R A Wahab, A W Alcock, *Report of the Proceedings of the Pamir Boundary Commission*. Office of the Superintendent of Government Printing, Calcutta, 1897.

12   D L Gilbert, 'The First Documented Report of Mountain Sickness. The China or Headache Mountain Story'. *Respiration Physiology 52*, 315–326, 1983.

13   S Hedin, 'Attempts to Ascend Mustagh Ata'. *Geographical Journal 6*, 350–367, 1895.

14   S Hedin, *Through Asia*. Methuen, 1899.

15   S Hedin, *Central Asia and Tibet*. Hurst and Blackett, 1903.

16   S Hedin, *Southern Tibet*. Lithographic Institute of the General Staff of the Swedish Army, Stockholm, 1917.

17   T Holditch, *Tibet, The Mysterious*. Alston Rivers, 1907.

18   M Jardine, 'An Electrifying Experience'. *AJ92*, 117–122, 1987.

19   M Jardine, 'North Muztagh: Xinjiang's Forgotten Peak'. *AJ93*, 84–87, 1988/89.

20   'Journal of Carey and Dalgleish in Chinese Turkestan and North Tibet, and General Prejevalsky on the Orography of Northern Tibet'. *Royal Geographical Society, Supplementary Papers, Vol 3, Pt 1*, 1890.

21   St G R Littledale, 'A Journey Across Tibet, from North to South'. *Geographical Journal 7*, 453–482, 1896.

22   E Maillart, *Forbidden Journey*. Heinemann, 1937.

23   K Mason, 'Johnson's Suppressed Ascent of E61'. *AJ34*, 54–62, 1921.

24   R Michell, 'The Russian Expedition to the Alai and Pamir in 1876'. *Proceedings of the Royal Geographical Society 21*, 122–140, 1877.

25   P Molnar, 'Ulugh Muztagh: The Highest Peak on the Northern Tibetan Plateau'. *AJ92*, 104–116, 1987.

26   G Morgan, 'China's Highest Mountain'. *AJ88*, 65–69, 1983.

27   *Mountains of Central Asia*. Royal Geographical Society/Mount Everest Foundation, London, 1987.

28   V A Obrucheff, *Central Asia, Northern China and the Nan Shan*. (Russian), 1900.

29   C H Pai, 'The Ascent of Amne Machin'. *AJ66*, 274–283, 1961.

30   N Prejevalsky, *Mongolia. The Tangut Country and the Solitudes of Northern Tibet, Being a Narrative of Three Years Travel in Eastern High Asia* (2 vols). Sampson Low, Marston, Searle and Rivington, 1876.

31   C G Rawling, *The Great Plateau*. Arnold, 1905.

32   J L D de Rhins, *Mission Scientifique dans la Haute Asie (1890–1895)*. Le Roux, Paris, 1897.

33   J F Rock, *The Amne Ma-Chhen Range and Adjacent Regions*. Istituto Italiano per il Medio ed Estremo Oriente, Roma, 1956.

34   W W Rockill, *Journey Through Mongolia and Tibet*. Smithsonian Institute, Washington, 1894.

35   G Rowell, *Mountains of the Middle Kingdom*. Century, 1985.

36   R Shaw, *Visits to High Tartary, Yarkand and Kashgar*. Murray, 1871.

37   E Shipton, *Mountains of Tartary*. Hodder & Stoughton, 1951.

38   C Skrine, 'The Alps of Qungur'. *Geographical Journal 66*, 385–411, 1925.

39   C Skrine, *Chinese Central Asia*. Methuen, 1926.

40   M A Stein, *Mountain Panoramas from the Pamirs and Kun Lun*. Royal Geographical Society, London, 1908.

41   M A Stein, *Ruins of Desert Cathay*. Macmillan, 1912.

42   M A Stein, 'Johnson's Map and the Topography of the Kun Lun, South of Khotan'. *AJ34*, 62–68, 1921.

43   M A Stein, *Memoir on Maps of Chinese Turkestan and Kansu from the Surveys made during Sir Aurel Stein's Explorations, 1900–1, 1906–8, 1913–15, with Appendices by Major K Mason, J De Graaff Hunter*. Trigonometrical Survey Office, Dehra Dun, India, 1923.

44   'The Central Asian Expedition of Captain Roborovsky and Lieut Kozloff'. *Geographical Journal 8*, 161–172, 1896.

45   *The Geological Evolution of Tibet. Report of the 1985 Royal Society – Academia Sinica Geotraverse of the Xizang-Qinghai Plateau*. Royal Society, 1988.

46   H W Tilman, *Two Mountains and a River*. Cambridge, 1949.

47   H W Tilman, *China to Chitral*. Cambridge, 1951.

48   J Town, 'Amne Machin: A Closer Look'. *AJ93*, 77–83, 1988/89.

49   H Trotter, *An Account of the Survey Operations in Connection with the Mission to Yarkand and Kashgar in 1873–74*. Foreign Department Press, Calcutta, 1875.

50   H Trotter, 'On the Geographical Results of the Mission to Kashgar under Sir Douglas Forsyth in 1873–74'. *Journal of the Royal Geographical Society 48*, 173–234, 1878.

51   E E Vaill, 'Mountaineering in China'. *AJ90*, 23–34, 1985.

52   J T Walker, 'Four Years' Journeyings through Great Tibet, by one of the Trans-Himalayan Explorers of the Survey of India'. *Proceedings of the Royal Geographical Society 7*, 65–92, 1885.

53   J T Wang, E Derbyshire, 'Climatic Geomorphology of the North Eastern Part of the Qinghai-Xizang Plateau, Peoples' Republic of China'. *Geographical Journal 153*, 59–71, 1987.

54   M Ward, 'The Kongur Massif in Southern Xinjiang'. *AJ86*, 7–16, 1981.

55   M Ward, 'The Kongur Massif in Southern Xinjiang'. *Geographical Journal 140*, 137–152, 1983.

56   M Ward, 'Across Tibet'. *AJ91*, 84–89, 1986.

57   M S Wellby, *Through Unknown Tibet*. Fisher Unwin, 1898.

58   A Wylie, 'Notes on the Western Regions, Translated from the Tseen Han Shoo Book, 96, Pt 1'. *Journal of the Royal Anthropological Institute 10*, 20–73, 1881.

59   F Younghusband, *The Heart of a Continent*. Murray, 1904.

60   F Younghusband, *Peking to Lhasa (The Narrative of Journeys Made by the Late Brigadier General George Pereira)*. Constable, 1925.

61   S Q Zhao, X C Xia, 'Evolution of the Lop Desert and the Lop Nur'.
      Geographical Journal 150, 311–321, 1984.

Information may also be obtained from the 'Area Notes' sections of the *Alpine Journal*, and the *American Alpine Journal*.

Chinese Chequers in Shiwakte

GEOFF COHEN

(Plates 33, 34)

All expeditions are hard work. What makes them memorable? Surely not Tom Patey's description of the summit of Rakaposhi: 'ten minutes of shivering misery as the climax to a year's preparations'. Nor, in our case, the long see-sawing of hope and dejection as we tried to reach our goal in the face of Chinese inscrutability and Kirghiz incomprehension. But we will certainly not forget the moments of horror as we clung wide-eyed to our camels in the midst of the seething Chimghan river; nor our strange evening entry to the summer settlement of Sekya under the vast E face of Kongur, never before seen by Western eyes; nor the afternoon in our tiny tent, poised between crevasse and cornice near the summit of Shiwakte II, while clouds enfolded the rock fangs around us.

It all started with a desire to celebrate the centenary of the Scottish Mountaineering Club by going to an unusual area of China which would involve us in exploratory mountaineering as well as interesting climbing. Our negotiations with the Chinese were lengthy and frustrating, and with only three months to go we abandoned our designs on Gurla Mandhata and opted instead for the Shiwakte peaks, which lie just east of Mt Kongur in western Xinjiang. Though much lower than their neighbour, they were reputed to be steep, rocky and exciting. We travelled by road from Islamabad up the Karakoram Highway, over the Khunjerab Pass and on to the broad Pamirean plateau. Encamped by the Karakul Lakes we were told that camels could not cross the Karatash Pass to reach our Base Camp, while horses were expensive and in short supply. After a week's attempt to resolve this problem we were provided with two camels, two horses and three fur-hatted Kirghiz drivers – none of whom, it transpired, knew the way! As predicted, the camels found glacier moraines tricky; so it was only eight days and many negotiations later that we arrived at Base Camp, with a different set of animals and a different driver, the redoubtable Hari Beg.

En route we had survived what was probably the most dangerous moment of the whole expedition at the crossing of the Chimghan River, which drains the whole of the east side of Kongur and the Shiwakte group. It was late afternoon when we reached it, a turbid torrent several hundred metres wide. Hari Beg engaged a local camel herder who rode with the panache of a cowboy, to lead us across by the safest route. The water was well up to the camels' bellies and the horses' shoulders on the first ferry across with the baggage. But Hari Beg was too frightened to return to get us and the cowboy, for some inexplicable reason, took a different line on his second crossing. In the middle of the river the animals got out of line and began to panic, horses and camels pushing against each other and leaning against the force of the current. Mistakenly I fixed my eyes on the grey swirl near my knees and, mesmerized, felt as if I was being carried backwards. A horse broke free and was swept away. We felt disaster close at hand, but by some miracle the cowboy guided the stolid camels to safety.

The huge basin on the south-east side of Kongur had many attractive challenges, but, basing our plans on the map of Shiwakte given by C P Skrine in 1925, we had decided to put our Base Camp by the Aq Tash glacier on the E side of Shiwakte. As it turned out, the peaks were even more difficult on this side, though we did have access to the lower, gentler peaks of the Aghalistan range. Skrine's numbering of the Shiwakte peaks, to which we adhered, was somewhat eccentric. Shiwakte I was reputedly the lowest of the group, II the highest and III and IV intermediate; while subsidiary summits were labelled IIa and IIIa. At the head of the Aq Tash were two cols separating Shiwakte IIIa from the long summit ridge of Shiwakte I. To approach Shiwakte III from this side required climbing a steep mixed ridge to the subsidiary top IIIa, and then following a long serrated horizontal ridge. Both flanks were extraordinarily steep, and the face of Shiwakte III on the Aq Tash side was subject to enormous rockfall, so that no more direct approach was possible.

Four of us attempted this ridge with a minimum of gear, having rather underestimated it on casual inspection. From the col we had 20 pitches of exciting rock and ice climbing, some quite difficult (IV/V), to a tiny bivouac ledge. Next day, after several pitches up hard ice to a shoulder, we got a clear view of the last 500 or so feet to Shiwakte IIIa – ice steps formed of strangely impending seracs and cornices. The halo round the sun provided the excuse for those who wanted to retreat. In such situations it is they who hold the aces. In any case it was quite clear that we could not reach beyond IIIa to the true summit of Shiwakte III in the time available, as the intervening ridge looked horrendously complicated. We descended to another exposed bivouac and abseiled down the next day, beating the storm by about 18 hours.

Meanwhile two of our colleagues had climbed an easy but beautifully shaped snow peak in the Aghalistan range which gave them a good view over the whole Shiwakte group.

The snow kept us in camp for nearly a week, and when it began to clear we had only seven days left to achieve something, our time at base having been sorely reduced by the delays *en route*. Shiwakte II was our official objective, and the only feasible approach from the Aq Tash side was a long and crenellated snow and ice ridge that looked decidedly tricky. Hamish Irvine and I preferred to return to the other (SW) side of the mountain, facing Kongur, and attempt a line we had seen briefly on our first arrival. Our route turned out to be technically straightforward, though exposed to considerable objective danger. On the second day, climbing as fast as we could, we passed around several huge serac barriers with only the odd steep pitch, and finally emerged on the horizontal ridge between Shiwakte II and IIa. Our camp-site gave us a magnificent viewpoint – sadly the Aq Tash basin was filled with cloud, but to the SW we could see the splendid snowy southern satellites of Kongur. The following morning we found our way through the final barriers and finished up an elegant alpine ridge. There were shafts of sunlight and patchy views of the

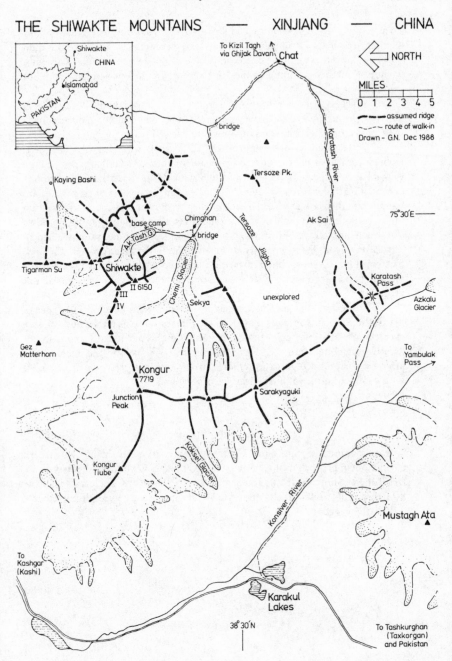

THE SHIWAKTE MOUNTAINS — XINJIANG — CHINA

Shiwakte
CHINA
Islamabad
PAKISTAN

To Kizil Tagh
via Ghijak Davan
Chat

NORTH

MILES
0 1 2 3 4 5
assumed ridge
route of walk-in
Drawn - G.N. Dec 1988

bridge

Karatash River

Tersoze Pk.

Kaying Bashi

75°30′E

Chimghan

base camp

Ak Sai

Ak Tash G.

bridge

Tersoze Jilgha

Tigarman Su

I
Shiwakte
II 6150
III
IV

Chemi Glacier

Sekya

unexplored

Karatash Pass

Azkalu Glacier

Gez
Matterhorn

Kongur
7719

To Yambulak Pass

Junction
Peak

Sarakyaguki

Koksel Glacier

Kongur
Tiube

Mustagh Ata

To Kashgar
(Kashi)

Konsiver River

Karakul
Lakes

38°30′N

To Tashkurghan
(Taxkorgan)
and Pakistan

savage Shiwakte III, which seemed slightly higher than us. The great bulk of Kongur, dwarfing the Shiwaktes, never cleared completely. It was colder than on a comparable peak in the Karakoram. We shouted to our companions who, we hoped, might be coming up the other side where there was thick cloud, but we got no reply.

In fact both the other ropes of two, who had stayed on the Aq Tash side, had experienced heavy, dangerous snowfalls in the bad weather and had retired frustrated from their bivouacs on Shiwakte I and II respectively.

We were all reunited at base on 10 August, with just two days left. Ironically, the weather turned fine again, and Hamish and Grahame crossed the Kepek Pass which Skrine had taken from Kaying Bashi 60 years ago. The woods of which he had written so lovingly, a rare sight in this part of the world, are happily still there, and so are the Kirghiz shepherds. The rest of us ascended two minor peaks of the Aghalistan range on our last day, obtaining fantastic views of Kongur and all the Shiwaktes. Our climbing was over and sadly we had to retrace our steps. There were so many attractive climbs we had to leave behind, frustrated by the short time at base that fate had dealt us. After two years of planning and two months away we had only ten days of climbing, and that at great expense.

To the traveller in Asia, managing the obstacles becomes a challenge which the connoisseur may enjoy. As a German put it to us on the bus, 'in Asia everything is possible and nothing is certain'. On this particular trip possibility greatly outshone actuality. Nevertheless, we will savour the memory of afternoons sipping yoghurt in remote yurts, the bright green pastures dotted with camels and the untouched snows of Kirghizia.

Summary

Scottish Mountaineering Club Centenary Expedition to China. Members: Geoff Cohen, Hamish Irvine, Grahame Nicoll, Barry Owen, Stan Pearson, and Des Rubens. Shiwakte II, c6250m, climbed by SW face by Cohen and Irvine on 8 August 1988. Shiwakte IIIa attempted by E ridge. Three peaks climbed in the Aghalistan range.

Eagle Ski Club Tien Shan Expedition

STEPHEN GOODWIN

(Plates 35–37, 63)

*G*lasnost, it is to be hoped, will mean more to us in time than seeing Our Lady of Finchley doing her party-political broadcasts on Russian television. Mountaineers, no less than other seekers of new horizons, physical or intellectual, stand to gain from Mr Gorbachev's drive for openness. For bureaucracy, or fear of it, has kept that sizeable portion of the world's mountains which lies within the USSR largely untrammelled by Britons.

Sifting through the archives of the Alpine Club and Royal Geographical Society for information on the north-western Tien Shan, the realization dawned that our six-strong party looked like being the first British mountaineers to probe this distant corner of Kazakhstan. Confirmation was provided by our Soviet hosts last March over an ample meal at Moscow's Sport Hotel – an alcohol-free base for those physiologically remarkable products of People's Athletics.

According to Boris – chief of the Kazakh alpine scene, but no desk-bound *apparatchik* as the stumps of three frost-bitten fingers testified – we would be the first Brits to attend a Soviet International Mountaineering Camp in the Tien Shan. He wondered why. Perhaps part of the answer lies with that very British bureaucracy – the BMC. The Manchester Kremlin has a full list of the camps and the dates, but this seems to have a 'classified (unless specifically asked for)' stamp on it. I only learnt of its existence after our return.

Not that we were complaining about being pioneers. We were about to enter a central Asian range only two days' travelling from Heathrow where every ascent would, by *reductio ad absurdum*, be a British first, and virtually every ski descent a first ever. The Soviets are only just catching on to ski-mountaineering, and our Eagle Ski Club and MEF-sponsored visit apparently provided a pretext for the import of a batch of Silvretta touring bindings. How else could Grisha, Master of Sport and our 'consultant' for the 16-day trip, accompany us up 4000m peaks? In the event, to our relief, he did not try, but seemed pleased with the performance of his new equipment on the slopes closer to base.

The title 'International Mountaineering Camp' was something of a misnomer. It has the whiff of canvas and the sound of many tongues about it. But the 'camp' at Chimbulak was the hostel of a rudimentary ski resort. Here again, language is being stretched. There is, for anyone fancying something completely different from Verbier, a two-stage chair-lift from 2200m to 3000m and two T-bars. The concrete and steel hostel is bedecked with banner exhortations to the USSR's ski protégés, who are its main business. As for 'international', our party comprised three Scots – leaders Dave and Moira Snadden and Eric Pirie – and three English – Nim Rodda, Steve Lenartowicz and myself – and no one else. A group of about 30 West Germans had pulled out at the last minute: I will not dwell on the immense grief this caused us.

Chimbulak is 25km south of Alma Ata, a city of about 1.2 million souls and capital of the republic of Kazakhstan. The name means 'Father of the Apples', a rustic touch that hardly fits with the grey, post-war reality of the place, though there are orchards beyond. It stands on the edge of the Kazakh steppe, where industry and topography have combined to create a smog trap. Only as our battered yellow 'sport bus' sputtered up above the murk and into the valley of the Alma Atinka river did the mountains appear at all. But then, rising above the hurrying stream, the birches and the higher spruce, what mountains they are.

The greater Tien Shan stretches for 2450km west to east, half in the Soviet Union, half in China. The highest peaks, Pobeda (7439m) and the imposing spire of Khan Tengri (6995m) – where Boris lost those fingers – stand on the border. The central zone of these Celestial Mountains (to translate their Chinese name) has seen limited international effort, and the Chinese side has seen rather more. But look in the Alpine Club Library for information on the 1200km length of the Soviet Tien Shan and, despite Mrs Johnson's persistence, you will look in vain.

The bus, clawing its way up through the snow in four-wheel drive and repeatedly overheating, was taking us into the Zailiyskiy Alatau, a range which runs 250km west to east and about 30km across, with peaks up to 5000m. John Cleare refers to the range in *The Collins Guide to Mountains and Mountaineering* (p 151). He does not name it, but accurately describes the peaks as 'jagged, icy and alpine in character'. Cleare also notes Hot Henry Barber's visit in 1976 and his ascent of Free Korea Peak (4800m). The Americans also put up new routes around Pik Talgar (5017m), the highest peak in the range and some 20km east of Chimbulak.

Heights should be treated cautiously. The only useful map for mountaineering that the RGS had was a line drawing of the Zailiyskiy Alatau by Jerzy Wala, who is Polish. The Soviets were very interested to see it! They offered no map at all until several days into our visit. It was another sketch map. Heights differed and so did the alignment of some ridges. There is also a certain Kazakh chauvinism which pushes up Talgar to keep it over 5000m. I used Cleare's figure above; the undiplomatic Pole marks it down to 4973m. The Kazakhs also keep Khan Tengri above the magic 7000m barrier.

The yellow bus finally crashed into a stationary twin, cooling its engine in the middle of the track. Plainly a hopeless optimist, our driver believed that there was room to squeeze by. We walked the rest of the way.

Though we had missed a night's sleep somewhere between Moscow and Alma Ata, we were keen to loosen our ski-legs on what remained of our first day. There had been perhaps 50cm of fresh snow over the preceding days, and the temperature out of the sun had remained well below freezing. Conditions on the *piste* were good. To our shame, early embarrassment over our privileged status to jump the lift queue did not last long. But then neither did we have more

28. *Peak 6104m to the E of the Tanggula Pass, Central Tibet.* (p 82)

29. *On the shore of Gozha Co (Lake Lighten), 1906–08.* (p 84)

30. *Burhan Budai range, Kekesaijimen (6179m) and the Xidatan valley, from the W. (p 84)*

31. *Namcha Barwa, Gyela Peri and Namla Karpo from the N (SE Tibet).*

32. *Landsat photograph of part of N Tibet, showing in R lower part the Burhan Budai range, with Xidatan valley to N. The photograph of Kekesaijimen (plate 30) was taken from the clearly shown gap between E Kun Lun and Burhan Budai.* (p 84)

33.   *SW face of Shiwakte II from Sekya. Route followed snow ramp on extreme R, then glacier in cloud (summit is hidden).* (p 97)

34. *Shiwakte III from the SE. Shiwakte IIIa is the snow shoulder at the R.
Route followed ridge on extreme R to smaller snow shoulder below Shiwakte
IIIa.* (p 97)

35. *Skolnik from the N, showing NE ridge.* (p 101)

36.   *Approaching Pogrebetskogo from Tuyuk-Su glacier.* (p 101)

37.   *Descending the E ridge of Pogrebetskogo.* (p 101)

38. *20th October Peak, N face.* (p 109)

39. *Looking towards summit of Suphan Dağ.* (p 115)

40. *Kurdistan village (Cilo Sat range).* (p 115)

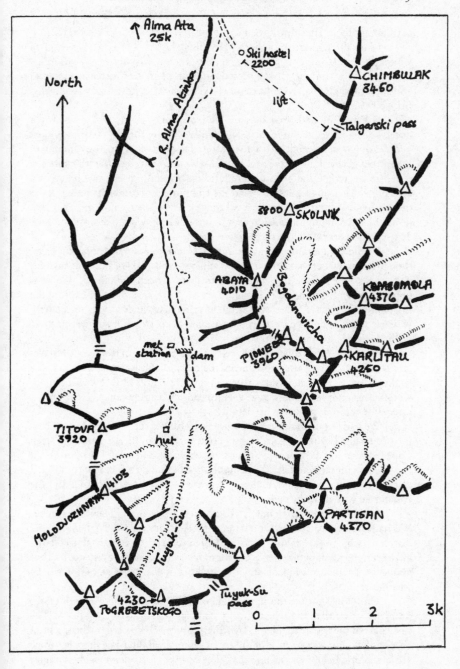

↑ Alma Ata
25k

○ Ski hostel
∧ 2200

lift

CHIMBULAK
3450

North

R. Alma Atinka

Talgarski pass

3800 △SKOLNIK

ABAYA
4010

Bogdanovicha

KOMSOMOLA
△4376 △

met □
station   dam

PIONEER
3960

KARLITAU
↑4250

TITOVA
3920

hut

MOLODJOZHNAYA
△4103

Tuyak-Su

4230 ▷
POGREBETSKOGO

Tuyak-Su
pass

PARTISAN
4370

0   1   2   3k

than a handful of runs down the main *piste* before cutting our own tracks.

From the col above the lifts, the Talgarski pass (3165m), we climbed Chimbulak peak (3450m), part way on skins, then an easy snow and rock ridge scramble to the summit. Grisha accompanied us at an ever-increasing interval and we picked him up on the descent. However modest, it was, we presumed, a British first.

If Day One had proved some kind of fitness point, Day Two was a necessary exercise in diplomacy. We had to get it through to the almost overbearing host 'committee' that we wanted to get away from the Chimbulak hostel to a glacier base. Dave and Moira, who had conceived the trip and then toiled to overcome the bureaucratic hurdles, pressed the message home at a mealtime head-banging session. And the committee succumbed, content to let us first do a day-tour to learn the local geography and to acclimatize. They did, however, seem mildly shocked to hear that we did not want to return for lunch. These Soviets seemed to be three-square-meals-a-day mountaineers.

Grisha accompanied us to the Talgarski pass to point out possible peaks, though he knew them as summer routes and not at all as ski peaks. Talgar stood out 20km to the west, rather out of practical reach from Chimbulak. We went opposite ways from the col; Grisha down to the *piste* and we to explore the Bogdanovicha glacier. A little over 3km long, it curves in descent from a north-westerly track to north-east, ringed by 4000m peaks; on at least three of these we had designs for the days to come.

However, the Bogdanovicha was not quite the piece of icing-sugared cake it appeared. Not long after skiing from the col and putting on skins, Steve was leading a zigzag up a short slope when a room-sized area settled with a thump, an ominous crack spreading across its top side. Warned again as Dave tried a direct line on foot, we began to detour.

We had hoped to reach a col to the west of Pioneer Peak and look across the promising Tuyuk-Su glacier system but, loaded with fresh snow, the steep slope below it looked too risky. Four of us climbed to the cleft between Abaya and Skolnik on the glacier's W side in the hope of finding a different route back to the hostel; but we could not see a clear line and did not want to alarm the committee with an early epic.

Next day we left for a hut at 3500m on the edge of the Tuyuk-Su glacier. We had decided to split our remaining 10 days between the Tuyuk-Su and Bogdanovicha peaks, taking tents and operating from a high glacier base. However, the night before we set out the Soviets disclosed the existence of a hut above the Tuyuk-Su, and later still admitted that it was manned, radioing back weather reports.

The 6km skin up the upper valley of the Alma Atinka presented no problems other than the sweat of a 1300m height gain with 20kg packs. The early part of the trail through the Tien Shan spruce was crossed by the tracks of deer and fox, but we saw little of the area's reputed wildlife. The shapely spruce are left behind below 3000m and the valley opens out to what must be summer pasture. Like the Bogdanovicha, it is ringed by 4000m peaks – 13 abutting the glacier itself – but in a much wider arc which allows the eye to take in a magnificent sweep of spires, snow-caps and shattered granite ridges.

There is a small dam at 3016m, redundant in winter, below which shelters a second met hut and a spinney of radio masts. The two observers were clearly expecting us and laid on a welcome cup of tea and bread with apple jam. A large fish was less enticing: we left it for the committee, three of whom we understood to be following.

Another couple of hours' skinning brought us to our base for the next three days. Described as the Geographical Society hut, it was in fact only one of a collection of wooden shacks. Viewed from the surrounding hills it looked like a movieman's deserted gold-rush settlement, set in a frozen wasteland. In summer it is a centre for field study and outdoor pursuits.

Igor the met man housed the six of us in a bunk-room and the varying numbers of our 'support team' on his kitchen floor. Five in all visited the hut; none ventured out far, but the evenings were convivial. Nice work if you can get it! This is what the state apparently paid them to do. They certainly brought up plentiful supplies – including whole chickens, several pounds of beef and a salmon – but then they had little to do all day except to eat.

Against this novel background the mountaineering itself was positively familiar. Our first objective was Molodjozhnaya (4103m) or 'Peak of Young Persons'. A massive mountain, its steep northern slopes and hanging glaciers fill the south-western aspect from the hut. We intended to approach it via a small col on the ridge which runs north to Titova (3920m), unmarked on our Polish map. But a snow-pit dug as Dave zigzagged warily up to the col revealed a disturbing profile – 25cm of soft snow overlying a hardish slab, beneath which was an air-layer and then a deep bed of cup crystals. Time and again we found similar conditions, with some crystals up to 7mm across, the perfect roller-bearing slide. In contrast to the Alps, where frequent freeze and thaw speed consolidation of the snowpack, the constant sub-zero temperatures of this part of the Tien Shan result in prolonged instability.

We took Titova as our consolation prize, carrying skis up to the ridge, then trudging to what we judged to be the S (3900m) and middle (3920m) summits. Unpronounceable or unnamed peaks stretched away into the hazy distance, all unvisited by Brits. The crust over the air-gap and crystals held for our descent of a wide, south-facing couloir, and we had time before dusk to nose into the main Tuyuk-Su glacier. At its head, Pogrebetskogo (4230m) looked an impressive snow mountain, maybe skiable; it became our next goal.

It was −14°C when we set out at 8.30 next morning. But we could not complain. An incongruous pair of mongrels and their roly-poly pup lived outside the hut, one in an old barrel. The glut of food-scraps we presented gradually won over these noisy guardians and made trips to the distant bog less fraught.

The steady skin up the Tuyuk-Su to the hub of a wide circle of 4000ers with the early sun breaking over the jagged eastern rim was one of the most satisfying moments of the tour. Pogrebetskogo's ice-laden ramparts appear to close the head of the valley, but tucked behind a spur lies the shallow Tuyuk-Su pass (4100m). The ramp up to it is crevassed, and we roped up. As it steepened we put harscheisen on the skis; but the ice hardened to green and we turned to front-points, with skis on our packs. The 1.5km ridge from the col was curiously crevassed – Eric and Steve plunged through to their shoulders – and culminated in a mixed snow and rock scramble. The Kazakh name means 'enclosed pools': a sort of Three Tarns under the ice and snow. From the summit, reached in just over six hours, we looked south over the parallel Kyungey Alatau to distant thin cloud, probably above the inland sea of Lake Issyk-Kul. Not only was this a first British ascent, but the first ever ski descent of the Tuyuk-Su glacier from the col.

That night in the hut Igor opened up on weather conditions. The session ended more philosophically, correcting East–West stereotypes and damning Trident and SS20s in equal measure. It seemed that we had hit on the best of a rather limited season for ski-mountaineering. According to our guardian there is ample snow by February, but it is extremely cold and the days are short. The March window of settled weather is followed by more snow in April, with high winds piling up an avalanche risk. Or, rather, a greater one! We noticed the next day that our descent pattern on Titova had been partially erased by the fan of a moderate slide. We also crossed the debris of two sizeable new avalanches on our return down the Alma Atinka valley two days later.

After Pogrebetskogo, named after the geographer who first climbed Khan Tengri, we turned again to Molodjozhnaya. This time we approached it from the long E ridge, ascending by a gully of exhaustingly unconsolidated snow on its southern side. Skis were redundant, though we carried them to the ridge: an almost futile exercise, as it turned out. It was a classic 2km stretch of winter mountaineering – mixed rock, ice and energy-sapping deep snow – with steep snow-fields and hanging glaciers on the N side and rock walls and icy gullies to the south. The summit itself is fairly nondescript and almost flat.

Next day we ski'd down to the Chimbulak hostel where the committee subjected us to the dubious pleasure of their basement sauna. A Kazakh sauna is to ordinary saunas what vindaloo is to curries.

In our finaa week we returned to the Bogdanovicha glacier, needing the tents this time, and pitched camp at 3430m on what we assumed to be moraine above the ice. Soon after settling in, however, we stumbled, literally, on a small crevasse under the snow in our brew-up zone. Our foundations were, apparently, a less sound amalgam.

From this high base we made attempts on three peaks: Komsomola (4367m), the highest in the Bogdanovicha group, Karlitau (4250m), its southern neighbour, and Pioneer (3960m), rearing majestically from the ridge directly south of our camp and plainly no ski peak.

Memory has abbreviated the weather during those few days to 'cold and clear'. But a reread of my diary shows this to be a gross simplification. A typical entry reads: '8am, it's −16°C. But clear blue sky offering us another chance at Komsomola. Melting snow for tea and semolina. Trying not to dislodge the rime frost on the inside of the tent.'

The first attempt at Komsomola ground to a halt at 4130m after a tedious slog up 200m of slippery scree and snow from the col with Karlitau. Readers of the heavy press may be familiar with the word Komsomol (youth) from regular quotes from *Komsomolskaya Pravda*, official organ of the party youth wing. Not that this nugget of intelligence was much use to us. We were expecting a rock and ice route of about Scottish Grade II. So, perhaps, we were lost. Anyway, cloud was building up, it was windy and, as ever, damn cold.

Karlitau looked a stroll from this vantage point, if a somewhat nervy one on crampons. One slip on the bare ice of its dome-like W side and a long slide would ensue, one or two hundred metres either to the soft snow below the col or to the not-so-soft boulders also waiting there. Karlitau means 'snowy mountain', but its E face falls away sheer with huge cornices along the summit ridge. About 25m below the top, Dave decided that the risk of a slab avalanche was too great. Between Karlitau's snowy cap and the ice were our old friends, the cup crystals. The consolation of ski-mountaineering, though, is the descent. We had left the skis not far below the col and were able to ski easily down the glacier to our tents.

Next morning the camp was enveloped in cloud and fine snow was building up on the tent sides. Things improved by midday, leaving time for a look at Pioneer. It is approached by Pioneer pass, a col at around 3700m which provides at least a summer way over to the Tuyuk-Su glacier. A granite pinnacle stands on the col, looking rather like a sea-stack. Russian imagination sees it not, however, as an Old Man but as entwined dancers, calling it the Bolshoi.

20 metres before we reached the dancers' feet, skis had to be abandoned as we tried to thread our way round narrow crevasses. Mixed climbing followed from the col, up a steep gully, briefly front-pointing and then swimming in loose snow, and finishing grandly from side to side along an airy castellated ridge.

An abseil and rapid descent of the gully was followed for Dave and myself by a fall into a crevasse below the col; Dave managed this feat with his skis on. Seen from the end of an embedded axe, it looked an evil slit, fortunately not too wide. Back at the camp we had a visitor. Consultant Grisha had come up from the hostel, full of good cheer and with three not particularly useful provisions: half a kilo of porridge, a box of sugar lumps and a grotesque sausage. Perhaps, despite the groaning packs we had carried up, we were falling behind Sovintersport's statutory calorie intake.

Our last day on the Bogdanovicha was the one my diary recorded as 'clear blue sky' etc, but the second shot at Komsomola was only marginally more successful. It petered out after some Grade II or III climbing, about 60m above our previous point, myself perched on a narrow ramp casting around in vain for a way ahead. We abseiled down the blocky wall which had been our only advance, leaving another first British ascent waiting for whoever divines the true route to this confusing summit.

After extricating our tents we ski'd back to the Talgarski pass in dense mist. It was not easy to locate, and it was dark before we rattled down the Chimbulak *piste* and into the hostel.

With one day left before returning to Moscow we settled for Skolnik (3800m), the 'Scholar,' which had the attraction of being both a good-looking peak and easily accessible. It lies on the ridge south of the Talgarski pass and so – let's admit it – we were able to get a leg-up on the chair-lift. From the col it took about four hours to the summit, most of it on foot after leaving the skis at 3360m. Rock ribs provided pleasant climbing but soon gave way to unconsolidated snow. Dave and Steve negotiated a way across the top of two exposed gullies and shared the trail-breaking through deep snow to our last Kazakh top.

By evening Eric Pirie had won the Eagles' Tien Shan Downhill Trophy in our last dash down the *piste* – a hard hat spotted below Skolnik and found, to our relief, to be empty. And by midnight he was pretty 'tired and emotional', to use a parliamentary euphemism. Nor was he alone. Perhaps it was the Kazakh champagne or the Armenian brandy or the vodka (drained from scrapped SS20s), or maybe it was just the speeches and song, which helped the Tien Shan International Meet to break down some final barriers.

Siberian Adventures

The 1988 British Altai Expedition

DUNCAN TUNSTALL

(*Plate 38*)

The temperature is rapidly heading towards the high 90s, the humidity has long since passed 100%. I am trying to control my imagination and thus, hopefully, my body's responses to the stimuli it is receiving. Numerous articles in the climbing press stress that mountaineering is a head game and that controlling one's mental processes is the key to big numbers, fame and fortune. But I never imagined the circumstances that would prove these theories correct.

The problem was simple. The birch twigs which were striking my back with frequent regularity and considerable force were wielded not by the 'Blond Swedish Air Hostess' of my dreams but by Mick Fowler, famous London bureaucrat, mountaineer and leader of the British 1988 Altai Expedition. Mick, relishing the role of a 'Naked Civil Servant', was introducing us to the delights of a Russian sauna – Fowler style!

Fortunately, the mental struggle is soon over and I am bundled out of the sauna to stagger the few painful yards before plunging ungracefully into the glacial Ak-Kem lake. The sudden immersion into the freezing meltwater quickly removes all thoughts of handcuffs and, prompted by my most basic survival instincts, I hasten back to the sauna. Here, not without considerable pleasure, I wreak my revenge on the now prostrate Fowler.

It was after several rounds of this self-inflicted torture that my constitution finally gave up, resulting in the involuntary ejection of a half-bottle of vodka which had been consumed earlier. On recovering from this mild setback, I was horrified to discover that our honourable leader had left, in a state of total undress, on a mission to raise the female members of the camp to join in the fun. Not surprisingly, his unsubtle pitch was rejected and we retreated to our tents without further ado.

You may well enquire how a well-balanced yuppie like myself happened to get embroiled in this bizarre scene of medieval brutality. It was a question I regularly asked myself during the three weeks spent at the 1988 International Mountaineering Camp in the Altai Mountains in Siberia.

Indeed, this question of why I had chosen the Altai nudged into my consciousness as early as the first night of the trip, while I was tucking into my fourth bowl of boiled cabbage in the aptly named Hotel Sport in Moscow, the starting point of our adventure, and trying to ignore the looks of disdain sent in our direction from the Adonis-like physiques of our fellow-guests: a rare mixture of Olympic shot-putters, pole-vaulters and weight-lifters.

Inevitably, so it seems in hindsight, it was Mick Fowler's fault. Mick needs no introduction and he had already thrown off his respectable Civil Servant image, becoming completely immersed in his *alter ego* of manic adventurer. His partner, Phil Thomas, is by contrast a quiet, thoughtful Welshman, short and stocky, probably described by everyone who knows him as 'solid'. Phil is a fully-fledged mountain guide and looks the part. Alas, the B team will never be described as solid. My partner Paul Allison's greatest contribution to the trip was to attract the attention of a passing American tourist who, captivated by his Gothic/hippy appearance, insisted on taking numerous photographs of this 'fine specimen of Gorbachev youth'.

If the official British Altai team was not incongruous enough, our fellow attendees on the camp also added to the colour. We were joined by four compatriots: Andy 'Gusher' Bond, 'Shifty' Steve Gould, Gerry Bumford and his wife Caroline. There were also eight Germans, one in traditional lederhosen, eight Swiss and a lone Austrian temptress who intimidated us all by doing pull-ups at every possible opportunity.

After being shown the sights of Moscow we were whisked away via two internal jet flights and a terrifying helicopter ride to Base Camp on the Ak-Kem lake at 2000m. Here we were introduced to our Siberian hosts.

The Altai mountains are alpine in scale, Bielukha at 4506m being the highest peak. They must resemble the golden age of alpinism as there are no fixed huts, cable cars or crowds. Despite this and their renown for beauty and rare flora, the mountains have received little Western attention. John Town was the first Briton to take advantage of the camps (*AJ90*, 47–53, 1985) and has, until this year, been followed only by Alec Erskine and Mark Phillips who, amongst other achievements, made the first British ascent of the N face of Bielukha.

Home for the next three weeks was the delightfully situated Ak-Kem camp. Unfortunately the infamous Altai weather set in with a vengeance and prevented us from taking full advantage of the place. Apart from one good day early on when we made the obligatory training ascent of Ak Ayuk by the N face (Russian 3b or Alpine AD), it rained heavily in Base Camp for 12 days, denying us the opportunity to climb anything worthwhile.

Despite our forced inactivity we surprisingly managed to avoid the normal 'Snell's Field/Expedition' depression. This can be put down to two reasons – the sauna and our Russian friends. The sauna has been adequately described already, but a few words are needed about the latter.

They can best be described by the Russian word *korrosho*, which roughly translates as 'the business', 'sound' or 'all right'. From Slava, the camp leader, through our translator, Victor, to Tanya the cook, they did everything possible to make our stay entertaining. Apart from providing three cooked meals a day, they engaged us in many a happy hour discussing ideology, Russian climbing trends, *glasnost* etc, all lubricated by copious amounts of vodka. In marked contrast to two Americans who later joined the camp, they enthusiastically participated in the series of outrageous games we concocted (although, to be honest, a session at cricket did appear to leave them rather bewildered). Not even a massive landslide which almost destroyed the camp managed to subdue the atmosphere.

Alas, all good things come to an end and, although there was no improvement in the weather, we were forced to set off for our main objective. Our decision to go was based on the simple estimate that we would need six days to complete the traverse of Bielukha via the N face of the superbly named 'Twentieth Anniversary of the Glorious October Revolution' peak. There were only six days left until the helicopter, our only form of return, was due to arrive.

Fortune didn't favour the stupid. For on Day Two, shortly after leaving Advanced Base under a starlit sky, the clag set in; beginning as a heavy mist, it quickly turned to snow and then developed into a full electric storm. Self-preservation and the sheer misery of the occasion led to a unanimous decision to return to our Advanced Camp.

Six hours later we re-emerged from the claustrophobic shelter of our Geminis to the stark realization that we had failed in our objective without even reaching the bergschrund. The face was still shrouded in heavy cloud and, even if the weather was to clear, we had run out of time. The humorously written message of warning from Victor could not raise our spirits and we were a sorry crew lounging around the boulders by our camp.

We now had only four days left. Rejecting the option of a further few days' dossing we decided on a repeat ascent of Bielukha by the *Voie Normale*, a hopefully achievable objective. Two impressive avalanches in quick succession down the N face reconfirmed our decision to ignore the added challenge of that approach.

Our ascent was remarkable only for its lack of incident. We left the Tomsk bivouac at 6am and crossed the Delone pass to gain the beautifully secluded Men Su glacier where the early morning gloom lifted over distant Mongolian peaks to provide a stimulating backdrop for our endeavours. We pressed on past the tents of the other British team also attempting Bielukha that day, completing the tedious plod up to the Borelski saddle. More than grateful to be following their tracks, we struggled up the long, complicated approach in deteriorating weather. A brief stop to chat with the others provided welcome relief before we continued up the striking final 300m of the E ridge. A total whiteout ensured that for us the summit would not be 'the tremendous viewpoint providing tempting panoramas of distant Chinese, Mongolian and Siberian landscapes' so enjoyed by John and Sheila Town. Instead we had to be content with snatched glimpses of our closer neighbours, as we hurriedly collected our summit pictures cuddling up to Lenin's bust.

The blizzard continued as we hurried back down the route to begin the familiar routine of ignoring numb digits while struggling with uncooperative poles and frozen Goretex in a mad rush to erect our Geminis. It seemed ages before I could join Paul in the shelter of our portable home.

We were somewhat surprised to wake the next day not to the expected storm, but to a silent dawn: no wind, no snow and not even a distant cloud in the crystal-clear skies. Even the walk back up and over the Delone pass, now on crisp névé, was a pleasure. The descent to the Tomsk was marred by the distressfully clear views of the Twentieth October Peak and the Bielukha N wall. Once again the dreaded phrase 'if only' entered our heads.

Mick and Paul shared my feelings. The weather was too good to waste.

Good sense prevailed over ambition and we rejected the obvious challenge of the Twentieth, dismissed the N face of Bielukha as boring and plumped for the Tomsk ridge on Delone. This fine-looking line took the obvious ridge in the centre of the impressive N face. Giving 1200m of Russian 4b mixed climbing, it seemed the ideal choice for a day of fine alpine climbing. More important, it started less than 10 minutes' walk from our camp.

After lounging away the rest of the day, sunbathing and binging on American delicacies, we retired early. An uncharacteristically prompt start saw us above the initial 40-degree ice-fields and established on the ridge proper at first light. Mick had changed out of his sluggish mode of the last few days and was racing ahead, relishing the challenge of steeper mixed ground. We caught him up at the central rock buttress where he appeared to be having some difficulty. Noting the 500m drop below and leaning on the hard-earned experience that 'what Fowler struggles on I can't do', I unselfishly offered Paul the rope. The only problem was that Mick had the gear and, having disposed of the rock step, he was already disappearing out of sight. A hurried shout resulted in the gear being deposited at the top of the pitch, leaving us to make do with a classical spike-belay for protection.

With the comfort of the rope above, the pitch went surprisingly easily, and we chased Mick's crampon-marks around the corner. Paul had only stopped to place a runner and this set the pattern for the climb, Mick soloing ahead with the B team following, moving together and placing gear every 40m or so. We knew from studying the face from below that there appeared to be a line up an icy ramp to the left of the crest. With this in mind we made a descending traverse leftwards (Scottish 4) which we hoped would lead to the ramp.

Our predictions were correct and the ramp provided the ideal route to the summit. The climbing was a delight, giving Scottish-type mixed action at a consistent Grade 3 with an unnecessary deviation to include a short section of unprotected 4. Our joy on reaching the summit was only slightly marred by Mick's gloating that he had been waiting for an hour or so (we didn't remind him that we had waited for a similar time on Bielukha). However, his enthusiasm for summit photos showed that he had enjoyed the climb as much as we had.

The descent down the Delone (E) ridge provided a fitting conclusion to a classic mountain day. Our eventual return to the Tomsk bivouac was once again met with instant helpings of Boris's mouth-watering soup, our first food for 12 hours. This is a delight we would all like to return to the British scene.

To the total shock of the Russian trainers, we ignored the pull of an early night, packed our rucksacks in the inevitable evening hailstorm and set off for the three-hour retreat to Ak-Kem Base Camp. The next few hours are best forgotten. We literally ran down in a headlong and frequently uncontrolled gallop, hoping to cross a treacherous boulder-field before dark. Needless to say we all failed, and none of us escaped the ignominy of at least one bone-shaking fall which, in Mick's case, could have led to drowning. Apparently he ended up, at one stage, suspended from his rucksack straps above a raging whirlpool!

The rapturous greeting we received in the arms of Tanya and the others made it all seem worthwhile and we were treated to a feast befitting heroes returning from the Eastern Front. We finished the night warming ourselves by the fire, polishing off the last of the vodka and listening to the sounds of Russian harmonies drifting across the still shores: the ideal climax to a wonderful few days.

My only footnote is that, if you have the good fortune to visit the Altai, please listen to the locals' advice and take your sauna *before* gorging yourself with endless courses of Russian delicacies, vodka and champagne – and not afterwards.

Ropes

HAMISH M BROWN

Coloured ropes, deflecting witness eyes,
coloured ropes, securing the insecure,
dragging zigzags up red rock.
Even with so many crabs
you could feel the quivering
through the speckled strands.
The rope should have acted
like a lightning conductor,
jolting my second
but it was a warm day and she snoozed
on a safe stance.
I yanked out three runners
and my partner had burnt hands.
The yellow rope wasn't noticed.
I wish I could untie it
and climb free
of me.

Wanderings in Eastern Turkey

An Ascent of Suphan Dağ

KARL SMITH

(Plates 39, 40)

Eastern Turkey is a land differing enormously from the more developed west of the country. While hotel-building à la Costa Blanca proceeds apace along the coasts, the east remains relatively free from the impact of mass tourism. Economically impoverished, it nevertheless possesses a great charm, the inhospitable nature of the land often more than compensated by the hospitality of the inhabitants. Frequently, while walking, one is invited to drink tea or be a guest at a family gathering.

Apart from Mount Ararat, which has been well-known since at least the time of Noah, there are numerous other peaks and ranges to attract the mountaineer. But despite the massive army presence, this is still a lawless region; the rugged, inaccessible terrain makes it ideal for smugglers, bandits and Kurdish separatists.

Unfortunately for the climber, the central base for the Kurdish rebels lies in the Cilo Sat mountains, straddling the borders of Turkey and Iraq. This range possesses some of the most impressive mountain scenery in the Near East, with huge dolomitic faces, small ice-fields, and it includes Resko Tepesi (4170m), Turkey's second-highest peak. Access to this region has been banned to visitors for some years, and going there one risks being arrested, or worse. The nearest I managed to get to the Cilo Sat was Hakkari, the capital of this region, a small mountain town facing the northern slopes of Resko Tepesi.

Catching the bus down to Yuksekova to gain a better glimpse of the range, I was arrested within minutes for photographing a military installation. The soldiers are understandably sensitive, and on the road through the mountains westwards to Cizre there were numerous army checkpoints. Locals were subjected to full body-searches on several occasions. I, being a Westerner, was offered tea instead.

If ever this area becomes more stable, there is immense potential for new routes. Northwards from here, the mountains continue in a wide band as far as the border with Russia. But here they are mainly volcanic in origin and therefore offer little scope for more technical routes. For giving a sense of wildness and isolation, however, ascents of these peaks can be very rewarding.

Approaching Eastern Turkey from the Black Sea coast, I had not intended this as a climbing trip; but on seeing Mount Ararat my desire to escape from buses took hold. Hiring gear was possible in Dogubeyazit, but obtaining a permit to climb was not. Permits took at least a month to arrive from Ankara. Each group is accompanied on the ascent by a liaison officer, and as there is only one normal ascent route avoiding detection seemed unlikely.

Continuing south by bus, I was struck by the sight of a snow-capped volcano on the western shore of Lake Van. Like Ararat, it rose in splendid isolation and seemed to provide a suitable challenge. A glance at the map confirmed it as Suphan Dağ (c4010m), the highest mountain in this part of Turkey. A week or so later, after a mixture of dissipation and walking, I was on the road heading north along the western side of the lake.

Things were not looking too promising. I had already spent most of the afternoon in the shade of the mosque, waiting for a lift. Eventually a truck stopped and I climbed in, sandwiched between the burly driver and his equally large mate.

As we followed the shores of the lake, Suphan Dağ came into view. I knew precious little about my objective – the idea of climbing Suphan Dağ having only occurred to me a couple of days earlier as a consolation for being unable to climb Ararat. Seen from this angle, it appeared to offer little technical difficulty – a definite plus in view of my equipment (training shoes, a thin jersey and no bivvy gear). Dropped in the dusty little town of Adilcevaz, I found a room in the only available hotel, a building I had twice walked past, believing it to be derelict.

On my way down to the lake for a swim, I tried to buy a few plastic bottles of mineral water – none were available. Reluctant to haul glass bottles up a 4000m peak, I reasoned that I might at least enjoy the contents. With this in mind I called at the town's sole 'off-licence'. It sold one type of beer, one type of wine (red) and, somewhat improbably, a single bottle of Napoleon brandy. Judging by the accumulation of dust, this had probably been left there by Napoleon himself.

As I prepared to leave with my three bottles of Efes Pilsen, the owner became agitated and asked me to drink them on the spot. After agreeing to return the empties as soon as possible, I escaped.

Swimming out from the shore, I was surprised to see how much snow was still lying on the hills surrounding the lake. Although it was only the end of June, the temperature was well into the eighties.

As I walked back into town, the off-licence owner jumped out of the shop and asked for the bottles again. 'Tomorrow!', I replied.

A few miles beyond the town there was a small lake, Lake Aygir. I vaguely recalled seeing in an old guidebook that it was supposedly a three-day ascent from here. Obviously, an early start was required if I was to avoid a night on the mountain. The lake was reachable by a dirt track, so I arranged for a taxi (at extortionate cost) to take me at 5am.

Next morning came, and there was no taxi anywhere. The only sign of life was in the village bakery, so I went in and was offered tea while a young lad ran off to get the taxi-driver out of bed. As time passed, I became less enthusiastic about the whole enterprise. Surely a day on the beach, or with the delectable Kate back in Van, was preferable?

Shortly before 6, however, the taxi arrived. I jumped in, and we set off . . . in the wrong direction. 'Where are we going?' 'Petrol, petrol!' By this stage, I was not in the mood for accepting any more excuses, so I told the driver to turn round and we headed at last toward Suphan Dağ. Leaving the town behind, we drove over a drab level plain, sparsely covered with yellow grass.

Suddenly the car started to splutter and, an instant later, it died. We had run out of petrol. After paying the driver off (needless to say, the full fare), I started towards Lake Aygir, on foot. As I climbed the long ridge below the lake, I looked back. The driver appeared as an ant-like speck, pushing his taxi before him across the plain.

It was already mid-morning by the time I skirted the lake again to begin the ascent proper. As with many other volcanoes, the route-finding presented few problems. Smooth, tussocky slopes led ever upwards, unrelieved but for an occasional outcrop of obsidian. Ahead of me in a slight hollow lay a nomad encampment, the low, dusty black tents draped web-like in a cluster of about half a dozen. I made a wide detour to avoid the camp; the novelty value of being used as a moving coconut-shy by young Kurds wielding rocks had worn off during the previous week.

Higher up the mountain, the grazing became ever more sparse, the bedrock now showing through everywhere. Despite this there were still the occasional shepherds, dressed in cloaks supported at the shoulders by a broad wooden bar. This presented a strange spectacle when first seen from a distance.

I shared my bread and cheese with one of the shepherds before pressing on. Despite my misgivings, I was making fast progress, and by 1pm I had reached the beginning of the snow-slope which I thought led to the summit. Half an hour later, I reached the crest of a sharp ridge. Here I was met by a stunning sight, in complete contrast to what there had been below. To my right, separated from me by a deep trough containing two frozen lakes, lay an expansive plateau of snow-filled hollows and bare rock. Ahead lay a sharp ridge leading to a col, and then a shallower ridge leading to what I presumed was the summit, half a mile from where I was standing. The views from here were very extensive; across the turquoise-blue Lake Van I could pick out the mountains leading eventually to Iran, while southwards Nemrut Dağ (Mount Nimrod) and its crater lake stood out clearly. At its foot I could pick out the town of Tatvan, where, a few days previously, I had encountered an Englishwoman riding down the main street on her horse.

More significantly, though, an ominous-looking wall of black cloud was coming in from the north-west. It was time to make haste. The ridge proved fairly awkward in places and, by the time I reached the col leading to the summit, the ridge behind me was already enveloped in swirling mist. Loud thunder rang in my ears as I hurried up to the top, and as I arrived a heavy shower of hail started. There was no sign of any other visitors having been there recently, and I saw little benefit in hanging around. Taking a more direct line down I soon found myself beneath the cloud level, and in another 10 minutes the clouds themselves had dispersed as quickly as they had arrived. I sat down on a convenient rock and broke into the beer, revelling in the isolation.

Going down was easy, the route being laid out before me, and by mid-afternoon I was trudging back along the dirt-track leading into Adilcevaz. After a short while a tractor came along, heading into town. I climbed on, to be greeted by a German with a huge rucksack. Throughout my trip, however unlikely the place, I encountered fellow travellers.

'So, you have climbed Suphan Dağ!' he said. He had bivvied overnight and reached the top by mid-morning, which accounted for our not seeing each other up there.

Back in Adilcevaz, feeling fairly shattered, I didn't want to waste a beautiful evening in the less-than-salubrious surroundings of the hotel. A swim was clearly the answer.

Passing through the main street, I believed I had escaped the attentions of the off-licence owner, but as I walked by he ran out of his shop. 'Where are the empties?' I pointed. 'On top of Sulphan Dağ.' He looked at me for a moment, then we both roared with laughter. When I went past an hour later, he was still laughing.

One Man's Fourthousanders

PETER FLEMING

(Plates 41–47)

No one in my family had ever shown more than scant interest in hills and mountains, and none could see any sense in climbing them. During my schooldays, as I never took an interest in sport and hated football and cricket, I was written off on school reports as an unmotivated weakling when it came to competitive games. But a new world opened up for me suddenly and dramatically when, at the age of 14, I discovered the Lakeland hills almost on my doorstep, and so it all began.

Twelve months after I had left school the headmaster proudly announced at morning assembly that an Old Boy had made headlines in the local paper, upholding the school's high standards of initiative and achievement, and setting a fine example which he hoped everyone would remember and strive to maintain. This Old Boy had entered the first mountain trial in the Lake District as the youngest competitor and had come third over the finishing line, ahead of seasoned marathon and mountain runners. At last I had found a challenge, and it seemed that I had a natural affinity towards mountains.

Four years later, in 1956 – after an intensive apprenticeship, summer and winter, on Lakeland and Scottish hills – I made my first venture to the Alps. Four of us from our local rambling club – Doug, Colin, Bill and I – drove out in a Ford Popular to Randa in Switzerland, where we took the rack railway to Zermatt. My neck ached with gazing at those awesome mountains. For our first season we did fairly well. Doug and I climbed the *Matterhorn* by the Hörnli Ridge. (There was no cable car to Schwarzsee in those days.) The ascent presented us with no problems, but we were over-cautious and late coming down. Having done the steepest and most improbable-looking mountain in the district, we turned our attention to the highest – the *Dom*. All four of us succeeded on this, but the Festi glacier unnerved us somewhat. For most of us it was the first time on a high snow-covered glacier.

This short introductory taste of alpine mountaineering left me in no doubt that I would return. I could not resist the adventure and the physical challenge that these mountains offered. However, my profession as a marine engineer dictated otherwise, and for a number of years my leave did not coincide with the summer season. Most of my time was spent in the Far East where I had to be content just to look at jungle-clad volcanoes in Indonesia or the unforgettable shape of Mount Fuji, its snow-capped cone rising high and aloof through layers of cloud. A truly beautiful sight, but, alas, I never had a chance to climb it.

It was 1960 before I again visited Zermatt, this time travelling out by rail. The return fare was £21.10 from London, which was good value even then. The only 4000er climbed on this short holiday was the *Zinalrothorn* by the S ridge in perfect weather. We also traversed the Wellenkuppe, which involved descending its N ridge to the Triftjoch. This was a mistake. The ridge was extremely loose and shattered and, as we were a fairly large party, it took ages. On reaching Zermatt late that evening, we learned that it was the first descent of the N ridge for three years. By the summer of 1962 I had abandoned my career on the high seas, and I took a long break before looking for alternative employment. A lot of time was spent in Scotland and the Lakes before I returned to Zermatt once again. This time I went with a girl-friend, Vi Tyson. We stayed at the Hotel Bahnhof which was owned by a retired chief guide, Bernard Biner, and his sister Paula, who were very well known and respected at that time by most of the British alpinists who frequented Zermatt, for their friendly and helpful attitude and inexpensive accommodation. We had great plans for our stay, and luck proved to be with us. The main objective was to make sure Vi got to the summit of the Matterhorn as it was an ambition she had dreamed of achieving for a long time. We were both at the peak of fitness, and on our arrival in Zermatt the weather and conditions on the mountains were ideal. We set out for the Hörnli hut next day, but before we reached it a storm swept in, putting down six inches of snow at the hut. To dampen our spirits further, when I enquired as to the whereabouts of the guardian we learned that he had just died and was to be carried down to Zermatt the next day. He was Matthew Kronig, a powerfully-built ex-guide, reputed to have climbed the Matterhorn over 100 times. We retired to our beds in the Belvedere next door, feeling rather depressed, and thinking that we had wasted our time in coming up to the hut.

I looked out at 3.30am and, if one ignored the fresh snow, it was a perfect morning. The essential ingredients were there – the '3 Cs': clear, cold and calm. Very few other people were stirring. I said, 'Right Vi, this is it. Let's get going' – and it went well; we were high on the ridge before the sun rose with a welcome warmth. We stopped at the Solvay Refuge for breakfast and soon the snow was melting. We were the first to arrive on the summit at 10am on a beautiful day. Vi could hardly believe that she was there, barely 36 hours after arriving in Zermatt. Her first Alpine peak! Good lass, I knew she would do it. The ascent had actually taken only four hours 45 minutes, despite the snowfall.

After this there was no stopping us. We traversed the Wellenkuppe and *Obergabelhorn*, descending by the Arbengrat accompanied by another friend, David Winstanley. A very good route full of contrasts. We followed this with the *Weisshorn* via the E ridge, and then two days later we went to the Mischabel hut, climbing the 1800m in well under three hours. Next morning we set out in unsettled weather to traverse the *Lenzspitze* and *Nadelhorn*. As we reached the point of no return – the col between the two peaks – we were caught in a storm which was very alarming. It was snowing heavily, the air was charged with electricity and our ironware was alive and buzzing. Visibility was very poor and there was no way of getting off the exposed rocky ridge without going over one of the 4000m summits. We had to sit it out, leaving our axes, pegs and karabiners some distance away until after about an hour or so it blew over, leaving everything in a treacherous and icy state. We continued over the Nadelhorn and descended the S face very cautiously, reaching the Hohberg glacier safely. Unknown to Dave and myself, Vi had silently been suffering in the storm. Her fingers had been frost-bitten and later they turned black at the ends, but fortunately there was no permanent damage. We arrived at the Dom hut with great relief, and later back in Zermatt Herr Biner informed us that our conquests were the only successful ones on any major peaks in the whole of the valley that day.

While Vi took time off to recover, David and I walked to the Rossier hut from Zermatt in one day – not a hut walk to be recommended unless you are in training for the Olympics! Next day we climbed the *Dent Blanche* via the S ridge and descended to the Schönbiel hut to stay the night.

To round off this holiday we planned to traverse the 'Big M' (our affectionate label for the Matterhorn), this time via the Italian Ridge and down the Hörnli. We arranged that Vi, if she felt fit enough, should meet us at the Italian hut which she could reach, via the Furggjoch and the Col du Lion, in the company of a climber we had met in the Bahnhof who also wished to make the traverse of the 'Big M'. Meanwhile, Dave and I were to try to reach the same hut from the Swiss side by a route, not in our guidebook, which had been recommended to us by Bernard Biner. This involved descending from the Schönbiel hut, crossing the Zmutt glacier and climbing into the large snow-basin below the W face of the Matterhorn. The right-hand side of the basin was bounded by what appeared to be a very steep snow-ridge running up the face to an area of seracs just beneath the Col Tournanche. Viewing this from the Schönbiel, we wondered if Bernard had overestimated our capabilities. As we got closer to the ridge the angle eased off, and all went well. We reached the col, and the traverse round the Tête du Lion across the steep névé was quickly made. We were mindful of Edward Whymper's fall just here and wondered how he had escaped with his life. When we reached the hut – which in 1962 was no more than a creaky and grotty shack – we were glad to find that Vi and her companion were already there. That night the atmosphere of the overcrowded and smoky hut was intolerable, and I finished up sleeping outside under the stars to escape the thick fug and general inconsiderateness of some of the occupants. At first light we set off, making good progress. The scenery was magnificent and the weather perfect. The climbing was exposed but not too difficult. We reached the summit cross at 7.30am, the first there again. Two miles below our feet Zermatt lay still in the shadow of the great peaks. Full of exhilaration and the joy of being alive, we remained on the summit for over an hour, soaking up the splendour of our elevated position and greeting the climbers arriving from the Swiss side. This holiday was a great success, and Vi went home in seventh heaven, having achieved her ambition twice over and done much more besides.

Dave and I returned to Zermatt in 1964. We got off to a slow start because of unsettled weather. On the first fine day we once again made the long climb to the Rothorn hut and next day we traversed the Zinalrothorn from the Triftjoch via the Trifthorn and Rothorngrat. A long, sporty rock-route. We descended via the normal SE ridge, and were back at the hut exactly 12 hours after starting out.

We had planned to climb the Täschhorn via the Mischabelgrat, but on reaching the Weingarten glacier we had to turn back when Dave felt ill. The day was not wasted, however, as I made a solo travese of the *Alphubel* via the Rotgrat and Alphubeljoch, descending to the Täsch hut for midday.

Our next objective was Monte Rosa via the Grenz glacier. In the early morning light we spotted a body encased in the ice, and reported this to the authorities on our return. We had now been joined by Jim Bury and Roy Whittaker, and it was a group of four that traversed the *Dufourspitze* and *Zumsteinspitze*, staying the second night in the uniquely situated Margherita hut on the summit of the *Signalkuppe*. Next day we traversed the *Liskamm* and descended by the Zwillings glacier, which provided difficult route-finding through the badly crevassed sections. The weather for the last week had been very good but now storms were forecast, which thwarted our plans to climb the Zmutt arête of the Matterhorn, and we returned instead to the Täsch hut and traversed the Leiterspitzen, a superb little rock-peak which involved climbing some exposed gendarmes. It is possible to do this from Zermatt in a day, but a very early start is recommended. Jim, Roy and I stayed on at the Täsch hut for another attempt at the Täschhorn next day. This time we reached the N branch of the Weingarten glacier before turning back again because of the deteriorating weather and poor visibility.

My companions left Zermatt next day and I took the opportunity to solo the *Rimpfischhorn*, taking three hours to do it from Fluhalp. Two days later I thumbed a lift in a contractor's 'cement bucket' from the Schwarzsee to the Gandegg hut while they were building a new extension to the cable-car system. I continued on up to Testa Grigia. On the following day, in beautiful weather, I soloed the *Breithorn*, the Kleine Matterhorn and the whole of the Frontier Ridge to the base of the Matterhorn, traversing the Theodulhorn and Furgghorn and descending via the Furggjoch back to the Schwarzsee. Thus ended the 1964 season with eight 4000m peaks (seven new ones) and four smaller ones.

Having now spent four seasons in the Valais, and satisfied that I had served a reasonable alpine apprenticeship, I decided to have a change of scenery in 1965. So I travelled out to Chamonix, again by rail and then by bus to Courmayeur, to meet Jim and Roy who had come out earlier by Land-Rover. Our first climb was the Aiguille de Triolet by the normal Italian Route. Two days later I was introduced to the 'delights' of the Torino hut, the first of many visits in the years to come. We made the classic traverse of the Rochefort arête as far as the *Aiguille de Rochefort*. On the way back Jim and I climbed the *Dent du Géant*, which we had to ourselves. Even in 1965 this surprised us. We later discovered the reason in the shape of a notice in the Torino warning climbers to keep off the Tooth because of the state of the fixed ropes; we had mainly avoided these anyway. We had in fact seen the notice before leaving, but none of us understood Italian. The weather was not too kind to us this season, but before it completely broke down we ascended *Mont Blanc* via the normal French Route from the Tête Rousse and the Aiguille du Goûter.

That brought to an end my first season in the Mont Blanc region. For the next two seasons I was unable to persuade any of my climbing friends that the Alps were the place to go, so I decided to go alone, hoping to meet someone out there looking for a companion. It seemed reasonable to assume that if I went back to Zermatt and stayed at the Bahnhof this plan might work. Sadly, Bernard Biner had died the previous year, but his sister Paula was running things as smoothly as ever.

I was introduced to Dr Hal Taylor from Aberdeen, and we made plans to traverse the Adlerhorn and *Strahlhorn*, starting at Fluhalp. All went well until we reached the summit of the Strahlhorn, where thick clouds swirled in very quickly and, before we had descended very far down the NW ridge, it began to snow heavily. Soon we were in classic whiteout conditions, off route and surrounded by crevasses and ice-walls. What good a compass here? The situation was dangerous and we just had to stay put. After an hour with no sign of improvement we were becoming very cold, so we embarked on excavating a snow-hole. The exercise and shelter it provided helped to restore circulation, but we were soaked by the falling snow and it was doubtful whether in our wet state we could survive the night in our snow-hole at 3900m without bivi gear. Another hour passed and it began to brighten; soon we could make out shapes and detail on the surrounding slopes, and before long we were able to resume our way down to the Adlerpass and make the long trudge down the glacier to the Britannia hut. We spent the next day drying out and recovering. On our return journey we traversed the *Allalinhorn* via the NE ridge and down by the Alphubeljoch to Täschalp.

A few days later we arrived at the Monte Rosa hut, our sights set on *Castor* and *Pollux*. We ascended Castor via the badly crevassed Zwillings glacier, but we were too late to carry on over Pollux and returned by the same route.

Next day we attempted Pollux via its N ridge and got to within 350m of the summit before deteriorating weather forced us to retreat down the Schwärze glacier, which required care in the steep ice-fall. We got our own back later in the week when we climbed Pollux and returned in one day from Zermatt by using the cable-car and snow-cat facilities to reach the Theodulpass first thing in the morning. We then made the long traverse around the S side of the Breithorn to the Schwarztor and climbed to the summit from there. It is much easier, of course, to approach Castor and Pollux from the Quintino Sella hut on the Italian side. Dr Taylor then returned to Scotland. I stayed on and went to the Schönbiel hut, where I knew a British party was planning to traverse the Pointe de Zinal and Mont Durand. I soloed the route behind them with their permission, knowing that they would assist with a top-rope if required. The views of the Dent Blanche were magnificent and the route was well worthwhile, with some sporting pitches on the arêtes.

The Matterhorn again and a tragedy

Towards the end of my holiday in 1966, another lone climber arrived at the Bahnhof looking for a companion. He was introduced to me by Paula; his name was Dave Baldock. 'How do you fancy the Zmutt Ridge of the Matterhorn?' he asked. This suited me fine; I felt on top form, the mountain was in good condition, and it was a route I had long wished to do. We set off next day for the Hörnli hut and bivvied outside. We were too keyed-up to sleep much, and long before dawn we started climbing the steep ice in the dark to gain the Matterhorn glacier plateau by first light. A quick traverse beneath the towering N face on our left brought us to the steep approach to the lower section of the Zmutt Ridge. We chose to continue our traverse at a low level rather than to climb directly up to the ridge, and this proved to be quicker and easier. On reaching the rocky section, we unroped and soloed as far as the overhanging Zmutt Nose. From here I remembered instructions given by Bernard Biner some years previously: 'traverse across the W face for two rope-lengths, then climb an exposed couloir for two more rope-lengths. You will find a ledge rising to the left, which will bring you back to the crest of the ridge immediately above the big overhang. The rest is straightforward.' We enjoyed every minute of the climb and on 12 August 1966 I found myself on the summit of the 'Big M' for the fourth time.

We started the descent by the Hörnli Ridge and were soon caught up in the throng of guided and unguided parties on the ordinary route. Hold-ups were frequent. On reaching the Obere Moseley Platte, we joined a queue behind two Germans. Because of the delay they became impatient and decided to bypass the queue by descending an icy chimney to the right. The first man was almost down when he slipped; his second, unbelayed and unprepared, was pulled off the ledge and went head-first down the chimney. They were beyond our help and we watched, frozen in horror, knowing that they stood no chance if they failed to arrest their fall in the first few seconds. They never got that chance, and I will never forget the sight of them disappearing in great bounds down the E face of the Matterhorn, the snow staining red along their path. They fell 750m and their bodies were recovered the following Sunday by the Zermatt guides. This tragic accident marked the end of my 1966 season.

I was back the following year, but it turned out to be rather unproductive in terms of peaks ascended. My third attempt on the *Täschhorn* via the Kin Face failed, and I finished up with sunstroke. On recovering, I set out again with Robin Collomb to have another go via the Mischabelgrat, using the newly-erected bivouac hut situated on the Mischabeljoch. We shared this with a group of Polish climbers. Next morning, after an enjoyable climb up the long ridge, we reached the summit where the Poles carried on to traverse over the Dom.

Robin and I returned to the Mischabeljoch and decided to traverse over the summit of the Alphubel rather than descend the Weingarten glacier which, we considered, would be rather treacherous. We reached the Täsch hut via the Alphubeljoch, to end the only worthwhile expedition of this holiday.

Marriage in 1968 curtailed my alpine activities until 1970, when the first visit to the Bernese Oberland was made with Tony Gough and Susan Carline. We did it in style, hiring our own chalet in Meiringen. The first route was a traverse of the Wetterhorn from the Gleckstein hut and down to Rosenlaui via the Dossen hut.

We then made the expensive decision to go up to the Jungfraujoch by rail, to climb the *Mönch* and *Jungfrau* by the ordinary routes. All this went according to plan and in very good weather, the Mönch taking 1½ hours and the Jungfrau 2½ hours. We then set our sights on something more ambitious and decided to traverse the Eiger via the Mittellegi Ridge. Leaving the Jungfrau

Railway at Eismeer Station, we stepped out of the tunnel on to the glacier and were committed. The rickety wooden Mittellegi hut stood precariously in its vulnerable position on a level section of the ridge overlooking Alpiglen, as it had done, withstanding the batterings of many storms, for at least 50 years.

Next morning, off at first light, we were soon grappling with the steep exposed buttresses high on the ridge. To our dismay, we found the fixed ropes encased in thick ice and of little use. This slowed us considerably. We were impressed by the exposure and narrowness of the ridge, and caution had to be the order of the day. Susan did very well, considering that this was her first alpine season. Three on the rope was not a good number for this route, and it was 2pm when we reached the summit. We were, however, well ahead of the parties which had left the hut shortly after us.

All that remained for us was to descend the W face to Eigergletscher Station, but this was more easily said than done. I was not familiar with the route and a layer of cloud had moved in below us, obscuring our line of vision. We seemed to spend ages route-finding in the gloom and were expecting to have to spend a night out on the face, when at the last minute we found our way down the steep slabs via a chimney on to relatively easier ground below, reaching the station at 7pm. The parties behind us were forced to bivi out for the night.

1971 and 1972 were not good years, because of unsettled weather. With Tony Gough I visited Courmayeur and climbed Mont Blanc once again via the Italian Route from the Gonella hut, which was closed because of the poor conditions. We returned down the Aiguilles Grises Ridge and had the entire route to ourselves, except for the section between the Dôme du Goûter and the summit of Mont Blanc.

Following this we climbed the *Grandes Jorasses* via the SW flank to Pointe Walker, and came down the Rocher de Whymper back to the Jorasses hut. We were surprised at the number of parties descending, having climbed the Walker Spur; we counted at least 13. The weather rapidly deteriorated and prevented any further mountaineering for us that season.

1972 was even worse. We were based at Lauterbrunnen with a party of Fell and Rock Climbing Club members, consisting of Pat Fearnehaugh, John Wilkinson and Tony Howard. At the first sign of good weather we made the long flog up to the Silberhorn hut. Our plan was to climb the N face of the Silberhorn, followed by a traverse over the Jungfrau, and to catch the train down in time for the Swiss National Day celebrations on 1 August. We made a rather late start next morning, watching a fiery sunrise light up the clouds around the Eiger. Pat led the first rope, cutting a line of steps straight up the face. We pitched it out 45m at a time, belaying on ice-screws. This seemed to go on for ages, until suddenly we were on the summit of the Silberhorn. By this time the weather was threatening, with clouds gathering around the Jungfrau, and a change of plan was called for. The problem was that there is no easy route off the Silberhorn, and it was decided to reverse the Guggi Route down to Kleine Scheidegg. This sounded an exciting prospect – it is described in the guidebook as 'expressly the best known ice-route in the Bernese Alps'. We abseiled down the Silberlücke into the snow-bay below, then went north to the summit of the Kleine Silberhorn, and descended the steep ice-crest down to the upper snow-plateau of the Giessen glacier below the NE ridge of the Jungfrau. It started to snow here, and daylight was fast diminishing. On reaching the Schneehorn we spotted a rock outcrop some 60m below the cornice. It was the first rock we had seen for some time, and it lay on our descent line, marking the end of that day's activities. A forced bivi ensued. It was a cold and uncomfortable one, made worse by the fact that the Jungfraujoch Hotel was only half a kilometre away to the east, and we could clearly hear the festivities and fireworks and imagine the people tucking into their fondue. Next morning, after nursing stiff and cold limbs back into working order, we carried on down through the tricky ice-fall of the Kühlauenen glacier to the easier terrain of the Guggi glacier and so returned to civilization and our wives.

I decided to try a fly-drive package in 1975 and flew to Geneva with Ray Parkinson on his first trip to the Alps. We collected a new Simca at the airport and away we went, through Chamonix, over the Col de la Forclaz, along the Rhône and up to Les Haudères where we met Peter Howard. We spent a few days in this area and climbed Mont Collon, then moved on to Courmayeur where the weather made us decide that the big peaks were better left alone, and so we only climbed the Tour Ronde and Petit Mont Blanc. From there we motored to Grindelwald, where conditions were much better. Ray had decided that the high peaks were not for him, so I decided to go up to the Strahlegg hut and solo the *Schreckhorn*. At the crowded hut I met Mike and Sally Westmacott with a Canadian friend, and they very kindly invited me to join them. They planned to traverse the Schreckhorn, climbing the SW ridge and going down the SE ridge. According to our English guidebook, the SE ridge was the normal route up and the easiest of the ridges, but we were to find that this was incorrect. The approach in the dark lay up steep snow and rock. Daylight saw us on the plateau of the Schreckfirn, with a full view of our objective. The rock on the SW ridge was extremely good and sound, which made the climb most enjoyable. On reaching the summit we noticed the other parties returning the same way and thought that this was rather odd. We set off along the airy SE ridge. Soon it steepened and became more difficult, and before we reached the Schrecksattel the climbing became more exposed and serious, with vertical pitches and icy chimneys overlooking the sheer Elliottwand. We then realized that the guidebook was wrong. We reached the saddle with some relief, but we still had to descend 350m of steep ribs and couloirs and cross a large bergschrund to regain the Schreckfirn. However, all went well despite the occasional stonefall. I was most grateful in retrospect to Mike and Sally for their company.

Ray and I left Grindelwald to finish our holiday at Saas Almagell. I reasoned that I could solo the *Lagginhorn* and Fletschhorn, so I went up to the Weissmiess hut and traversed them both the next day in cloudy conditions – a boost to my ego. The next day, in better weather, I traversed the *Weissmiess* and was impressed by the superb scenery on the way up, and by the easy way down on the other side. A mountain with two completely different faces.

(*Editor's Note*. It is reported that enlargement of the summit cairn has converted the Fletschhorn (3996m) into another 4000er.)

The decision is made to go for them all

By now I had reached the stage where I had climbed a comfortable majority of the major alpine summits and when asked, as I often was, which of the big peaks in the Alps I had climbed, I found it easier to name those which I had not climbed. In 1976, therefore, I made the decision to do them all. Some of the remaining peaks were the more remote and difficult ones. The idea of climbing all the 4000ers was exciting and not unreasonable. In addition, I could find no evidence at that time to suggest that any living British mountaineer had climbed them all. I was aware that Eustace Thomas had completed them in 1928 with guides, and that Frank Smythe was a strong contender. I acquired a copy of Robin Collomb's book 'Mountains of the Alps', published in 1971, which provides tables of all summits over 3500m. It listed a total of 52 separate mountains over 4000m, which seemed to agree with maps I had studied. This left me with 23 more to do.

With renewed interest and an ambitious goal to achieve, July 1976 found my wife, Margaret, and myself on the way to Courmayeur by a fly-drive package again. We travelled out with Mike Kenley and Margaret Mitchell, and on arrival at the Aiguille Noire camp-site in Val Veni we met Peter Blezard and Anne Danson. Our first excursion into the hills was thwarted by bad weather, when we were repulsed from the Aiguille de Trélatête. The next day, despite the continuing unsettled weather, we went up to the Torino hut hoping to traverse the Rochefort Arête as far as the Dôme de Rochefort. We reached the summit of the Aiguille once again and decided to go no further because of the poor conditions.

When the weather improved the three males in the party embarked on a three-day high-level traverse which was very successful and enjoyable. It involved the long march up the Miage glacier from Lac de Combal to the Col de Miage, where we spent the night in the Refuge Durier. Next day we continued over the sharp crest of the *Aiguille de Bionnassay* and the Dôme du Goûter; the second night was spent in the crowded Goûter hut. On both evenings we saw splendid sunsets. On the third day we traversed Mont Blanc (my third ascent), *Mont Maudit* and *Mont Blanc du Tacul* in super weather. At the Aiguille du Midi we caught the cable-car system back to Italy, across the Vallée Blanche, and so to our camp in Val Veni.

Peter and Anne left for home next day; the rest of us drove over the Great St Bernard Pass to Sembrancher. From here Mike and I traversed the *Grand Combin* from the Valsorey hut. Dawn broke as we reached the Col du Meitin. The W ridge went well despite icy conditions. We crossed the summit of the Combin de Valsorey and reached the highest point, the Grafeneire, in a bitterly cold wind on a beautiful clear day. We returned to the hut via the Corbassière glacier, passing under the dangerous ice-cliffs on the N face. The two Margarets met us in Bourg St Pierre, from where we drove back to Italy and set up camp in Val Savaranche. There was time for one more climb before returning our car to Geneva and flying home, and it was to be the *Gran Paradiso*, the highest mountain entirely in Italy. This, and the fact that it is a very easy 4000m peak, makes it a popular mountain with the Italians. The day we climbed it was no exception. The views were superb, with cottonwool clouds filling the valleys and the whole Mont Blanc range clear as a bell in brilliant sunshine. This ended another successful season – with seven 4000m peaks ascended, five of them new ones.

It was a good start towards the achievement of my recently adopted ambition, but distractions occurred in 1978 and 1979 when I was trekking and climbing in the Himalaya.

In the meantime, I had met Leslie and Barbara Swindin at an Alpine Club meet in the Lakes, and we realized that we had a lot in common as far as alpine mountaineering was concerned. Les had done almost as many 4000ers as I and quickly agreed that to do them all would be a worthwhile feat.

The next time we met was in Grindelwald on a very wet day, late in July 1980. The Lauteraarhorn was our first objective, but the weather dictated otherwise and we turned back at the Strahleggpass. Two days later we traversed the Mittelhorn from the Gleckstein hut. As we arrived at the summit, two jet aircraft of the Swiss Air Force flew close by and dipped their wings in salute. The weather remained unsettled, and our attempt at the Nollen route on the Mönch was cut short at the Guggi hut by a storm that night. What a superb little place the new Guggi hut is.

A week had gone by, and we had not topped a single peak on our list. We moved to Chamonix and went to the Couvercle, intent on climbing the *Aiguille Verte*. At 1am next morning we set out and ascended the steep Whymper Couloir in the dark, reaching the summit ridge at sunrise. There was a splendid view from the summit, looking right up the Mer de Glace to Mont Blanc. We also had a good look at the nearby Les Droites, which neither Les nor I had yet climbed. After a careful descent of the couloir, we reached the safety of the Glacier de Talèfre and the Couvercle hut before 10am. The only other route we did was the N face of the Tour Ronde, in order to study the Aiguille Blanche and the Peuterey Arête of Mont Blanc from the summit. We planned to do this great ridge at some future date, since the Aiguille Blanche qualifies as a 4000m peak.

I was unable to visit the Alps in 1981, for this was the year when Margaret and I had planned a holiday in the Far East. Normality was resumed in 1982, when we drove out to Brig in the Rhône Valley to meet Les and Barbara. We had unsettled weather again in which to go up to the Oberaletsch hut. Our training climb next day took us up the Gross Fusshorn by its SW ridge. It was becoming obvious that age was beginning to tell; we had never bothered about training climbs before, we had always made a beeline for the big peaks. From the summit of the Fusshorn we had a good view of our objective for the next day – the *Aletschhorn*.

The following morning dawned, but only just. We were high on the steep SW arête of the Aletschhorn with more cloud than blue sky above, but all went well and the summit cross was reached just after 10am. No other peaks were visible. As we began our descent a shaft of sunlight beamed down on us and actually followed us all the way down the ridge to the glacier. We were lucky and suspected that our mountain was one of the few major ones climbed that day.

Next day we moved camp to Randa in the Zermatt valley and met

Andrew Hodges, who joined forces with Les, Barbara and myself for an ascent of the *Dent d'Hérens*. The route from the Schönbiel hut is long and difficult to follow in the dark, but Andrew's previous knowledge of the terrain was a great help. The climb up the WNW face through the ice-cliffs and serac barriers was spectacular, as were the views from the sharp summit crest to the Matterhorn and the Dent Blanche.

Two days later Andrew and I set out for the Monte Rosa hut, leaving Les to rest a leg he had hurt returning down the moraine on the way back from the Dent d'Hérens. Our objective was the *Nordend*, but we took enough provisions for three days in case conditions were good enough to traverse the other main tops of Monte Rosa and spend a night at the Margherita hut on the Signalkuppe. After following the usual treadmill route towards the Dufourspitze, we branched off to reach the Silbersattel where an icy wind encouraged us to move quickly along the arête to the summit of the Nordend. We then attempted a direct ascent of the Dufourspitze from the Silbersattel, but the strong wind and steep ice, combined with our heavy sacks and lack of a second ice-tool each, forced us to retreat. When we reached the Gorner glacier it was obvious that a big storm was brewing and we had barely reached the path to Riffelalp when it broke. The crashes of thunder were deafening as they echoed around the Liskamm and Breithorn. Flashes of lightning seared and hissed through the gloom, and the rain poured down. The gods were very angry! We considered ourselves lucky to have retreated, but this feeling was short-lived when a bolt of lightning struck the crags on the Gornergrat high above our heads, and suddenly we saw a volley of rocks about the size of armchairs hurtling straight towards us. They struck the ground above us and bounced over our heads, finishing up on the glacier 300m below. We scuttled back to the safety of Zermatt with our tails between our legs.

A storm on the Peuterey

After a rest-day we drove to Chamonix, where the Weather Bureau assured us that the next four days would be settled and fine. So Les and I decided to go for the *Aiguille Blanche de Peuterey*, which is regarded as being the most serious and difficult of all the 4000m peaks. From there we planned to traverse over the summit of Mont Blanc. We set off through the Mont Blanc tunnel to Val Veni and climbed to the Monzino hut for the night. Next morning we went over the Col de l'Innominata and sought a route across the notorious Frêney glacier. This behind us, we avoided the stone-swept couloir, descending from the Brèche Nord des Dames Anglaises and climbing the higher and safer ledge-system to the left below Pointe Gugliermina known as the Schneider Ledge and Couloir. The route was enjoyable on reasonable rock, with no great difficulties. After a short but futile attempt to find the Dames Anglaises bivouac, we reached the base of the SE ridge of the Aiguille Blanche, high above the Brèche, and after crossing several exposed and loose ribs and couloirs on the Brenva side, we climbed directly up towards the summit ridge taking great care on the very loose steep rock. We reached the crest in a gap above the Pointe Gugliermina and followed the rocky arête to the snowy SE summit of the Aiguille Blanche. The time was about 5pm. We were aware of cloud swirling around and this puzzled us, in view of the good forecast. We prepared a bivouac site on a rock-ledge with snow on one side and absolutely nothing on the other, except for a 1200m drop to the Brenva glacier. By the time we had prepared and eaten a hot meal conditions looked decidedly worse, with thunder in the distance. At 8pm it began to snow and we got into our Zarski bivi sack for the night. The snow fell more heavily and the storm drew nearer. Lightning played around us. Soon we were caught right in the centre of the storm amongst blinding sheet lightning and deafening explosions of thunder. The snow fell so thick and fast that we had to keep sweeping it off the bivi sack to enable us to breathe. The continuous sheet lightning was so intense that it was possible to read a book. Ever hopeful, we thought, 'Oh, it's probably just a local storm. It will pass over in an hour. After all they told us in Chamonix. . . .'

The storm raged unabated all night. We had plenty of time to ponder on our dangerous situation since sleep was impossible. Witnessing nature in a very angry mood from our lofty perch, we felt very much at the mercy of the elements. We could not believe our bad luck. Here we were on the summit of what Frank Smythe described as the most difficult of all alpine peaks at 4000m in the middle of a storm. How could the weather forecast be so wrong?

At first light, about six, the storm began to disperse. We were unscathed. Two hours later we emerged from our snowy cocoon to survey the scene. Visibility was poor. We estimated that 15cm of snow had come down. To carry on over Mont Blanc was out of the question and we were faced with reversing our ascent route – neither of us was looking forward to this. After a leisurely breakfast and with a brightening sky, we started down. A lot of time and effort went into uncovering and selecting safe abseil points for our 90m of rope. It was impossible to know what was safe and what was not under all the powder-snow. We abseiled hundreds of metres down the steep ribs and couloirs on the Brenva flank. Occasionally large blocks were accidentally dislodged and went crashing down a thousand metres to the glacier. The most nerve-racking section was the traverse to regain the Brèche des Dames Anglaises, where one or two slips had to be checked. By now the weather was rapidly improving, and the views of the Aiguille Noire and the sharp needles of the Dames Anglaises were spectacular; but the Frêney glacier was still a long way below. We set off down the Schneider Couloir with water cascading all around from the melting snow. It was decided to bivouac on a safe ledge some 150m above the glacier; it was a beautiful night with bright, shining stars. In the bitter cold all our wet gear froze solid. Next morning we soon reached the Frêney glacier and found that it had greatly changed in only three days. The crevasses were now too wide to jump, so we abseiled into them from snow-bosses cut in the ice and climbed out the other side. After crossing the Col de l'Innominata with its gallery of memorial plaques commemorating the tragic Bonatti epic on the Central Pillar, we soon were in sight of the Monzino hut, green grass and a well-earned rest.

In retrospect, after our safe return, our three-day epic on the Aiguille Blanche de Peuterey and the night spent on its summit in the eye of an electric storm was a worthwhile and interesting experience, but not one I should care to repeat.

In August 1983, Margaret and I motored to Chamonix to rendezvous with Les and Barbara. Because of a recent operation Barbara did not take part in this season's activities. Les and I climbed the Dômes de Miage from the Trélatête Hotel as our training route, followed by the Aiguille de la Bérangère from the Conscrits hut the next day.

The only two 4000ers in the Mont Blanc massif which neither of us had climbed were the *Droites* and the Dôme de Rochefort and so, two days later, we set out from the Couvercle for the S face of the Droites. The route was mixed, on steep ground and, like the Whymper Couloir on the Verte, it should be avoided when the sun gets up. We arrived on the rocky summit after an enjoyable climb. We took care on the descent to avoid the stonefall which raked the couloirs at seemingly regular intervals. Once on the Glacier de Talèfre, we soon regained the Couvercle hut and then went back to Chamonix.

A breakdown in the weather prevented us from attempting the Dôme de Rochefort, so we moved to the Oberland hoping for better conditions. We planned a three-day traverse taking in the *Lauteraarhorn* and Schreckhorn, which Les had not done. Starting from the Grimselpass we walked to the Lauteraarhorn hut, and in the morning faced the long march up the Finsteraar and Strahlegg glaciers, most of this being done in the dark. The ascent to the summit of the Lauteraarhorn was rather loose and tedious, until we reached the terminal arête which was on better rock. On the descent we planned to traverse the link route across the S face to the SW ridge and down to the new Schreckhorn hut; but we failed to find the correct line across the face, wasting time, and so we reversed the S couloir and crossed the Strahleggpass to the hut. It had been a long day and we could not face the ascent of the Schreckhorn next morning, so we descended to Grindelwald.

I had never been too happy about my ascent of the Jungfrau by cheating and using the railway to the Jungfraujoch and, as Les wanted to climb it, we decided to start from the lowest point. We set out from Lauterbrunnen for the long ascent to the Rottal hut; we had the place to ourselves and were surprised by the trusting nature of the absent guardian, who had left out wine and beer on a self-service basis. In the morning we climbed the Inner Rottal ridge to the summit of the Jungfrau in unsettled cloudy weather and descended for the night to the Obermönchjoch hut. We intended to climb the Gross Fiescherhorn next day, but a blizzard set in overnight, forcing us to retreat to Grindelwald.

With time for one more climb, we returned to the Schreckhorn hut and repeated the ascent of the Schreckhorn that I had made previously with the Westmacotts, except that we returned down the SW arête.

1984 was a frustrating year. It started out with a heatwave in the Dauphiné, where we met once again with Les and Barbara in La Bérarde. Our first mountain was Les Bans from the Refuge Pilatte. This went well, in spite of a cloudy start on the glacier, and it was my introduction to the rock of this region, relatively sound compared with the Central Alps. We then went to the Temple Ecrins hut and ascended Pic Coolidge for a view of the *Barre des Ecrins*, which we traversed in perfect weather the next day. Our route lay up the S face of the Ecrins from the Col des Avalanches, but we strayed a little too far to the right and missed the fixed cables. Soon we were on very steep and sensationally exposed rock, high above the col, but the rock was so good, with deep incuts, that we carried on, taking small overhangs in our stride. It was not long before we regained the correct route. Higher up we crossed two or three snowy couloirs and rock-ribs to reach the sharp summit arête. The view was remarkable: Mont Blanc was as clear as a bell 110km away. Our descent lay down the normal N face route to the Col des Ecrins, followed by the Bonne Pierre glacier, and so back to La Bérarde. It had been a most enjoyable traverse of the highest peak in the Dauphiné, and a day to remember.

Next day we drove to Courmayeur in beautiful weather, but by the time we reached our camp-site in Val Veni rain was pouring down. During the next five days, we made two abortive attempts on the Dôme de Rochefort from the Torino hut – each time the weather turned us back. On the only fine day, Les and Barbara climbed the Grandes Jorasses, while Margaret and I traversed the low hills on the south side of Val Veni, which give splendid views of the Mont Blanc massif.

I had not yet climbed two 4000ers on the NW end of the Lenzspitze/ Nadelhorn ridge; the *Dürrenhorn* and *Hohberghorn*. We therefore moved on to Randa and ascended the endless zigzags to the Dom hut. Next day, in still unsettled weather, we crossed the Festijoch and descended the Hohberg glacier to gain a steep ice-filled couloir descending from the ridge. It was ice of the worst kind – rock-hard and impregnated with stone. After a long ascending traverse to the left we gained the col between our two peaks. We soloed the Dürrenhorn and then traversed over the Hohberghorn, regaining the glacier by descending the steep flanks of the Stecknadelhornjoch in snowy conditions, 22 years to the day since I had last come down that way.

Les was keen to have another go at the Dôme de Rochefort. It was his last 4000er: he had overtaken me since 1977 because of my trips to the Far East, and because he and Barbara had climbed some on their winter ski-touring holidays. So off we went back to Chamonix, and once again we made the expensive journey to the Torino hut, this time via the Midi and Vallée Blanche cable-car system. The weather was poor and the following morning it was no better, but we started out just the same, hoping that our cheek would pay off as it had done occasionally in the past. After two hours with no sign of a break in the cloud, we gave up on the Dôme de Rochefort for the third time in two weeks and headed for home. Les would have to wait for another year.

The following season, for a change, everything went according to plan. For obvious reasons we started off in Val Veni and our training route this time was the Aiguille de Trélatête via Petit Mont Blanc from the Giovane Montagna bivouac. The ugly structure on the summit of the Trélatête built in the interests of science was the only blot on an otherwise excellent day.

Our next stop was – yes, you'll have guessed – the Torino hut. The traverse of the Rochefort ridge went smoothly this time, on over the Aiguille, and then Les Swindin, on 27 July 1985, stood on the summit of the *Dôme de Rochefort* – his last 4000m peak. Congratulations were exchanged and a celebration dinner was enjoyed later in Switzerland. It was a great relief to have done it at last. We could not have faced another night at the Torino hut, and we badly needed a change of scenery.

We split up for a few days, arranging to meet again in St Moritz, and Margaret and I drove up Val Sesia to Alagna. There were still two summits on Monte Rosa outstanding on my agenda, and this was the most convenient starting-place for the ascent. Next day we went to the Gnifetti hut, and the following morning I left Margaret there while I set off to solo the *Parrotspitze* and *Piramide Vincent*. It was a fine day, but a very strong and bitter wind was roaring across the high tops; on reaching the Lisjoch, I had to put on all my spare clothing. About this time a helicopter passed by and I found out later that it was about to recover a lone climber who had been blown off the summit of the Piramide Vincent. I continued on towards the Parrotspitze and could hear the wind blasting over the terminal crest. Unfortunately the highest point was at the far end, and I had to decide whether to risk going on or not. In view of the fact that the wind speed was constant, I decided that I would proceed on all fours. If the wind had been gusting, I would have turned back. I reached the highest point, clinging to anything and everything. The noise of the wind on the nearby Signalkuppe sounded like an express train. I learned later that the wind speed recorded at the Margherita hut that morning was 130km/h. I made a hasty retreat via the Balmenhorn and Piramide Vincent, back to the Gnifetti and one relieved wife.

The next day we joined Les and Barbara in St Moritz and were surprised to find that they had not done any routes because of wet weather. They were equally surprised at my success on Monte Rosa.

We were in the Engadine to traverse the only 4000er in the area, *Piz Bernina*, so we went up to the Tschierva hut at what turned out to be the start of four days of fine weather. The Biancograt was in good condition, but busy. We were ahead of most parties on this popular classic route, so we avoided the worst of the queuing at the difficult rock-step high on the ridge, and we gained the summit in good time. We descended the SE ridge, passed under Bellavista and went down to the Morteratsch glacier via the Fortezza ridge. It was another outstanding day on a superb mountain, and a route I can recommend.

Two days later we were watching the sunrise lighting up Piz Bernina as we crunched our way across the glacier from the Berghaus Diavolezza on our way to Piz Palü. We were keen to climb the North Pillar of the East Peak. It looked to be the best way up the mountain from the northern side and there was nothing difficult on it, despite its appearance. The lower section was on rock, while the upper half provided splendid ice and snow scenery all around. From the summit we descended to the Diavolezza via the ordinary route. Piz Palü, while not a 4000er, had a certain attraction for me. It was the alpine peak which had first stirred my imagination as a schoolboy in an old black-and-white film 'The White Hell of Piz Palü'! An archaic film by today's standards, but the drama of alpine mountaineering came through to me, little knowing then that I would one day climb that mountain along with 100 other peaks throughout the Alps. So this had been another day to hold as special.

We returned to our camp-site at St Moritz, and overnight the weather changed dramatically. We awoke to a winter wonderland of snow – except that it was August. St Moritz was under 10cm of snow and this spelt the end of our activities in 1985.

1986 was an unusual year. It was my 18th season and I had never seen so little snow in the Alps; there was rock showing where it had never been seen before. The weather was never completely settled and cloud was present on most days, but it never interfered with our plans. We met once again in Val d'Anniviers, high above the Rhône, in the village of Vissoie. Our training climb was the N face of the Pointes de Mourti, which is in full view of the Moiry hut where we stayed. A good route, but I broke a front-point off a crampon on it: not a good start to the season.

We then went on to complete the long, easy traverse of the Pigne de la Lé, Pointe de Bricola and Dent des Rosses. This done, we returned to Vissoie. The final 4000er I had to climb in the Pennine Alps was the *Bishorn*, which to my mind is merely the terminal spur of the N ridge of the Weisshorn. It looks quite insignificant when seen from Täschalp or the Dom, but it featured in Collomb's tables of Alpine Peaks, so it had to be done.

We drove round to the Turtmanntal and up to the Turtmann hut, a smart and well-appointed little hut of which the guardian must be proud. It also boasts a view of an unusual rock-peak called the Barrhorn, which is the double of Half Dome in Yosemite. (Climbers please note!) Next morning our route was a long one, up the Turtmann glacier to the Bisjoch and then to climb the NE ridge to the summit of the Bishorn. We had the ascent to ourselves, and it is probably the best route up this mountain. The view of the N ridge of the Weisshorn, with its huge gendarme rearing up, is very spectacular. After pausing for photographs, we descended the normal route to the Tracuit hut and on down to Zinal.

Our next project was carefully worked out and was entirely dependent on good weather lasting for at least six days. My final three peaks all lay in the Oberland, so we planned to traverse them from the remote huts in the area.

We left Fiesch in the Rhône valley and reached the Aletsch glacier at Märjelensee. The trudge up the glacier seemed endless; on the way we passed a fine perched glacier table. At last we were climbing the iron ladders to the Concordia hut, which was busy with guided parties on glacier tours. Barbara was not feeling well, and only Les and I set out next day for the *Gross Grünhorn*. We ascended the badly crevassed lower part of the Ewigschneefeld to gain the western flanks of our peak. A complicated route was ascended through an ice-fall which gave access to the lowest point of the N ridge descending from the summit. The steep ridge was followed to the highest point on good rock at about Grade III. There were distant views of the Zermatt giants, and much closer was a full view of the W face of the Finsteraarhorn. We descended the Grünhorn via its SW arête and the Grünegghorn to gain the Grünegg glacier and so arrive back at Concordia.

By the next morning Barbara had improved, and the three of us set off up the remainder of the Aletsch glacier towards the Jungfraujoch, where construction work on the new hotel complex was very evident. We made our way across to the Obermönchjoch hut for the night, and were rather dismayed when a snowstorm swept in and deposited a fair amount of fresh snow. However, the next morning we were off before first light to traverse the *Gross Fiescherhorn*. We reached the crest of the NW ridge at 3605m just in time to see a fiery sunrise

41.   *Aiguille de Bionnassay (4052m).* (p 119)

42.   *The Pinnacles of Mont Blanc du Tacul (4248m).* (p 119)

43.   *Return from Mont Maudit (4465m).* (p 119)

44. *Mönch (4099m) and Eiger (3970m)*. (p 119)

45. *Les and Barbara Swindin on the summit of the Aiguille Verte (4122m)*. (p 119)

46.   *Aiguille Blanche de Peuterey (4107m).* (p 119)

47.   *Finsteraarhorn (4273m), seen from the NW.* (p 119)

48. *Piz Badile (3308m) and Piz Cengalo (3370m).* (p 136)

49. *Monte Disgrazia (3678m).* (p 136)

50. *The snow arête just below the summit of Monte Disgrazia (3678m).* (p 136)

51. *Frontier Ridge from below the Pic d'Arres (1983), Maladeta Massif beyond.*
(p 142)

52. *Taillon 1983.* (p 142)

53. *Brèche de Roland 1983.* (p 142)

54.   En route *to Pujol hut, 1987.* (p 142)

55.   *Canigou N ridge, 1988.* (p 142)

behind the Schreckhorn and Lauteraarhorn. The fresh snow was not causing any problems. The last section to the summit was up steep ice overlooking the exposed Fiescherwand. On our arrival we expected to see the other parties which had set out that morning to make the ascent via the Fiechersattel, but we guessed that they had found problems with deep powder snow on the lower approach slopes. Our descent took us east towards 'Ochs' and then south-east down the badly crevassed ice-fall of the upper Fiescherhorn glacier. A couple of hours later we entered the Finsteraarhorn hut and at last I was within striking distance of my final objective, the mountain of the same name. We were all praying that the weather would hold; we did not want a repeat of the Dôme de Rochefort saga.

We had intended to traverse the *Finsteraarhorn* but, in view of the fresh snowfall and unsettled weather, we decided to follow the ordinary route. It was just as well for me that we made this decision, for in the morning I awoke with a chest cold which affected my breathing. The odds were mounting against a successful outcome. We went off up the steep SW slopes, up the tedious, inclined snow-fields. I was pleased to reach the Hugisattel; my wheezy lungs had done well to get me that far. The rock-climbing on the NW ridge required less effort and was more enjoyable. The higher we got, the cloudier it became. By the time we reached the summit the view had gone, but what did that matter? My ambition had been achieved – 30 years almost to the day since the first 4000er, the Matterhorn. My feelings were mixed: elation, relief and, perhaps, some sadness. It was the end of an era for me. However, I did not have time to dwell on my thoughts. The weather was rapidly deteriorating, a wind had risen and it had begun to snow. We hurried off down the ridge and soon caught up a group of four German climbers whom we had met on the summit. They were equipped with unnecessary hardware and were slow. By now it was snowing heavily and, not wanting to be caught so high on the ridge in a storm, we bypassed them down chimneys and ledges to the left. After one more night at the Finsteraarhorn hut, we faced the long march out to civilization once again, over the Grünhornlücke and down the Aletsch glacier, where I could not help but notice that the top had fallen off the glacier table – symbolic in some way? I had returned, having climbed all the big alpine peaks. Perhaps it had doffed its cap in salute!

On the Southern Slopes of the Bregaglia

JOHANNA MERZ

(Plates 48–50)

. . . The eye rests on one of those wonderful landscapes which tell the southward-bound traveller that he has reached his goal and is at last in Italy. The great barrier is crossed, and the North is all behind us. The face of the earth, nay the very nature of the air, has changed, colours have a new depth, shadows a new sharpness. The hills seem to stand back and leave room for the sunshine . . .

Douglas Freshfield, *Italian Alps*, 1875

The Italian valleys which pierce the southern slopes of the main range of the Bregaglia are still unspoilt and beautiful. Everywhere there is water: in the Val di Sasso Bisolo, cows graze peacefully among flower-filled water-meadows, with rocks and trees for shade. Nearby, in the Val di Mello, water rushes down from the mountains in great streams and torrents and a huge waterfall plunges down into a sparkling amethyst rock-pool.

The villages hum with life. In the morning the food shops overflow with housewives replenishing stocks for their large families. By midday the bars and cafés are full and in the evening the local people put on their best clothes and walk about the village, chatting in groups, for the traditional *passeggiata*. Higher up the valleys and in the more remote villages, the day starts early in the summer. People there are up and about by 6 o'clock or earlier while, higher still, the cowman leads a lonely life following his herds up the valley, as the snow recedes to reveal the fresh new grass beneath.

Even the mountains show a more human face on their southern sides and provide some compensation for those, like myself, who have reached that stage in life where we seek out, without shame, the easiest route up a mountain rather than the most difficult. Three great peaks rise above the southern slopes of the Bregaglia and have their 'normal' routes on the Italian side of the range: the Badile, the Cengalo and the great Disgrazia itself. Last summer I had the opportunity to climb them and also to explore some of the side-valleys off the Val Masino. A very old friend, Steve Jones, came along too to act as leader and guide.

I had arranged to meet Steve in Sondrio, a pleasant spacious town with the river running through it and several large open squares with solid buildings. There had been serious flooding in the area a few weeks earlier, and along the river banks there was much evidence of flood damage. All along the approach roads, crops had been devastated and were covered with yellow sludge. The loss and suffering of the local people must have been very great. However, we put such thoughts behind us as we started on the long walk up the Val Porcellizzo to the Gianetti hut, involving a height gain of well over 1000m. It was very beautiful – first through forest and then more open boulder-filled meadows. At one point our way lay along the river where it widened to form large rock-pools. I went to sleep in the sun while Steve had a swim. He reached the hut at least an hour before I did. Coming straight out from England and doing a five-hour climb with a heavy rucksack to 8000ft or so made me realize how unfit I was compared with people like Steve who are climbing all the time.

The Gianetti hut is a large and good one with a nice guardian, a pleasant free-and-easy atmosphere and no tiresome rules. We were allowed to choose where we wanted to sleep and take our rucksacks upstairs, so that I was able to make up my mattress properly with plenty of blankets and get all my gear arranged for the morning. We left the hut early to climb the Badile (3308m). It was a glorious morning, the superb friction of the granite made climbing a joy and we reached the summit in the guidebook time of three hours. Mostly it was hard scrambling, with a few pitches which had to be properly belayed. From the top we watched people struggling up the great N ridge. Beyond them, the main artery of the Bregaglia snaked away towards St Moritz while, to the south, range upon range of mountains stretched towards the Apennines. We spent nearly two hours on the summit enjoying the sun and the view before making the descent, which was slightly more tricky and needed firm concentration, and returning to the Gianetti hut.

Next morning was cloudy and stormy, but after a leisurely breakfast it cleared a little and we set out, as planned, for the Cengalo (3367m). This was a very different route from yesterday's – longer, more serious, with mixed rock and snow. Again we achieved the guidebook time of 3½ hours to the summit. We could hardly believe that, on the first ascent, Douglas Freshfield and his party, *starting from the valley* at Bagni del Masino, had taken only 4 hours and 40 minutes. On the way down we discovered that the first couloir between the Badile and the Cengalo is much safer than the second one, recommended in some guidebooks, since the latter – when snow cover is thin or non-existent – is full of very loose rock. So we came down the first couloir without difficulty and, after a brew of tea at the hut, walked on down to the valley. We felt we deserved a treat after a long day, so we had a terrific supper at an albergo of pasta, steak, ice cream and coffee, washed down with a bottle of wine. *Meraviglioso!*

Next day we drove to the top of the Val di Sasso Bisolo and found an idyllic spot by the stream for our lunch picnic. The path to the Ponti hut zig-zags steeply up above the valley until it comes out on an open boulder-field. Now the magnificent Disgrazia came into view – a real large-scale mountain with ridges and arêtes and rock-faces and glaciers. *This* was what our two previous climbs had been working up to!

We were the first to get away next morning, but were soon passed by a party of fast-moving men. After boulder-hopping to the moraine, we followed a long track on a raised ridge of shale to the edge of the glacier. The sky behind the rock-masses surrounding us was passing through all the changing colours that presage the dawn; finally the tips of the crags turned golden and the sun lit up the glacier above us. Here we put on our crampons and started on the long slog up to the col. Two parties behind were slowly gaining on us. Recognizing that my competitive instinct was not yet quite dead, I made a special effort to keep moving steadily upwards and to take no rests. At 9am we stood on the col, with me panting like a landed whale, and stared with awe down the precipice on the other side.

Meanwhile, the parties which had been following us up the glacier were trying to reach the ridge more directly, via a snowy couloir, and were dislodging a lot of loose stones. I watched a rock the size of a football go leaping and crashing on its way down to the glacier. Rather than risk climbing beneath this barrage, Steve decided to go straight up the ridge. This involved many interesting moves, interspersed with hard scrambling, and I was now able to benefit from Steve's expert leading and wide experience. Several times we were able to forge ahead of people younger and stronger than myself, either because of Steve's immaculate route-finding (though he had never been on the mountain before), or because we left others behind making complicated and unnecessary belays, where moving together or a few cut steps would have answered the problem more quickly and efficiently. At last we arrived below the classic snow ridge leading up to the summit. Steep, narrow and sparkling, it soared towards the sky. There remained 'the bronze horse', a tooth of rock which you have to get past as best you can – in my case, inelegantly, à cheval. A few more yards of scrambling and we were on the top.

The summit of the Disgrazia (3648m) is somewhat marred by a metal structure like a climbing-frame from a child's play-ground, but the views all around us were wide-ranging and majestic. To the north, the immense Corda Molla ridge swept down from the summit. To the east, beyond a couple of inaccessible-looking towers of enormous domed rock, I recognized the Bernina and its satellites, the Piz Roseg and the Palü. To the west, we could pick out the Badile and the Cengalo, as well as the Passo di Mello (2992m) where we intended to bivouac that night. Beyond these, the familiar Zermatt peaks stood out with great clarity.

Having climbed down to the col, we then paused to decide what to do. Both of us were disinclined to return to the Ponti hut; it was only 3pm and we felt like tackling something more exciting. At the same time, our original idea of climbing down to the Passo di Mello by first scaling the Monte Pioda (3431m) seemed less attractive, now that that rock pile was actually towering above us. Instead, we continued to the edge of the glacier and traversed round to the Bocchetta Roma (2898m) which overlooks the Val di Mello. From here we hoped to pick up the Sentiero Roma running down into the next valley, after which a short climb should bring us to the bivouac hut. Steve had estimated that we would need an extra three hours to complete all this, but we could now see that it would take far longer. From here we could have returned quite easily to the Ponti hut; but I persuaded Steve to continue. What we did not realize was that the Sentiero Roma is less a footpath, more an obstacle course, with steep rocky descents protected only by swinging pieces of wire, icy snow-slopes at hazardous angles and, at best, enormous never-ending boulder-fields. All this was taking time and we were getting extremely tired – at least, I was. Finally, on an icy traverse, I slipped. With his quick reactions, Steve held firm and stopped me slipping further; but then he tried to pull me back up by the rope like a sack of potatoes. 'For Christ's sake, Steve,' I called up, 'let me stand on my feet!' and I finished the traverse by cutting steps for myself. This was the only time during the whole week when voices were raised between us!

We had another conference at the point where we should have turned uphill for the bivouac hut on the pass. We could just see it, a tiny doll's house, high – very high – above us. I knew that to climb up there would take me at least two hours, and we were likely to run out of light before that, so there was nothing for it but to plunge down the Val di Mello and try to get as low as possible before bivouacking in the open. Soon it was nearly dark and we were facing the unattractive prospect of a cold and uncomfortable night under a rock. We passed a herd of cows which loomed up, stolidly impassive, in the gathering darkness. Then suddenly we heard a dog barking and by the light of our head-torches we saw a primitive stone hut with an elderly man standing, a shadowy figure, in the doorway. He indicated that we were welcome to stay there for the night and of course we accepted thankfully. The old man now set about lighting a fire inside the hut; the smoke curled up and disappeared through holes in the roof. The path to the village, he said, was *pericoloso*. When he asked us how we came to be so high up the mountain at this late hour, we could give no adequate explanation, especially as the conversation had to be conducted in my inadequate Italian.

The hut was even more basic than those I had seen in Nepal. In one corner was a mattress on the floor with a few rough blankets. There was a large copper cheese-maker and a huge cheese maturing in a press. A petrol lamp had run out of fuel, but by now the fire was burning merrily with a pan of water heating over it. Steve made a wonderful brew of tea, a life-saver, and the old man offered us some home-made wine. Neither of us felt very hungry – just infinitely thirsty – and we ate no more than a couple of cheese rolls before settling down for the night. The old man spread some sheets of plastic on the ground and sacrificed one of his larger blankets. I must have been fast asleep in seconds. Later in the night, the dog came in and lay down near the embers of the fire.

At first light we all got up and made some more tea. The elderly man was 65 years old, he told us, and had no family at all. Once a week he went down to the village for supplies and to sell his cheese. He had 21 cows up the mountain, and would shortly have to go and milk them; he showed us how to put up a rudimentary barrier across the door to keep animals out. It was hard to know how best to express our gratitude for his hospitality.

After the old man had gone, we collected our things together, washed up the mugs and spoons in the stream and set out into the early morning mist. I caught a last glimpse of the dog who was large, old and shaggy, climbing slowly up the rocks, unsteadily, on stiff rheumaticky legs.

Now, with plenty of time, we made our way down the Val di Mello. At first the path was rough but soon it passed through a village of old stone houses, after which it improved. Sometimes the path crossed a fast-moving torrent, by way of a bridge of logs lashed together, or ran along the side of a clear emerald stream. Looking back up the mountain everything appeared indistinct and mysterious but, in the lower valley, camp-sites were coming to life and Italian family parties were setting out for a day in the mountains. We could feel the heat rising – it was going to be another warm day.

In the afternoon I left Steve washing his clothes in the river and drove down to Sondrio, where I was impressed all over again by the instinctive kindness one constantly meets in Italy. First, the bank changed my travellers' cheques at 3.17pm when they were supposed to close at 3.15pm. Would that ever happen in Switzerland or, indeed, in England? Then the man in the hardware shop took immense trouble to find a bulb suitable for my head-torch (by removing one from something else). Finally, the man in the photo-shop removed the jammed film from my camera in his dark-room and returned it to me, without charge, in a sealed cassette.

That evening we had another excellent meal and a bottle of wine; the latter seemed to enable us to talk of many things which we don't normally mention. We had, of course, already held a post-mortem on yesterday's adventure – or débâcle (whichever way you look at it) – and we now progressed to lots of other things like friends, commitments, freedom, happiness and the good life. Next morning I saw Steve off, with promises to try to arrange another week in Italy next year. Then I went down to the village and bought some petrol for the old man's lamp.

At about mid-day I set out for the Omio hut. I took it very gently, not having really decided whether or not to go all the way. But the sun filtering through the beechwoods kept persuading me to go a little further, to see what lay on the far side of the forest. The path led through real rock-climbing country, past great cliffs with obvious lines up them and nobody on any of them. By this time a cup of tea was an enticing prospect and I pressed on to the hut (three hours up and two down) which is magnificently sited in a great cirque of rock peaks and is another staging post on the Sentiero Roma.

In the evening I treated myself to a thermal bath at the Bagni del Masino. These baths date from the 13th century and the water comes up through a spring from deep in the earth at a constant temperature of 38°C. It is supposed to be excellent for rheumatism and skin diseases. The baths are like small swimming-pools; a timer is set for 20 minutes and, for full benefit, you must stay in the water until the time is up. The old woman was quite cross with me for emerging five minutes early! After the bath I felt renewed and energetic. The building in which the baths are housed used to be the old albergo and dates from the 15th century. Only one room is still as it was before the war – the walls covered with beautiful carved wood-panelling and the ceiling with hand-painted wallpaper. During the war the albergo had been used as a prison camp and the rest of the panelling was chopped up for firewood. No one knew how this one room had escaped.

On my last day I left early for the long walk back up the lovely Val di Mello to deliver the petrol to the old man. The morning was warm and misty, but the upper reaches of the valley looked remote, lofty and inaccessible. However, I carried a compass in my pocket and took a bearing on the general direction in which the hut ought to be. Beyond the turn-off to the Allievi hut the way became wilder and the path less distinct. At one point I lost it altogether, but continued on my compass bearing until I picked it up again. After about three hours I suddenly saw the old man high above me, coming down with the dog and carrying a huge basket on his back. We both waved and he looked pleased and astonished to see me. I gave him the petrol for the lamp and asked for permission to take a couple of photos of himself and the dog. He asked me to send him copies and I wrote down his address in a village down in the valley. He only spent three or four months of the year in mountain huts, he said; at the beginning of October the cows would come down to the valley and he would go home.

By now we were approaching one of his lower huts and the old man unlocked the door and invited me to look inside. Rows and rows of enormous cheeses, like loaves of bread in a huge oven, were stacked on shelves which ran the whole length of the hut. He went round prodding them and eventually selected one from which he cut me a massive slice as a present. He also poured me a glass of his strong home-made wine. The excellent cheese was similar to gruyère, but of lighter texture. The wine, though delicious, gave me a small throbbing headache above my right eyebrow! I gave the old man what few provisions I had with me – a fruit loaf, some apples, a bar of chocolate. He produced some pictures of himself as a young man, a soldier in the war, with black hair and moustache and dark inquisitive eyes. Born here in the Valtellina, for most of the war he had been a prisoner of the British, but obviously that fact no longer rankled. In 1951 he had started his herd of cows; the dog was 15 years old. We wished each other 'Arrivederci!' 'Buona fortuna!' and I watched the old man and the dog disappear into the mist up the mountain.

On the way back down the valley it started to rain and there was a violent thunderstorm, but I found shelter under an enormous leaning rock. Another rock lay at an angle to it and deflected the water dripping off the larger one. Here I waited, in great comfort, for the storm to pass and gave thanks to the fates for allowing me, over the past few days, such generous measures of good luck, ranging from superb weather to instant shelter. Now the weather had broken and my holiday was over, but I had absorbed a rich store of memories to take home with me from the beautiful southern slopes of the Bregaglia.

Pyrenean High Route

J G R HARDING

(Plates 51–55)

Once upon a time the high-level ski route from Chamonix to Zermatt had a cachet for British ski mountaineers. It was also unfrequented; on a 1964 east-west crossing we met but one other party *en route*. Today this grandest of alpine ski tours has been packaged. At the end of a trail littered with the caravans of guided parties are huts filled to bust serving meals à la carte, table d'hôte or whatever else you fancy.

However, there is another 'Playground of Europe' and all good *Pyrénéeistes* will echo the pronouncement of their precursor, Count Henry Russell: 'The Alps astound, the Pyrenees attract and soften us.' That is as true today as it was a century ago, and, if the Pyrenees are built smaller, their character is better preserved. There is no easily definable watershed, but the French and Spanish versants are wholly different in character. The French Pyrenees, rising abruptly from the Gascon plains, are only accessible via deep gorges or *garves* which lead to high basins surrounded by steep peaks. The Spanish Pyrenees, split by transverse valleys creating isolated montagnard communities, flow southwards in a series of undulating ridges, eventually to merge into the Iberian Plateau. The French slopes are wetter, lusher and heavily wooded. The Spanish, drier and gaunter, embody both the promise of the Mediterranean and the harshness of the meseta. But common to both are the granite pics and crenellated *crêtes*; limestone cirques and vertiginous canyons; torrents and waterfalls and, above all, a multiplicity of lakes both large and small, in this land touched by the wand of enchantment.

I first came to the Pyrenees in the summer of 1974 to climb Perdu, Aneto and Vignemale. I returned a devotee nine months later, in March 1975, as a member of an Eagle Ski Club party, after a break of five years from ski-touring. Ski mountaineering in the Pyrenees was as unfashionable for the British then as it is now. The party's object was to cross the western half of the *Parc National des Pyrénées*. Since the previous October virtually no snow had fallen but, from the day before we arrived, it fell continuously for the next six days. Starting from Lescun, we climbed the Pic 'Anie (2504m), most westerly marker of the main range, in a whiteout. Thereafter, in unremitting bad weather, a route was pushed on compass bearings from Urdos to Gabas via the Ayous and Pombie huts. At Gabas the expedition halted and took stock. Because of avalanche risk the key passage between Gabas and Cauterets was abandoned. And here, with my holiday run out, I had to retire prematurely. Of the Pyrenees in winter I had seen but one summit, the Pic du Midi d'Ossau, emerging momentarily through the cloud. The weather had been dreadful and the skiing unmemorable. Yet a seed had been sown and, with a fringe of curiosity unsatisfied, I determined one day to discover for myself the country that lay beyond Gabas in that wild knot of granite peaks – Balaitous, Palas and Arriel.

Another three years were to pass before that seed germinated in 1978. From the original kernel of myself and Alan Wedgwood we swelled to four and set off from Pau on 20 March, with the addition of Richard Morgan and Alan's brother Nick. Our plan was first to get the feel of the place by repeating the 1975 section, Urdos to Gabas: thereafter to broach new ground from Gabas to Cauterets. The weather broke after the first day out, but we surprised ourselves by making faster times than had the 1975 guided party and successfully navigated the difficult cols of Ayous and Suzon in blizzard and whiteout. But not without hostage. In descending the Col Suzon, Richard badly injured his back and had to retire home hurt, five days out.

Now reduced to three, we sat out a depressing 36 hours at Gabas awaiting a break in the weather. A local guide, Monsieur Dodu, recommended a stolen march to the Arrémoulit hut and a secret route into Spain. The Arrémoulit, nestling in a cup of the great cirque formed by Palas, Balaitous and the Frondellas, exemplifies reinforced concrete Gothic. Here, demoralized, we spent Easter Sunday comatose and frozen, while outside the storm heaped snow roof-high to block out all light. The arrival of three *Toulousiennes* late that evening dispelled a bad attack of British phlegm. With Gallic *élan* they dispensed beer, claret and *boeuf en daube* to enliven our staple diet of porridge, cake and char.

After another night of storm there dawned a perfect day and with it a change of fortune. From the Col du Palas we swooped down the upper Arriel valley, skimming frozen lakes to plunge ever deeper into Spain. Here was new country dotted with tiny lakes, studded with dwarf pines and surmounted by a galaxy of Puntas and Picos with unpronounceable names. We climbed the Grande Fache (3005m) in the last of the good weather, and that evening were reunited with the *Toulousiennes* at the Wallon hut.

The night's interminable toasts in Ricard accounted for the morning-after pledges, but we still made the Oulettes hut with a blizzard at our heels. Next morning, 30 March, snow was coming over the roof, so we renounced both the Vignemale and a proposed grand slam finish to Gavarnie. A guided party of 24 Swiss had got out early, leaving the hut *guardienne*, her dog, two elderly aides, two Parisian doctors, Jean-Pierre Leire (a montagnard Pau hotelier) and ourselves to make a *Sturm und Drang* escape to Cauterets. Avalanches, mainly heard rather than seen, were fusillading down the Val de Gaube, but we reached the Pont D'Espagne by mid-afternoon at the cost of only one ski pole. That evening, with our party now expanded to 11, we celebrated safe release and *la vie montagne* with a *grande bouffe* in French gastronomic tradition. The Urdos to Cauterets traverse had been accomplished, and in Jean-Pierre we had made a friend who became an automatic selection for the next three tours.

The 1978 tour first sparked in me the concept of a complete Pyrenean ski traverse. Although Pyrenean mountain exploration generally lagged behind the Alps, the first summer traverse of the range was ahead of its time. In 1817, two years after Waterloo, Dr Frederick Parrot linked the Atlantic with the

Mediterranean in a 53-day crossing. The same year, the remarkable Dr Parrot almost climbed Monte Rosa, and 10 years later he made the first ascent of Mount Ararat. Coast-to-coast foot traverses, whether by the French Low Level GR10 or the High Level *Haute Randonnée Pyrénéenne* in 45 stages, are now well established. But the Pyrenean High Route on ski is a different proposition. The complete ski traverse of the main range from Canigou to Pierre St Martin was first accomplished in 1968, in 35 days, by Charles Laporte. My aim, tentative at first, was to make a west to east traverse, but not until 1981, three years on, did I become aware of Laporte's achievement.

The 1979 tour started from Cauterets where the 1978 tour had ended, establishing a pattern for all subsequent expeditions. We planned to climb the Vignemale *en route* to Gavarnie and then to push eastwards to Gèdre. The party of five comprised Susan Baldock, my cousin Alain Bevan-John, Richard Reynolds and Jean-Pierre Leire who endorsed the plan as *très classique*. We started on 9 April, a month later than the 1975 tour. On a sullen, brooding day, with the contours of the frozen Lac de Gaube barely discernible, we reached the Bayssellance hut after a long hard march. Set high below a col at 2651m the hut had been abandoned to winter, with spindrift enfilading every door and window.

Next day, deteriorating weather precipitated a retreat to the Oulétes hut, 500m lower. Descending from the Hourquette d'Ossoue under the dark cliffs of the Petit Vignemale, occasionally visible through shifting cloud, a thunderous roar from on high confirmed an uneasy feeling. Nothing could be seen but in a moment of frozen time everything heard and felt. Instinctively we ski'd downwards but, scarcely started, a rush of wind and a wall of snow overwhelmed, buried and carried us along in its irrepressible tide. Tossed in a dark void, inexorable forces crescendoed. Yet, as the torrent of snow kept moving, a vestige of hope was preserved, and when it stopped my head had come to the surface. The wet snow had frozen like concrete. Another hour passed before Richard had traced and dug out both Susan and myself. A snow-slide off the seracs of the Petit Vignemale glacier had triggered an enormous avalanche. Its path stretched upwards into the mist; its debris, seared by deep runnels, filled the entire couloir. It stopped at the very floor of the cirque, consolidated in huge mounds. Searching frantically with 'Autophons' we traced Jean-Pierre deeply buried, badly shocked but alive. Eventually Alain's body was located beneath a metre of hard-packed snow; he had been killed almost instantly. We spent a stormy night at the Oulétes hut, shocked and silent, and next day marched out to the Pont d'Espagne. Only one pair of skis was left between us: Susan's had been laminated.

Death offers no easy explanations and in its aftermath one reassesses mountaineering mores. In memory of Alain's brilliant qualities I determined to pursue the traverse, but to try in future to get a better measure of these mountains. To date, three tours totalling 24 days had yielded four with good weather, three with indifferent and the rest thoroughly bad. In summer, at much the same latitude as Rome, the Pyrenees are not serious mountains, and from mid-June to early September conditions are usually settled. But winter tells a different tale and, whereas Alpine weather is continental, Pyrenean is Atlantic.

Glaciation may be sparse, but heavy winter snowfall transforms benign summer peaks and passes into serious obstacles. This and variable temperatures make avalanches the most serious Pyrenean ski-mountaineering hazard, particularly in the steep-sided French valleys amongst which Gaube, Ossoue, Couplan, Moudang and Rioumajou are notorious. In France, local weather advice is usually available in major centres from guides bureaux or the excellent Pyrenean gendarmerie. Nevertheless, forecasts in themselves do not wholly resolve the dilemma that bad weather poses to touring parties with limited time, pre-set holiday dates and itineraries involving complex planning and logistics.

Most parts of the Alps have well-developed hut systems, each within the compass of a day's tour. In the Pyrenees, quantity and quality are infinitely variable and many huts are closed in winter. Overall, the Catalan Alpine Club's are the best huts in the range, with the best French concentration in the Néouvielle Reserve. Some huts have winter quarters (often cramped and primitive); there are also 'granges' (shepherds' summer quarters), 'cabanes' and 'abris' which are sometimes no more than concrete cubes. Few will have cooking facilities or water; many will be partially or totally snow-filled. Self-sufficiency in cooking and bivouac equipment are essential.

The Pyrenees are significantly lower than the Alps, but height is only one measure. Verticality is another, and Pyrenean ski touring is nothing but ups and downs. The axis of the main range follows the frontier, but any number of transverse and lateral ridges form separate massifs of which Maladeta and Posets, the highest and biggest, are both in Spain. In bad weather, retreat down the steep French valleys is invariably exposed to serious avalanche risk. You may escape into Spain, but then the logistics of getting back to the frontier ridge and France can throw a tight schedule.

Although the quality of Pyrenean maps has improved over the past few years, neither France nor Spain concedes to the cartographical needs of the other. Frontier maps tend to cut off just where continuity is crucial, so you may need both the French and Spanish. Most of the range is now covered by the new 50m French IGN *Edition Randonnées Pyrénéennes* series (though in some respects the old 1:50,000 series is clearer). But for touring in the Posets, Maladeta, Ribagorca and Val d'Aran areas, the Spanish Editorial Alpina series is still indispensable.

Essentially, Pyrenean ski touring is mountaineering on ski. The ground is steep, route-finding across remote country is complicated by inaccurate maps and a paucity of good huts means heavy packs. On only 10 days in 63 were we to meet other ski parties; on some tours, never. One lesson, learned the hard way, is never to push routes in bad weather. But these very characteristics and the uncertainty of the outcome lend a special flavour to this splendid range.

The 1980 and 1981 tours were international. The core of the 1980 team was Alan Wedgwood, Walter Good of the Swiss Avalanche Research Institute, Davos, Jean-Pierre Leire and myself, but at times we went up to seven when Jean-Pierre's family and friends joined in the fun. Our plan was to follow part of the 1979 itinerary as far as Gavarnie; thereafter, to explore the three great limestone cirques of the Pyrenees – Gavarnie, Estaubé and Troumouse – and come out through the Néouvielle Reserve. To better the weather, we left

Cauterets only four days off May Day. In the nine energetic stages that followed we climbed Cambales (2965m), Taillon (3144m) and – almost – Perdu (3355m); descended the mysterious Rio Ara; crossed by the Brèche de Roland into Spain; and were unwittingly introduced to Ski Extreme by Walter when descending Perdu's NE face and the Tuquerouye Couloir. The weather gave some reasonable breaks but finally ran out in the snowy wastes of the Troumouse Cirque. Here, in the cold comfort of a concrete cube that awaits the traveller in the guise of the Cabane Aires, Alan's bivouac was a hammock of skis suspended from the roof. Exit north to Barèges through the Néouvielle was frustrated by avalanche danger, but we had covered over 100km, accomplished our objectives and pushed the route eastwards.

The 1981 tour – last of the international experiments – started with seven but finished with two. Alan and Janet Wedgwood and I represented the British contingent, Colin Chapman the Irish and Jean-Pierre Leire, Jacques and Jean-Claude *La France*. The sports plan Barèges to Luchon was ambitious, but preparations had been painstaking and elaborate. In the preceding months, Jean-Pierre had made four separate food caches along the route, including two by helicopter. The catch was that, before engaging the main range, he insisted that we should see something of his *magnifique* Néouvielle Reserve. Though well north of the watershed, the Néouvielle has much in common with the Catalan Pyrenees. The northern approach up the Glère valley, a typical *garve*, is austere but, once the sharp containing ridges that guard the heartland of the reserve are breached, a classic Pyrenean landscape dotted with solitary dwarf pines unfolds to the foot of shapely granite peaks. But pre-eminently this is a land of lakes: big lakes such as Orédon, Aumar, Aubert, Oule and Cap de Long; little lakes that dance up the valleys in steps. In summer like blue beads in a necklace; in winter merging imperceptibly into the landscape.

We started well enough but, on the second day out – almost within sight of our *abri* on the shores of Lac d'Orédon – I scored an own goal by falling into a hole and coming out with concussion and amnesia. Fabian, the nearest roadhead, was over 10km away down the notorious Couplan Gorge. Jacques and Jean-Claude, both good skiers, made Fabian in three hours. At 1am, 7½ hours later, Captain Fons with eight mountain gendarmes of Section 29 SRS Lannemezan plus doctor arrived, having ascended the Couplan in 2½ hours. With bad weather forecast, a helicopter rescue next day could not be guaranteed and the doctor ordered immediate evacuation by blood wagon. Trussed like a chicken and usually belayed fore, aft and above; at one stage shouldered as on a tightrope by bearers moving gingerly along the bollards that demarcated the outer edge of a snow-bank and the lip of a black void; at other times furrowing through the snow like a bobsleigh, the surrealistic descent to Fabian took 6½ hours. It brought home what it takes to organize a mountain rescue over difficult ground, even with the most professional of rescue teams.

After a reassuring brain scan at Tarbes and three days in Lannemezan Hospital, I contrived an escape on April Fools' Day. Despite indifferent weather the others had already got up the Pics de Néouvielle (3091m) and Campbieil (3051m). But four crucial days had been lost, Jacques had already returned to Toulouse and, with Alan's feet irreparably damaged by new plastic boots during the 30-hour rescue epic, the original *équipe* was reduced to three. Now, paradoxically, the weather improved. In the four days that remained, Jean-Pierre, Colin and I completed a circuit of the Néouvielle via the Bastanet and Aygues-Cluses huts, a succession of cols and the Pics Contade (2714m) and Quatre-Termes (2724m). Colin then retired to Waterford and on what sadly turned out to be our last expedition together, Jean-Pierre and I climbed the Turon de Néouville (3035m) from Lienz accompanied throughout by the patron of the Chez Louisette's dog. It had been a tour of the unexpected, embellished with exits and entrances. The original objective might not have been achieved, but there had been incident enough, and in climbing five peaks and traversing a dozen passes we had come to know a delectable corner of the Pyrenees.

In 1982 I reverted to the Alps and a Verbier/Zermatt High Route with Alan and Elsbeth Blackshaw, only to have my Pyrenean prejudices confirmed. The 1983 True Brit party included Alan and Nick Wedgwood, Julian Lush, John Wilkinson and David Williams. We left Gèdre on 7 March just ahead of the spring squalls, bound for Luchon or bust. On the second day out, Campbieil (3051m) fell to us from the south and, in the wake of the matchless Williams, the whole team survived the first British ski descent of the 850m WSW couloir intact to finish a memorable day at St Lary with a tally of 1535m ascent and 1620m descent.

Between the Cirque de Troumouse and the Spanish Ribagorca lies the Sobrare. This is still one of the remotest stretches of the Pyrenees, with an unavoidable four-to-five day passage between St Lary and Benasque. Even in good weather with a flying start from the Bielsa tunnel, the route to the Refuge Trigoniero in Spain, traversing a succession of cols, is tricky. By mid-morning on 10 March, at about the half-way mark, 15cm of new snow had already fallen. At this point, on a delicate passage above the cliffs that overlook the upper Hechempy valley, John Wilkinson dislocated a shoulder and fractured an arm. With such handicaps, the descent of the Hechempy in poor visibility, variable snow and outlandish sacks was serious stuff. Nick and Julian took the last 30m of the exit couloir direct in tandem, with Nick riding Julian's head. Escape to Fabian down the Moudang valley gauntlet, its flanks seared by the debris of avalanches past and present, is best avoided in any conditions. 13 hours after starting we were back in St Lary recasting plans. Unbowed and imperturbable, John returned to England next day. To lighten the gloom and allow the weather to settle, the rest of us took a mid-week break in the Néouvielle. Far from the harsher realities of the main range 25km to the south, we climbed the Portarras (2687m) from the Campana de Cloutou hut in perfect weather, to finish a superb day with a 6½km, 1350m descent to Aulon.

The past 48 hours had left the original schedule in tatters, but by making the Hospice de Rioumajou that same night we were back in contention. The passage Rioumajou-Viadós demands good weather. A steep climb leads to the Port de Madère which offers both a gateway into Spain and one of the grandest views in all the Pyrenees. From here the entire eastern horizon was filled with the lazy mass of Posets (3375m), objective for the next day. But after a dawn start from Viadós, the weather turned so we broke our tryst, humped up the

vertiginous Cinqueta de Añes Cruces and were chased up the gun-barrel gully
below the Col Gistaín by storm clouds. Though virtually gutted by arsonists in
1979, what was left of the Estós hut provided sanctuary. Relaxed in the evening
sun on a green sward, we peered eastwards beyond a herd of grazing chamois
towards the brooding bulk of Maladeta shrouded in cloud.

Heavy snow that night finally put paid to Posets. In a landscape
transformed, we slipped down the Estós valley to Benasque to expunge the taste
of five days Accelerated Freeze-Dried with a feast laced with olive oil and
lubricated with Rioja. Aneto (3404m), the apex of the Pyrenees, was still in our
sights until a tentative attempt to reach the Renclusa hut was aborted by a black
storm. Driven out of the Esera and Spain by the weather we taxied through the
Biella tunnel, lodged in a rude refuge above the Col du Portillon and next
morning were over the Col du Barèges in bright sunshine. Aneto, now due
south, its flanks glittering with fresh snow, seemed tantalizingly close. Had
caution lost the venture? The question which had nagged me ever since leaving
Benasque was comprehensively answered even as we pipped the Pic d'Arres
(2161m). Lenticular clouds curling sinuously over Aneto were precursors of a
mighty front rolling in from the Atlantic that was stretched tight like a black
band across the western horizon. The flawless sky and brilliant colours of early
morning had already faded to flat monochrome as Aneto vanished into the
clouds and we quit that last summit for Luchon in a spiralling snow descent.

1984 was another gap year enforced by my dislocating a shoulder during
an east-west Cairngorm traverse. The 1985 team – Patrick Baily, Roger Childs,
Rupert Hoare, Julian Lush and David Seddon – introduced new blood, and in
Childs we had an expert on Spanish mores and *morales*. Starting from Luchon
on 9 March, we planned a tilt at Aneto before pushing on eastwards to Andorra.
But the crossing into Spain by any one of three avalanche-prone routes should
not be underestimated. Although the weather was unexceptional, it took two
bites to complete this first stage, climbing Montjoie (2164m) twice and
Escalette (2466m) *en route*. With a key passage behind and the weather still
holding, Aneto was surely in the bag; but nothing is certain in the Pyrenees, and
an unremitting 48-hour storm sent us scuttling down to Benasque as food ran
out. One venture and two days lost, the next stage was leapfrogged by copying
the 1983 taxi trick. By this stratagem we reached an exceptionally well
appointed valley hut, the Parador Don Gaspar, Artiges, at the threshold of the
Aigües Tortes National Park. This tangled area of rugged granite peaks,
delectable lakes and odorous pine forests is peerless even by Pyrenean
standards.

The Restanca is of blessed memory for the guardian's ham and eggs. *En
route* from here to the Ventosa we were stopped 150m short of Montardo's
(2830m) summit when the weather delivered what the forecast had predicted.
By a series of frozen lakes dropping in steps past the fabled Aiguilles de
Travessani we reached the Ventosa as the evening sun at last burst through
retreating clouds that streamed in banners off the Besiberri. Perched on a spur
above the Estany Negre, in an ensemble of gnarled pines and granite slabs
encircling a lake petrified by winter snows that simulates a Japanese print, few
huts can compare with the Ventosa, and no *guardienne* in all the Pyrenees with

Carmen. Carmencita! The Circe of Catalunya; mistress of her refuge; winner at 'Hearts' and next day's leader of a column of medieval mountaineers, struggling in her wake to maintain a semblance of machismo, up the Punta Alta (3014m).

Sadly, all such idylls are ephemeral and, as weekend tourers trickled into the Ventosa, British morale stiffened and with it a genuine attempt was made to regain momentum and reach the Colomers hut. But now the weather led the ball and waist-deep snow, two duckings in the Estany Travessani and a horizontal blizzard precipitated a terminal retreat down the Upper Riu Malo and exit via Boí. The Oread's spell had blunted our spearhead, but made a return to her domain inevitable.

1986 was the year of the Picos de Europa, but in 1987, with David and Anna Williams and Carmen *aficionados* Roger Childs and Julian Lush, I determined that we would crack the crux of the Pyrenean High Route from the Val d'Aran to Andorra by a route wholly in Spain. The upper reaches of the Nyiri, Mollas, Tavascan, Noarre, Lladore and Ferrera valleys in that part of High Catalunya above the Pallars Sobira were for long the most inaccessible in the Pyrenees. Undisturbed even by the early British pioneers Packe, Russell, Spender and Belloc these parts are still little visited, despite the recently constructed line of Catalan Alpine Club huts. From the decline of Rome to the Union of Aragon and Castile, the peoples of these remote valleys had pleaded their own laws. Even today they boast their own customs and retain the Catalan tongue.

It was unthinkable not to revisit the exquisite Aigües Tortes National Park before engaging on this crossing. But Carmen had moved on, and so it was from the Colomers rather than the Ventosa that we climbed the Aiguille de Travessani (2755m) as a curtain raiser. In descent David effortlessly reversed on ski our earlier labours on foot, pre-jumping the col's corniced lip as a final flourish. Next morning we set off from the palatial Amitges hut in steady snow to stop just short of the St Maurici lake as the clouds parted to bare the twin spires of the Encantados – the two shepherds of Espot petrified in limestone for disregarding the church bells' call to prayer. The Encantados, mystical object of Robin Fedden's Pyrenean pilgrimage, we circumnavigated in a long 10½hour day via the steep Monestero Col, descending the Peguera valley to experience, at the Hotel Roya, Espot hospitality three generations removed from Belloc's Pyrenean inns with fleas that tease.

And now for the key passage. From the deserted *contrabandista* village of Alos de Isil in the upper Noguera Palleresa, the route shadows a 55km arc defined by the frontier ridge that pivots on Mt Rouch (2858m), before swinging SE to Coma Pedrosa (2946m). On the four committing stages Alos de Isil–Pujol–Certescan–Val Ferrera–Arinsal, we averaged just under 10 hours per day and, for the last two days, survived on a cheese cube, sliver of salami, rasher of bacon and flapjack. Throughout, Anna soldiered on with a damaged knee soothed by snow compresses.

The initial stage, Alos de Isil to the Pujol hut, is the most serious. A steep climb up the Barranco de Comamala takes in two intermediate cols before reaching the Col de Pilas, 2500m high on the SW ridge of Mt Rouch. After a sharp drop into the Nyiri Valley, a rising traverse across the Sierra Mitjana to the Col Galena tots up 1450m of ascent. The longest stage, Certescan-Val Ferrera, involved a steep *mauvais pas* above the Lower Etang Romedo, where a 10m free fall into the lake would have been unrescuable; 1½ hours with ski atop sacks like prehistoric insects sporting outsize probosces plunging, rearing, backing and thrusting through dense thickets at the confluence of the Romedo, Broate and Canedo Gorges; a sly snow-slide just below the Col Sellente; and a final stage engulfed by night. On the last day, with a mantle of fresh snow reflecting the fierce southern sun, our dehydrated and distended column inched upwards in long traverses to the frontier col, the Porteille de Baia. The exit couloir, steepening to a rock pitch, justified the rope, but at last we had reached Andorra and, fittingly, at 2790m, the high point of the tour. From this grandstand we could trace our route of the past four days by the frontier ridge that curved in a bow to the cornerstone of Mt Rouch still dominating the western horizon. Our timing was lucky. For once, when it really mattered, we had enjoyed settled conditions. The day after we left the mountains it started snowing for a fortnight.

The Eastern Pyrenees, covering 130km as the lammergeyer flies from Andorra to the Mediterranean, make up a quarter of the entire range. Russell once remarked on their 'oriental grace and languor', but a rustic Catalan put it more prosaically when he told David Williams that anything east of Andorra was a 'cow hill'. Certainly, there are the Pics de Vache, but even these cows have horns, and half a dozen others *en route* nudge the 2800/2900m mark. In truth, these closing stages of the Pyrenean High Route coursing through Andorra, Spain and France should not be underestimated. To ring down the curtain, the last two days aggregate 52km, with each rating a guidebook time of 12 hours. For me, this Catalan country with its alliterative catalogue of unfamiliar names – Carlitte, Carole, Cerdagne, Capcir and Canigou – had the fascination of unfulfilled ambition. In Roger Childs, Rupert Hoare, David Seddon and David Williams we had a team for all seasons.

Statistically, the closer the Mediterranean, the better the weather. As it turned out, the 1988 tour got some of the worst on offer. From the day we landed at Le Havre it scarcely stopped snowing for a week, with high winds persistent throughout. In compensation, the skiing was excellent and never once did we resort to trainers. In theory the first half of the tour, El Serrat to Font-Romeu, promised hostel accommodation; the second, Font-Romeu to Fillols, an element of hairshirtery. The route from El Serrat to Ransol, crossing the treacherous Col de la Mine with thigh-deep snow accumulating stealthily windward, gave a clue to what might later be in store. Next day, in a storm which closed every lift in Soldeu and El Tartar and the road from Andorra to France, we battled along to the Col de Puymorens with the *tramontana* blowing off Carlitte in paroxysms of rage. At 1920m the Col de Puymorens, an historic Pyrenean passage, forms a weathershed between the Atlantic and Mediterranean and has an evil reputation in winter. From here we planned to traverse, or at least circumnavigate, Carlitte (2921m), Charlemagne's namesake. In the event, the only possible outcome of the six-hour epic ascent up the Lanous valley to the Baraque des Ingénieurs – snow-filled but friendly – was to reverse the ground so hardly won the following day and count our blessings to have reached Font-Romeu, weather-battered but otherwise intact.

Seven days into the tour but barely at the half-way mark, we had only four days in hand, with the prospect of serious avalanches after so much bad weather. But when on the morning of 9 March the sun appeared for the first time in a week, flooding the length and breadth of the Cerdagne and etching the myriad villages of this glorious upland valley in unfamiliar clarity, our venture took wings. The next two stages – Err-Nuria-Ull der Terr, traversing Puigmal (2910m) and the Pics de Vache (2826m and 2821m) en route – took only 4½ and 5¾ hours respectively. Any avalanche threat was literally blown away by the north wind – our companion for the next three days – which either scattered the snow as chaff or froze it solid. But when David Williams, spearheading the attack with Rupert Hoare, went down to a bug in the grotty winter quarters under the Ull der Terr hut, what odds the morrow's 25km stage? Happily, the extra hours in bed so restored our hero that for most of the next day he was never more than a speck on the sastrugi skyline. These exceptional ski conditions made for a bumpy ride but a fast one. Under a flawless sky we sped eastwards along the snow-spine of the Esquerdes de Rotja, set high above sprawling forested ridges that now fanned out north to France and south to Spain. Only Canigou barred our way.

Progress was such that we arrived at the newly constructed Pla Guillem hut in a mere seven hours, shaving five off guidebook time. But the prospect of spending those five hours gained on digging out of the hut justified a 560m descent for a night of comfort at the idyllic Mariailles hut. A lovely evening with twinkling stars promised fair for tomorrow's traverse of Canigou (2784m). This, the last great mountain of the Pyrenees, long regarded as its apex and sacred to Catalans, is a world unto itself. Like Etna, Vesuvius or the Thessalian Olympus, it springs from the sea and aspires to heaven. It inspires the lives of those who live within its sight as it has the imaginations of generations of artists and writers.

An early start saw us skinning up the awkward path that delicately skirts the sinister avalanche shoot of the Pic de Sept Hommes to gain the great basin of the Cady, and thence to climb steadily upwards to the back of Canigou's rocky southern cirque. That day was unlike any other. The sky was darkest blue, the sun was brilliant and, though unruffled by a breath of wind, the air stayed cool. From the Porteille de Valmanya we cramponned 150m to an airy brèche and so on up a narrow snow couloir culminating in an ice-encrusted rock chimney rating PD with ski. At exactly 12.30pm on 12 March 1988 I stood exultant on the summit.

Canigou is visible from Marseilles, and its immense summit panorama is justly famous. To the east, beyond the stark rock precipice of the Crête de Barbet's 350m N face, only a blue-tinged coastal plain lay between us and the Mediterranean. To the west, the Pyrenees stretched away in an endless succession of white waves. That was now a theatre of the past. Nine separate winter tours, 63 individual stages, 20 peaks and over 70 cols were gone as yesterday. Driving back to Font-Romeu as dusk was becoming night, we stopped for a final look back to the snow-pink beacon of Canigou's summit fading in the last of the sun's afterglow. Inevitably Count Russell has the last word, for he it was who said that 'it is to the Pyrenees that the smiles of the artists and the heart of the poet will always turn'.

Summary

There is no one way to traverse the Pyrenees on ski, but the most direct west-east traverse from Mendive to Fillols in 34 stages with variants is well described in the Ollivier-Peres CAF guide *La Haute Route d'Hiver des Pyrénées*. For further variants and general touring the FFM's *Pyrénées Itineraires Skieurs* in four volumes (ed: Ollivier) and various Catalan Alpine Club publications complete the picture. In retrospect, an east-west traverse might give better snow for skiing. The ideal would be a continuous traverse but, fitness and logistics apart, few amateurs could find time for such a project. My compromise was to do it by stages. Part of the 1978 tour was a repeat; 1979 was abortive and others (1980, 1981, 1985 and 1987) involved significant variations through the Three Cirques, Néouvielle and Aigües Tortes. In other respects, the Ollivier–Peres line was generally followed. For the record, our stages measured by entry and exit points and intermediate huts or other accommodation en route were as follows:

1975 (9/16 March)
Pau: Urdos: Ayous: Pombie: Gabas: Cauterets.

1978 (17 March to 1 April)
Pau: Larry: Ayous: Pombie: Gabas: Arrémoulit: Penelara: Wallon: Oulétes: Cauterets.

1979 (8/13 April)
Cauterets: Bayssellance: Oulétes: Cauterets.

1980 (26 April to 6 May)
Cauterets: Wallon: Gavarnie: Sarradets: Gaulis: Estaube: Des Aires (Troumouse): Gèdre.

1981 (27 March to 8 April)
Barèges: Glère: Orédon: St Lary: Bastanet: Aigues Cluses: Lienz: Barèges.

1983 (6/18 March)
Gèdre: Le Sausset: St Lary: Campana de Cloutou: Rioumajou: Viadós: Estós: Benasque: Portillon: Luchon.

1985 (7/19 March)
Luchon: Poulane: Renclusa: Benasque: Artiés: Restanca: Ventosa: Boí.

1987 (18/29 March)
Salardu (Val d'Aran): Colomers: Amitges: Espot: Can Trues (Isil O Gil): Pujol: Certescan: Val Ferrera: Arinsal (Andorra).

1988 (3/13 March)
Font-Romeu: El Tartar: Col de Puymorens: Baraque des Ingénieurs (Lanous): Font-Romeu: Nuria: Ull der Terr: Marialles: Fillols.

Although one tends to remember the bad weather in the Pyrenees, over an aggregate period of 67 days only 36% were really bad, 43% good and the remaining 21% indifferent. On balance, the middle weeks of March probably give the best conditions. At the end of the day, everything depends on one's companions. Of 20 friends who took part in the eight tours I organized, those who made the most frequent appearances were Alan Wedgwood, anchorman of the early expeditions, David Williams, the complete ski mountaineer, Julian Lush and Roger Childs – these and all the others the best of *compagneros*.

In the Footsteps of Mackinder

NIGEL C GATES

(Plates 69–73)

Mount Kenya was first climbed in 1899 by Sir Halford John Mackinder, 'the father of British geography', with César Ollier and Joseph Brocherel, both from Courmayeur. As a geographer and mountaineer I had long wished to follow in Mackinder's footsteps. Therefore I was delighted when Lieutenant Steve Jackson of the Royal Navy & Royal Marines Mountaineering Club (RNRMMC) offered me a place on his expedition to Mount Kenya and Kilimanjaro. The aims of the RNRMMC expedition were to carry out both medical research and mountaineering in East Africa during January and February 1987.

Mackinder, the first lecturer appointed specifically to a post in geography at a British university, became Reader in Geography at Oxford University in October 1887. Because, as he stated, 'at that time most people would have no use for a geographer who was not an adventurer and explorer', he organized an expedition to East Africa in 1899 with Campbell Hausburg. Mackinder's ship left Marseilles on 10 June and reached Zanzibar on 28 June. He proceeded to Kenya, then part of British East Africa, then travelled on the newly-completed railway from Mombasa to Nairobi. Today one normally flies non-stop between Europe and Nairobi overnight. Mackinder's 170-strong expedition, comprising six Europeans, two Masai, 66 Swahili and 96 Kikuyu, left the Nairobi area on 26 July. They made the overland journey, then slow and difficult, to the base of Mount Kenya on foot during the heavy summer rains and arrived some three weeks later, on 15 August. In 1899 few man-made tracks existed on Mount Kenya, and Mackinder's party had to force a route – which his Italian guides called *la grande route du Mount Kenya* – through the belt of dense bamboo and forest which cloaks the lower slopes of the mountain. Although Mackinder expected this to take three days, it was actually accomplished in a single day. Today one normally drives from Nairobi to the Meteorological Station (3048m), near the top of Mount Kenya's forest belt, in a few hours.

Mackinder's expedition utilized a large number of porters. However, as his description demonstrates, this was not without problems. Not only had Mackinder's expedition to contend with stores theft, porter mutiny and porter desertion; two Swahili porters were actually killed in an attack by hostile Kikuyu tribesmen. Many Kikuyu now work as porters on Mount Kenya and porterage is a thriving and lucrative business. The RNRMMC expedition, with large quantities of equipment and stores to move up the mountain, employed 70 Kikuyu porters. However, we soon discovered that each porter will only carry a maximum of 18kg and has to be paid four days' wages for just one day's work. In addition to the entry fee and daily charges that all mountaineers must now pay to the Mount Kenya National Park authorities, one must also pay similar fees for each porter employed. In 1899 Mackinder did not experience these particular bureaucratic problems.

From the top of the forest belt, Mackinder's expedition reconnoitred its way up the mountain to a position roughly half-way between the mountain's base and the foot of the central peaks, and standing camp was made at 3139m. On 22 August the site of the highest camp was chosen; this was in the Teleki valley, probably very close to the position now termed 'Mackinder's Camp' (4328m). Unfortunately, because of a smallpox epidemic which Mackinder encountered on arrival in Zanzibar, which had forced a precipitous departure from Nairobi, the expedition had been mainly unable to purchase stores and was forced to live on what the land could provide. Although the mountain party had food supplies for about three weeks, the Base Camp below the forest belt was nearly devoid of supplies, and Mackinder descended the mountain on 24 August to return to the camp. The personnel were dispatched to cross the then unexplored Aberdare Range to buy food at a Government station on Lake Naivasha, and Mackinder and Hausburg reascended the mountain on 26 August.

On 30 August, Mackinder and the two Italians made their first attempt to climb to the summit. They climbed the eastern face of the southern arête but were delayed by various difficulties and, caught high on the mountain by nightfall which occurs early in the tropics, were forced to spend the 12-hour equatorial night in an unplanned bivouac at 5121m. Next day they continued up the arête but were eventually stopped by an impassable difficulty, and the first attempt was abandoned.

Mackinder then left the mountain to watch for the return of the party he had sent to Naivasha, while Hausburg and the Italians made a traverse around Mount Kenya's central peaks to see if they could spot an easier route to the summit. They did not find one, so Hausburg and Ollier attempted to climb the mountain by cutting their way up the Darwin glacier. However, stopped by bad weather and unable to climb higher or to retreat the way they had come, they were lucky in being able to traverse to the S arête and descend the route followed earlier by Mackinder. By 5 September the Naivasha party had still not returned, and the food supply situation was getting desperate. Mackinder sent word for all to descend to Base Camp so that they could themselves depart for Naivasha on 7 September. Thus it was indeed fortunate that the Naivasha party returned on 7 September with supplies of food.

Mackinder returned to the mountain to make a final attempt to reach the summit. On 12 September, he and the two Italians again followed the now familiar route up the face of the southern arête. However, this time they spent the night inside a Mummery tent near the top of the arête. Early next morning they left the arête, traversed across the head of the Darwin glacier and then followed a rock-rib to a glacier which descends from the Gate of the Mist, the high col between Mount Kenya's twin summits of Batian (5199m) and Nelion (5188m) – all names given by Mackinder. They had hoped to cut steps in this glacier and traverse it in 20 minutes, but the glacier proved very steep and its ice was intensely hard. Step-cutting was extremely arduous, the traverse took three hours and Mackinder named this adamantine glacier the Diamond Glacier.

From the Gate of the Mist a final rock scramble took Mackinder, Ollier and Brocherel to the summit of Batian, which they reached precisely at noon on 13 September. They stayed on the summit for about 40 minutes and then, in mist, descended cautiously by the same route. The lower section of the descent was completed in darkness and the three finally reached camp after 10pm, 'exhausted, but victorious'. Mackinder remained on Mount Kenya for several more days before descending to Base Camp on 20 September. While on the mountain the expedition also undertook scientific experiments and other research; this included altitude studies, botany, cartography, geology, glacier surveys, meteorology, photography and zoology. Mackinder left Mount Kenya on 21 September and arrived back in London on 30 October.

Reading Mackinder's account of the expedition in the *Geographical Journal* of the year 1900, one cannot fail to be impressed by the dynamism and personality of this quite remarkable British Victorian geographer. In fact, Mackinder did not climb Mount Kenya by its easiest route. Mackinder's Route (now graded IV) diverges from today's normal route (pioneered by Shipton and Wyn Harris in 1929 and graded IV Inferior) at the half-way point, and then follows an exposed ascending line across steep rock and ice. The glaciers are shrinking fast on Mount Kenya and, in 1899, Mackinder's route may have been somewhat easier than it is today, as there may well have been more snow and ice than rock. There are now two tiny bivouac huts which climbers on the normal route can utilize if necessary; one is near the top of the S arête, probably at the position where Mackinder spent the night in his tent, and the other is beside Nelion's summit. However, even today Mount Kenya still remains a 'mountaineers' mountain'. It is not to be attempted lightly and there are many serious routes on the mountain, such as the famous Diamond Couloir. There are no easy routes up and down Mount Kenya and, having climbed it myself, I can only applaud Mackinder's incredibly bold first ascent. His 1899 climb was quite outstanding. Although many now attempt the ascent of Point Lenana, Mount Kenya's third highest summit (4985m) which does not demand climbing skills, the walking circuit around Mount Kenya's central peaks – first followed by Hausburg and the Italian guides – is not walked by many but is certainly well worth following. I walked it comfortably in eight hours and Steve Bell, our Royal Marine, ran it in under three hours.

Mount Kenya, an extinct volcano with a central core consisting of syenite on which 15 small glaciers exist, literally straddles the equator. However, we soon discovered that Mount Kenya's weather was not typically equatorial; each day started cold and clear, but by mid-morning clouds usually covered the sky and it frequently rained, hailed or snowed. Equatorial climates are normally without distinct seasons but, surprisingly, this does not apply to Mount Kenya. In January and February the northern side of the mountain has a winter season while the southern side has a summer season; in August and September these positions are reversed. The unusual combination of high altitude and equatorial latitude has resulted in quite incredible vegetation, such as the Giant Heather, Giant Groundsels and Giant Lobelias, all of which Mackinder noted in 1899. These are among the most spectacular of all mountain plants. Some lobelias grow to eight metres, while another variety forms a giant rosette close to the ground filled with water containing pectin which reduces evaporation and inhibits freezing. The rock hyrax found on Mount Kenya, small animals surprisingly related to elephants, supposedly eat lobelia but they also find mountaineers' rations very attractive!

On the RNRMMC expedition, a main aim was medical research into Acute Mountain Sickness (AMS) which was carried out under the personal direction of Surgeon-Captain Michael Beeley and Dr Jim Milledge, both experts in high-altitude physiology and medicine. By normal expedition standards the medical input to the RNRMMC expedition was very high-powered; there were four doctors, two paramedics and one nurse. Eight medical research protocols involving many separate tests were involved, and all 22 members of the expedition, including the seven 'medics', provided data as subjects. Many mountaineers experience AMS problems associated with ascent to altitude. AMS can be mild or severe, and can take several forms such as headache, nausea, sleep disturbance and loss of appetite. In particularly severe cases, death can occur with great rapidity from pulmonary or cerebral oedema. Many of the reasons for AMS are not yet fully understood, and a major aim of the RNRMMC expedition was to gather medical data, take blood and urine samples and undertake other medical tests on the expedition members at various altitudes. No RNRMMC expedition members used Diamox, as its use would have negated our research protocols.

The amount, although not the actual proportion, of atmospheric oxygen decreases with increasing altitude, and this lack of oxygen is the root cause of AMS. The accepted way to avoid or minimize the symptoms is by acclimatization, and this is best achieved through a leisurely ascent to altitude. Surprisingly, Mackinder's expedition report does not mention symptoms of AMS, and it is therefore likely that acclimatization took place on the long slow walk from Nairobi to the top camp on Mount Kenya. Long-term acclimatization is achieved because the bone-marrow produces additional red blood cells in response to oxygen lack. This process is slow; the body's red blood cell count has only increased by about 10% after ten days, and it takes about six weeks to achieve the maximum increase of about 30%. However, the modern medical view is that increased haemoglobin is not an important aspect of acclimatization; other factors and mechanisms are also involved in the process, particularly in the short term. The main process of acclimatization is the change in the control of breathing. As one ascends, and the amount of atmospheric oxygen decreases, one becomes more sensitive to carbon dioxide; this results in increased ventilation. Several hormones are believed to be involved in the body's response to altitude: renin (produced in the kidneys), aldosterone (produced in the suprarenal glands), and atrial natriuretic peptide (produced in the heart). Ascent to altitude may result in fluid retention or loss, and it has been said that those who get AMS tend to retain fluid, while those resistant to AMS have increased urine output. There have therefore been a number of studies of aldosterone, which causes salt (and water) retention. However, the newly-discovered hormone atrial natriuretic peptide had not (until the RNRMMC expedition) been studied at altitude.

Mount Kenya is an excellent location for medical research into AMS because mountaineers usually drive straight to the Meteorological Station and then make the ascent to Mackinder's Camp in a single day's walk. This ascent of 4328m is extremely rapid by mountaineering standards and symptoms of AMS are, therefore, very common on Mount Kenya. Half the world's annual cases of pulmonary and cerebral oedema are reputed to occur there!

Since all the medical protocols were related to AMS, the recognition and scoring of its symptoms was crucial. For the first six days at Mackinder's Camp, all expedition members were questioned in detail about their AMS symptoms and their responses were recorded. Headache, loss of appetite, nausea, sleep disturbance, Cheyne-Stokes breathing and photophobia symptoms were scored each morning on a scale ranging from no symptoms to severe symptoms. Two subjects were virtually unaffected by AMS. Another member was so sick that he required rapid evacuation to low altitude; after a few days at 2000m, however, he recovered and rejoined the expedition with no ill effects. Few members experienced any Cheyne-Stokes breathing or photophobia, but I observed that over half the expedition members experienced definite signs of the remaining four AMS symptoms. Thus, as far as our AMS scores were concerned, we had a good spread of severity of AMS against which other medical observations could be compared.

Before leaving the United Kingdom, all expedition members attended the Lung Function Laboratory at Northwick Park Hospital where our routine pulmonary functions and our ventilatory responses to both hypoxia (oxygen lack) and carbon dioxide were measured. Publication of results showing any correlation between the hypoxia and carbon dioxide ventilatory responses and the AMS symptoms which members experienced on Mount Kenya is still awaited.

Haemorrhagic phenomena in various organs, including the eye, are known to occur on exposure to altitude, and it has been suggested that these might be related to AMS. We tested capillary fragility, using the technique of mucosal petechiometry where suction is applied to the inner surface of the lower lip for one minute. This process causes a few petechiae (pinhead-size haemorrhages) which are then counted. Base levels of the subjects' petechiae were established in Nairobi, and the process was again carried out at Mackinder's Camp. The expedition hoped to relate petechiae scores to AMS. However, the results show that there was actually a decrease in petechiae, and there was no correlation between petechiae scores and AMS.

The most unpleasant aspect of the medical tests involved giving frequent blood samples. Blood was drawn from our veins and spun for 20 minutes in a hand centrifuge to separate the blood into plasma and red cells. This was undertaken to measure plasma volume increase relating to altitude from measurements of haematocrit (the ratio of the volume of red cells to the total volume of a blood sample) and haemoglobin (the chemical in the red blood cells which combines with oxygen). Sampling was carried out on two days at Nairobi to establish subjects' base levels, and again for two days on arrival at Mackinder's Camp. Blood pressures were also measured daily. Plasma volume change was inferred from the haematocrit increase assuming a constant red cell mass, an assumption probably valid over the short period during which the blood samples were taken. In an attempt to study the effect of posture, samples were taken at 4am and compared with samples taken at 9am when subjects had been up and about for at least an hour. As expected, haematocrit rose in the group as a whole. However, the final results show no correlation between individuals' AMS scores and changes in their plasma volume, haemoglobin and haematocrit.

Symptoms of AMS have been reported to correlate with water retention. To examine this, each member's weight and urine output was recorded daily; this commenced in Nairobi. All urine passed by each individual in 24 hours was collected, and this meant that one's personal 'pee-bottle' had to be within easy reach at all times. As expected, on ascent to altitude, and following a fairly strenuous day's walking from the Meteorological Station to Mackinder's Camp, urine outputs were diminished. The final results show no correlation between individuals' AMS scores and urine volume. There was, however, a significant negative correlation with individuals' 24-hour urine sodium output. No correlation was found between AMS scores and changes in body weight.

AMS is thought to be related to the body's fluid balance, and another reason for taking blood samples was to analyse the changing levels of aldosterone and atrial natriuretic peptide. These hormones are believed to be important in regulating sodium excretion and are thus related to the body's fluid balance. Each sample of the subjects' blood was centrifuged. The resulting plasma was marked with date and time, preserved by freezing in a cryostat containing liquid nitrogen and solid carbon dioxide, and returned to the United Kingdom for analysis. Most expedition members gave their blood at 4am and 9am but a small and dedicated subset of five gave their blood four times a day, at 4am, 9am, 4pm and 9pm, in order to provide more detailed data on the body's circadian rhythm and hormone release cycles. Small samples of each member's daily urine output were also dated and frozen in the cryostat, so that an individual's sodium output could be isolated and measured. The process to assay the hormones is sophisticated and tedious and the many samples of frozen plasma and urine took considerable time to analyse. The final results show a significant correlation with aldosterone, and a negative correlation with atrial natriuretic peptide, on arrival at altitude. However, most unexpectedly, the Nairobi atrial natriuretic peptide value seemed to be predictive of AMS; subjects with high values had little AMS and vice versa.

The final test undertaken by the expedition was concerned with the treatment of AMS headache. This was a trial between Ibuprofen (Brufen) and paracetamol. The test was carefully controlled, and subjects never knew which of the two drugs they were taking; they merely took a tablet and scored the headache's severity after 30, 60 and 120 minutes. If the headache was unresolved a second, different, tablet was taken, and the same scoring process was again followed. The trial's findings have still to be published. However, on completion of the medical research, when we could freely take analgesic drugs, many expedition members discovered empirically that they got good relief from their AMS headaches after taking Brufen (usually prescribed for rheumatoid arthritis).

After completion of our medical research and mountaineering on Mount

Kenya, the RNRMMC expedition moved to Kilimanjaro. For anyone thinking of climbing Kilimanjaro, let me immediately point out that it has now become prohibitively expensive; it cost us about £500 each for our six-day trip, starting and finishing in Nairobi! The Tanzanian and Kilimanjaro National Park authorities appear to make as much money as they can out of Kilimanjaro; certainly the people we saw on the mountain seemed to be mostly affluent Germans and North Americans. The genuine mountaineer will probably baulk at paying the considerable sums now being demanded for visas, Kilimanjaro National Park entrance fees, guides' fees, porters' fees and hut fees, and I fear that the Tanzanians may well be rapidly killing the goose which lays their golden eggs. Nevertheless, I greatly enjoyed my quick trip to Uhuru Peak (5986m), the main summit of Kilimanjaro, by the Marangu route (the normal tourist route via the Mandara, Horombo and Kibo huts). Having spent almost three weeks at altitude on Mount Kenya, we naturally thought that we were well acclimatized. However, many of us still found the final 600m of ascent quite tough going. Although many people start the ascent of Kilimanjaro, a substantial proportion never reach the summit; many give up on the seemingly never-ending scree leading to Gillman's Point, the subsidiary summit on the crater rim at 5681m. Although many members of the RNRMMC expedition ascended Kilimanjaro by much more difficult ice-climbing routes, such as the Heim glacier route, it does need stressing that the Kilimanjaro National Park authorities actively discourage deviation from the Marangu route. Those wishing to climb the mountain by other routes must pay substantially more in fees.

The RNRMMC expedition was very successful. The insights into AMS will hopefully advance our understanding of acute mountain sickness. Personally, I was very pleased to have walked and climbed in the footsteps of Mackinder but, I wonder, did he also return to England suffering from amoebic dysentery?

The author acknowledges, with much gratitude, the assistance given by Dr J S Milledge, Consultant Physician at the Clinical Research Centre, Northwick Park Hospital, Harrow, Middlesex, in the preparation of the medical sections of this article.

REFERENCES

I Allan, *Guide to Mount Kenya and Kilimanjaro*. Mountain Club of Kenya, 1981.

F Benuzzi, *No picnic on Mount Kenya*. Kimber, 1952.

H Lange, *Kilimanjaro: the white roof of Africa*. Mountaineers, 1985.

H J Mackinder, 'A journey to the summit of Mount Kenya, British East Africa.' *Geographical Journal XV*, 453–487, 1900.

J S Milledge, J R Broome and J M Beeley, 'Microvascular fragility and acute mountain sickness.' *British Medical Journal* 296, 610, 1988.

J S Milledge, P S Thomas, J M Beeley and J S C English, 'Hypoxic Ventilatory

Response and Acute Mountain Sickness.' *European Respiratory Journal I*, 948–951, 1988.
P Robson, *Mountains of Kenya*. East African Publishing House for Mountain Club of Kenya, 1969.

Laymen on Lenana

ANN VENABLES

(Plate 74)

Or Kenyan Kapers? With my penchant, indeed passion, for alliteration I can hardly be expected to resist this sort of title, and personally feel that all books on, say, Everest should have titles such as Everest Epic, Sagamartha Saga, I Chose Chomolungma, and so on; this might lead to Mad Moments on Menlungtse, Ruwenzori Raptures – the possibilities are endless.

To return to Mount Kenya, my title is entirely apt since neither my husband nor I are climbers, nor had we been to Kenya before, and the business of getting up this mountain appeared to be unnecessarily fraught with problems. From England, it appeared to be impossible to get the sort of information we wanted on costs, equipment, the best place to start from, how to get there and time needed. First we tried to arrange our 'expedition' as part of our package holiday but were told (although prices – exorbitant – were quoted in one or two brochures) that there was 'no demand' for a tourist ascent of the mountain at this time (July). I then wrote to the Mountain Club of Kenya, who answered that it could not help us in any detailed way. Their Secretary did send us a short printed leaflet containing what seems, with hindsight, quite adequate information on how to set about an ascent. However, at the time this didn't feel sufficiently reassuring and we were not told, for instance, whether one can just turn up at Naro Moru Lodge – probably the best-known valley base for tourist ascents – and be sure of finding porters and/or guides as well as camping space (at the lodge), or must one book in advance? And is Naro Moru the best or easiest starting place? Just how much equipment can one hire there? How likely are the huts on the way up to be full, or would it be better to camp? Which huts does one need? What are they like? Must food be brought from Nairobi, or can anything be purchased at Naro Moru – lodge or village? What choice of transport is there from Nairobi to Naro Moru? How cold might it be, and what sort of footwear does one really need? How complicated is the whole thing to organize once in Kenya, and how long will it take? We only had one week to spare; would this be enough to organize the thing and to get up and down the mountain? To all those seasoned travellers who are readers of the *Alpine Journal* this may seem an awful lot of fuss about rather little, but to us, arriving in a strange country, indeed a strange continent, it was hard to know where and how to start, given our shortage of time. Fortunately Dick Hedges, who was the organizer of our particular safari, was able to point us in the right direction. We found that there was a perfectly adequate bus service from Nairobi to Naro Moru, easily booked and full of all those people wanting to go up Mount Kenya – no demand? It was perfectly simple to buy adequate food in Nairobi, the only slight problem being to find paraffin for our primus. We had brought our own tents and (warm) sleeping-bags, basic cooking utensils, walking boots, duvet jackets and the odd item of thermal underwear; all this was providential as it turned out.

So we – that is my husband Richard, son Philip, daughter-in-law Caroline and I – set off on an MSP (public) bus from Nairobi to Naro Moru Lodge on the W side of Mount Kenya and some 42km from the mountain. To call the bus full would be a gross understatement – it was packed solid in every nook and cranny with people and luggage. We were dropped some hours later at the entrance to the lodge, found the office and, in a leisurely way – thinking we had till the next morning – set about booking a guide (partly because it was impossible to buy a large-scale map of the area) and two porters. Strangely, the office manager tried to persuade us that we needed fewer days to make the ascent than I, personally, thought we required to allow for acclimatization. I say strangely, since it must be in the African interest for tourists to make the maximum bookings, so bringing in more badly needed revenue. However, he did persuade us against our better judgement that we could do the whole thing, up and down, in three days and nights. A cursory look at the equipment on offer for hiring was enough to make us glad that we had brought our own. The 'leisurely' bit stopped there and then as we found ourselves whisked away, within a quarter of an hour of arriving, in a van *en route* for the Met Station at 3000m which was to be our first night's stop. We picked up our two porters and young guide on the way. Since we were putting in quite a lot of motorized altitude gain (from 1800m to 3000m), we decided to walk the last bit in a half-hearted attempt at starting to acclimatize. This was no hardship on a warm sunny afternoon in a beautiful forest with occasional fantastic views. The Met Station, which is also the roadhead, is a large grassy clearing attractively situated with wood cabins for hire and plenty of camping space. We pitched our two extremely small tents and cooked a tolerable supper on the primus while it was still sunny. By dusk it was cold and we were glad of our good quality down sleeping-bags.

We were away next morning by 7.30, having sorted out what we would need over the next two or three days into two porter loads and four small loads for ourselves. Anything spare we left at the Met Station until our return. We set off on a fine sunny morning through the bamboo forest which soon gave way to the most amazing giant heathers – I mean giant, they were three-metre trees. Part of this Heather Zone consists of a region aptly called the Vertical Bog where wellingtons would have been more appropriate than walking boots. By lunch-time I was flagging slightly and was glad to see the terrain levelling out into the long gently rising Teleki valley. What I did not then know was that 'long' was the operative word! By this time the sun had gone and rain looked likely. Our guide, Stephen, was continually urging us on to beat the expected afternoon shower. I was past urging and was only too glad to stop frequently to examine the giant cabbage-like groundsels (*senecios*) and lobelias which lined our way. The notion of a more-than-head-high 'cabbage' is surely worthy of contemplation. Indeed, the almost surreal vegetation more than compensated for my increasing weariness. Richard seemed less affected by the altitude, though Caroline was in little better shape than I was. The only one totally unaffected was Philip, bouncing ahead with increasing contributions from my

rucksack. It took us a fairly gruelling seven hours to reach Mackinder's Camp at
4300m. I, personally, was certainly tired enough to realize that I was unlikely to
be getting up at 2am to go to a 5000m summit, so we simply told Stephen that
we needed an extra day at Mackinder's to acclimatize. Because he agreed to this
so readily, it was obvious that the length of booking was a pretty fluid affair. At
Mackinder's, wooden platforms are provided for tents. There are also, at a
fairly modest price, the ropiest, smelliest, most moth-eaten scout-type tents for
hire, and at a far-from-modest price a half-finished hut (1985) not yet equipped
with bunks so that the inmates had to put their bedding straight on the concrete.
(This hut must be the permanent bunkhouse mentioned in *AJ*93, 225, 1988/89.)
Having paid a small camping fee, we were allowed to use the hut for cooking
and eating. By this, I mean only as shelter (draughty and cold) in which to put
our primus and food. At the lowest price we were certainly, in our tents, far
warmer and more comfortable than the tenants of either scout tents or hut.
There was an outside tap with running water; running, that is, until dusk when
it froze until well beyond sunrise. Mackinder's, though rather a dump, was
quite an entertaining place with constant comings and goings of a variety of
types. Perhaps the best were the Spaniards with their brand-new camping and
(extensive) climbing equipment, who appeared never to leave the camp even for
a short walk. There was an enormous variety of fascinating bird life (though
there was even more variety at a lower altitude) and very tame hyraxes (a sort of
giant guinea-pig) were everywhere, presumably in search of food. And the
nearest relation to the hyrax is. . . ? Yes, the elephant!

We must have adapted very readily to high camp life, as supper at 5.30pm
didn't seem at all odd. Our aim was to finish by dusk (6.30–7), to be in bed
before the temperature was much below freezing. Next morning I felt distinctly
under the weather and decided to rest as much as possible, hoping I might
recover sufficiently to attempt the summit the following day. The other three
went off with Stephen to Two Tarns, small lakes 270m higher, to limber up for
the morrow. Later in the morning I went for a short walk along the beginning of
the route to Lenana (our summit), noticing Point John towering above me and
knowing that it was a lot lower than Point Lenana. The route, though set in this
rather arid valley-head, was very attractive with giant groundsels lining the
path. There were slight flurries of sleet, but the usual afternoon rain never
materialized. I slept quite a lot and suddenly, at 4pm, I felt different and knew I
was all right. I don't know if this is usual, but it wasn't at all a gradual effect, just
a sudden feeling of having acclimatized. Supper was early again. Our delicious
(?) freeze-dried sweet-and-sour was spurned by Caroline, who found eating at
4300m difficult: at least, eating what was on offer; what was more serious, she
tended not to drink enough.

We slept fitfully until 2.30am when Stephen woke us. He had brewed
some hot sweet tea for which we were all very grateful before setting off at 3.
There was a full moon, so we didn't need torches. An easy track winding along
the valley gave way to a steep scree-slope up which we zig-zagged. Stephen set a
slow pace which was easy to follow. In fact, Philip found our pace too slow and
went on ahead with the army, in the shape of three very charming young men
whom we had met on and off since leaving Nairobi. They, lucky chaps, were

paid to climb Mount Kenya, in the name of Adventure Training. After a second scree-slope and a short rocky snowy section which was almost level, we reached Top Hut at 4790m. I had thought this would be our top camp – and for those who would rather rise at 5.30 than 2.30 and still be on Lenana by dawn, it would of course seem preferable. We were given no choice in the matter. I imagine that the guides and porters prefer the lower altitude and greater space of Mackinder's. For us it was also much cheaper, as we could not have camped at Top Hut. We had made such good time that we were too early if we wanted to reach the summit at dawn, so we had a half-hour rest at the hut, trying not to disturb its sleeping inmates.

As it started to get light we set off over rocks which were followed by a gentle snow-slope. Next came a much steeper snow-slope (part of the Lewis glacier) where we followed steps kicked by Stephen, occasionally using a hand to help the balance. The last section was a very short steep scramble over rocks on to a broad rocky summit – Point Lenana (4985m). Sunrise was at 6.30 bringing with it, on this perfectly clear morning, views in all directions which can only be described in clichés. Peaks, valleys and, far below, cloud. There was a wind and it was very cold but I, in my ample clothing including a duvet jacket, could have stayed there for hours just . . . looking (I daren't say 'savouring the view'!). It was wonderful but Stephen, totally inadequately dressed and to whom it was just another day's work, couldn't wait to start down. So, after about 20 minutes' 'savouring' and taking photographs, we set off again. The descent was easy and, though we obviously had to tread carefully on the top part, we went fast and were back at Mackinder's in time for a late breakfast. We could have gone on down to the Met Station but not to Naro Moru, as transport only comes up to the Met in the late mornings and we would have been too late for this; so we pottered at Mackinder's for the rest of that day, reading a bit, sleeping a bit, talking to the camp inmates.

Next morning we were up at 6.30, to a much colder start than at 2.30 the previous day. The tents were so solid with ice that we couldn't pack them properly, so we just draped them on top of the pack-frames. The fine sunny dawn deteriorated into a cool misty morning. It had clearly rained lower down and the Vertical Bog was even boggier than three days earlier. The journey down from Mackinder's to the Met took us 3¼ hours without hurrying or effort, allowing time to stop and look at the spectacular bird-life. Our truck eventually appeared and took us back to the lodge where we basked in the warmth of its mere 1800m as we set up our tents in the perfectly adequate and very reasonably priced camping-field. After our exertions we felt justified in eating at the lodge itself where the food was good, plentiful and fairly cheap, as opposed to the accommodation which was very expensive. Since it was very difficult to be in any way sure if and when a bus might pass the lodge on its way to Nairobi, we opted for a Matatu which is a sort of taxi – with emphasis in every way on the 'sort of'. The driver tried to cram nine people and their luggage into his vehicle, at exorbitant cost. In our opinion this particular quart just would not fit its pint pot, so Philip and Caroline left us to make their own way back to Nairobi. The remaining seven were somehow squeezed in, though the nerves, had they not been toughened by two weeks in Africa, might have become a trifle frayed by the African style of driving which was as exciting and unorthodox as we had been led to believe.

In between the onslaught on our nerves we had time to reflect that we now had answers to all those questions about cost, equipment and what to do when and how. Our week had cost in total, for four of us, exactly the same as the advertised cost for one person that we had seen in an English brochure. If any reader would like more detailed information I have it all, with costs (for 1985). Rather more interestingly, I have a list of all the numerous different birds we saw, and I could easily be persuaded to go into rhapsodies over the vegetation, but not here as I have already exceeded the space I am allowed as a mere layman in this august journal.

(*Editor's Note*: Laymen – and laywomen – who write as well as Ann Venables are allowed as much space as the most accomplished tiger.)

69. *Sir Halford Mackinder (1861–1947). (p 154)*

70. *At de Graaf's Variation, the crux pitch (IV−) of the normal route up Nelion. Climber: Jim Milledge. (p 154)*

71. *Approaching Baillie's Bivi near the crest of the southern arête on the normal route up Nelion. It is probably close to this point that, in 1899, Mackinder and his two Italian companions spent the night in their Mummery tent. (p 154)*

72. *At Mackinder's Camp with Mount Kenya in the background, showing (L to R) Batian (5199m), the Gate of the Mist, Nelion (5188m), Point John (4883m) and Point Lenana (4985m). (pp 154, 162)*

73. *The central peaks of Mount Kenya seen from the S across the Lewis glacier. The normal route up Nelion ascends the face below the southern arête until the arête is reached. (pp 154, 162)*

74.   *Giant groundsel* (senecio) *near Mackinder's Camp.* (p 162)

75. *Ascent of E face of Mount Poi: Ron Corkhill at tree niche belay.* (p 167)

76. *Mount Poi (Kenya), S crack approach.* (p 167)

77. *Looking E: Mawenzi from rim of crater.* (p 175)

78.   *Kilimanjaro from Amboseli.* (p 175)

79. *Mount Speke from the W.* (p 177)

80. *S face of Alexandra from the Stanley Plateau.* (p 177)

81. *Ruwenzori: Bob Knapp in the Bigo Bog.* (p 177)

An Expedition to Mounts Kulal and Poi in Northern Kenya, 1977

BARRIE CHEETHAM

(Plates 75, 76)

It is interesting to note, on reading the 1984 and 1985 *Mountain Club of Kenya Bulletins*, that the traverse of the remote Mount Kulal at the side of Lake Turkana (previously Lake Rudolf) has now been well documented. Furthermore, in 1983, the previously unclimbed E face of Poi, in the Ndoto Mountains nearby, was finally climbed (650m, VI+) by A Wielochowski and R Corkhill.[1]

Ed had been working for three years with the UN at the mission station in this remote part of Kenya. He infrequently visited the MCK club house at Wilson Airport in Nairobi, bringing with him fascinating tales of this remote area.

For myself, Robin and Bob, the prospects of a safari climbing trip to the Northern Region of Kenya was very attractive, as we had climbed almost everywhere else in Kenya that was popular at the time, and we knew of several unclimbed peaks to be 'bagged'.

A Cessna Navajo was hired from my benevolent employers, Kenya Breweries, and we made our plans to leave. The lads were most disgusted when we found that two crates of Tusker Lager had to be jettisoned because of the heavy climbing gear and provisions which filled our tiny seven-seater aircraft.

Our first look at Poi, after two hours' flying-time, was from the air. It was daunting to consider climbing such a remote, large, steep face that pointed tantalizingly skyward at our small Cessna.

We landed at Lolengalani for our last taste of civilization and a cool swim in the crystal-clear pool of the hotel, based at an oasis amidst the volcanic debris of this barren region. A day's visit down to Lake Turkana amongst the Turkana people was well spent, and we feasted on the day's catch of Nile perch and tilapia. Evening fell and the odd Rendile tribesman was seen driving camels back to the kraal as we set off for the hills in our long wheel-based Land-Rover. We passed on and upward through the barren land until we reached the grassy foothills of Kulal with their herds of kudu. We arrived at our rest camp among the lush trees of the mission station at Gatab late in the evening for a welcome shower.

Gatab is situated in the foothills of the Mount Kulal range which runs north and south adjacent to Lake Turkana in this desert region.

We had it on good advice from the mission that no successful traverse of the Mount Kulal ridge had been recorded, and as we had recently learnt of the 'silent lions' which were terrorizing the local Rendile tribesmen in the Ndoto mountains, the Kulal Range seemed a very attractive alternative to start with.

A local tribesman was hired to assist us in finding our way through the rain-forest to the Kulal ridge proper. We then set off alone on our memorable traverse.

The complete traverse of the Kulal ridge must be treated as a very serious undertaking. Technically it is not difficult. Rock climbing on it rarely exceeds Very Difficult standard, and the pitches are all quite short. There are also several abseils, which need not be long.

Very little technical equipment is needed, as the rock is generally not suited for chocks and pitons; trees and shrubs are usually the best belays and runners. The seriousness arises from several sections where long traverses have to be made on steep slopes of very loose soil with extremely steep drops below. The worst section in this respect was the drop down into the Cow Path Col. The dense bush sections were very tedious and unpleasant. Water must be carried, as there is none on or near the ridge.

Situations on the ridge are incredibly beautiful, especially the views towards Lake Turkana and down the great gash of the El Kajarta Gorge. The scenery compensates for the more unpleasant sections of the ridge. There are some sections where the walking is very good; these are either in the beautiful shady forested parts or on the more open northerly end of the ridge.

Access to the ridge is best from Gatab, where there is a well-run mission. The road to Gatab is spectacular; a saloon car with good clearance should get up it. The walk from Gatab to the southern summit takes about four hours and is mainly through very beautiful, shady rain forests. The southern summit provides excellent views over the ridge.

The most memorable incident, on our return after three days, was the sight of four grown men fighting over a single tin of sardines and one packet of biscuits as they tried to negotiate their lost tracks through the forest during late evening. Fortunately, we eventually discovered the marks we had made by our panga on the bark of nearby trees, and these helped us to get home safely.

Beer was a scarce luxury and, from our location high in the Northern Region of Kenya, the nearest brewery was well over 1000km away. Nevertheless, Ed was organized and we had a promise that two teetotal friends of his, who were establishing a work station in the Ndoto mountains, had left a full crate of White Cap Lager 'in the stream' at the side of their Base Camp. This incentive was enough to send us packing the following day and to make the day-long, hot, dusty journey by Land-Rover to the promised land. The terrain between Kulal and the Ndotos is semi-desert scrub, and several snakes were disturbed as we followed the vehicle tracks of the local missionaries.

Word had got back to Nairobi of a pack of man-eating lions which made a habit of plunging through native mud-walls of the kraals to drag away and devour their unsuspecting victims. The walls of a Low and Bonnar canvas tent were not even a match for the mud and thatch dwellings of the tribe.

We arrived in late evening with much trepidation, particularly as the 'Askari' at the camp showed us the remains of a domestic cow which had been half eaten by lions the previous night.

After such a hot, thirsty day in the bush, the White Cap mirage turned into reality as it lay there among cobbles of the gurgling stream. What a luxury!

It couldn't have been planned better! We soon forgot about the marauding lions as the White Caps raised our spirits.

Having slept uneasily we set off at the crack of dawn, led by our 'warrior' tribesman. After several exhausting hours we came upon the E face of Poi as can be seen in the photograph.

The most significant feature of the face, which looked well over 650m high, was the smoothness and lack of protection for the climber. The gas holes inhabited by those rarest of birds, the lammergeyers, were very significant. We realized that several days of hard exposed and unprotected climbing would be necessary, with the prospect of several bivouacs on the way. Unfortunately, we were ill-prepared for such a climb, and as we had the added excuse that Ed had to be back in Nairobi within a few days, we retired to leave this unclimbed peak to the solitude of the lammergeyer.

REFERENCES

1   *Mountain Club of Kenya Bulletin 80*, 26–30, 1983; *82*, 39–40, 1985.
     Maps of Kulal Main Ridge: *MCK Bulletin 81*, following p41, 1984.

Kilimanjaro and its First Ascent
– 6 October 1889

JOHN TEMPLE

It is a huge mountain. The volume of lava erupted over its million years of activity exceeds 4000 cubic kilometres. Dumped on the Home Counties (the southern bias of the AC would necessitate this), it would spread from Reading to Rochester. The summit crater alone would have its eastern rim 5800m above Tower Bridge and the western rim somewhere above South Audley Street, appropriately a few metres higher. It would seem to be the biggest land-based volcanic cone and, until the top 600m or so collapsed forming the summit crater (strictly: caldera), it may well have been the highest.

With side slopes averaging seven degrees, classic Gothic mountain scenery is limited to the Western Breach of Kibo and to the older, more deeply eroded eastern peak Mawenzi, especially its E face. Both have been termed 'The Eiger of Africa'. The summit crater, however, is like nowhere else on earth. A formal pattern of concentric cone/crater structures in sombre blacks and ochres is decorated by the terraced remnants of the ice-fields. Fretted and fluted, glittering silver in the sun or smouldering blue in the shadows, it looks like a moonscape. The sweeping dome of the sky and the absence of any distraction from rival peaks reinforce the sense that you are indeed standing on the edge of space. On a moonless night illusion and reality meld and you can reach out, over the edge, to the stars.

Kilimanjaro is best seen from some distance to the north or south. The graceful sweep of the forested slopes provides a majestic pedestal for the three summit areas. The oldest, imploded Shira to the west is now a plateau rather than a peak. Rugged Mawenzi, to the east, is a shipwreck of a mountain. Between and above them stands the symmetrical cone of Kibo. The whole massif is a balance of contrasting shapes, a scenic unity from the spreading thorn trees on the steppe in the foreground to the ethereal and seemingly inaccessible ice-capped summit.

The shape of the hill and its equatorial position give it a benign character, considering its Himalayan scale. In contrast to neighbouring Mount Kenya, it is a democratic mountain, its summit accessible to all. If you can get to the bottom and pay fees rather steeper than the mountain itself, and can walk uphill for four or five days, you can get to the top. The crowded huts, the sparse oxygen and the execrable scree may make it less than totally enjoyable. The summit – tatty unless the rubbish is hidden by fresh snow – is likely to be reached with relief rather than euphoria. But the mountain will not have tried to kill you.

Wilful negligence on a suicidal scale is needed to make Kilimanjaro even averagely dangerous. The greatest hazard Meyer faced once he was climbing was that of falling into a well-concealed eight-metre-deep elephant trap.

Homicidal leopards have been reported in the forest (as well as the freeze-dried specimen found on the crater rim). A lone hippy did die of exposure in the Western Breach but he had set out alone, ignorant of the route and apparently with only a few oranges as supplies. Serious climbing is available – Messner is reported as saying that his ascent of the Breach Wall Icicle was the most dangerous thing he had done. And Barber and Taylor had an epic accident on that route, but their trip could be re-run as a soap opera – a kind of 'Dallas on Ice'.

Kilimanjaro lacks the vindictive bad weather of serious mountains. Go up in March or in one of the other rainy-season months if you must have your mountains wet, but even then you could be disappointed; the upper slopes get less precipitation in a year than some parts of the Sahara.

The lower slopes get a couple of metres of rain a year. For the people of the area, Chagga on the southern side and Masai to the drier north, Kilimanjaro acts like a great water tower, storing and supplying a huge oasis as fertile as the surrounding steppes are barren. The Masai in their prime – before they were wasted by disease and expropriation, shackled by Pax Britannica and, ultimate indignity, subjected to the 'democratic' control of the more numerous tribes – had an uncompromising way with visitors. Convinced that their way of life was the best of all possible ways, they were not to be seduced from prehistory to the 19th century. They neither feared nor coveted its gadgets. Happy to steal from caravans, they had little interest in trade, valuing their cattle more highly than trinkets. Well-armed caravans kept clear of their side of the mountain. The Chagga, in contrast, were deeply involved in trade – the East Coast slave trade. With their numbers and mountain stronghold they should have been safe; but the rivers which cut deep dividing valleys helped to produce a political geography of 20 or so clans, each in a state of hostility towards its neighbours. Travellers could be a source of weapons and might even be recruited as allies. Meanwhile, if they could be detained, they could be milked.

In 1848 Johannes Rebmann was the first European to report the snow-capped mountain, 3°S. The Chagga he questioned revealed that attempts to collect the 'silver' from the mountain failed because it turned to water when it was carried down in a container. Considerable scepticism was expressed, especially by an Irish 'armchair' geographer, Cooley. He had made a reputation refuting other travellers' tales and, provoked perhaps by the gross under-estimate of Kibo's height (3800m), he was positively abrasive in his disbelief of the missionary. Indeed, it seems that he had a 'passage at arms' with the next European visitor, Baron von der Decken, over the latter's report of an overnight snowstorm at 4300m in 1862.

The next would-be conqueror of Kibo was the English missionary New, in 1871. His problems were with the wily one-eyed Chagga chief, Mandara. It is fitting that Mandara's name was given to the former Bismarck hut when it was expropriated by the Tanzanian Government and the fees for its use vastly inflated. Mandara was delighted to have visitors. He would provide a camp-site near his village. Gifts would be exchanged and Mandara would affect dissatisfaction in sulk or rage. More gifts would appease him. Trade in fresh food would resume. Mandara would pay his visitor a call and inspect or rather mentally catalogue property not well hidden and ask for anything that took his fancy. Refusal produced rage and a crisis. Food trade ceased. Arrogant spearmen would jostle and intimidate the porters. The water supply, an irrigation leat sourced in a distant deep ravine, would be diverted. The traveller could trim or cut and run. If he looked serious about leaving, Mandara compromised.

New eventually got Mandara's permission to start up the mountain, but found that his own men were largely psyched out by Chagga horror stories and few would go with him. The Chagga guides regarded the journey as a chance to do some private-enterprise slaving and it must surely be a unique record for a missionary's mountaineering expedition that a woman was enslaved, though but briefly. New did reach the snow-line, but his second expedition in 1873 was a total disaster. Mandara, bolder, robbed him of everything but his life, and that he lost on the way back to the coast.

Johnston, in 1884, spent six months in the area on a mainly scientific expedition sponsored by the British Association and the Royal Geographical Society. Mandara effectively obstructed his efforts to get up the mountain and Meyer is distinctly sceptical of his claim to have reached over 4900m. Johnston's expedition does mark the intrusion of imperialism as the Scramble for Africa speeded up. Kilimanjaro was briefly involved, as it was located in the disputed zone where the German and British spheres of influence overlapped, like badly fitted carpet.

Mandara distinguished himself by concluding treaties recognizing the suzerainty, first of the British-backed Sultan of Zanzibar and then, a few weeks later, that of the Germans who promised greater rewards. The eventual acceptance of this by the British reflected perceived gains elsewhere in the wider diplomatic game. That the mountain was not a gift from Queen Victoria to Kaiser Wilhelm seems to be an established fact. The job of journalists then and since has been to process the news and the myth persists. I quote an example from *East Africa* by Read: 'The division of British from German East Africa was, with one exception, drawn along a ruler edge . . . That exception was Kilimanjaro . . . It may or may not be true but it is at least *ben trovato* that the youthful Kaiser Wilhelm, when staying at Osborne, took the map of East Africa and tearfully entreated Queen Victoria thus: "Oh please, Grandma, do let me keep that big mountain." '

Sportsmen explorers such as the Hungarian Count Teleki visited the area; he reached 5300m. When he met the inbound Meyer in 1887, he was able to give him up-to-date advice. Meyer was already well prepared; he had climbed in the Alps and the Himalaya and had travelled extensively in tropical Asia and Central America. Also he was powerfully motivated. As a geoscientist he had an academic interest; his patriotism urged him to promote German imperial interests which the authorities seemed to be neglecting; the publicity that a successful ascent would bring would be gratifying; but, above all, he was going for the adventure. His addiction to safari life shows through, and he certainly gives the impression of being more at home travelling than on what was surely very straightforward ice-climbing. Without any obvious technical problems Kibo must have seemed like a ripe plum, a happy combination of duty and pleasure. 'Kilimanjaro,' he wrote, 'was discovered by a German . . . , it was first explored by a German . . . , it seemed to me to be almost a national duty that a German should be the first to tread the summit . . . certainly the highest in the German Empire.'

Meyer did, however, have to take three bites, and he admits to an obsessive hunger as his appetite was sharpened by failure. His first expedition of 1887 went very well up to 4300m, where his companion gave up with mountain sickness. Meyer went on, reaching the edge of the ice-cap at 5400m. An ice wall, typical of the mountain, barred his way. Alone and without ice gear he retreated, confident that he had found the solution to the problems of getting to and getting up Kilimanjaro.

He immediately organized a second expedition. As the conquest seemed rather a formality other objectives were included, involving the exploration of mountain areas as far inland as the Ruwenzori. A commercial caravan was engaged to place a depot of supplies near Lake Victoria. An army of 230 porters left Tanga and, while most of them slowly followed the caravan route, Meyer went to explore the delightful Usambara range.

His caravan was not at the rendezvous. Without proper leadership, it had been sent back and disbanded as the coastal people rose in armed revolt against the Germans. Meyer went in pursuit to try to salvage his expedition but was 'overpowered, maltreated and loaded with chains until eventually I was able to purchase our freedom by the payment of a heavy ransom'.

Relieved to escape with his life, he immediately started to organize the third expedition. He recruited the outstanding Austrian amateur mountaineer Ludwig Purtscheller as companion, generously but justly giving him credit for his major contribution to their success. When some of their baggage went on to India in error, depriving them of their tents and some climbing equipment, he was able to have replacements made in Zanzibar, except for his crampons. Through the good offices of the British commander in Zanzibar, he was able to circumvent the ban on gun imports and get a lift on a gunboat to Mombasa.

Meyer craftily nursed his caravan for the first few stages, until it was far enough into the wilderness to discourage desertion; then he drove it forward quickly. He based himself briefly at Mandara's court where his gifts bought a few days' goodwill, but he soon relocated his party further east with an old friend, Chief Mareale, at Marangu.

He adopted the classic siege tactics of Base Camp, Advanced Base, Camp 1, etc, to ensure the regular supply of food to the Saddle between Kibo and Mawenzi. The first assault, on 3 October 1889, had probably not allowed enough time for acclimatization. Despite a 2.30am start, it was 10am before they got on to the ice. Some of their impetus had been lost in a route error. There are hints of disagreements as to the best line. Meyer favoured a direct line towards the summit, but the more experienced Purtscheller appears to have preferred a route which avoided height loss by keeping to a curving ridge on the NW side of the SE valley. In the event, at least an hour was lost descending into and across the SE valley. The only technical problem was a steep bulge of ice up which Purtscheller, happily in possession of crampons, cut steps to reach the fissured surface of the Ratzel glacier. The crater rim, at 5870m (Meyer's estimates are understandably inflated by about 120m), was reached at 1.30pm. The summit was 150m higher and 1500m away. Their hunger for success was blunted by altitude sickness and the prospect of a bivouac, so they retreated, consoled to be the first to see the summit crater, and they got back to camp after dark, very weary with headaches, slight snow-blindness and considerable sunburn. Their experiences have been unwittingly re-enacted by thousands since who reach the crater rim and give up.

Recuperating next day, they set out at noon on 5 October, making for a bivouac in the SE valley at about 4600m. After a 3am start on the 6th, in welcome moonlight, dawn found them shivering with cold at the edge of the ice. When the sun rose behind Mawenzi they resumed, relieved to find their steps still serviceable. By 9am they were at their previous high point and at half-past ten, 'I was the first to set foot on the culminating peak . . . Taking out a small German flag . . . I planted it on the weather-beaten lava summit . . . and in virtue of my right as its first discoverer christened this hitherto unknown and unnamed mountain peak – the loftiest spot in Africa and in the German Empire – *Kaiser Wilhelm's Peak.*'

Snow on the Equator

A memory of Kilimanjaro

CHARLES WARREN

(Plates 64, 77, 78)

Not quite on the equator, like Mount Kenya, Kilimanjaro is nearly there and is incomparably the highest mountain, with snow on it, near the equator, in Africa. From the mountaineering point of view it is by no means difficult to climb. Yet it is very high; and for that reason alone it poses problems for many aspiring ascensionists through mountain sickness.

We (William Spiers, Douglas Scott and I) made the ascent from the Kenya side in 1966 and, my word, what an entirely delightful experience it was. A last-minute dash to climb the highest mountain in Africa while still within reach of it. We were very fit at the time, having just come off Mount Kenya.

Seen from the plains of the Amboseli game reserve to the north, with the big game just wandering about in the foreground, what a splendid backcloth to the scene the great mountain makes. There is nothing really quite like it in the world. It is impossible to realize how high it actually is until you sit and tell yourself that that band of cloud is only half-way up.

Our launching-pad for the ascent was Loitokitok where we were hospitably put up, entertained and helped with advice as to how to get a pass through the forest on to the mountain by the Outward Bound establishment there.

How nice they all were. We were invited to watch one of their character-training exercises which now – looking back on it in old age – I can't help finding faintly ridiculous. However, I must admit that most of the young men seemed to be enjoying it all. But surely they must have been really glad to get up on to the great mountain itself!

Water is a problem on Kilimanjaro; it has to be carried up from low down. We had two porters and a boy who helped to take us up through the forest; and then up over the dried-up moorland to Kibo hut, where they left us.

How marvellous was the walk up through the forest zone. No game seen; but elephant spore everywhere. And birds chattering in the trees all around us. On Kilimanjaro there was no frightening bamboo zone to go through, as there was on Mount Kenya. So we reached with ease that marvellous bivouac cave, beneath a great sheet of volcanic rock, just above the forest zone. Surely the most comfortable bivouac site in the world! From here we had to go some hundreds of yards to get water from a spring and stock up for the next two days. And then, to bed; leaving the mountain pink in the sunset glow.

The next day we arose from our perfect bivouac cave to find Kilimanjaro white with newly fallen snow right down its slopes to the foot of the volcanic cone, but in bright sunlight.

Having packed up, we all then set forth for Kibo hut, a trek over an extensive volcanic moorland but one greatly enhanced by the beauty of the everlasting flowers. Arrived there at last, we let our porters go and were then on our own.

Kibo hut was a miserable place. After a short, cold night, we arose before dawn, having put on all our spare clothing. Then we stamped our way up the interminable but blessedly frozen scree slopes to the rim of the crater at Gillman's Point, having watched the sunrise above a sea of cloud below Mawenzi. Thence, in the warm sunshine, we walked the next mile or two round the rim of the crater to the highest point.

The summit of Kilimanjaro is not, scenically, a very inspiring place, but it is fascinating because you are above the world and because the glacial formations at the edges of the volcano's crater are so strange. It is marked by a plaque to commemorate the political event of *Uhuru*, which spoils the scene unnecessarily. It is a flat shaly platform. Here, in the sun, we lay for an hour or two above the clouds and remote from the world below. 'Alone on a wide wide sea.'

The crater of the great volcano is not of much interest apart from its curious serac formations, like *nieves penitentes*. But the mountain is still alive. Tilman descended amongst the seracs and moraine heaps there where he found hot holes. So the old mountain still only sleeps. But the great glaciers which flow from the rim of this volcano, almost on the equator, for thousands of feet are of much technical interest to mountaineers.

The journey back from the mountain and down through the wonderful forests to Loitokitok was uneventful. We had climbed our mountain; not a difficult one. And we had had it entirely to ourselves – something which it is almost impossible to achieve in these days of commercial tourism. So that is why I have written this piece.

Our party had now returned to Kenya, whence Spiers and I left for home, leaving Douglas Scott, a professional photographer, camped alone in the Amboseli game reserve to take photographs of big game. And perhaps to be eaten by lions!

I believe that this ascent of a great mountain possibly gave me more pleasure than most things in my mountaineering career, even those in the Himalaya. But what was it that I liked so much about it? Well, it was the mountain's isolation in the heart of a continent. To find Kilimanjaro, 'Snow on the Equator', way out in Central Africa, is a unique experience even for a sophisticated mountaineer, unless he has no romance in his soul.

Ten Days in the Ruwenzori

JOHN NIXON

(Plates 66, 79–81)

Entebbe presented an eerie and sur-
real scene in the early hours of 22 December 1987, as Bob and I disembarked
from the long-overdue Ugandan airliner. Dark shapes were waving from the
balcony of the airport terminal in the distance, across the dimly-lit tarmac, and I
could hear Jeff's welcoming cheers carrying clearly in the still, humid night air.
We struggled towards Customs and Immigration, dreading the impending
interrogation as to why we were each carrying 15 kilograms of climbing gear in
our cabin luggage, as well as monstrous rucksacks stuffed full of strange and
incomprehensible items of equipment. Inside the building, the drab arrival hall
was buzzing with the sound of anxious passengers negotiating their path
through numerous desks controlled by surly officials who would stamp papers
grudgingly and only after superfluous questioning. The noise of human activity
was accompanied by a resident insect chorus which seemed to build to a
crescendo as if anticipating the apprehension and nervousness of the travellers
in the last stages of their bureaucratic journey. There were tense moments as
Bob and I were separated from the main group of arrivals and ushered sinisterly
into an office where we were questioned about our medical documentation.
After discussion and threats of new injections, we were released, but only when
a few dollars had been paid for 'administrative costs'.

When we finally emerged from Customs, a little shaken from the
experience, Jeff greeted us with a broad grin and 'Welcome to Uganda!' After
much back-slapping and vigorous shaking of hands we were ushered to his
company car where his driver, Moses, comically awoke with a start when Jeff
rapped sharply on the roof of the vehicle. 'There are a couple of roadblocks on
the way into Kampala,' said Jeff cheerfully, 'so we'll drive back in convoy.' Not
far from the airport we were stopped at the first roadblock and ordered out of
the car. Young, over-zealous soldiers carried out a thorough search of our
vehicle and the equipment which we had to explain patiently, particularly the
ice-axes. Their enthusiastic examination was no doubt encouraged by the
proximity of the President's residence. There was a commotion at the car in
front when a resident tea-planter refused to allow the soldiers to extricate his
elderly parents from his vehicle, pointing out that they were both in their
eighties, and that the father was blind. The European used an impressive,
authoritative manner, carefully measured in order to convince the soldiers that
it would be more trouble than it was worth to upset the *wzungu*. It was a fine
balance and events could easily have turned very nasty, but the tea-planter and
his family were reluctantly waved through. Our small procession of cars rolled
on to the next checkpoint where there was less obstruction.

As we approached the capital my first impressions of the night-time city

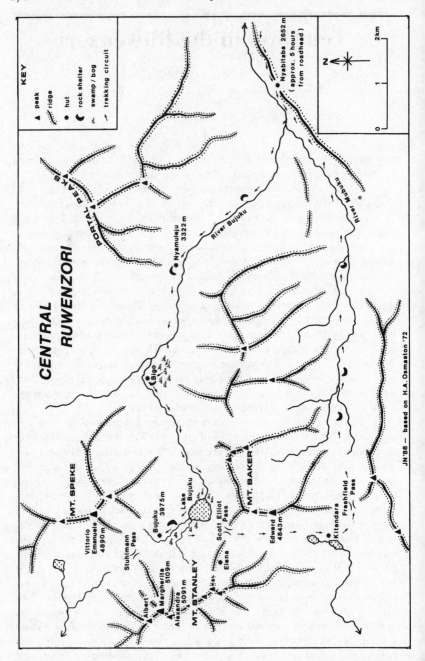

KEY

▲ peak
   ridge
★ hut
☽ rock shelter
☽ swamp / bog
⌁ trekking circuit

N

0   1   2km

*CENTRAL
RUWENZORI*

PORTAL PEAKS

Nyabitaba 2652 m
(approx. 5 hours
from roadhead)

River Mubuku

River Bujuku

★ Nyamuleju 3322 m

★ Bigo

MT. SPEKE

Vittorio
Emanuele
4890 m

Bujuku
3975m

Lake
Bujuku

Stuhlmann
Pass

Albert
Margherita
5109 m

Alexandra
5091 m

MT. STANLEY

Elena

Scott Elliot
Pass

MT. BAKER

Edward
4843 m

Kitandara

Freshfield
Pass

JN'88 — based on H.A.Osmaston '72

were of a beautiful location nestling amongst low hills. Daytime Kampala, however, turned out to be a reflection of the country's troubled past and present, with a dowdy, run-down atmosphere amongst the bustling, dusty streets full of empty shops. We finally arrived at Jeff's apartment at 4am, three days after having left our homes in England, and after a catalogue of frustrating delays. I was beginning to question the wisdom of a climbing expedition to the Ruwenzori mountains of Central Africa. My doubts were further fuelled by Jeff's announcement of an acute petrol shortage due to the border conflict with Kenya, and news of rebel insurgency in the north-west of Uganda, suspiciously close to where we were planning to climb. Jeff, who had become known as 'Our Man in Kampala', is an irrepressible, danger-loving character, and his vibrant enthusiasm had played a vital role in all our previous expeditions. On this occasion, though, I was starting to feel that he was living up to his Graham Greene counterpart by having been a little economical with the truth in his letters about the prevailing political stability. It had been, he solemnly assured us, far worse when he first arrived, and our minor inconveniences so far – and any recent trouble we might have read about – were insignificant in comparison with the excesses of previous regimes. The thought of roadblocks and searches by soldiers under Amin or Obote was indeed frightening.

The decision to climb in the Ruwenzori mountains was prompted partly by Jeff's residence in Uganda, and also by the appeal of a remote area with a difficult approach and its own unique mystical charm. The 'Mountains of the Moon', as they are romantically called, rise in a number of glaciated massifs from steamy rain-forests on the Uganda/Zaire border. For most of the year the peaks are shrouded in mist, and there are heavy rains which collect and feed the headwaters of the River Nile. During late December and early January, however, there is usually a short respite in the downpour and we were hoping for a couple of weeks of dry weather. It was with some surprise that Stanley sighted these snow-capped mountains, so close to the equator, in 1876. 30 years later, in 1906, the Duke of the Abruzzi led a large expedition to the range and managed to climb all the major summits. The region has been popular for exploration, trekking and climbing, but there have been fewer visitors since the political troubles of the early 1970s.

Two days after our arrival in Uganda we were at the roadhead of Nyakalengija, preparing for our trek into the mountains. I was pleasantly surprised to find how easily things had gone. In Kampala, Jeff was able to obtain enough fuel for our trip, despite the shortage, by mysterious means which he referred to as *magendo*. He even had a letter of permission from the Minister of Energy to carry extra fuel so as to avoid arrest at roadblocks, should the soldiers find our jerrycans. A Kampala-based friend of Jeff's, who owned a suitable short-wheelbased vehicle and was also a keen climber, had been recruited to join our team, so that we were four in number. The friend was also called Bob and, as he was nearing the grand old age of 40 (although he turned out to be the fittest member of the group), we decided to call him 'Musee Bob' (or 'Old Man Bob').

The road westwards from Kampala had long, straight sections cut through the rain-forest, and we made reasonable time. The further we travelled

MOUNT STANLEY - FROM THE EAST

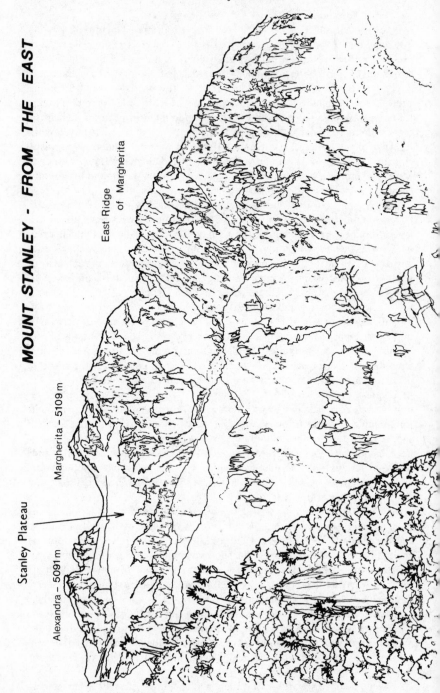

Stanley Plateau

Alexandra – 5091 m

Margherita – 5109 m

East Ridge
of Margherita

from the capital, however, the more the road deteriorated. A combination of neglect, heavy lorry traffic and seasonal rains had resulted in stretches of road with large potholes and craters which drastically reduced the speed of travel. There was much activity along the road, and the ubiquitous banana crop was being transported either by creaking, ancient bicycles, or in perfect balance on the tops of peoples' heads, or by heavily laden, listing trucks with gangs of grinning men perched precariously on top. Occasionally a brightly-coloured *matatu*, or minibus taxi, would impatiently overtake us and speed past, full of bouncing, worried passengers. At each village we passed through, groups of naked, cheering children with swollen bellies would run to the roadside and shout their friendly greeting, 'Jambo, Wzungu!' After eight hours we reached Fort Portal, a moderately-sized town, and sought refuge in the only apparent hotel. Inside we rested in low chairs under the cooling draught of whirling fans, beneath the smiling, benign picture of the current President which would doubtless be hastily replaced should there be a *coup*. From the courtyard came the distinctive guitar sounds and rhythm of Central African music.

At Ibanda we were able to hire seven porters at favourable fixed rates with the help of John Matte, guardian of the once-active Mountain Club of Uganda. He is a friendly man, with dark features softened by greying hair and a wide toothless grin. We were able to leave our vehicle with him, parked behind his ramshackle office.

We set off with our porters and sacks of equipment just after midday and foolishly, perhaps through pride, we elected to carry heavy rucksacks weighing about 25kg. In the open fields close to the village the sun's rays beat down mercilessly, but even in the shade of the tall elephant grass and then in the *Podocarpus* forest there was no relief, as the transpiration from the vegetation produced a high, stifling humidity. It felt as if I was walking in a sauna, and after a few hours I could feel my strength ebbing fast. The final section of the first day's trek is a long, uniformly steep slope along a ridge crest to the Nyabitaba hut. Both Jeff and I found this section to be purgatory and we finally dragged ourselves up to the hut at 6.30pm, long after the others, and very exhausted. We were revived with mugs of coffee which we thankfully sipped as we gazed at the magnificent evening view of the Portal Peaks opposite our ridge.

The next day was Christmas Day and we gaped with incredulity as Bob ceremoniously produced a smartly-wrapped package from his rucksack and proceeded to open a number of small presents. A half-bottle of whisky received an appreciative response from the rest of us, although we hoped that we would have no need for the next present, a tube of ointment for piles!

After a hurried breakfast, Jeff and I set off first, descending through tall bamboo to the confluence of the Bujuku and Mubuku rivers. There is no longer a bridge at this point and, when the rest of the team arrived, we carefully waded across the rapids to the N bank. Not far from here Musee Bob was struck down with a bout of nausea and we waited for a couple of hours until he was able to continue. Our rest enabled us to talk and joke with the porters and to get to know them better. They were a friendly, cheerful bunch, dressed in ragged, patched clothing; most of them spoke a little English. A character called Cornelius, however, assumed the role of interpreter and also established himself as shop steward. He described the poverty that they all lived in and was clearly pushing for higher wages. Although Cornelius was perhaps the most educated of the porters, he was certainly also the most gullible. The others – and particularly the headman, Baluku George – quickly realized that we were forever pulling Cornelius's leg. Jeff imaginatively announced that he would be dining with the President of Uganda when he returned from the mountains and would be reporting on the efficiency of the porters in the Ruwenzori. At this, Cornelius swiftly shouldered his load and set off at quite a pace to show how keen he was, amid giggles from the rest of the porters.

We continued through a dense jungle of *Mimulopsis*, where the porters would occasionally resort to hacking a better passage with a large machete, or *panga*. Towering over us were the umbrella-crowns of large trees, and we were greeted by the wild chattering of a troupe of monkeys. There were also giant tree-heathers, some over 10 metres high and draped in curtains of lichen. Nyamuleju, our overnight accommodation, in fact means 'Place of Beards' and consists of a rather dilapidated hut and a remarkable natural rock shelter, one of many which abound in the area.

Our third and final day's march to a base at Bujuku led us through more open terrain towards the infamous Bigo Bog. I was secretly dreading this part of the trek as I had read stories of waist-deep glutinous slime with squirming giant earthworms over half a metre long. However, the bog was a little drier than usual and, although unpleasant, was only knee-deep. There are two levels to the Bigo Bog before a final marshy area beside Lake Bujuku leads to the Bujuku hut. Throughout this zone there are fantastic giant varieties of vegetation, such as groundsel and lobelia, with tall hollow spikes up to eight metres high. The reason for such colossal plant forms is a combination of high rainfall and humidity, moderate temperatures and rich, peaty soils. There are in fact two huts at Bujuku, one usually used by the porters, guarded by an army of silent tree groundsel like grotesque triffids on parade, some up to five metres high. From here there is a spendid view of Mount Stanley and Mount Baker. Upon arrival, we paid four of the porters and handed them a good bonus; they seemed well-pleased, warmly shook our hands and wished us luck with our climbing. We decided to keep George, Cornelius and a porter called Alfred at Bujuku so that they could help carry gear over to Kitandara in a few days' time.

Stirrings in the hut at 5am, 28 December, awoke me from pleasant dreams. Dark figures were shambling about in the gloom attempting to pack rucksacks and prepare breakfast. A candle was lit and ghostly shadows danced across the walls and roof of our temporary home, accompanied by primeval grunts as my companions struggled with boots and gaiters. I closed my eyes, hoping that it was all a bad dream, but to no avail. Chances of breakfast in bed were extremely slim and the mental struggle to convince my body to leave the warmth and security of my sleeping-bag had to begin. A petrol stove was happily purring away, its sound remarkably resembling a 'doodlebug' bomb. If, for any reason, the noise had ceased, I'm sure we would have dived for cover.

I wearily went through the motions of preparation like an automaton, declining conversation and brooding over the merits of an early start. A steaming mug of tea was thrust into my hand and I was awarded a brief release from reality as the fluid warmed my inner self and the condensation produced a localized fog which obscured my immediate surroundings.

We emerged from the hut just before 6am into the pre-dawn darkness, and eased our rucksacks on to aching and bruised shoulders. Limbs were stiff from the previous day when all four of us had ascended the Shipton/Tilman route of 1932 to the summit of Vittorio Emanuele (4890m), the highest point of Mount Speke. The climb was relatively easy, consisting of scrambling and a short ice-field which led to the summit ridge, and the exertions had provided an opportunity to begin to acclimatize to the higher altitude. Now, however, we were stumbling down a rough path, past Cooking Pot Cave sheltering snoring porters, on our way to attempt the E ridge of Margherita (5109m), the highest summit of Mount Stanley and the Ruwenzori range.

As we crossed the Bujuku stream and headed westwards towards the bulky massif of Mount Stanley, we encountered a very boggy area which required an exhausting series of leaps from one tussock of dry coarse grass to another. The ground became drier as the gradient sharply increased on the mountain flank, and our route became less obvious as we threaded our way through a vast stand of giant groundsel. The two Bobs forged ahead while Jeff and I struggled and staggered through the increasingly tangled vegetation, pulling ourselves up the steep slope by using branches from the thicket of helichrysum and heather, and easing carefully past the top-heavy, swaying groundsel.

Four hours after our start we reached the Irene Lakes hut, situated on a flat rocky area above the dense vegetation zone. Musee Bob had already pushed on higher and was sending rocks clattering down a stony gully leading to the crest of the long rocky E ridge which descends from the icy summit of Margherita. Jeff and Bob, however, were suffering from headaches and nausea caused by the altitude and decided to return to base, hoping to attempt the mountain at a more leisurely pace over the next few days. I had no choice but to continue and made a lung-bursting effort in order to catch up with Musee Bob.

At first the ridge presented long sections of pleasant, airy scrambling until a steeper rock step was reached. After a few rope-lengths of good climbing on sound rock, the angle eased once more and mixed ground led up to the summit cornice. Crampons were fitted and we moved awkwardly with our clumsy footwear screeching on icy rock. The cornice was fearsome, a gigantic frozen wave draped with rime, and we had to climb through massive hanging icicles like the jaws of a monstrous Venus Flytrap. We managed to exit to the right and a short steep ice pitch brought us close to the summit. At the top we ceremoniously shook hands and Musee Bob attempted to cure his rasping cough with a couple of cigarettes. The wind was blowing mist across the summit, but as we rested there were clearings which gave us tremendous views of the whole range. We were slightly higher than the neighbouring peaks Albert and Alexandra, and to the east and south-east were the majestic Mount Speke and Mount Baker. Down to the west we could see the startling emerald-green colour of Lac Vert at the foot of the face of Margherita, and beyond were the forests of Zaire.

After half an hour on the top we descended the ice wall on the S side of our mountain, carefully threading our way through a couple of crevasses and down on to the extensive Stanley Plateau. Although the ground is reasonably flat, the walk across the plateau was tiring as there was fresh snow on the glacier. Eventually we climbed down the steep glacier margin to reach the small Elena huts where we were greeted by Clive Ward, a visiting Briton, who handed us a welcome mug of tea. With some advice on the descent from Clive, we decided to push on down to Bujuku rather than spend an uncomfortable night at Elena. I began to regret this decision as I was desperately tired and forever slipping and falling over on the boggy path in the base of Groundsel Gully. In the fading light Musee Bob went on ahead, while I sat down to rest a little. 30 minutes later I awoke with the ominous feeling that I was being watched by the sinister groundsel and I quickly continued my journey, spurred on by my imaginary observers. I finally stumbled into the Bujuku hut at about 8pm, much to the relief of the others who were about to set out to search for me – or so they said! Despite my fatigue, however, I was elated at having traversed the highest peak of the Ruwenzori with Musee Bob in one day, and I certainly slept well that night.

After a well-deserved rest day, Musee Bob and I returned to the Stanley Plateau and made an ascent of Margherita's slightly lower sister peak, Alexandra (5091m), by the SE ridge. Meanwhile, Bob and Jeff successfully completed the E ridge of Margherita, and we all met that evening at the Elena hut. A day later, on 31 December, we followed a rocky path down to the Scott Elliot Pass from where a delightful track led down, under the impressive rock-wall on the W face of Mount Baker, to the beautifully sited Kitandara hut. Although it was New Year's Eve we all retired early in anticipation of an early start for our final objective, the S ridge of Edward (4843m), the highest point of Mount Baker.

Next morning we were away by 7am and found it hard going up the steep muddy track to the Freshfield Pass. From the col our route followed an extensive broken rock ridge which led up into mist and cloud. The climbing was absorbing but easy enough to solo, and, after crossing an ice-field, we picked our way along rubble-littered ledges and short rock walls to the windswept summit. Our team had now climbed the four highest summits in the Ruwenzori, mainly thanks to a spell of good weather, but as we descended from Mount Baker and prepared for our two-day return trek, it was obvious that the weather had broken and that true Ruwenzori conditions of mist, sleet and rain were returning.

We celebrated Musee Bob's 40th birthday on the veranda of Mweya Lodge in the Queen Elizabeth National Park. A hippo was grazing the lawn 10 feet away, and a herd of elephants had come down to the lake edge. Despite the political upheavals, Uganda is a beautiful and unique place in which to trek and climb.

The Land Below the Wind

ERIC WARBURG

(Plates 65, 82, 83)

Sabah, at the northern tip of Borneo, means 'The Land below the Wind' in the local language. It is just celebrating 25 years of its independence, acquired at the same time as Sarawak when both joined the federated states of Malaysia.

Prior to that Sabah has appeared on occasional pages of history, recording a visit by Ferdinand Magellan's fleet as early as 1521 and the establishment of a post by the East India Company in 1763; this was subsequently attacked by Sulu pirates and abandoned. The British flag was again hoisted at Labuan, an island off the West Coast, when the Sultan of Brunei ceded it to Britain in 1845. Some years later he ceded the West Coast of Borneo to the 'American Trading Company' which established a colony at Kimanis called 'Ellena', but this did not prosper and was abandoned. Eventually, in 1881, the 'British North Borneo Chartered Company' was formed and one of the directors of this company, Sir Charles Jessel, gave his name to the capital, Jesselton, now renamed Kota Kinabalu. The town was occupied by the Japanese in January 1942 and, as a Japanese base, it was heavily bombed by the Allied Forces and almost totally destroyed. After its liberation in September 1945 it became the capital of the British Crown Colony of North Borneo, which included Labuan Island.

Today it is a thriving little town of some 220,000 people, with its own high-rise buildings, a modern airport with international flights to eight other centres and a seaport which is visited by international cruise-ships from all over the world. From London it is reached by a 22-hour flight, with a change either in Singapore or in Kuala Lumpur.

Borneo itself, covering 72,500 sq km, is the third largest island in the world. The territory of Sabah is 70% jungle, and timber is one of the main industries. Its economy is otherwise basically agrarian. The population of 1.3 million covers over 31 ethnic groups and over 80 different languages or dialects. The largest group are the Kadazans, who are also called Dusuns, and who used to be headhunters; their trophies are still to be seen hanging from the rafters of their longhouses. Today their main activity is farming, rice-planting being most important. This can be 'supplemented' by fermenting the rice into a fiery liquid called 'tafai', served on all occasions which call for a celebration. Another large group are the Bojaus, who used to be a sea-roving people, but who have also gravitated to farming and rearing buffaloes and ponies. They are largely responsible too for promoting Sabah's pony-racing which takes place at the weekends.

The Chinese are known to have had trade and diplomatic dealings with Brunei since 600AD, and archaeologists have found evidence of their settlements on the island near Kota Belud. Arab traders from Sumatra and Malacca also came to Borneo in the 14th century. Today the Chinese form the largest non-native group in the state, having started to immigrate more or less since the British opened up the territory. They are the shopkeepers, the office workers and the professionals, recognized for their business acumen. Whilst Sabah was known by travellers from faraway lands in the 18th and 19th centuries as the 'island of plenty', modern day economics are starting to catch up, and in the search for new sources of income a big effort is being made to build up the tourist industry. It is ideally suited for this in many ways. The daily average temperature is 30°C, dropping to 25°C at night, and in the highland interior there is a variation between 28°C during the day and 18°C at night.

With two luxury hotels, the Hyatt Kinabalu International and the Tanjung Aru Beach, the bodily comfort of the traditionally pampered tourist is catered for. The miles of sandy beaches and coral reefs open up all the usual water-sports possibilities, with one outstanding diving 'secret' at Sipahan Island, where scuba divers can descend up to 600m within a few metres of the shore. Whitewater rafting down the Papar river has just been introduced and is a natural fun experience which will undoubtedly grow in popularity. Interests obviously vary from one individual to another, and I myself had always had the hope of climbing Mount Kinabalu which at 4101m is the highest mountain in South-East Asia. Set in the 724sqkm Kinabalu Park, 80km from Kota Kinabalu, which is rich in vegetation and a centre for the typical and varied flora and fauna of Sabah, this huge chunk of granite was pushed up through the earth's crust some one million years ago and then eroded by glaciers and heavy rains. It offers the trekker a superb climb.

The interpretation of the name 'Kinabalu' has been the subject of much ingenuity in the theories of various writers. One suggestion was that the summit had a mythical lake, guarded by a dragon. As numerous Chinese came to an untimely end up there, the Dusun words *Kina*, meaning 'Chinese', and *Balu*, meaning 'widow', gave it the name of 'The Chinese Widow'. The accepted meaning today, however, is 'The Revered Place of the Dead', denoting a resting place for the spirits of the Dusun dead. Indeed, until comparatively recently one was only allowed up if accompanied by a priest who had to offer propitiation to the spirits (on one's behalf and at one's own expense) in the form of the sacrifice of five chickens and five eggs. Today tourists usually climb the mountain in two days, with a two-to-three-hour ascent on the first evening for the overnight stay in the Panar Laban hut. They then rise at 2am, complete the three-hour climb to the summit in time to witness the sunrise and then return to the base.

This was the scene in September of the 'First International Climbathon '88', a promotion by Malaysian Airlines, the Sabah Tourism Promotion Corporation and the Sabah Parks Trustees, who sponsored an all-comers competition to climb the mountain – of course, it was to be a 'straight up-and-down'.

Numbering some 244 competitors, with 27 from abroad, we all gathered in Kota Kinabalu and were bussed out to Kinabalu Park the evening before. Rising at 4.30am, we breakfasted and set off for the starting point at 1830m, again by bus, and were flagged off by the Minister for the Environment at 6am sharp, the ladies starting 15 minutes later.

As a senior citizen myself I just watched in awe as the confirmed joggers sped out of sight, and I was soon overhauled by the jogging ladies. The first objective was the Panar Laban hut at 3353m, which male competitors had to reach in three hours and ladies in four in order to justify their entry in the competition and thus to qualify for the prizes. My great worry was that the times of the various sectors which I had noted at the park entrance, which were of course designed for the normal tourist, gave a combined time of six hours to the point which I was supposed to cover in three! I therefore had to keep going at a rate considerably enhanced over that to which I am accustomed, and that took a lot out of me. My wife overhauled me after one hour, and to our relief we reached our reporting point in 2½ hours. The lower part of the course was through thick jungle, up an incredibly steep path. There were few flat stretches, but lower down the steps were reasonably shelved. As we went up, however, the steps got deeper and, as small people, we both found them very exhausting. Then, as the path zig-zagged higher up, we came to wooden ladders with wooden bars as steps. Fortunately many of these had wooden frames which one could use as handrails, some of them highly polished by use but at any rate giving assistance to the climber. Against the younger joggers I stood out in any case as an anomaly, wearing a rucksack and carrying a walking-stick, but both came in remarkably handy. After the Panar Laban hut one got on to solid granite rock slabs which cover the summit. On the steeper faces there were ropes to help pull oneself up. Away to our right we could see the impressive *gendarmes* of the Donkeys Ears Peak, with the South Peak to the left. It was a long tiring haul up the centre slab, where we hoped to find the turn-round point, but we were flabbergasted suddenly to be faced with Low's Peak (4101m) sticking up in front of us, on the top of which we could see the final reporting point. Climbers are always faced with unforeseen summits which they have to surmount one after the other before achieving their goal, and this was no exception. So, after a rest and another drink of vitamin juice from our flask in my rucksack, we staggered on. In actual fact we were surprised at the relatively short time we did take to the summit: at last we were there!

Then came the descent: this was none too easy as a heavy mist had come down, and it started to rain. Even in the tropics at this height it can snow, and I guessed that we were only a couple of degrees above 0°C. We followed the cairns down the summit slab, but these suddenly petered out and we were quite lost – making in fact for a precipice – but fortunately a Climbathon official saw us and redirected us to the right path. Coming down the wet rock and then the wooden ladders was a tricky operation, and with our tired and trembling knees it seemed an eternity until we reached the bottom.

The 'real' competitors however had had a field day. Led by three Gurkha soldiers, they had run up to the top and had passed us on their way down after we had been going for some 2½ hours, leaping surefootedly down the trail as though they were flying. The extraordinary winning time of 2 hours 42 minutes was hard to believe, when we returned having ourselves taken some eight hours – it was certainly the toughest climb we have ever done. Any chagrin we might have felt at this time was however dispelled by my wife winning the silver medal and I the bronze in the Veterans' category, there being no other contestants! The organizers of this race can be well pleased with its success. They will undoubtedly wish to include it in their annual calendar, and as it becomes better known it is bound to attract more participants, especially from overseas.

The organization was of a high order. The Park authorities are to be commended for having prepared the trail to such a superb degree, the Tourist Promotion Board for the external organization and Malaysian Airlines for getting everyone there, and on time.

As time goes on, younger and tougher competitors will no doubt appear and break the record time and again. My good wishes go with them, but for myself I think this is a timely end to climbs like this, and my wife and I will keep to the flatter trails in future!

In Memoriam
Claud Schuster (1869–1956)

EDWARD SMYTH

*M*ountaineering is not life in the round, but it is a very fair emblem of life as it should be considered and as it should be lived . . . to find the reward rather in the performance than in the accomplishment; not to court danger for her own bright eyes, but not to shrink from her unduly when she bars the path; and above all and in all to preserve a high serenity of mind.

Presidential Address to the Club, 10 December 1940.

The sport of mountaineering is the use of skill and experience in the avoidance of danger.

Letter to *The Times*, April 1939.

Stumbling is the start and the talk surly
Monosyllables
Fumbling in the dark, awake too early
Stale crusts across the tables . . .

Somehow we go
The boot's first bite
At the snow
And on first light
The peak – bleached white
And then aglow . . .

Exertion on the slope
Elation on the steep
Cohesion on the rope
Calculation in the leap –
Incalculable hope . . .

To find – who knows – in this our questing
A recompense, success apart
And – come what may – the moment testing
The moment of content of heart?

A Century of
Mountaineering in Scotland

W D BROOKER

(Plates 84–86)

It is always curious to read as history what one has experienced oneself.

Max Beloff

Although there had been ephemeral precursors, it was in 1889 that the first mountaineering clubs in Scotland held their inaugural meetings: the Cairngorm Club in Aberdeen on 9 January and the Scottish Mountaineering Club in Glasgow on 11 February. They are thus the oldest clubs in Britain, apart from the Alpine Club itself.

They began differently, with the Cairngorm Club actually being founded on 22 June 1887 by six friends who were passing the night at the Shelter Stone of Loch Avon, in order to celebrate the Golden Jubilee of Queen Victoria with fireworks on the summit of Ben Macdui. They resolved to form 'a Cairngorm Club' and 18 months later the new club was formally constituted. The SMC, on the other hand, owed its origin to a letter in the *Glasgow Herald* from W W Naismith, suggesting a Scottish Alpine Club. This led to further letters and a public meeting at which 'The Scottish Mountaineering Club' was constituted.

As the origins of these clubs differed, so did their character. The Cairngorm Club was focused on Aberdeen and the Cairngorms, with the emphasis on hill-walking activity often involving large-scale club excursions. Although there were no ladies initially, it has always been open to both sexes. Today, with over 400 members, it is the largest of the 100 or so clubs in the Mountaineering Council of Scotland. The SMC was founded in Glasgow, but nearly half of its membership came from other parts of the country and its role has been more of a national club. It was exclusively male and still resists occasional attempts to make it mixed. The Ladies' Scottish Climbing Club was founded in 1908 and continues to flourish alongside its brother organization. In its original tally of 94, the SMC included no fewer than 17 members of the AC and from the outset it was involved in a wide range of mountaineering activities. Slightly smaller than the Cairngorm Club, it is not particularly large in today's terms but still plays a prominent part in Scottish mountaineering affairs and is the principal source of information and record, with about 25 titles currently published through the Scottish Mountaineering Trust. Both clubs were to produce journals which continue to this day, the *SMC Journal* appearing annually and the *CC Journal* with rather less frequency. In their pages is to be found a large part of the history of mountaineering in Scotland during the last 100 years.

Of course Scottish mountaineering began long before 1889. Occasional

ascents are on record from the late 16th century, and by the end of the 18th
notable peaks like Ben Nevis and Ben Lomond were on the itinerary of the
adventurous traveller doing the Scottish version of the Grand Tour. The 19th
century saw increasing changes in attitudes to the Highlands. The Romantic
concept of mountain scenery was fostered by Scott and the Lake Poets, fauna,
flora and geology were being studied and the mountains mapped by ordnance
surveyors, who performed some prodigious hill-walking feats in the course of
their duties. The development of sporting estates – fashionably encouraged by
the Royal interest in upper Deeside – saw an entrenchment of landowning rights
with attempts to limit access by the closure of some traditional routes which had
been used by drovers and others. One incident in 1847, when a party of
botanists from Edinburgh University was confronted by the Duke of Athole and
his ghillies, has come down through history as 'The Battle of Glen Tilt'.
However, the real conflicts took place in the law courts where this and other
similar disputes were resolved, usually in favour of the public's right of way.
Present-day hill-walkers and climbers owe a great deal of the 'freedom to roam'
we enjoy today in the Scottish hills to the efforts of these stravaigers of the 19th
century, and to organizations like the Scottish Rights of Way Society which
defended their interests. The case of 'Jock's Road' in Glen Doll even reached the
House of Lords. The early membership of the SMC and the Cairngorm Club
included several protagonists of these rights and the latter elected as its first
president James Bryce, MP for South Aberdeen, later Viscount Bryce, who
waged a long parliamentary campaign for free access to mountains for
recreation. His efforts were partly successful, but his farsighted proposals for
national parks were never realized.

Anyway, by 1889 the scene had been set, the Highlands had been mapped
and investigated – yet little was known about their mountaineering potential. It
was not until the 1860s that the rival claims of Ben Nevis and Ben Macdhui for
primacy in height had been resolved. No one knew how many mountains there
actually were, or how many were major peaks with summits over 3000ft. The
Highlands were probably less well known and certainly much less documented
than the Alps.

An exception was Skye, where the jagged peaks and narrow rocky ridges
of the Cuillin had largely repulsed the early tourists, scientists and surveyors.
They had, however, attracted mountaineers. In the 1870s and 1880s the
summits were all reached, some by AC members like the Pilkingtons who
climbed the Inaccessible Pinnacle of Sgurr Dearg in 1880. In the alpine manner,
Skye even had its own professional mountain guide, the famous John McKenzie
after whom Sgurr Mhic Choinnich, the last Scottish Munro to be climbed (by
Charles Pilkington in 1887), is named. The last phase of this primary
exploration of the Cuillin was completed by SMC members in the 1890s.

The special character of the Cuillin has given them a mountaineering
history different from other parts of Scotland. English climbers have played a
more prominent part in their climbing exploration than elsewhere. To do justice
to their story is beyond the reach of this short article, which must give more
attention to the mainland.

It is convenient, if simplistic, to divide Scottish mountaineering history into four roughly equal parts: the first phase up to 1914, 1915–1939, 1940–1965, and the modern period. In a brief account of this kind it is only possible to present a summary, and I shall avoid listing over-many climbs and climbers which, although important in themselves, may make for tedious reading to readers unfamiliar with the Scottish mountaineering scene. Instead I shall try to emphasize those aspects which are distinctive to mountaineering in Scotland.

The Golden Age

This is an appropriate label for the first phase, when nearly every excursion was an exploration and merited a record in the *SMC Journal*. Some of them covered impressive distances through the hills on foot. The first complete traverses were made of inspiring summit ridges like the Aonach Eagach, An Teallach and Liathach, as well as ascents by flanking spurs like the Ciochs of Applecross, the NE ridge of Aonach Beag and the Northern Pinnacles of Liathach, which gave more challenging approaches.

However, cataloguing the mountains by height and general character was the primary task. Its chief agent was Munro whose 'Tables giving all the Scottish Mountains exceeding 3000ft in Height' were published in the *SMC Journal* in 1891. Munro identified 283 separate mountains with 538 tops and, although his original list has been slightly modified in later editions, the word 'Munro' has entered the language. In this way Sir Hugh T Munro is today the best-known of all the SMC pioneers, although as a mountaineer he was overshadowed by some of his contemporaries. In early SMC parlance, Munro was a 'Salvationist'. There was no derogatory implication in this term which was used as a convenience, along with 'Ultramontane', to indicate preferred activities. Circumstances usually make most Scottish mountaineers a bit of both.

The outstanding Ultramontane was Harold Raeburn, a highly talented mountaineer with a remarkable bent for exploration. He climbed extensively in Norway, the Alps and the Caucasus, but is mainly noted for his ubiquitous discoveries on Scottish crags, from the Shetland sea-cliffs to the volcanic scarp of Arthur's Seat. 'Raeburn's' gullies and buttresses abound, some even appearing on today's Ordnance Survey maps. Although Raeburn was a masterly rock-climber, it was in the winter arena that he made his most important contribution. By the early 1900s the ascent of ridges, buttresses and gullies in snow and ice conditions was becoming the cornerstone of Scottish mountaineering. What had begun as alpine training had become a mainstream mountaineering objective, and what may have been lacking in the height of the peaks was compensated for by limited daylight and the nature of Scottish winter weather.

The climbs themselves might well involve 1000ft or more of difficult ground and require a level of commitment fully satisfying to those engaged on them. Raeburn's ascent of Green Gully on Ben Nevis in 1906, and Crowberry Gully on Buachaille Etive Mor in 1909, both involved steep ice of over 75° and technical difficulty which was as high as anything done elsewhere.

1914–1939

The First World War created a hiatus in the progress of Scottish mountaineering, not only during hostilities but through the decade which followed when climbing society – small enough to begin with – had been depleted by the loss of some of its main activists and may have seen little merit in pushing the frontier in a succession of snow-poor winters. Anyway, it was not until the 1930s that the standards set by Raeburn and his contemporaries were regained. In 1929 the Charles Inglis Clark Memorial Hut was completed and led to a major wave of exploration on Ben Nevis. This was mainly rock-climbing, but its principal activists, G G Macphee and J H B Bell, were also involved in ascents which heralded a renaissance in winter climbing. By the late 1930s a group of young Glasgow climbers which included Bill Mackenzie and Bill Murray was extending the winter frontier by ice climbs like Garrick's Shelf on the Crowberry Ridge, and firmly established this type of climbing as a Scottish speciality. It was climbing which demanded one-handed axework and this in turn led to the use of short axes, usually by modifying ordinary long ones.

There had been some fundamental changes in the social make-up of the climbing world in Scotland, just as there were elsewhere. The growing availability of motor vehicles and leisure (sometimes enforced) brought the mountains within reach of many young people from the cities. The result was a big increase in climbing and the birth of new local clubs. Alastair Borthwick's well-known book, *Always a Little Further*, gives a splendid yet amusing account of the atmosphere of this outdoor world of the 1930s. It is a book of colourful characters, of tramps and tinkers, for this was a world of hitch-hiking, tents and caves, not of hotels, tweeds and railway stations like the pre-1914 era.

1940–1965

The Second World War restricted mountaineering to a much lesser extent than the First, and in its aftermath the flood of ex-WD clothing and equipment encouraged growth and continued social change in the Scottish climbing world just as elsewhere in Britain. In Scotland, where W H Murray's *Mountaineering in Scotland* had inspired a post-war generation, an important development was the climbing exploration – largely by Aberdeen climbers – of Cairngorm granite which had earlier been generally regarded as unsuited to rock-climbing. All over the Highlands other major climbing grounds were developed during the 1950s, among them the Torridonian sandstones of the north-west, the quartzites of Foinaven, the gneiss of Carnmore and the granite slabs of Etive. Rock-climbing techniques and standards generally lagged a little behind those south of the Border, except perhaps in Glencoe where some outstanding routes were established by Glasgow climbers, particularly members of the Creag Dhu Club. Among these climbs was John Cunningham's Carnivore, which still retains Extreme grading.

However, it was the winter developments which were the most significant. Aberdeen climbers had continued to use nailed boots in preference to vibram soles in order to cope with the algae-clad Lochnagar granite which becomes slippery when wet. They applied themselves to the winter buttresses, so that this type of mixed winter climbing to which tricounis were well suited became a major feature of the Scottish scene. A by-product was the establishment of the numerical Scottish winter grading still used today in preference to the adjectival rock-climbing system. Tom Patey was the outstanding member of the Aberdeen school, and he was to remain in the forefront of Scottish mountaineering until his death in 1970. Many of these Cairngorm mixed climbs have retained their standard and some, like Eagle Ridge, Mitre Ridge and Sticil Face, have become classic winter routes.

In the late 1950s vibram soles replaced nails even in the Cairngorms and this meant that crampons, which had long been resisted by the Aberdonians, were now essential for winter climbing. An impressive example of their use on Lochnagar granite was given on the first winter ascent of Parallel Gully B, a VS route in summer, by the Edinburgh pair of Jimmy Marshall and Graham Tiso in 1958. Marshall was to prove one of the finest all-round climbers in Scottish history, and his winter achievements on Ben Nevis together with Robin Smith represented the peak of what was possible in ice-climbing by means of single axe step-cutting supplemented by pitons. Among their fine winter first ascents on Nevis were Minus Two Gully, Gardyloo Buttress and the Orion Face direct. Robin Smith was one of a group of Edinburgh climbers who made some remarkable rock climbs on both rock and ice in the late 1950s and early 1960s. These included Shibboleth, the classic Extreme on Buachaille Etive More and the Needle on the Shelterstone Crag.

The Modern Period

By the mid-1960s rock-climbing had seen the adoption of specialized footwear and the development of protection. As elsewhere, these were to contribute to the rising technical standards which today have transformed this sector of mountaineering into a very different activity from that practised by earlier generations. The number of new routes being recorded is greater than ever, but they are necessarily harder and are increasingly located on smaller crags, quarries and sea-cliffs. This is no different from other parts of Britain, and other developments such as indoor climbing-walls and the use of training to improve standards are also present in Scotland.

In snow- and ice-climbing the technical changes began modestly with better crampons, ice screws as an improvement over ice pitons in providing anchorage, and the tentative use of ice daggers to assist the short ice-axe. In retrospect it seems incredible that it took so long to make the obvious discovery that the traction from an ice-axe pick would be enhanced if the pick is dropped enough. Yvon Chouinard and Hamish MacInnes appear to have reached this conclusion independently on opposite sides of the Atlantic. After Chouinard visited Scotland in 1970 the new ice tools were launched, curved pick hammers and axes by the former and the dropped pick Terrordactyls by the latter. In 1971 Cunningham and his Glenmore Lodge colleague Bill March demonstrated the potential of the new methods by ascending the Ben Nevis test-piece of Point Five Gully in less than three hours. This had taken 29 hours of siege tactics on its first ascent in 1959, and even Marshall and Smith who repeated it in good style in 1960 had taken seven hours. In 1973 it was soloed by Ian Nicolson along with Zero Gully in a combined time of three hours! By the mid-1970s front-pointing with two axes was in wide use and 'pick and stick' had transformed Scottish winter climbing. The technique is now used all over the world, with refinements such as the replaceable banana-shaped pick as the current front-runner.

Today Scottish ice-climbing is a popular sport and the winter corries where only 20 years ago solitude was almost guaranteed are now crowded with climbers, not only from all over Britain but occasionally from Europe and even North America. Many of the classic ice gullies have been downgraded and a Grade VI has been added for the harder climbs (with tentative extension beyond this). The ice frontier is now on ice-falls and icicles where vertical and even overhanging ice occurs. A notable practitioner in the 1980s is Mick Fowler, who has achieved many fine first ascents on weekend visits from a base in London.

At this point we may well ask what remains that is still distinctive about mountaineering in Scotland. There are two particular features which lie at opposite ends of the mountaineering spectrum.

The first is the cult of Munroing. Huge numbers who go hill-walking and who in other countries would just be hiking in the hills are bent on reaching 'the tapmaist elevation' of their peak and eventually on ascending all 277 Munros. Although A E Robertson, the first Munroist,[1] finished his round in 1901, it took another 50 years for the number to reach 20. There are now over 600, and they are increasing by more than 50 every year. Whether one approves or not, 'Munrosis – the Scottish disease' – is a fact.

The second is mixed climbing involving rock-climbs under winter conditions. This is suited not only to the classic ridges and buttresses where thick deposits of hoar crystals may be an embellishment, but also to places where moisture and vegetation may impair rock-climbing in summer but enhance it in winter. In these conditions the Lochnagar buttresses, the great Torridonian walls of the North-West and even the mica-schist of the Fannaichs come into their own, providing not only conventional snow and ice but pick and stick in frozen turf, delicate work on ice-smeared slabs and the wedging of axe heads in cracks known as 'torquing'. Outstanding Scottish climbers like Andrew Nisbet who served an apprenticeship in general mountaineering, and Dave (Cubby) Cuthbertson who began as an accomplished pure rock-climber before developing his ice-climbing, have different backgrounds. It is significant that today both seem to seek their ultimate challenge in mixed routes of the highest standard. New stars like Graeme (The Brat) Livingston are enjoying the same experience, as did Tom Patey on the Winter Traverse of the Cuillin ridge and even W W Naismith on the NE Buttress of Nevis in 1896. It is a dream that has been shared by many; above all else it is the most distinctive and special feature of Scottish mountaineering.

REFERENCES

1   AER completed all the 283 separate mountains on the original list but almost certainly did not do the Inaccessible Pinnacle of Sgurr Dearg which was then listed only as a Top.

Tysfjord and Lofoten

RUPERT HOARE

(Plates 68, 87–89)

The Arctic Highway south-west of Narvik passes through a relatively low-lying and uninteresting area beyond Ballangen; then suddenly, on rounding a corner, the whole dramatic profile of the Tysfjord mountains is revealed. These stark ice-sculpted granitic peaks rise so abruptly that they look quite unreal, as if part of a fantasy landscape. The road passes between the precipices of Stortinden to the north and Huglehornet to the south. Here John Evans and I left the bus: our long journey was at an end.

We had both decided that we needed a change from the Alps for our summer holiday in 1986. Eventually we chose to travel to Norway and spend one week in Tysfjord and one week in Lofoten. I had been to Arctic Norway 12 years earlier and had always wanted to visit the Lofoten Islands since having seen their jagged profile in the distance from a mountain near Narvik. Our journey was via Stockholm, with 21 hours on the train to Narvik. By the time we stepped out of the bus we certainly felt a long way from home. Indeed, John remarked that it had taken considerably less time to reach Kashmir!

Our first objective was the E ridge of Huglehornet. The foot of the ridge is reached by walking easily up an extraordinary slab of granite gneiss set at an angle of about 25 degrees. This single slab must be half a kilometre long and several hundred metres wide, and is a unique feature.

At the foot of the ridge, 'the party' fell noticeably silent. The narrow rock ridge rose at a steep angle to a huge capping overhang, with massive slabs dropping away almost vertically on each side. Had we not known in advance that the technical grade is only V Diff/Severe, I expect that we might well have made an excuse to find an easier-looking objective. As it was, the climb was highly enjoyable and the summit was a tremendous viewpoint. The weather was perfect and all around were fiords, islands and fine peaks. There is a special magic about the combination of mountains and sea. In the distance we could see the Lofoten Islands and nearer at hand to the south-east was the unmistakable profile of Stetind.

Stetind (the 'Anvil Peak') is one of the most distinctive mountains in Norway. It has the shape of a very steep-sided triangular pyramid with a flat top. Described by Priestman as 'probably the most remarkable and at the same time the ugliest mountain in Arctic Norway', and by no less an authority than W C Slingsby as 'a grim monolith', it nevertheless looked highly attractive to us and immediately became the next feature of the 'sports plan'.

The first problem was how to approach the peak, which has a remote location at the head of Stetfjord. The obvious answer was to try to charter a boat. The next day, after a hot and rather tedious walk from Skardberget to Lysvold with heavy packs, it proved surprisingly easy to arrange for a local

fishing-boat to take us about 12km to the head of the fiord. As we chugged up
the fiord with Stetind growing ever closer, we looked at the impossible terrain
on either side and realized that we had definitely made a good decision to
approach by sea!

That evening we pitched the tent on a patch of grass beside a stream near
the shore and boiled up some fresh fish, kindly given to us by a local fisherman,
in a billy of salt water. Long after we lost the sun, it continued to light the
granitic slabs which soared up to the summit of Stetind high above.

The ordinary route leads round the back (south) of Stetind and over a
subsidiary peak called Hall's Fortopp, and then up the S ridge (Sydpillaren).
This is the route on which a strong Alpine Club party consisting of Collie, W C
and A M Slingsby failed in bad weather in 1904. The route was first climbed by
a Norwegian party the following year.

From our camp, a path led through birchwoods beside a stream, then
gradually it gained height passing over bilberry slopes until it reached a small
lake at 700m. It was an exhilarating morning with perfect sunny weather and
good views back to the fiord. From the lake the route led over large scree up to a
col below Prestind, and then it continued north-west mostly up easy-angled
scree. We began to wonder if it was just a walk to the top of Stetind until having
at last reached the top of Hall's Fortopp, we gained a view of the final ridge: the
rope and gear would certainly be needed after all!

The crux pitch of the ridge was a very exposed but well-protected hand
traverse; on the descent we avoided it by an abseil. The summit was a curiously
flat bouldery area about the size of a football pitch: a most unsummit-like
summit. Needless to say, the views were marvellous.

After Stetind, I was naïvely concerned that the Lofoten Islands might be
an anticlimax, but I needn't have worried. The peaks are completely different
from those of the Tysfjord area but are no less spectacular. We chose to visit
Austvågøy, and just the crossing from Narvik to Svolvaer is a memorable
experience. The ferry has been replaced by a jet-boat which weaves between the
rocky islands at 30 knots. We made the three-hour trip on a fine evening, and
the fantastic beauty of the mountains and fiords in the low sun was one of the
highlights of our holiday.

From Svolvaer we travelled north to camp in a secluded spot at the head
of Ostpollen Fiord. We were saddened to find a lot of rubbish lying around close
to our camp-site, especially when we discovered that it was obviously British
and must have been left by a large group.

The peaks in Lofoten are extremely steep. What looks at a distance like
grass is really a tangle of birch scrub, bilberry and ferns hiding ankle-breaking
scree. Because of the steepness and the difficult vegetation the lower slopes
take an incredible effort to climb. The rock above looks superb from a
distance, but in fact it is covered in lichen which can make even simple moves
feel very insecure. The extreme steepness means that particular care is
necessary whilst scrambling, especially in places where the rocks are only held
together by moss. The rock peaks of Austvågøy have been likened to the
Chamonix Aiguilles, but I was more reminded of a bigger, steeper and rockier
version of the Cuillins. The detailed topography of most of the peaks is

82.   *Two up, one down: competitors passing each other along the fixed ropes near the top of Mount Kinabalu during the Climbathon '88. (p 185)*

94.   *A M Kellas (1862–1921)*. (p 207)

95.   *Sir Arnold Lunn in Mürren, 1974*. (p 214)

extremely complex, and it would take weeks if not years to become familiar with the area.

Having made these excuses, I have to admit that our own climbing was not notably successful. On the first day we failed to pass a gendarme on the N ridge of Rorhoptinden. Later we saw that the whole section of ridge could have been avoided. Next we tried to climb Geitgaljartind, a most impressive rock peak, by a new route from the south-east. After a nerve-racking day we ended up on top of a pinnacle with a huge drop between us and the final peak. Norman Collie's pronouncement that 'these precipices are entirely unclimbable' was quite true – for us at least.

On the final day, desperate to reach a summit, we climbed Geitgaljartind by the NE ridge, the route taken by the first ascensionists, Collie, Hastings, Priestman and Woolley, in 1901. The summit views were as magnificent as any I have seen.

Before leaving Lofoten we climbed 'The Goat', a rock pinnacle situated, it seemed vertically, above the Svolvaer town cemetery. Climbing on clean rock without a rucksack made a pleasant change. The top consists of two horns; the lower horn is reached by an airy jump through space from the upper horn. I was never keen on jumping, and the look on my face after I had successfully made the leap was enough to make John burst out in hysterical laughter!

We were lucky to have almost perfect weather and very few mosquitoes throughout our two-week period in Arctic Norway. It was a great pleasure to sit outside the tent by a camp-fire watching the sunset each evening. On our final night in Lofoten the cloud-base came right down and it started to rain, just to show us what might have been, but by then we were already on the boat, starting our long journey home.

Fact Sheet

Travel   There are many alternatives. We went by Apex return to Stockholm and train to Narvik. An obvious, but longer, option is to travel via Bodø and coastal steamer to Narvik. A more expensive option is to fly to Narvik. The boat between Narvik and Svolvaer goes daily.

Both Narvik and Svolvaer have tourist information offices. Try to avoid the official camp-site in Narvik: it has no grass! The youth hostel offers very good value B & B, but gets full at peak holiday periods.

Weather   There is 24-hour daylight from mid-May to mid-July. Out of the sun, the air temperature is quite cold and warm clothing is necessary. Insect repellent can be necessary on warm windless evenings, and a tent with a mosquito net is a great bonus.

Maps   Joint Operations Graphic   1:250,000 SERIES   34–10 (Svolvaer)
34–11 (Narvik)
Army Map Services M711   1:50,000 series   1331–III (Tysfjord)
1131–I (Oddvaer)
(Available at good UK map shops and in Narvik.)

REFERENCES

Rock Climbs in Norway. Norway Travel Association, 1953.

T Weir, *Camps and Climbs in Arctic Norway*. Cassel, 1953.

Royal Navy & Royal Marines Mountaineering Club Nordland Expedition, 1978.

'Huglehornet.' *Climber and Rambler*, September 1978.

J Norman Collie, 'Lofoten.' *AJ22*, 3–15, 1905.

Dick Turnbull, 'Northern Norway – a personal view.' *AJ87*, 46–53, 1982.

Kahiltna Travels

JULIE-ANN CLYMA

(Plates 67, 90–93)

In 1988 the Payne 'family' – myself, husband Roger and a clutch of ice-tools – found that its plans to visit the Himalaya had gone awry. However, a favourable exchange rate against the dollar, a special offer on North American air fares, the lack of bureaucracy in gaining access to climbing areas – and the novelty of climbing in a country where we spoke the same language as the locals – made Alaska our choice of venue for our annual 'Greater Ranges' foray. Roger had already visited Alaska in 1983 and related dire tales of strong winds, temperatures of −45°C, man-eating crevasses and terrible snow conditions. It seemed a ridiculous place to have chosen – from these accounts we would surely perish! – but I had seen pictures of the Denali National Park, and the isolation and beauty of the area were undeniable. Some more reading and the timely arrival of the 1987 *AAJ* provided us with an objective in the shape of Mt Foraker (5300m) and, after considering possible routes, we selected an unclimbed line on the S buttress of the SE ridge for our attempt. Mt Foraker is a comparatively little- climbed mountain upon which only 29 expeditions have been successful, as compared with more than 5000 individuals who have summited on nearby McKinley. A common reaction on hearing our intentions of climbing this mountain was cautionary; H Adams Carter wrote of the huge avalanches which pour off the mountain.

As we flew over Greenland, we reflected that it was taking us less time to get from London to Anchorage than it often took to get from London to Fort William! Having left at 1pm on Wednesday 18 May, we arrived in Anchorage at 1.30pm the same day (the 9hr time difference having been lost somewhere between time zones). While this made us feel very efficient, it also caused us to feel extremely tired. We almost literally stepped off the plane and into the supermarkets (open 24 hours a day) to buy provisions, and did the round of the climbing shops for miscellaneous equipment. By the time we stopped to eat dinner (10pm local time), we had been up for 24 hours. We collapsed that night at the home of a local woman, Jean, who had been working on the information counter at the airport when we arrived. When we explained to her that we needed some help to find a motel, supermarkets, equipment shops and transport to Talkeetna, she proceeded to arrange our transport to Talkeetna the next day, and then offered herself as chauffeuse and her home as our temporary place of residence. Alaskans are hospitable and friendly people.

The following morning we were on the road to Talkeetna, the jumping-off point for flights into the Denali National Park. A 2½-hour journey saw us arriving at midday in showery weather. We called in to K2 Aviation to meet Jim and Julie Okonek; organized the loan of sleds, bought wands and fuel, and arranged to fly on to the glacier as soon as the weather cleared sufficiently. Then it was over to the Ranger Station to register and undergo a briefing. After another repacking of all our gear and an excellent dinner at the 'Latitude 62', our second hectic day finished at the K2 Bunkhouse. The following morning dawned (a relative term with 24 hours of daylight) beautifully clear and sunny, and Jim started at 6am to fly parties on to the glacier. We were scheduled for 10am. Nothing can quite prepare you for the disorientation of standing at one moment in the balmy spring air at Talkeetna airport, and an hour later being dumped alone in the wilderness of the Denali National Park.

We had elected to land in the W fork of the Kahiltna glacier, immediately beneath our objective, Mt Foraker. Two possible reasons for the low success-rate on this mountain soon became apparent. First, the least technical routes on Foraker are extremely long and, second, all the routes we examined had high objective danger from serac fall and avalanche. During the six days we spent beneath the mountain, we examined it from a number of angles. On 21 May, using our touring skis, we skinned up to a pass SW of our camp to get a better look at our proposed route. What had not been clear in our photographs of the route was an ice-cliff separating the rock buttress from the summit snow-slopes above. Somehow the route lost its immediate appeal, and we began looking for alternatives. From the col we could see down into the Lacuna glacier and towards the SW ridge and Infinite Spur routes. We already knew from earlier parties in the area that season that the approach and lower reaches of the Infinite Spur were in poor condition, and the SW ridge is extremely long, so we discounted these. The only other route to be considered was the French ridge (SSE ridge) but, as the first (and only) ascensionists had placed 7300m of fixed rope, we discounted this also!

Back at our camp, on another afternoon, we saw four simultaneous serac avalanches on the SE face; for us this marked the end of making any attempt from the W fork of the Kahiltna glacier. On 22 May, by ski and sled, we moved camp to a bay between Mt Foraker's E face and Mt Crosson (3900m), and on the 25th we climbed a small peak behind our camp to examine the E face and NE ridge routes. The two existing routes on the E face looked difficult and, we observed, were both threatened by huge active seracs. The NE ridge route, which initially climbs over Mt Crosson, began to look like the most likely option – but, again, it was very long. We decided as a warm-up to climb the S ridge on Mt Crosson to assess snow conditions and the feasibility of continuing on to Mt Foraker. The weather during this time had been mixed, with some days of clear blue skies and others of snowfall. We set off to climb Mt Crosson at 3am on 26 May; it seemed a long walk to the foot of the route, and the initial couloir we had picked to gain access to the upper ridge turned out to be most unpleasant. What had looked like one pitch of straightforward climbing turned into a hour-long struggle through bottomless sugar-snow beneath tumbled seracs. By the time we reached the top of the couloir we were thoroughly demoralized. Cold, tired and not impressed with either snow conditions or weather prospects, we turned round and headed back for camp.

Having spent a week looking at options on Mt Foraker, we felt we had to make a decision. In view of the high objective danger, neither of us could raise much enthusiasm for any of the routes we had seen. So we finally decided to turn our backs on Foraker and move towards Mt McKinley.

Armed with photocopied extracts from various journals and magazines, we searched through them and settled with interest on an account of the ascent of the NW ridge of McKinley. It has only been climbed twice and has not had a British or NZ ascent – it seemed ideal. Our approach lay over the Kahiltna Pass (3145m) at the head of the Kahiltna glacier, and then dropped down into the Peters Basin to reach the foot of the route at about 2400m. On 27 May we moved camp to a new base at around 2200m near the entrance to the E fork of the Kahiltna glacier. The following day we packed up eight days' food and ski'd towards the Kahiltna Pass, following the usual Mt McKinley W buttress trail. After 6½km and six hours on the glacier we had to stop beneath the pass, overcome by the intense heat. We were dismayed to discover when we stepped off the trail that the snow was over our knees. It was a struggle to set up camp for the night, and just as we crawled inside the tent it began to snow again. The following morning (29 May) hardly a word needed to be spoken before we agreed to abandon crossing the pass (now an avalanche hazard), and to opt instead for the only other route close to hand – the W buttress of Mt McKinley.

We discovered that many of the guided parties on this, the standard route, take about three weeks to make a summit attempt. They adopt a siege approach to maximize the chances of success, but land themselves with days of load-carrying between camps. We now had seven days' food and, trusting to luck as to weather and our acclimatization, we set off from 3000m towards the camp at 4300m. The weather was cloudy and cool: ideal travelling conditions. We used skis and sleds up to the 3400m camp and from there continued on foot. Stopping two or three times for longish breaks and a brew, we reached 4300m at about 8pm. The weather was deteriorating as we put up our tent.

Despite our tiredness, we spent a restless night listening to the rising wind. The 30th brought a calm day but whiteout conditions. We both had mild headaches and settled in for a well-earned rest day. Lots of parties were dropping down from higher camps reporting very strong winds of 80–130km/hour. The 31st brought improving weather, but we were both still feeling the altitude and opted for another rest day. The camp at 4300m is unique in having a manned medical station from which Dr Peter Hackett and colleagues collect data on high-altitude sickness from the great pool of afflicted mountaineers passing their door. They even offer a 'haemoglobin-oxygen-saturation reading' service which gives some indication as to whether one is wise to continue gaining altitude. We could not resist submitting ourselves to this test, and were delighted to find that we were above the recommended level.

We woke at 4am on 1 June to find the day clear and cold. We set off at 6.30am up the steeper slopes towards the 4900m camp on the ridge above. Although the ground was not excessively steep, a fixed rope was in place, presumably to make load-carrying safer and easier and to protect guided parties. We arrived at 4900m at 9am and stopped to have a drink and to warm our cold hands and feet. The wind was gusting more strongly, and parties were still dropping down from higher camps. Within 30 minutes the cold drove us to set up camp there in order to see what the day would bring. It took a long time to dig out a platform and to erect the tent; and even longer to get warm again. However, the day improved and by 3pm it was sunny, calm and warm. We decided to continue our ascent to the camp at 5200m. It was perhaps the most memorable day's climbing for sheer enjoyment; winding our way on hard névé between beautiful granite blocks, enjoying the views of peaks and tundra dropping away on both sides. We arrived at 5200m at 8pm and, feeling extremely tired, we put up our tent and collapsed into our sleeping-bags. Again the weather deteriorated and the night brought very strong winds and more snow.

2 June was cold, windy and miserable, but the weather was supposed to improve, so we sat and rested and hoped. On the morning of the 3rd we woke late at 9am to find calm weather and sunny skies. We had a leisurely breakfast, and then there suddenly seemed nothing else for it but to set off for the summit. It was very cold on the traverse of the shaded slopes up to Denali Pass at 5500m, and we feared that our summit attempt had ended when I had to stop to rewarm seriously cold feet. However, after some brisk rubbing and a change of socks we were able to continue. Progress was steady over moderate slopes until we reached about 5800m, but from then onwards the altitude began to feel like a physical barrier. Our footsteps were weighted and slow, and soon our range of vision had narrowed to just the few feet in front of us. The last few hundred feet up a suddenly steeper slope and along the summit ridge felt like being on a treadmill – the summit was in view, but never seemed to get any closer. Finally, at about 7pm, we reached the top. The last 300m of climbing had been extremely trying, and the arrival on the summit was an emotional moment. We hugged each other and stood together for a while, feeling a great weight being lifted from our limbs as we rested. Except for one other person just ahead of us, we were alone; the weather was calm and clear; and, incredibly, we felt properly warm for the first time that day. Soon we had recovered enough to become fully aware of our surroundings, and we were infused with an enormous sense of well-being and contentment. Beyond us in all directions stretched row after row of mountains, tinted blue and pink; beyond them again lay the tundra, a deep brown, with small lakes glistening silver in the reflected light; and above it all stretched a sky of palest blue and green. We stayed on the summit for nearly an hour, and it was with the greatest reluctance that we turned to make the descent. We paused often to sit and talk and to take in the changing view, and we made good time back to camp at 5200m.

The following day we descended to 4300m in the morning. Again it was one of those exceptional days, and the spell of the previous day seemed stronger than ever. We lingered on the ridge between 5200 and 4900m taking photographs, stopped at viewpoints at 4300m and did not continue on to our dump at 3400m until the afternoon. We had heard stories from parties passing us on their way up about a big avalanche at the 3400m camp in which many people had lost equipment. However, nothing had quite prepared us for the sight of a deep fracture-line which extended along more than 1km of ridge above the camp. Had it not been for the very large bergschrund at the bottom of the slope, the whole camp and all its occupants would have been engulfed. Freshly fallen snow had buried our skis to within a foot of their tips, and a long session of digging was required before we could reload our sleds and ski off down to a safer haven. Tiredness and frustration from falling over under our heavy loads finally led us to stop at 2700m for the night. A final morning's effort saw us reach our cache at 2200m on 5 June. We were both starving and spent the next four days luxuriating in good food and lots of sleep and rest.

It was not long, though, before we felt that we were squandering our time and began to cast about for another peak to climb. A small 'peaklet' (Pt 2800m, a satellite of Kahiltna Dome) across the glacier from our camp seemed to offer just what we were looking for: 400m of nice-looking technical climbing on a 50°+ ice and mixed face. We called it *Kahiltna Gnome*. We set off at about midnight on 8 June and skinned across to the foot of the route on crisp snow. We made good progress, moving together on the face up to two pitches beneath the summit. Here the snow was deep 55° windslab, deposited beneath the cornice. We tiptoed across to a firmer rib of snow which led through the cornice, unable to relax even as we moved on to the rounded summit, as the snow settled and creaked beneath our feet. We decided that it was an unhealthy place in which to linger and made for the mixed SE ridge for our descent. This was straightforward and gave wonderful views of the peaks further down the glacier, turning pink and blue in the morning sun. At 6am we were back in our sleeping-bags, happy with a good night's work.

After a further night's rest we decided on another attempt on McKinley by the NW ridge. We left camp at 10.30pm on 10 June and skinned up to beneath Kahiltna Pass. Leaving our skis at 3000m, we continued on foot. The snow was more consolidated, but now we had to contend with a breakable crust. It was a struggle to get to the top of the pass, with sacks containing eight days' food and with every other step collapsing beneath us. The view into the Peters Basin and on to the snow-laden NW ridge was extremely disappointing. The weather was deteriorating again, and we could only see the upper 150m of the slopes descending to the glacier below. The visible ground was littered with serac debris and loaded with windslab. Again a tactical retreat was agreed and we slogged back to camp in a whiteout, arriving at 8.30am. We later learnt that a party of Italians was avalanched, luckily without serious injury, descending near this point.

By this stage we were getting fairly tired of carrying heavy loads up and down the glacier to little effect, but with time running short we decided to make one last attempt on McKinley. Two days later, on 13 June, we set off at 10.30pm, this time up the NE fork of the Kahiltna glacier towards the Cassin ridge. The NE fork has a somewhat fearsome reputation for danger and, although there was no debris on the trail, the size of the seracs which line this narrow passage is such that, if something big were to come down, one would not want to be there to see it! We skinned, and later walked, on up to the head of the glacier without incident, hoping that the worst was over, but in fact the most appalling line of seracs was sitting above the final part of the trail which we needed to follow to reach a safe camp-site. It was already 6.30am and the sun was beginning to touch the upper slopes, so it was with heart in mouth that we practically ran to the safety of a point under a rock-wall near Kahiltna Notch (3650m). By 8am a great spectacle had begun: enormous avalanches exploded across the glacier from the serac-band above. We spent the day resting in our tent, trying to find relief from the oppressive heat. The next day (15 June) the altimeter showed a large drop in pressure and the weather was deteriorating, with light snow falling. Suddenly it seemed a good time to be going home and, happy to be leaving that oppressive place, we raced back down to our base at 2200m to pack up our equipment.

The weather continued to deteriorate and we continued in heavy snowfall on to the landing strip in the E fork of the Kahiltna glacier to wait for a flight out. A mass exodus seemed to be under way, with a party of 14 Spaniards in front of us, and four or five parties in front of them. It was a rude shock to be suddenly surrounded by so many very vocal people, and we ruefully recalled the solitude of the Kahiltna glacier. Our trip was over and, although we had not achieved our initial objective, we had enjoyed a successful and immensely satisfying time. For us the two days above 5200m on Mt McKinley had had all the essential elements which make mountaineering worthwhile.

Conditions seemed to preclude any chance of flying out for a couple of days but, incredibly, late the next morning small aircraft were appearing beneath the cloud-base to land with a roar outside our tent. With the long queue of people in front of us, it was not until 5pm that we lifted off from the glacier. The flight out was spectacular – spring had taken hold and the landscape was clothed in a forest of fresh green, with great areas of golden marshland holding small lakes coloured deep blue.

Talkeetna was bathed in sunshine and our heavy mountain clothing was shed without delay – it was such delight to walk barefoot on the grass.

A M Kellas: Pioneer Himalayan Physiologist and Mountaineer

JOHN B WEST

(Plate 94)

A M Kellas (1868–1921) has a special place in the early history of climbing Mt Everest, but his contributions have not been fully appreciated. First, he was an indefatigable Himalayan explorer; when the 1921 Reconnaissance Expedition was being planned, he probably knew more about the physical approaches to Everest than anybody else. But Kellas also excelled in another area: in 1920 he had almost certainly given more serious thought than anyone to the physiological challenge of the immense altitude of Everest.

In spite of these two special attributes, relatively little has been written concerning Kellas. Apart from a few obituaries which appeared immediately after his death, the only extensive article about his mountaineering achievements was one in German in 1935 which is not easily accessible.[1] Recently, a paper on his physiological contributions was published in an American physiological journal.[2] In the present article, I hope to show why Kellas deserves more attention.

A good place to start is the meeting of the Royal Geographical Society on 18 May 1916, when Kellas delivered a paper entitled 'A consideration of the possibility of ascending the loftier Himalaya.' A R Hinks, Secretary of the Society, had written to Kellas as follows, inviting him to prepare the lecture: 'If you could give us a paper with some general title like "The possibilities of climbing above 25,000 feet" it would be a subject of first-rate interest . . . especially since no one perhaps in the world combines your enterprise as a mountaineer and your knowledge of physiology.'[3] Hinks was remarkably perceptive. Indeed, Kellas was probably unique in his knowledge of the physical problems of approaching Mt Everest, and of the physiological difficulties of climbing at these enormous altitudes.

Alexander Mitchell Kellas was born in Aberdeen on 21 June 1868. His father, James Fowler Kellas, was Secretary and Superintendent of the Mercantile Marine Company in Aberdeen and married Mary Boyd Mitchell. There were nine children, of whom Alexander was the second. One of his brothers, Henry, was a lawyer in Aberdeen and looked after Alexander's affairs when he was abroad. Alexander never married but Henry had four children, two of whom are still alive; one, A R H Kellas, was British Ambassador to Nepal from 1966 to 1970.

A M Kellas was educated at Aberdeen Grammar School and at the University and Heriot-Watt College in Edinburgh. He then moved to University College London, where for a time he was a research assistant to Sir William

Ramsay. He later went to Heidelberg University, where he obtained his PhD degree in 1897. In 1900 he was appointed Lecturer in Chemistry at the Middlesex Hospital Medical School in London, and he held that appointment until 1919.

Kellas began hill-walking when he was young, first in the Grampians and later in Wales and on the Continent. In 1907 he made his first expedition to the Himalaya, spending the months from August to October climbing first in Kashmir and later in Sikkim. There followed a remarkable series of climbs in the summers of 1909, 1911, 1912, 1913, 1914, 1920, and the early spring of 1921. The period between 1914 and 1918 was ruled out because of the war; however, we know that Kellas planned expeditions to Sikkim for both 1915 and 1916 because a typewritten proposal for these still exists.

Table 1.   Kellas's Expeditions to the Himalaya

1907 August–October	Kashmir: Pir-Panjal range
	Sikkim: Zemul glacier, Grunsee, Simvu (6816m, unsuccessful) (*AJ34*, 408)
1909 August–October	Sikkim: Pauhunri (7065m, unsuccessful), Jongsong La (6120m), Langpo (6950m), Jongsong Peak (7459m, unsuccessful) (*AJ34*, 408)
1911 April–August	Sikkim: Sentinel Peak (6470m), Pauhunri (7065m), Chomiomo (6835m), Dhanarau Peak (5790m) (*AJ26*, 52,113; *GJ40*,241)
1912 July–September	Sikkim: Kangchenjhau (6920m) (*AJ27*,125)
1913 Summer	Kashmir: explored access to Nanga Parbat via branch of Ganalo Peak (little information available)
1914 Summer	Garhwal: approaches to Kamet (little information available)
1920 August–December (with Morshead)	Garhwal: Kamet (7755m, unsuccessful by 500m) Sikkim: Kang La (*AJ33*,312; *GJ57*,124, 213)
1921 Early spring May	Sikkim: Kabru (7338m, unsuccessful) Start of Everest Reconnaissance Expedition

(*AJ*: *Alpine Journal*; *GJ*: *Geographical Journal*)

Table 1 summarizes some of the regions and peaks explored by these expeditions. Notable first ascents included Langpo (6950m), Pauhunri (7065m), Chomiomo (6835m) and Kangchenjhau (6920m). Kellas was not a prolific writer, but accounts of most of his expeditions were published in the *Alpine Journal* and the *Geographical Journal*. Very little information is available about the expeditions of 1913 and 1914.

Kellas usually climbed alone, accompanied only by some native porters. An exception was in 1907 when he was accompanied by two Swiss guides, but this was not a success because they were badly affected by mountain sickness. It was not until 1920 that he chose another companion, Major H T Morshead. Kellas is credited with being the first Himalayan explorer to recognize the great value of the Sherpas. He stated that one of the purposes of his attempt on Kabru in the early spring of 1921 was to train Sherpas for the forthcoming Everest reconnaissance.

It is remarkable that Kellas, a full-time member of the Middlesex Hospital Medical School until 1919, was able to find time for this extensive series of Himalayan expeditions. On every expedition he must have been away from London for some four to five months, counting the time taken to sail to India and back. Nevertheless, he was described as a conscientious staff member and a good teacher.

Kellas must have been exceptionally tough to withstand the rigours of these small expeditions to great altitudes, although his appearance did not suggest this. Mallory described him in a letter to his wife during the early stages of the 1921 Everest Reconnaissance thus:

> Kellas I love already. He is beyond description Scotch and uncouth in his speech – altogether uncouth. He arrived at the great dinner party ten minutes after we had sat down, and very dishevelled, having walked in from Grom, a little place four miles away. His appearance would form an admirable model to the stage for a farcical representation of an alchemist. He is very slight in build, short, thin, stooping and narrow-chested; his head ... made grotesque by veritable gig-lamps of spectacles and a long pointed moustache. He is an absolutely devoted and disinterested person.[4]

Kellas gradually became increasingly interested in the physiology of extreme altitude, which is not surprising given his scientific background and his great personal experience. It is believed that he probably made more ascents over 20,000ft (6100m) than any of his contemporaries. The early part of this century was a colourful period in the physiology of extreme altitude. In the late 19th century, many people believed that it would be impossible to climb above about 21,500ft (6500m).

T W Hinchliff, President of the Alpine Club, wrote in 1876 after a visit to Santiago as follows:

> I could not repress a strange feeling as I looked at Tupungato (21,550 feet) and Aconcagua (23,080 feet) and reflected that endless successions of men must in all probability be forever debarred from their lofty crests ... Those who, like Major Godwin-Austen, have had all the advantages of experience and acclimatization to aid them in attacks upon the higher Himalaya agree that 21,500 feet is near the limit at which man ceases to be capable of the slightest further exertion.[5]

However, in 1909 the Duke of the Abruzzi reached an altitude of 7500m without supplementary oxygen on Chogolisa in the Karakoram. This feat astonished climbers and physiologists alike. The Duke's biographer, de Filippi, remarked that the expedition was designed 'to contribute to the solution of the problem as to the greatest height to which man may attain in mountain climbing'. Kellas became interested in the factors limiting man's performance at extreme altitudes and the causes of mountain sickness, though he himself seems to have been remarkably unaffected by great altitudes. In 1917 he wrote a tentative proposal for a medical scientific expedition to remain for several months at an altitude of 20,000ft (6100m) in order to study the physiology of acclimatization. He even suggested that it might be possible to carry the parts of a small wooden hut to the summit of Kangchenjhau (6920m) to use as a laboratory. This proposal could be considered the forerunner of the Himalayan Scientific and Mountaineering Expedition of 1960–1961.

In 1918 Kellas collaborated with the eminent physiologist J S Haldane on a study of acclimatization over three days in a low-pressure chamber at the Lister Institute in London.

From a physiological point of view, the most remarkable contributions made by Kellas were in an unpublished manuscript entitled 'A consideration of the possibility of ascending Mt Everest.' This was apparently finished in the summer of 1920 just before he left for another Himalayan expedition, and he never returned to England. Two copies of the manuscript are extant – one in the archives of the Alpine Club and the other in those of the Royal Geographical Society. The two manuscripts are very similar, though not identical; the Alpine Club version appears to be slightly later, with more notes and corrections.

A French translation of the manuscript was published in a very obscure place, the Proceedings of the Congrès de l'Alpinisme held in Monaco in 1920.[6] Kellas may have presented the paper at this meeting when he was en route to India, but this is not certain.

Kellas began by stating his main question: 'Is it possible for man to reach the summit of Mount Everest without adventitious aids [by which he meant supplementary oxygen] and if not, does an ascent with oxygen appear to be feasible?' He divided the problems to be overcome into two groups: 'I. Physical difficulties' and 'II. Physiological difficulties', and he considered each of these at some length.

It would be inappropriate to go into the details of Kellas's physiological studies here. The importance of his work was not that he obtained the correct answers to many of the questions that he asked; in fact he did, but this was in part by chance because he had so few data. The importance of his work was that he asked all the right questions, and indeed his probing of the important factors to be considered showed great insight.

Among the factors that he discussed were the altitude and barometric pressure of the Everest summit, the composition of the air in the lungs of a climber near the summit, the amount of oxygen in his blood, the maximal rate at which oxygen could be consumed by the body and the greatest ascent rate near the summit. His predictions for the last two were remarkably accurate. For example, he calculated that the maximal rate of oxygen consumption of a climber near the summit would be a little less than one litre per minute; the currently accepted value is only just above this. Again, he calculated a maximal climbing rate near the summit of 300–350ft per hour; this agrees well with calculations based on the maximal oxygen consumption and Messner's account of his first ascent without supplementary oxygen. Messner stated that 'The last 100 metres of height took us more than an hour to climb.'[7]

The last few lines of Kellas's manuscript are under the heading 'General Conclusion': 'Mt Everest could be ascended by a man of excellent physical and mental constitution in first-rate training, without adventitious aids if the physical difficulties of the mountain are not too great, and with the use of oxygen even if the mountain can be classed as difficult from the climbing point of view.' It took 58 years for his prediction of an ascent without supplementary oxygen to be proved true!

Six days after Kellas posted a copy of this manuscript to the Secretary of the Royal Geographical Society, he left for India never to return. The circumstances of his death make a poignant story.

Kellas was apparently under a great deal of strain during his last years as lecturer at the Middlesex Hospital Medical School. In a letter to Hinks, dated 21 October 1919, he referred to 'a peculiar and continuous annoyance . . . a disturbance which medical men tell me is due to overwork and which takes the form of malevolent aural communications, including threats of murder'.[8] This suggests incipient mental illness and was the reason why Kellas resigned his position. There is no other mention of this problem in Kellas's correspondence with Hinks, but Kellas told the well-known biologist J B S Haldane (son of J S Haldane) about his auditory hallucinations, and Haldane mentioned these at a high-altitude symposium: 'Some people hear voices at high altitudes. Dr Kellas also heard them at sea-level. Indeed he once told me that he wondered if a very sensitive microphone might not render them audible to others.'[9]

In 1920 Kellas nevertheless carried out an extensive climbing programme from August to December with H T Morshead, and since he had resigned from his job he remained in Darjeeling during the winter. While he was there he received an invitation to take part in the 1921 Everest Reconnaissance Expedition. This naturally elated him greatly, since he had spent much of the previous 15 years exploring the approaches to the mountain from the west and north. However, he was back climbing on Kabru in the early spring of 1921, and he wrote to Hinks that his main object was 'to obtain for your use a photograph of Mt Everest and all the peaks to the NW . . .'[10] He returned to Darjeeling from Kabru on 10 May, which only gave him nine days' rest before starting on the Everest Reconnaissance Expedition.

The trek from Darjeeling went north through the humid jungle of Sikkim and crossed into Tibet over the Jelep La. Kellas, who was almost 53 years old, became ill with severe diarrhoea and was so weakened that he had to be carried on an improvised stretcher. Mallory wrote to a friend:

> The most tragic and distressing fact about his death is that no one of us was with him. Can you imagine anything less like a mountaineering party? It was an arrangement which made me very unhappy, and which appals me now in the light of what has

happened. And yet it was a difficult position. The old gentleman
(such he seemed) was obliged to retire a number of times *en route*
and could not bear to be seen in this distress, and so insisted that
everyone should be in front of him.[11]

Kellas died as the expedition approached the Tibetan village of Kampa Dzong.
It was here that the expedition members had their first view of Everest. Mallory
wrote:

It was a perfect early morning as we plodded up the barren slopes
above our camp . . . ; we had mounted perhaps a thousand feet
when we stayed and turned, and saw what we came to see. There
was no mistaking the two great peaks in the west: that to the left
must be Makalu, grey, severe and yet distinctly graceful, and the
other away to the right – who could doubt its identity? It was a
prodigious white fang excrescent from the jaw of the world.[12]

Kellas was buried on a hillside south of the village in a place which looks out
across the arid Tibetan plain to the distant snows of the Himalaya where there
rose the three peaks of Pauhunri, Kangchenjhau, and Chomiomo, which Kellas
alone had climbed. Mallory described the scene to Geoffrey Winthrop Young:

It was an extraordinarily affecting little ceremony burying Kellas
on a stony hillside – a place on the edge of a great plain & looking
across it to the 3 great snow peaks of his conquest. I shan't easily
forget the 4 boys, his own trained mountainmen, children of
nature seated in wonder on a great stone near the grave while Bury
read out the passage from the Corinthians.[13]

So Kellas, who had spent much of the last 15 years of his life studying the
physical and physiological problems of climbing Mt Everest, and who probably
knew more about these subjects than anyone else alive, died just as the first
reconnaissance expedition had its first view of the mountain they came to climb.
It would be difficult to imagine a more moving end to the life of this remarkable
man.

ACKNOWLEDGEMENTS

I am indebted to Mrs C Kelly, Archivist, and other members of the staff of the
Library of the Royal Geographical Society and the Librarian of the Alpine Club
for research on the references.

REFERENCES

1   P Geissler, 'Alexander M Kellas, ein Pioneer des Himalaja.' *Deutsche
      Alpenzeitung 30*, 103–110, 1935.

2   J B West, 'Alexander M Kellas and the physiological challenge of Mt Everest.' *J. Appl. Physiol.* 63, 3–11, 1987.

3   A R Hinks to Kellas, letter, 14 April 1916, RGS, London.

4   Mallory to Ruth Mallory, letter, 17 May 1921, Magdalen College, Cambridge.

5   T W Hinchliff, *Over the Sea and Far Away.* London (Longmans, Green), 1876, pp90–91.

6   A M Kellas, 'Sur les possibilités de faire l'ascension du Mount Everest.' *Congrès de l'Alpinisme, Monaco, 1920. C R Séances, Paris, Vol 1,* pp451–521, 1921.

7   R Messner, *Everest: Expedition to the Ultimate*; translated by Audrey Salkeld. Kaye & Ward, 1979. (Caption to front end paper.)

8   Kellas to A R Hinks, letter, 21 October 1919, RGS, London.

9   *International Symposium on Problems of High Altitude, Darjeeling, 5–8 January 1962.* Organized by Director General, Armed Forces Medical Services. Gulabsons Offset Works, Delhi, p14.

10 Kellas to A R Hinks, letter, 18 May 1921, Everest Archives, RGS, London.

11 Mallory to David Pye, letter, 9 June 1921 (quoted in *George Leigh Mallory – A Memoir* by David Pye, OUP 1927).

12 C K Howard-Bury, *Mount Everest: The Reconnaissance, 1921.* Arnold, 1922. Chapter XII (by Mallory), p184.

13 Mallory to G Winthrop Young, letter, 9 June 1921, Everest Archives, RGS, London.

Sir Arnold Lunn (1888–1974)

EDWARD SMYTH

(Plate 95)

Arnold Lunn, whose centenary fell in 1988, was perhaps the most unusual and certainly one of the most distinguished Honorary Members of the Alpine Club. Mountaineer, ski-pioneer, tireless author and controversialist, fearless Christian apologist – what can be put into 1500 words that is not either already too well known or else totally inadequate? A few highlights at most. I only knew him a little – several meetings at AC functions, some correspondence over a contribution to one of his books and a delightful meeting at Mürren when skiing with his cherished friends Harold and Molly Davis – all towards the end of his life, but much better than not to have known him at all.

I think it would be true to say that his life revolved around three main themes – love of friends and family, mountains and thirdly (but he always put it first) his Christian faith. Three main themes, yes, but buttressed with a thousand lesser enthusiasms, each accurately compartmented in his otherwise notoriously absent-minded brain. In attempting to write briefly about each theme, I will mention some of his many books as appropriate.

On the first, I can only join with all his other friends in saying that the warm memories of his presence have not faded with the years. As James Riddell could say in his obituary (*AJ80*, 298, 1975) '. . . all my memories of Arni are connected with fun and laughter . . . Even if one argued with him . . . it always ended up in laughter.'

His passion for the hills dated from early days at the Lunn holiday home in Grindelwald, where he and his brothers very soon christened a local 30-foot boulder 'Hill Difficulty', making routes up every face whenever they could steal away from the nurse detailed to guard them. When aged 10, in 1898, Arnold learnt to ski at Chamonix, on primitive equipment. At Oxford he founded the Oxford University Mountaineering Club and became editor of a famous book, *Oxford Mountaineering Essays*, whose contributors included, besides himself, Julian Huxley, Hugh Kingsmill, H E G Tyndale and N R Pope. In 1909 he traversed the Bernese Alps – one of the first major ski-mountaineering journeys on record. Later the same year, on Cader Idris, he smashed his leg in a 100-foot fall when a rock flake he was holding broke away. The leg remained permanently two inches short and the wound did not heal for 11 years. Two years after the accident he climbed the Dent Blanche in 10 hours from the hut, triumphing over great pain; and thereafter he concentrated more and more on skiing as his means of mountain travel.

This is no place to dwell on his fame in the world of skiing. Let the titles, generic and otherwise, by which he came to be known tell their own tale: Father of Downhill Skiing, Ambassador of the Mountains, Inventor of the Slalom,

56.   *Makalu NW face, partially obscured by Makalu II, from Everest Kangshung Base Camp.* (p 1)

57.   *Menlungtse West (7023m), from NW.* (p 34)

58.   *Menlungtse West from SW.* (p 34)

59.   *Bhutan: rice planting in Paro.* (p 38)

60.   NE pillar of Mardi Phabrang from col. (p 63)

61.   *Cerro Kishtwar from Chomochior W ridge.* (p 63)

62.   *Julian Fisher flying off Kunyang Kish, Trivor behind.* (p 76)

63. *Approaching Pioneer Peak (L) from Bogdanovicha glacier.* (p 101)

64. *On Gillman's Point, early morning.* (p 175)

65.   *Typical village on stilts in Kota Kinabalu, Sabah.* (p 185)

66.   *Above the Bigo Bog, amongst giant heather and lobelia.* (p 177)

67. *Roger Payne and Julie-Ann Clyma on the summit of Mt McKinley. Mt Hunter L, Mt Foraker R.* (p 201)

68. *Lofoten: Ostpollen Fiord from Geitgaljartind.* (p 197)

President of the Ski Club of Great Britain and Founder of the Alpine Ski Club and the Kandahar – to say nothing of the *British Ski Year Book* which he started in 1920 and edited without a break until he died. And it was 'Services to skiing and to Anglo-Swiss relations' which earned him his knighthood in 1952.

In all, Arnold wrote about 60 books – not only about mountains and Christianity but also about politics, especially those which threatened the freedom of the hills such as the Nazi competitive and nationalistic climbing which preceded the Second World War. His firm stand in withdrawing the Arlberg-Kandahar Race from St Anton at the time of the 1938 Anschluss, in protest against the arrest of Hannes Schneider (his friend and partner in promoting the race), resulted in the latter's release to go to America but not – as the Nazis had hoped – in the return of the race to St Anton; this only happened after the end of the war.

Amongst all Arnold's works there was only one which he considered likely to survive as literature: *The Mountains of Youth*. Written in 1925, this was the book reviewed by Sir Martin Conway (*AJ38*, 140–141, 1926) in the words 'ought to take high rank among the best books ever written about mountaineering'. But amongst those I read myself, I would judge at least two others especially likely to live on: *A Century of Mountaineering* (the Centenary Volume, and so far the only history of the Alpine Club, 1957); and his splendidly reasoned defence of the Resurrection of Jesus, *The Third Day* (1945). His autobiographical works, *Come What May* and *Unkilled for So Long*, are also alive with interest. And of course there was *The Harrovians* (1913), which set a new trend in school stories but was dismissed by the Church Times with 'there is no excuse for Mr Lunn', and for which he is said to have been blackballed by three clubs! As all know, the Alpine Club – to its shame – treated him in the same way, despite his sponsorship by the current President. Arnold felt this deeply at the time, consoling himself with the thought that no one living had the power to exclude him from the deeper fellowship to which every true mountain-lover belongs. Later in life, he would describe himself, not without relish, as an HOB member of the Club. I leave the reader to work that one out.

No account of AL can omit reference to his prowess and indomitable courage in controversy and debate, always conducted with good humour, and the more endearing since he preferred – and nearly always took on – opponents and causes apparently stronger than himself. Mention has already been made of his successful confrontation with the Nazis at St Anton in 1938; others abound, such as the long battle for recognition and Olympic inclusion of downhill and slalom racing against the Norwegian inventors of the sport. It is said that their opposition collapsed when one of them remarked: 'We Norwegians were born with skis on our feet!' and AL riposted: 'That must be very awkward for your midwives.' He also contended with intellects which he considered superior to his own. Monsignor Ronald Knox, who eventually led him to become a Catholic (*Difficulties*, 1932); Professor C E M Joad, who became a Christian as a result of their debate (*Is Christianity True*, 1933); and J B S Haldane, who did not (*Science and the Supernatural*, 1935).

Arnold hated double standards and what he called 'fake alternatives' –

red herrings dragged up to confuse an argument with which they were unconnected – and he was quick to detect and expose the smallest whiff of dishonesty. He particularly disliked what he used to describe as 'selective indignation' – meaning to condemn in the weak what is condoned in the strong. On such a basis he fought his long fight with the Olympic Committee against 'shamateurism' which, though uncrowned by success, will not go unremembered.

The legend abounds with stories – there seems to be about as much 'Arnistory' as 'Churchilliana' – and it may not be inappropriate to include one or two of them in this peripatetic memoir.

At Oxford, despite being Secretary of the Union, he did not obtain a degree; partly, it is said, because he replied to an examination question about the social atmosphere of the court of James I with the couplet: 'No nice examiner would ever dream – To set a question on this sordid theme.' Then there was the lecture in the United States when he was introduced to the amazed and enthusiastic audience as the author of a guidebook on Montana. He failed to enlighten his hearers that the Montana in question was of course in Switzerland. He loved telling anecdotes and saying things against himself – such as: 'When it comes to humility, I'm tops,' or 'Pack your rucksack aided by the lively sense of fear we all possess.' Once, when travelling in America, he happened to meet a priest who advised him in the course of conversation to read a book called *A Saint in the Slave Trade*. 'It will do you good', said the priest. 'Ah', replied Arnold, 'it might, if I didn't know the author!' He always said that he had become a Catholic in spite of Torquemada, and had remained one in spite of Arnold Lunn.

At his requiem in Westminster Cathedral, Cardinal Heenan described Arnold as 'A great controversialist who did not allow sport to become a religion – whom mountains taught the emptiness of atheism.' After his death his wife found the following prayer hidden away amongst his things; it makes a fitting conclusion to this tribute:

> Let me give thanks, dear Lord, in the frailty of age for the beloved mountains of my youth, for the challenge of rock and for the joy of skiing, for the friends with whom I have climbed and ski'd, and above all, dear Lord, for those moments of revelation when the temporal beauty of the mountains reinforces my faith in the Eternal beauty which is not subject to decay.

From the Librarian's Shelf

CHARLES WARREN

This time I take down for comment two little books from the children's corner: the first by John Ruskin and the second by an almost unknown author, Caroline Bell.

One of the most charming books which Ruskin ever wrote, with a mountain setting, was a fairy story written for his future wife when she was still a child aged 11 (but not published until nine years later), called *The King of the Golden River. A legend of Stiria*. The opening paragraph reads as follows:

> In a secluded and mountainous part of Stiria, there was, in old time, a valley of the most surprising and luxuriant fertility. It was surrounded, on all sides, by steep and rocky mountains, rising into peaks, which were always covered with snow, and from which a number of torrents descended in constant cataracts. One of those fell westward, over the face of a crag so high, that, when the sun had set to everything else, and all below was darkness, his beams still shone full upon this waterfall, so that it looked like a shower of gold. It was, therefore, called by the people of the neighbourhood, the Golden River.

What a pleasant opening to the entirely charming and moral tale that follows. But what a charming little book our copy is, too, in its pretty blind stamped cloth binding of the period, and with its illustrations by Richard Doyle; and, above all, with its delightful inscription, in Ruskin's hand, to: 'Alice Pignatel with John Ruskin's love. 1864'.

My second book for comment has the title *Pictures from the Pyrenees*. This is a somewhat dull book to read unless you happen to be slightly interested in the history of children's books. It is dated 1857, the emphasis being upon instruction, both religious and otherwise. At that time, books were not being written purely for the pleasure of children. (Shades of Beatrix Potter later!) Yet the little book has its moments, such as the one when 'Nanny' notices one of the little girls looking pale on the channel crossing and puts her to bed to prevent seasickness. An interesting tale, but rather a priggish one.

But what a charming little volume this is, in its contemporary blind stamped cloth binding and decorative gilt cover; and with its hand-coloured vignette illustrations. Not the least interesting thing about it are the advertisement pages at the back of the book for Newberry's 'Children's Library', taken over by Griffith and Farran in 1857. One is reminded of a more famous one run by the radical reformer, William Godwin, in Skinner Street some years earlier; he published books written for children by famous writers such as Goldsmith. Godwin's 'Children's Library' is of great interest in the history of the publication of books for children. He it was who tried to give them better material on which to sharpen their wits.

However, it was not really until authors like Edward Lear and Beatrix Potter came on the scene that the children's pleasure was really catered for – God bless them.

One Hundred Years Ago

(with extracts from the Alpine Journal)

C A RUSSELL

(Plates 96–98)

The splendid weather in the Alpine regions during January – a marvellous contrast to the gloom and cold of the preceding summer – naturally induced mountaineers to undertake ascents, which were carried out under unusually favourable circumstances. The marked feature of the Grindelwald winter season was the small quantity of snow. Up to January 11 the village was reached by wheeled vehicles only, sleighs being quite useless.

The early months of 1889 were notable for the settled conditions experienced throughout the Alps, and many winter ascents were completed. During the first three weeks in January the Gross Schreckhorn, the Wetterhorn and the Mönch were all climbed, with local guides, by English parties staying at Grindelwald. On 21 January a large Italian Alpine Club party, with guides and porters, ascended the Gran Paradiso; a month later, on 19 February, Vittorio, Corradino, Erminio and Gaudenzio Sella, with Battista and Daniele Maquignaz, traversed the Dufourspitze of Monte Rosa:

> The party left the Capanna Gnifetti at 3A.M., crossed the Lysjoch, and gained the summit at 12.30 by way of the southern face, the rocks of which were somewhat iced. The sky was clear, but the cold not intense. The descent to the Gorner Glacier by the usual route was not difficult, though a strong wind was rather troublesome on the ridge between the summit and Sattel; but there was so much snow on the glacier, and it was so soft that progress was greatly retarded, and the Riffelhaus was not gained till 4A.M.

On 5 March Alfredo Dalgas and Guiseppe Poggi, accompanied by four guides, climbed the Lyskamm in very fine weather.

As the climbing season approached it was hoped that the unfavourable conditions experienced throughout the Alps during the previous summer would not be repeated, but these hopes were dashed by the bad weather which prevailed in most regions until the end of July. Although very little climbing was possible during the early part of the season, some expeditions were successful. In the Mont Blanc range on 3 June V Attinger, E Colomb and L Kurz – with Justin and Joseph Bessard and François Biselx – made the first ascent of the Grande Lui. On 25 July Attinger and Kurz, with Jean-Baptiste Croz and Joseph Simond, reached the summit of the unclimbed Aiguille de la Lex Blanche, above the Trélatête glacier. In the Pennine Alps on 20 July C Herzog, Samuel Junod, Henri Moulin and Paul Wittnauer, with Justin Bessard, completed the first ascent of the S ridge of the Combin de Corbassière, now the normal approach to the summit from the Panossière hut.

Further east Robert Hans Schmitt and Fritz Drasch, without guides, succeeded in forcing a route up the unclimbed S face of the Dachstein, a remarkable achievement for the period. Having overcome numerous difficulties, they were forced to bivouac after completing most of the route on 14 July and reached the plateau below the highest point on the following day.

Although conditions were far from ideal throughout the summer there was some improvement during the second half of the climbing season, and many parties were able to take advantage of short periods of fine weather as the search for new routes continued. In the Pennine Alps the first ascent of the W, or Ferpècle, ridge of the Dent Blanche – which had been descended five years earlier – was completed by Walter Gröbli, with Aloys Pollinger, on 29 July. Some weeks later, on 2 September, Oscar Eckenstein, with Matthias Zurbriggen, ascended the Dent Blanche by way of the dangerous SE face and the ENE ridge, 'a route which is believed to be the worst yet taken'. On 31 August H W Topham, with Pollinger and Aloys Supersaxo, completed a new route to the summit of the Dent d'Hérens by way of the Col des Grandes Murailles and the upper shoulder of the E ridge. By climbing the ridge from the shoulder, the party became the first to reach the summit from this direction, although many years were to elapse before an ascent of the entire ridge was achieved. In the same region George Broke, with Adolf and Xavier Andenmatten, made the first ascent of the W ridge, or Rotgrat, of the Alphubel.

Other ridges ascended for the first time were the Cresta del Marlet, the NE ridge of the Cima Ortles, on 22 August, by Otto Fischer, Ludwig Friedmann, Robert Schmitt, Edward Matasek and Albrecht von Krafft, without guides; the N ridge of the Bessanese, a classic ridge climb in the Graian Alps, by Guido Rey, with Antonio Castagneri, on 2 September; and the SSE ridge of the Dôme de Rochefort in the Mont Blanc range on 14 September by William Muir, with Emile Rey and David Promont. Another climb of note, also in the Mont Blanc range, was the first guideless ascent, on 3 August, of the Aiguille des Grands Charmoz, by H W Henderson, G H Morse, J H Wicks and Claude Wilson. Five days later, in the Dauphiné, A Reynier, with Pierre Gaspard senior, Christophe Clot and Joseph Turc, made the first ascent of the central peak of the Ailefroide.

In August the Queen of Italy, who in the previous summer had demonstrated her enthusiasm for the high mountains by reaching the Col du Géant, stayed in the Gressoney valley and made many excursions among the neighbouring hills:

The most considerable expedition undertaken by her Majesty was an excursion to Zermatt, which was reached on August 20 by way of the Betta Furka, Cimes Blanches, and St. Théodule. The weather was, unfortunately, very bad during her sojourn at Zermatt, but on August 24 the Queen went to the Gornergrat, where she drank to the health of the Queen of Great Britain, in acknowledgement of the cheers of an English party on the summit. On August 26 her

Majesty ascended the Breithorn, spending two nights at the St. Théodule inn, and regaining Gressoney St. Jean next day by the same route as that by which she had come. The Breithorn is as yet the loftiest point which has ever been reached by a reigning European sovereign.

Following the disappearance of W F Donkin and Harry Fox – with the guides Kaspar Streich and Johann Fischer – in the previous year during an attempt to climb Koshtantau (5145m), no conclusive trace of the missing climbers had been found and, as rumours of foul play by the local inhabitants were rife, a strong search party consisting of C T Dent, D W Freshfield, C H Powell and Hermann Woolley, with Christian Jossi, Johann Kaufmann, Kaspar Maurer and Johann Fischer's brother Andreas went out to the Caucasus in July. Addressing the Alpine Club in the following February, Dent explained that 'our chief hope was that we should find a bivouac, and that we should be able to infer from this the probable movements of the party, and also the directions in which any further search that might be necessary should be prosecuted'.

It was clear from notes left by Fox which had been entrusted to a local porter that, after an unsuccessful attempt on the N ridge of Koshtantau, the party had intended to cross the Ullu-auz pass below the E ridge and seek a route from the south. The search party therefore decided to approach from the south, through the Tiutiun valley, in the hope of meeting the route taken by Donkin and Fox. After a careful reconnaissance by Freshfield, the pass and a steep but broken rock rib leading to it were identified. Dent recalled that during the ascent of the rib

> . . . from time to time an opportunity would be found of gazing to the right or left, but progress was tolerably continuous. Maurer, who was leading, looked upwards now and again as he worked out the best line of ascent, but the rocks were so steep that he could only see a very few feet. Just about midday, as he stopped for a moment to look upwards, I saw his expression suddenly change. 'Herr Gott!' he gasped out, 'the sleeping-place!' I think I shall never forget the thrill the words sent through me. A hurried glance up and we saw, some six or eight feet above the leader, a low wall of stones. In a moment we were all together within the little enclosure, or on the narrow ledge by its side. The suddenness of the discovery was for a few moments overpowering. We had felt certain that some such bivouac existed. We believed that we should find it. We knew for an absolute certainty that nothing more than evidence of a fatal accident could be obtained, and yet the blow came as if freshly inflicted.
>
> The sleeping-place consisted of a wall of stones, carefully built, about two feet high, and of horseshoe shape. The circle was completed by an overhanging rock at the back. The enclosure measured about six feet across, and some eight feet in length. Carefully arranged in this space, and almost entirely covered by the snow which had drifted and fallen into it, we could just make out

the sleeping-bags with two mackintosh coats spread over them. A cooking-pan half full of water was placed ready for use under a stone, and, close by, a loaded revolver hung from a projecting splinter of rock. There was a good store of provisions. No rope was to be seen. Donkin's camera too was absent. He had doubtless, according to his usual custom, taken it with him, intending to carry it as far as possible. I think none who were present will ever lose the power of recalling the scene in the minutest details. As we stood there the explanation of what had happened eleven months before was as clear as if we had found a written description. The character of the place has been reproduced for us by Mr. Willink's skill with surprising accuracy, the drawing being founded on a sketch made on the spot by Capt. Powell.

Freshfield and Woolley, with Jossi, continued to the pass where a small cairn was found. It was concluded that Donkin and Fox and their guides, after reaching the pass from the other side and bivouacking on the rock rib below, decided not to descend the rib to reach the Tiutiun glacier and fell to their deaths while attempting to traverse the steep cliffs below the difficult E ridge. This conclusion was greeted with relief by the local inhabitants, and it was accepted by the authorities that the missing climbers had lost their lives as a result of a mountaineering accident.

While in the Caucasus, Woolley, who had climbed Kazbek (5047m) on 13 July with the three guides and Fischer, reached, with Jossi, the unclimbed E peak of Mishirgi (4918m) on 5 August. This expedition provided another opportunity to examine the W and S ridges of Koshtantau and on 8 August Woolley, accompanied by Jossi, Kaufmann and a local hunter, set out with the intention of finding a route to the summit. On reaching the Tiutiun glacier the hunter could not continue and when he

> ... saw us preparing to cross the ice-fall he was obviously much impressed by the gravity of our undertaking, and showed his solicitude in various ways. First he asked me to give him a portion of his pay; then he produced his untouched breakfast (rye-bread and cold mutton), and pressed us to take it; finally he shook us each by the hand, making, for him, a long speech in the Tatar dialect, which we took to be a parting benediction; and after our departure he sat for a long time on a hillock watching our progress with evident misgiving and disapproval.

Woolley and the two guides bivouacked beside the Tiutiun glacier and on the following day continued up the glacier to reach the S ridge. After ascending for some way Kaufmann, who had been unwell, was forced to rest, but Woolley and Jossi went on up the ridge in deteriorating conditions to complete the first ascent of the peak. Woolley later recalled that 'the gloomy, threatening sky and driving masses of cloud gave to the scene a peculiarly impressive character of wildness and desolation'.

After being overtaken by darkness during the descent Woolley was relieved to regain the bivouac where 'as plenty of wood was left, a cheerful fire was soon blazing under our kettle. The soup was a brilliant success, and before long we were wrapped in sleep, sound enough in my case to defy even the sharp ridges of the miniature Schreckhorn, which formed such a prominent feature of my couch.'

Ten days later, on 19 August, Woolley, with Jossi, made the first ascent of Ailama (4523m), to the SE of Shkhara. Before leaving the range he also climbed Elbruz (5633m) with both guides and made two unsuccessful attempts to reach the S and higher summit of Ushba (4710m). Freshfield and Powell climbed the N peak of Laila and made a number of explorations in the Bezingi and Adyrsu regions. Another visitor to the Caucasus was Vittorio Sella who, with his brother Erminio, the guide Daniele Maquignaz and three porters, travelled extensively throughout the range, taking many fine photographs, climbing Elbruz and making the first ascents of Ullu-auz Bashi (4679m), to the N of Koshtantau, and the central, highest, peak of Laila (3986m).

In the Pyrenees an outstanding climb for the period was the first ascent of the Couloir de Gaube in the N face of the Vignemale by Henri Brulle, Jean Bazillac and Roger de Monts, with Célestin Passet and François Bernard Salles, on 7 August. It is recorded that while descending after the climb the party celebrated this remarkable achievement with drinks offered by Count Henri Russell, who was staying in one of his grottoes on the mountain.

Several expeditions of note were completed in more distant regions. In East Africa Hans Meyer, the Leipzig geographer, and Ludwig Purtscheller of Salzburg made the first ascent of Kibo (5895m), the highest peak of Kilimanjaro. Meyer, who had attained a height of approximately 5500m on Kibo two years earlier, and Purtscheller reached the main crater rim by way of the Ratzel glacier on 3 October, but were too late to continue the ascent and returned to their camp on the saddle between Kibo and the neighbouring peak of Mawenzi (5149m). Two days later they

> ... reached, after five hours' scrambling, a 'roomy lava-cave' much nearer to the peak. Starting thence at 3a.m. on the 6th, they gained their previous position by 8.45, and turning to the left followed the ridge to the summit. Three small rocky peaks rise through the ice, each of which they climbed, and found that the middle one was the highest. At 10.45 they planted the German flag and named the rocky tooth 'Kaiser Wilhelm-Spitze'.

Meyer and Purtscheller then turned their attention to the more difficult Mawenzi. Although the highest point – now known as Hans Meyer Peak – was not reached, they succeeded on 15 October in making the first ascent of one of the other Mawenzi peaks, identified from Meyer's account of the climb as the peak now named Klute Peak (5095m).

In Papua New Guinea, on 11 June, a party led by Sir William MacGregor made the first known ascent of the highest peak in the Owen Stanley range (4072m), some 75km north-east of Port Moresby. Starting on 17 May from a camp beside the Vanapa river the party encountered difficult terrain, including dense rain forest, during the long approach to the peak, which was named Mount Victoria.

In Mexico on 3 November James de Salis led the first recorded ascent of Ixtaccihuatl (5286m), one of the three high volcanoes to the south-east of Mexico City.

In the Karakoram Francis Younghusband, who had been sent to investigate raids on caravans crossing the Karakoram pass and to search for other passes in the range, continued his exploration of the region. Despite indifferent weather, Younghusband crossed several high passes with his ponies and a small Gurkha escort, discovering the Gasherbrum and Urdok glaciers in the course of his travels.

At home, on 17 March, Geoffrey Hastings made the second ascent of the Napes Needle, at the front of the Needle Ridge on Great Gable. The Needle, which had been climbed by W P Haskett-Smith nearly three years earlier, was also climbed by F Wellford, on 22 June, and John Wilson Robinson, on 12 August. In Scotland the development of climbing was given a considerable impetus by the foundation of two climbing clubs. The first of these, the Cairngorm Club, was formally constituted at a meeting in Aberdeen on 9 January. A few weeks later, on 11 February, at a meeting in Glasgow, it was decided to form a club which, it was suggested, should be called 'A Scottish Alpine Club'. As one of the original members later recalled, 'exception was taken to this on the grounds that it would possibly diminish its significance by contrasting it with "The Alpine Club". On the other hand, to call it "The Scottish Mountaineering Club" would give it a sufficiently distinctive designation and lead to no invidious comparisons.'

On 21 October the death occurred of John Ball, the first President of the Alpine Club, the editor of the first volume of *Peaks, Passes and Glaciers* – the forerunner of the *Alpine Journal* – and the author of the three volumes of the *Alpine Guide*. W A B Coolidge, writing in the *Alpine Journal* for November 1889, the last number to be published under his editorship, described the *Alpine Guide* as

> ... the first of Alpine classics. I have had over twenty years' experience of this guide-book, largely in those parts of the Alps least known even to Mr. Ball; and I wish to place on record my profound admiration of the amazing success with which the author has firmly grasped the main lines of the topography of the most unfrequented districts; so that all his followers have had to do has been to fill in the outline sketched out with so masterly a hand. I venture to state with the utmost confidence that no one man has ever possessed a wider or a more thorough knowledge of the entire chain of the Alps than Mr. Ball.

In conclusion, it seems appropriate to recall the following extract from Dent's valedictory address, read before the Alpine Club on 16 December 1889:

> I confess to agreeing with those who believe that mountaineering can never become wholly free from peril. The greater the experience and the more that experience is utilised the less will be the risk; but some risk there will ever be. Unfortunately the peril

has not yet nearly reached its minimum point. It can hardly be gainsaid that a small proportion of the accidents that occur are a reproach to mountaineering. Such as these it is the especial duty of this Club to guard against to the utmost of its ability. There is room for further efforts. By discouraging mountaineering which is but flashy athleticism, by bearing constantly in mind that a wholesome responsibility attaches to our Society which is at once a burden and a privilege not to be thrown off, and by maintaining a respect for a sport which even a golf-player has been known to admit to be in some points superior to that seductive game, we may not indeed wholly eliminate what is ineradicable, but we may whittle the element of reproach down to vanishing point. And this brings me face to face with the question so often asked by unbelievers – Is the game, then, worth the candle? To that my answer is, unhesitatingly, Yes! and still yes! even when the question is asked of mountaineering which can neither plead the excuse of scientific aims nor the justification of new exploration.

The game is, of course, still worth the candle.

Correspondence

Box 226
Revelstoke, B.C.
VOE 2 S O
Canada

The Editor
Alpine Journal

29 September 1988

MOUNT BONNEY, 1888–1988

(*Plates 99–101*)

Sir,

One hundred years ago, on 9 August 1888, two eminent members of the British Alpine Club made the first ascent of a peak on the North American continent for the sole purpose of sport. The Rev William Spotswood Green and the Rev Henry Swanzy climbed Mount Bonney (3107m) in the Selkirk Mountains of British Columbia in Canada (see *AJ93*, 210, 1988/89. This reference gives the height of Mt Bonney as 3050m. 3107m is the height according to the map sheet Mt Revelstoke and Glacier National Parks, Canada Map Office 1987.)

On 4 August 1988 this historic climb was re-enacted by the Rev Jack Greenhalgh and myself, the Rev Lloyd Northcott. The record of the first climb in Green's *Among the Selkirk Glaciers* (1890) served as our guide. Very few people have visited the peak since, let alone followed the original route. Heavy undergrowth for 4km leading to the alpine meadows acts as an effective filter to keep the less determined at a distance. It took us 10 hours to penetrate this growth which at times was as thick as a cedar hedge. As we followed Green and Swanzy's footsteps we found the landscape nearly as they had described it, and without any trace of human activity.

Several times we might have turned back, but for the encouragement Green gave us in his account. We knew that he had felt the same trepidation and that he had succeeded. There was a very steep headwall overhung by a cornice barring the obvious route to the ridgeline. Later there was a nasty forepeak composed of loose, wet, even in places muddy, rock. There was a long way to go to get to the peak and back off the ridge by nightfall. It was uncanny how the words of the first climbers rang in our ears as we made our way, and as we stood on the peak to honour William Green and Henry Swanzy, the fathers of mountaineering in Canada.

Fr Greenhalgh and I are Anglican priests, like the first two ascensionists. Jack was rector of Revelstoke in the 1970s, and I am the current rector. Both of us have enjoyed mountaineering for many years. We were sponsored in our anniversary climb by Parks Canada which arranged publicity and colour slide presentations in Revelstoke and Roger's Pass. I hope that it is not immodest to say that the photographs we took turned out to be of excellent quality. I thought that you might be interested and might care to print this letter for the benefit of your readers.

Yours faithfully,
Lloyd Northcott

Area Notes

COMPILED BY A V SAUNDERS

The Western Alps 1988

LINDSAY GRIFFIN

(*Plate* 102)

A prolonged spell of fine weather during August allowed British parties to complete a variety of routes in the Mont Blanc range. Most of the activity, however, again took place on the easily accessible, less serious and often heavily overcrowded rock walls which now offer some outstanding modern classic free climbs. At higher altitudes, Rob Durran and Jerry Gore repeated the Gabarrou-Long route on the Red Pillar of Brouillard, finding the free climbing to be less technical than that noted by the first ascensionists but having considerable problems with the hard aid pitch (first free climbed by John Sylvester in 1986!). They were not amused to find their car vandalized and equipment stolen on returning to the Val Veni parking lot – an occurrence which is now distressingly common on this side of the range and is certainly not unheard-of on the other. They also completed the Guides' Route on the Dru and thought it an excellent two-day outing, with only one or two sections on less-than-sound granite. The route was climbed virtually free as far as the 'Niche', after which an overnight storm dictated a more traditional approach.

Far from the madding crowd, on the quiet walls of Petit Mont Gruetta above the Frébouze glacier, Tony Penning and Peter Cresswell discovered a new line up slabs and grooves on the open face to the right of the Emery route. They found good quality climbing, especially in the lower third, with difficulties up to VII; a description will be included in the forthcoming Guide. There are now at least six routes on this slabby face, perhaps the best being the 1983 Grassi-Meneghin (V+). The vertical interval attributed to some climbs in the past is thought to be rather exaggerated.

At the time of writing the foundations of the Trident hut are far from stable: prospective clientèle are recommended to use the Col de la Fourche hut, or risk an early and somewhat unpremeditated descent to the Brenva glacier.

Unusually, the Dauphiné retained a lot of snow, and pure ice routes remained in superb condition until well into August. British parties climbed a number of these, and at least one new route was created. Not for the first time, a party completing the classic Gervasutti route on the NW face of the Ailefroide found it hard, loose and frightening.

North Face of the Brèche du Glacier Noir (Dauphiné)

A very steep piece of ice climbing taking the obvious shallow couloir that snakes down from the upper snow slopes, immediately below the brèche. The difficult middle section remains in the shade all day and is protected from stone-fall by a rock wall to its left. Belays are not easy to arrange and the climbing is reminiscent of routes on the Minus face of Ben Nevis.

First Ascent: L Hardy and N Parks, 17 July 1988, c500m, ED inf.

Follow the wide couloir of the Marmier-Rabet route on the N face of the Arêtes and where this forks, after 150m, branch left (the Marmier-Rabet route takes the right fork) and reach the 250m rock wall in the centre of the face. Climb a vertical ice smear in two 50m pitches to a shallow couloir. Four more pitches of gradually easing difficulty lead to the upper slopes and the brèche is gained after a further 100m (11h from the bergschrund).

Descent: Reach the summit of the Ailefroide Orientale easily in 20min, then follow the normal descent route to the Sélé hut (2½h).

Józef Nyka adds:

Rocchetta Alta (2412m) (Eastern Dolomites)

A Polish team composed of Władysław Kacorzyk, Jacek Kantyka and Janusz Skorek completed the first winter ascent (and probably second ascent) of the Martini route via the N face. Attempts on 9 and 11–12 February 1988 failed in bad weather at 80 and 120m height. Ropes were left. On 14 February they started the final push. On the 16th a shelf at the base of the overhanging upper part was reached where the team spent three nights, equipping the crux pitches via the great overhangs. Returns to the tent on the shelf demanded acrobatic manoeuvres. On 19 February they reached easier terrain and the summit ridge. The last bivouac was on the E side of the ridge.

The term N face really refers to the North Pillar of the Rocchetta Alta (survey point 2309m). It is some 750m high and has 25 pitches of UIAA V, VI, A3. Only three pitches are easier than V. There is no sun on it at all during the winter. The route was first climbed on 2–6 September 1978 by S Martini, P Leoni and M Tranquilini. There are seven other routes on the face. The Rocchetta Alta di Bosconero is located in the eastern part of the Dolomites – north of Longarone and Belluno. A good 'Base Camp' is the Bosconero hut at the foot of the mountain.

Because of the high technical difficulty of the climb and the hard wintry conditions during the ascent, this was one of the most notable achievements of the 1988 winter in the Dolomites.

Lindsay Griffin would welcome further information and new route descriptions for publication in these pages at: 2 Top Sling, Tregarth, Bangor, Gwynedd LL57 4RL.

Spain: The Sierra de Gredos 1988

LINDSAY GRIFFIN

(Plate 103)

Guidebooks: *Gredos mountains and Sierra Nevada* (R G Collomb), West Col 1987.

La Sierra de Gredos (Adrados), Guias de Montana 1981.

After last year's article by John Harding (*AJ93*, 141–145, 1988/89) which concentrated on the ski-mountaineering potential of the range, it is perhaps worth drawing attention to the very fine ice-climbing that is available from the conveniently situated Elola hut in the Gredos Cirque.

Jan Solov and Lindsay Griffin spent about eight days here at Easter (late March/April) in 1988. There was plenty of snow around and, without a track, the walk to the hut with heavy sacks takes five to six hours from the roadhead at La Plataforma. The hut, which holds 130, had at least this number of visitors for the national holiday, though there were apparently no other climbers. An AC card allowed half-price accommodation at £1 a night from the very friendly guardians. The weather was perfect for the first five days, with night-time temperatures of −3 to −4°C, giving ice conditions comparable with the best experienced in Scotland and crisp névé elsewhere. The rock is rough red granite. Summiteers are rewarded with beautiful panoramas across the vast expanse of the southern plains.

The normal route to the summit of Ameal de Pablo (2505m) was well plastered with a build-up of futuristically sculptured rime. It gave a short, enjoyable outing at Scottish 2, and so did the diagonal chimney line on the S face (mixed Scottish 3). Ice-falls on the direct approach to this peak from the hut gave several pitches of Scottish 2/3.

One of the most obvious lines in the area is the central gully on the NE face of Al Manzour (2592m). After a steady approach up perfect névé, the crux gave a pitch reminiscent of, though slightly easier than, the left fork of Clogwyn Du. The airy summit (and highest point) in the range was reached directly after a few more enjoyable pitches on mixed ground (Scottish 3/4).

Various parts of the main ridge were traversed and the spectacular crossing of La Galana was found to be particularly worthwhile. The complete horseshoe from Altos del Morezon to the Paso del Rey in the west would give a magnificent expedition, although it is possible to avoid many of the difficulties by descents on to the S flank. It is probably pretty good value in summer!

South of the hut the 300m face leading to the Campana crest sported an imposing free-standing icicle and several long and interesting lines leading on to the upper slopes. The N face of Cuchillar de las Navajas (2507m) lies above a snow basin that can be reached directly (Scottish 1/2) or traversed on to. Above lies a wealth of attractive gullies and ice smears. One of the more obvious lines was climbed in four pitches (Scottish 5), and there is obviously scope for some thin and sustained entertainment.

Great Britain 1988

The *Alpine Journal* has in the past reported British developments under the heading of Scottish Winter. It seems natural to extend these reports to other areas of the United Kingdom. The emphasis will be on mountaineering rather than cragging; this will tend to mean winter climbing. This volume of the journal adds to Scotland the current state of winter climbing in the Lake District and Wales; future reviews will be on an occasional basis.

Scottish Winter 1987–88

KEN CROCKET

Quiet rumblings about the present system of winter grading stayed at the ripple level, indicating that climbers were either content with the *status quo*, or could not be bothered to stick stamp to envelope. I suspect the former. The following notes will be shorter than of recent years, as Scotland suffered (?) a disastrous three-month spell of virtually constant thaw. Considering the number of climbs done during the thaw, it seems a miracle that so few teams were avalanched or bombed by falling ice. (This does not imply, however, that any of the following routes were climbed in such conditions.)

In the Northern Highlands, the continuing slow pace of research for the next edition of the *SMC Climbers' Guide* to this vast area has maintained a chronic confusion, the intensity of which is inversely proportional to the amount of *SMC Journal* reading an individual explorer is prepared or able to do. Thus we have three routes on Beinn Dearg Mhor which do not refer to pre-existing lines: Fat Man's Folly (220m III/IV), Broken Finger Gully (250m IV), and Spring Maiden (250m V), climbed by combinations of A Todd, D Curr and G Taylor in March or April 1987. Mick Fowler continued to bomb up the winding roads on quick raiding sorties which produced, among other routes, a IV and a IV/V on An Teallach (Bowling Alley and Bottomless Gully, in April and March respectively), and a V/VI on Beinn Dearg in March (Ice Bomb, on the Upper Cliff of Coire Ghranda, named after the prominent ice boss which forms on the cliff). Martin Moran, living in Strathcarron, found a 200m IV on An Coileachan in the Fannichs in December 1987 (The Turf Accountant).

In the Torridon Giants a dozen lines were recorded, including three at IV and one easier line on Liathach. The hard climbing was on Beinn Eighe, however, with the Far East Wall – thus far reserved for steep rock routes – now seeing outrageously steep winter climbs. Cunningham and Nisbet climbed the Grade VI Vishnu, a 100m line up a major fault-line left of The Rising Son. Protection was found to be poor. The same duo made a winter ascent of Kamikaze at V/VI, noting that because of much chimneying sacks were better left off. Both of these routes were climbed in February. On the Eastern Ramparts Cunningham and Nisbet climbed Gnome Wall in February, at V, finding the last pitch much harder than earlier ones. Finally, on 5 April Fowler and Morrison climbed West Central Gully on the Triple Buttresses at VI. The gully was easy except for the crux section, a 65m, ice-smeared, overhanging chimney.

On the SE Cliff of Fuar Tholl, Jenkins and Moran found the 220m, Grade V Evasion Grooves, providing a mixed alternative to Tholl Gate by climbing the large buttress to its right.

Further east, Lochnagar continued to provide winter ascents, with Findlay and Strange recording several routes, including Sepulchre on The Cathedral at IV in December, and Eclipse at IV/V on Shadow Buttress B in March. Postern Direct on Shelter Stone Crag provided a hard VI for Nisbet and

Cunningham in early March. The crux was the last pitch, climbed via the wide corner crack immediately right of the summer line. As the summer route is in a dangerous condition following a rock-fall in the spring of 1987, a winter ascent is probably safer. In January the same energetic duo avoided heavy powder snow conditions on other crags by climbing the 170m V/VI Windpiper on the Stag Rocks, a combination of Windchill and Sand-Pyper Direct.

S Richardson and R Clothier (he of the 12 axes a winter) had a great time climbing Citadel on the Shelter Stone, a four-hour wait just below the top allowing the moonlight to point out a finishing route via the Sticil Face (Citadel, Moonlight Finish, 60m V).

On Ben Nevis the thaws did climbing little good. We should go back to the previous winter, however, and mention the burst of soloing on 20 March 1987 by the French climber François Damilano. In one day: Point Five, Orion Face, Zero Gully, Sickle, and Smith's Route. There were things done on the hills surrounding the Ben by other energetics, including a V on Aonach Beag's W face by Everett and Richardson, in addition to several easier routes. Also requiring a long walk were the routes recorded on the N face of Ben Alder in January by Everett and friends, including a IV and a V, both about 250m in length.

Glencoe activity was confined to the Grade V Para Andy on Stob Coire nan Lochan's N buttress (Cunningham, Nisbet and Newton, January), Intruder at V by Rab Anderson and Grahame Nicoll on the same buttress (February), and two Grade VIs on the N face of Aonach Dubh. Against All Odds by Fowler and Watts lies between Kuf and Fingal's Chimney, and apparently had been a glint in Fowler's eye for a long time. It is very hard, and has much climbing on frozen tufts of grass, pitch three requiring three pegs for aid on an overhanging (and tuftless) section. Further right, Taylor and Anderson climbed the summer route Fall Out, Anderson providing his mathematical individual pitch grading: 140m, Grade VI (3) (7) (7) (7) (4). Apart from their unsightliness, one wonders how much such pitch gradings (and pitches) will be affected by varying conditions, and consequently how useful such a Ward-Drummondish grading system would be.

Finally, we have pleasure in seeing in print the new SMC Climbers' Guide to Arran, Arrochar and The Southern Highlands. Of interest to winter climbers will be the section on the Bridge of Orchy Hills, bringing to a wider audience the delights of Beinn an Dothaidh and Beinn Udlaidh, to mention only two hills. Recent exploration in this area has seen the maturation of the NE Coire of Beinn an Dothaidh, and several hard routes on the two cliffs of Coire an Dothaidh, facing Bridge of Orchy. Lucifer Rising at V by McEwan, Crocket and Walker, on Creag Coire an Dothaidh in March, was named partly to contrast with Messiah, VI, on the other cliff, Creag nan Socach, by Little in January. The 88m corner of Messiah had been eyed by a few teams for over a decade, but with virtually no drainage coming down the cliff little ice ever seemed to form.

At the left end of the same crag, a December ascent of The Glass Bead Game, V, by a party of five, with Bob Duncan leading the crucial slab pitch on this poorly protected cliff, made up for an earlier retreat during a snowstorm. The snow on the actual ascent was of just the right amount; too much, and toeholds for front points will be obscured. This was not the problem on Lucifer

Rising, where the sun was thawing the frozen turf and slowing the party of three. Once it was freezing again, the possible dangers of exposure to starlight forced a left traverse across the upper part of the cliff. By the time you read this, the wished-for finish will (hopefully) have been done. Buy the guide to find out about the other fine routes on this cliff, and the others of the region, including the wonderful ice-falls of Beinn Udlaidh.

The Lake District

BRIAN DAVISON

Recent winters have seen a change in the type of new routes being climbed in the Lakes. Following the trend of Scottish climbers, locals have moved out from the gullies on to buttresses. Al Phizaklea with Ed Cleasby and Dave Kay set the early pace with winter ascents of several Scafell classics, including Pisgah Buttress Direct (V) and the often-eyed Botterill's Slab (V). Abseiling into climbable ice on Scafell's E buttress gave dubious ascents of the top sections of a few climbs, including White Slab (III). While these were fortunately omitted from the recent guide they did indicate the possibilities, given the right conditions.

The 1985 winter saw Brian Davison and Richard Jones stepping in where the locals had failed to tread with ascents of Moss Ghyll Grooves (IV/V) and Engineers' Slabs (V). By now various groups were looking beyond Scafell, and excellent conditions in 1986 saw new routes throughout the Lakes. The eastern crag of Hutaple yielded an Accidental Discharge (V) to Dave Kay and Joe Grinberg, while Phizacklea and Hasley caught the Midnight Special (IV/V) at Scrubby Crag. Dave Kay's interest in Pillar gave Gomorrah (V), while Bowfell's Cambridge Crag saw ascents of the Left Hand (V) and the Right Hand (V) routes and Siamese Chimney (V) by Rick Graham. Crinkle Gill acquired a Wight-out (V), Whiteout (V) and a Rae of Sunshine (V) from Bob Wightman and John White, while Southern Corner (III/IV) on Pike Crag was climbed by Steve Howe. Various other routes were done throughout the region, but the major activity still centred on Scafell. Tricouni Slab (IV) was climbed by Phizacklea and Smith and quickly repeated by Jim Fotheringham and Vic Saunders, while Tony Stephenson climbed out of Steep Ghyll by its Grooves (V) and the Bridge of Sighs (V). The Pinnacle Face offered up a confusing array of Jones' and Hopkinson's routes, Age Concern (V) being Dave Kay's renamed winter version of Jones's Route from Deep Ghyll, not to be confused with Jones's Route Direct from Lord's Rake (VI) done in 1984 by Phizacklea. Hopkinson's Gully (V) received an ascent, as did Moonbathing (V), a Phizacklea line based on Hopkinson's Cairn. Two of the most impressive ascents caused controversy, when Tony Brindle and Adrian Moore took two days over Central Buttress, breaking the rules with an abseil into above the Great Flake on the second day, the flake being climbed without axes or crampons, so posing the question: was it in winter condition? An impressive lead, but surely no more impressive than Menlove Edwards's 1931 ascent. On the E buttress Fotheringham's ascent of Overhanging Wall (VI) showed that it is possible to climb from the bottom of this steep buttress if conditions are right. The climb, unfortunately, was tarnished by four aid points on the lower section.

The following season saw fewer routes, Grinberg and Kay adding Wall Climb (V) and Ginny Cleft (V) to Scrubby Crag, and Davison and Atkinson climbed Slanting Groove (IV) on Pike Crag before repeating Botterill's Slab. On Scafell Mulvaney and Davison's ascent of Harvest (V/VI) freed a normally aided summer pitch, while further up Moss Ghyll the groove of Clockwork Orange (VI) gave Jones and Davison a difficult and serious exit from the Ghyll.

Last year's mild winter saw little Lakeland activity, the weather not having the reliability of Scotland. Most of the routes are the work of a few local activists and the odd determined outsider, and as yet few have had repeats, so grades may vary with the individual.

Welsh Winter Climbing

MALCOLM CAMPBELL

In the 'Good Olde Days' climbing was climbing – whatever the season. Winter was merely a colder version of summer; the snow, a bit of an inconvenience; and the ice-axe still a tool and not a handhold. And so it was until the coming of the second ice age – around 1971. During these early years, the great snow gullies (not to mention some of the more difficult 'modern' buttresses) of Snowdonia were visited by the likes of Eckenstein, Archer Thomson, Owen Glynne Jones, Winthrop Young, Mallory, the 1953 Everest Men, and the Rock and Ice. But, in contrast to the case of rock climbing, there has been no tradition of recording or cataloguing climbs done under winter conditions – hardly surprising, given the marginal nature of the average Welsh winter. For who is to say when an 'ascent' becomes a 'winter ascent' – in the Alps, it's the date that decides it; in Scotland they have a 'proper' winter; in Wales, it's just climbing!

However, it's still worth remembering that Archer Thomson climbed out of the Devil's Kitchen in March 1895, and ascended Ladies' Gully and Cave Gully on Snowdon in the winter of 1898; O G Jones and the Abraham brothers climbed Central Gully on Glyder Fawr in 1899, and the right-hand branch of Clogwyn Ddu Gully in the same winter; Joe Brown plucked Western Gully on the Black Ladders and the classic South Gully in Idwal, in 1952 or thereabouts, and Slanting Gully on Lliwedd in 1964; Martin Boysen teetered up Cloggy's Black Cleft in 1963; and Dave Alcock assaulted Central Gully on Lliwedd and Ypres on the battle-scarred Black Ladders in 1968, while Jack Street and Paul Nunn attacked Ice-fall Gully on the same crag. And all this before the advent of the irremovable ice-axe, the irreplaceable Snarg, and the iridescent Koflach boot.

But, following the Chouinard/Cunningham revolution, everyone was at it! Climbing steep ice not only became possible, but it actually became *easy*! The masses moved in, and in 1974 Rick Newcombe produced the first edition of his excellent *Winter Climbs in North Wales* in response to this upsurge of interest. This book made no attempt to be 'definitive', consisting mainly of climbs undertaken by Rick and his friends from Bangor University Mountaineering Club, together with the well-known classics.

In the excellent winter of 1969, Newcombe was involved in early, if not first, ascents of Central Gully on Lliwedd, Snowdrop on the Clogwyn y Garnedd face of Snowdon, and Central Route on Clogwyn y Geifr in Cwm Idwal. But, as Rick himself says, '. . . first ascents on snow and ice occur every time someone makes an ascent – it's never the same twice, and I always like to think that some quiet, anonymous climber who climbs for his own personal enjoyment did the routes years ago . . .'

Following the publication of the guide, the winter weather went into retreat for a number of years (no suggestion at this time of the 'greenhouse' gases' getting out of hand, although a fair amount of methane and hot air could be detected escaping from the Padarn on a Saturday night), but it returned with a vengeance in the two great winters of 1978 and 1979.

While the Scots were busy bemoaning the 'too cold' conditions, Welsh ice took a quantum leap forward under the guidance of Martin Boysen, Tut Braithwaite and London raider Mick Fowler. But in 1978 Idwal's jewel, The Appendix, fell to local lad Mick Poynton, who just outdistanced some thoroughbred opposition in the race to embrace this fragile entrail. Mick has since shown that this was no flash in the pan, with stylish ascents of the best of Welsh ice. More recently, he starred in Alan Hughes's *Affinity with Ice*, an exciting video featuring some classic Welsh ice and some classic horseplay by Paul Williams. But back to the great freezes of the seventies!

In 1978, Fowler opened his account modestly enough with Cascade on Craig y Rhaeadr in the Pass, but the following year it was a one-horse race: Skid Row on Llech Ddu (the first winter breach of this imposing crag), Jubilee Climb, Brwynog Chimney, The Arête, Camus and Silver Machine on Cloggy, East Peak Direct and Central Gully Direct on Lliwedd, Central Ice-fall Direct, Chequered Wall and Grooved Slab on Craig y Rhaeadr – all succumbed to the mighty Fowler axe. And, with the exception of Jubilee Climb, none of the other routes on Cloggy have seen second ascents, unlike Cascade and Central Ice-fall Direct, which have tended to become stepped highways whenever they have formed. Indeed, both have suffered the ultimate ignominy – of being soloed by John Barry (as indeed has The Devil's Appendix, although not without recourse to a mind-gathering rest, clipped to both tools!).

Fowler apart, the remaining crumbs were fairly evenly distributed: Tut Braithwaite managed to steal Bloody Slab on Cloggy; Roger Baxter-Jones, in a less well-publicized effort, forced a winter ascent of neighbouring Great Slab, while Martin Boysen had to make do with The Somme (formerly known as Lost Gully) on the Ladders, and Maria, a little gem on Gallt yr Ogof, the crag behind Helyg. Meanwhile, down in deepest, darkest mid-Wales, local guru John Sumner, aided and abetted by John Codling, was busy proving that ice-climbing was not solely a phenomenon of the frozen north. Trojan on Cadair Idris, Sloose on Gist Ddu and the brilliant Maesglasau Falls near Dinas Mawddwy are three-star routes to rank with the best in Britain.

With all this frantic activity going on, Rick Newcombe rushed out a revised version of the guide to incorporate the new wave – and, predictably, the mild winters resumed. Winter climbing continued, but it wasn't until January/ February 1985 that the ice age returned, and once again Mick Fowler was very much to the fore, this time treading on the toes of John Sumner in his mid-Wales backyard. The big line to the left of Trojan became Colonial Virgin, after Fowler's Kiwi partner had completed his first British winter climb in some style. The obscure Craig Bodlyn in the Rhinogs was the next target, with Crag Jones and 'Slippery Vic' Saunders getting in on the Fowler act to record a quartet of 'modern Vs' in the form of Chain Gang, Cryogenics, The Screaming and Riskophilia. Meanwhile, Slippery Vic slipped off quietly to grab some action on Gist Ddu, where the groove next to Sloose became Magic Moss after the style of climbing on the crux!

Meanwhile, closer to the hub, the locals were stirring from their winter-long hibernation in Pete's Eats. Someone discovered that Aber Falls had gone and frozen, so Rock Godfather Paul Williams donned his hard hat and dragged Martin Crook off in search of fame. Together with the Poynton brothers, they were responsible for three of the four superb water-ice lines which resulted from these apparently freak conditions. In more traditional surroundings, Martin Crook added Y Chimney to Llech Ddu, Arcturus to the wet streak above the Grochan descent gully, and the very fine Aquarian Wall to the largely ignored but potentially superb Cwm Silyn crags. This last route was climbed with the irrepressible John Redhead, whose first venture into winter left a lasting impression – he seems not to have returned! Cwm Silyn also saw the rediscovery of the three-star Bedrock Gully, and Martin Crook gave it an equally fine and slightly harder finish up the steep, hanging left-hand branch. The Mask of Death typifies modern steep ice-climbing in Wales, and illustrates the new wave of winter route names from the twisted mind of Martin Crook – Deffing out the Ben, Fear of the Wagg and Broadmoor, to mention just a few more!

Malcolm Campbell dragged John Barry off to the remote Cwm Dulyn in the Carneddau to discover Quicksilver, while John Sylvester, thinking along similar lines, found Fairy Falls. This wet, slimy area has a number of other obvious winter lines for which there appear to be no recorded ascents, although it seems unlikely that others have not been there before. Meanwhile, Wil Hurford and Paul Williams whizzed off to the far west where a number of steep frozen streams in another Cwm Dulyn, just beyond Cwm Silyn, gave some excellent sport in the middle grades.

If 1985 was good, 1986 was outstanding. Aber Falls froze again and stayed frozen for most of February, as did Craig y Rhaeadr and every stream above sea level; but this time there was more snow on the mountain crags, and the emphasis shifted away from low-level water ice. The Black Ladders was where it was at, and with rumours of a new guide flying around, everyone was keen to get their name on the scoresheet – and, fortunately for the rest of us, Fowler was busy in the NW Highlands. Ian Sherrington with George Smith produced the fine Post War, a hard variation on The Somme and Chris Parkin with Dave O'Dowd fought their way up Flanders, the summer HVS rib to the left of Western Gully. Although this is a classic mixed arête in its upper reaches, the lower pitches involve hard wall-climbing on ground which doesn't ice, and this was probably a turning-point for Welsh winter climbing, along the lines of the Cairngorm experience. Also on The Ladders, O'Dowd followed the summer line of Cannon Rib to give another winter desperate, after Tut Braithwaite and Ian Carr had climbed The Polar Bear, a line of turfy grooves in the same area. Along similar lines, during the one good freeze of 1987, Manx Wall on The Nameless Cwm's Clogwyn Ddu received an ascent in partial winter conditions, just to confirm the direction in which things were moving.

Subsequent less severe winters have seen a remarkable number of hard ascents on crags whose condition would not be classified as 'winter' by the traditional yardstick. Ian Carr climbed Church Buttress on Clogwyn y Ddysgyl, and Arctic Fox, a variation on Ypres on the Black Ladders, whilst Tut Braithwaite – the old master of hard, mixed climbing – returned to the West Buttress of Cloggy with Ian Carr to force a winter ascent of Longland's Climb.

Ian reports: 'The route was climbed under optimum conditions of névé, heavy powder and verglas. In these conditions, together with good weather, the route took seven hours to climb . . . PLEASE NOTE THAT NO PEGS WERE USED (*sic*). The overall grade of the route is considered to be VI.'

And so, with the eventual appearance of the new guide signalling, perhaps, the end of the old order, the future 'development' of hard winter climbing is now clear. Most ice, and snow capable of consolidation, has been climbed, so the trend is bound to be towards more and more 'summery' ascents of harder and harder climbs. It may grind to a halt before axe and crampons skitter their way up a verglassed Cenotaph Corner but then again, it may not! In any case, there will always be plenty of fuel for argument and speculation in this curiously masochistic branch of our sport.

Canadian Arctic and Alaska 1988

TED WHALLEY

Until recently, almost all the topographical maps of the eastern Arctic were on the scale of 1:250,000 or smaller and had contour intervals of 500 or 200ft, i.e. about 150 or 60m. We are delighted that the Canada Centre for Mapping of the Department of Energy, Mines and Resources has recently announced its programme for new mapping on the scale of 1:50,000 for the years 1988–1992. It is particularly important for the eastern Arctic, because few maps on this scale have been published. The sheets derived from the 1:250,000 Clyde sheet will be mapped in 1988–89, and much of the eastern coast of Baffin Island is promised for 1989–90. The mountains of Auyuittuq National Park will be mapped in 1990–91, and similar mapping of north-west Ellesmere Island is promised for 1991–92. Many of these maps, when they are published, will be very useful for mountain climbers in the area. Almost all the 1:50,000 maps of Bylot Island have already been published.

We must realize, of course, that the new maps reduce the uncertainties of our mountain climbing: route-finding using a 1:50,000 map is quite different from route-finding using a 1:250,000 map. The 1:250,000 map causes us more surprises on the ground, and so may make the route-finding and the climbing more difficult. But we can always throw away the large-scale maps if we wish to challenge ourselves more.

A full account of a ski traverse of Bylot Island made in 1984 by Mike and Ulrike Schmidt, Fred Bushnell, Mike Wingham, and Dave Clay has at last been published.[1] The expedition flew from Pond Inlet on 7 May to the N coast of Bylot Island, one day inland from Maud Bight, and spent the next few weeks traversing the island and climbing about 56 mountains; half of the climbs seem to have been first ascents.

Christian Dalphin, Bernard Wietlisbach, Xaver Bongard and Peter Gobet, a group of Swiss climbers, left the settlement of Clyde, in the middle of the E coast of Baffin Island, with three Inuit and kamatiks and snowmobiles. They carried supplies for six weeks and reached the western side of Sam Ford Fiord after three days and 180km, and after abandoning a snowmobile with piston trouble. They climbed in seven days the S face of the 1000m rock tower that lies between Belvedere Ridge in the north and Broad Peak in the south. They graded it UIAA VIb, A3+. A few days later they climbed the 700m N buttress in 17 hours non-stop and graded it UIAA VIb, A3. Bongard and Gobet climbed the 1100m Beluga Mountain in two days. They then waited for almost three weeks while the Inuit tried to reach them on the ice-choked sea, and reached Clyde on 23 August.

Tom Elliot, the Chief Warden of Auyuittuq National Park – which is on the Cumberland Peninsula and has about the area of Wales – reports that the 1988 climbing season was busy, 30 people from five countries visiting the Park for mountaineering and ski-touring. There are many days each year when many more people are on the summit of Snowdon or Helvellyn at the same time: the Park really is (still) an isolated and remote place. Most, but not all, climbers and walkers go to the area around Pangnirtung Pass because that is where most of the spectacular mountains, such as Mount Asgard, are. But there are other fine places where there is only a remote chance of meeting anyone.

The principal pass across Auyuittuq National Park is between Pangnirtung Fiord and North Pangnirtung Fiord. It has been called Pangnirtung Pass, but its name has recently been changed by a decision of the North-West Territories Executive Council to Akshayuk Pass, after the Inuk Akshayuk who pioneered the pass in the late 1890s. At the same time, the name 'Frobisher Bay' for the town at the head of Frobisher Bay, which was built during the war to help fly DC3s to the United Kingdom, has been changed to Iqaluit, the traditional Inuit name for the town. It seems inevitable that there will be more introductions of Inuit names in the east Arctic mountains in the future. The names often seem strange to western eyes and ears, but we shall no doubt become used to them. Few collections of Inuit names have been reported, one of the more extensive being a list of about 132 names along the coast between Home Bay and Cape Dyer on the east coast of Baffin Island, collected by K F Dudley.[2]

Dave MacAdam continued his lone journeys on the E coast of Baffin Island, this time in the region of Narpaing and Quajon Fiords in late June and July. At first the snow was very soft and deep, but it improved later and he managed to reach several minor heights.

Bob Seibert, of Denali Park and Preserve, Alaska, reports three solo winter attempts on Mount McKinley, of which only Vern Tejas's was successful. The High-Latitude Research Project tested a lightweight portable pressure bag for treating high-altitude pulmonary oedema, and also tested vasodilatory drugs. The flow of blood and oxygen to the brain is critical. There were 12 search-and-rescue operations, in one of which three Koreans were evacuated by helicopter in two separate incidents, probably the highest hoist operation in North America.

Bob Seibert reports that 916 persons attempted Mount McKinley in 1988, of whom 562 succeeded. Almost all were on the W buttress route. 103 climbers had acute mountain sickness; 12 of these were in danger of death. More than 18,000 climber days were spent on the mountain, of which 15,000 were on the W buttress; it is a busy place.

Some noteworthy climbs on McKinley and other Alaskan peaks are reported by H Adams Carter below. In addition, Mounts Hunter, Brooks, Silverthrone, Ragged, Dickey and Dan Beard, and East Kahiltna Peaks, were climbed by one or more parties.

The annual 'Accidents in North American Mountaineering 1988', which is compiled by Jed Williamson for the American Alpine Club and by Jim Whitteker for the Alpine Club of Canada, reports accidents that occurred in 1987.[3] It is an excellent report and it should be studied by all climbers so that we can learn from others' mistakes. It can be bought from either the Alpine Club of Canada, PO Box 126, Banff, Alberta, TOL OCO, or the American Alpine Club, 113 East 90th St, New York (10128–1589). It continues to astound me that some mountain climbers are prepared to accept high risks of death in order to climb their mountain. Extreme climbing, particularly at high altitude, must be one of the more dangerous things that we do; too many of us, perhaps, adopt the philosophy that 'it cannot happen to me'.

The only accident that was reported in the Yukon Territory was the presumed death of Dave Cheesmond and Catherine Freer on the Hummingbird Ridge of Mount Logan. Much snow fell while they were on the ridge, and they probably died in an avalanche.

10 accidents were reported in our areas; a brief summary is as follows. Brian Zelenka and Ben Benson climbed Pioneer Peak in Chugach State Park. On his way down, Zelenka went off the route and tried to glissade, but fell to his death when he was tired and the light was poor. Dan Dougherty and Mickey Pratt set out to climb the SE ridge of Mount Foraker on 1 May 1987 and, independently, Ian Bult and Dan Guthrie set out the following day to climb the same route. All four men seem to have been swept to their deaths by an avalanche.

Ben Benson and Frank Jenkins were approaching the summit of Mount Hunter (4415m) when they triggered a slab avalanche which killed Benson. Victor Grosley and Thomas Jannik climbed quickly from 3000m to 4500 on Mount McKinley. Jannik contracted pulmonary and cerebral oedema and was taken down to 4000m, from where he was able to descend alone. Sachikie Tokada, one of a Japanese expedition of three to Mount McKinley, became ill at 5200m, so the party descended to 4300m. A French expedition noticed her and took her down to the medical office on a sled, as her partners seemed unconcerned. A day later she still could not walk. Hubert Eggert and his partner were on the W buttress. Eggert returned to the 5200m camp while his partner went to the top with another team. The following morning, Eggert was semi-conscious and had to be lowered to the 4300m camp. There he was treated with oxygen and Decadrin and was flown out the next day.

Charles Sassara and Dave McGivern were climbing on a double rope 50m apart, when a large snow-block collapsed on them. Sassara had a rope tied three times around his neck, and was blue and not breathing. McGivern removed the rope and gave mouth-to-mouth resuscitation; after several hours both could descend slowly. They were eventually picked up by aeroplane, flown to Talkeetna and then to the hospital.

Thomas Bohanon and Richard Strong climbed to 5000m on Mount McKinley, but retreated to 4300m because they felt the effects of the altitude. On the following day, Bohanon climbed solo to the summit but tripped and fell 450m. He was evacuated by helicopter.

Franziska Bracher and Ivan Seeholzer of Switzerland went to the summit of Mount McKinley, at −35°C, from their camp at 5200m. Both had frostbitten toes and had to be treated in the hospital in Anchorage. Piotr Jankowiak fell almost 800m to his death while descending the Messner Couloir on Mount McKinley.

One of the five tents of a guided party on the W buttress of Mount McKinley was buried under one metre of snow by a slab avalanche on 8 July 1987. Fortunately, all members of the party were recovered alive. However,

Brian Hoover started up the Cassin Ridge on Mount McKinley but failed to return. He was not found in an air search, and is presumed dead.

REFERENCES

1   D R Clay. *Can Alp J 71*, 26–28, 1988.
2   K F Dudley. *Arctic Alp Res 4*, 343–347, 1972.
3   J E Williamson and J Whitteker, editors. *Accidents in North American Mountaineering 1988*. American Alpine Club, New York, and Alpine Club of Canada, Banff, pp 17–25.

H Adams Carter adds:

In Alaska Vern Tejas started the season by becoming the first man to climb Mount McKinley solo in winter and return to tell the tale. This was the second solo winter ascent, but Japanese climber Naomi Uemura disappeared during the descent. Tejas was on the mountain from 16 February to 15 March. 'I probably had five sunny days,' said Tejas. 'One of them was the day I flew in and another when I flew out.' He spent much of the time holed up in snow caves, pinned down by storms. He carried a five-metre ladder as protection against crevasses. The entire Pioneer Ridge of McKinley was climbed for the first time by Randy Waitman, Rowan Laver, Chuck Maffei and Jim Cancroft. Starting on 10 June from Wonder Lake, they carried supplies to the mountain and made a cache part-way along the ridge on the Flatiron. They then descended to the Muldrow glacier and to the very start of the ridge. Much of the lower part was a knife-edge above the Muldrow and Peters glaciers with pitches of 70° ice. After a week they reached their cache. The broader, somewhat easier upper part of the ridge to the N peak took another 10 days. They were back at Wonder Lake on 13 July. Andy Carson and friends made a new variation on the S buttress ramp on McKinley to the right of the serac-fall line. They feel that, though their route was steeper than the 1965 Japanese route, it is safer. South of McKinley, Jack Lewis and Tom Bauman made the first ascent of the Eye Tooth. It took them three days to climb 22 difficult pitches. They reached the summit on 16 May. Nearby, Austrians Andreas Orgler and Thomas Bonaface made several remarkable climbs above the Ruth Gorge. These included the W face of Mount Barrill and the unclimbed E buttress of Mount Dickey. The latter involved 51 difficult pitches which took five days. They reached the summit on 16 July. Bill McKenna and Jim Sweeney did some excellent climbs on the elegant granite spires of 'Little Switzerland', including the E face of the Royal Tower. In April, John Bauman and Tom Walter made a fine new route on the E face of Mount Hayes, a 2000m-high face of 50° to 65° ice with occasional steeper rock bands. A three-day storm pinned them in a snow cave at the point where they reached the E ridge 250m below the top. After getting to the summit, they descended the E ridge.

In Arctic Canada's Cumberland Peninsula on Baffin Island, Earl Redfern and three companions finally managed to climb the very difficult W face of Asgard's S tower.

Bengt Rodin adds:

A Swedish expedition completed a 43-day, 730km traverse in East Greenland. Bengt Rodin (leader), Franz Fischer, Tommy Sandberg and Per-Gunnar Bjurman flew by Twin-Otter to a glacier 20km north of Gunnbjörnsfjeld (3708m) which they climbed on 25 July. On 27 July they started the 500km journey to Mount Forel, pulling 80kg pulks by ski. By 9 August the team reached the ice-cap to join the route of Martin Lindsay's 1934 Trans-Greenland Expedition. Per-Gunnar Bjurman developed chest pains and was evacuated by helicopter on 23 August. On 29 August the reduced team climbed a new route on Mount Forel (3360m). The route down to Kungmiut ran down snow-free glaciers. 'Down on the Paris glacier we threw our pulks in a crevasse. After that we did go back-packing.'

South America 1988

EVELIO ECHEVARRÍA

As if confirming the opinion about the future of mountaineering that David Lord advanced in the 1981 issue of this journal, the high mountain sports in the Andes are showing indeed a much less crowded scene overall, a greater concentration of climbing crowds at particular sites and a decline of public interest in climbing. Generally speaking, the Andean valleys seem to be now less visited, partly because the Himalaya-Karakoram represents a greater attraction and partly, also, because crowds tend to accumulate (or are accumulated by caravan managers) in a reduced number of more accessible valleys. Chosen areas are now, more than ever, the northern half of the Cordillera Blanca of Peru, Aconcagua and, for a short spell of three weeks, the Chaltén group in Patagonia. In addition, as far as foreign expeditions are concerned, there is also the slowly but steadily increasing fear of attack by guerrillas, terrorists and even farmers and miners.

On the other hand, at least in a few areas, Andean mountaineering has been displaying some unforeseen characteristics. Aconcagua and the great peaks of the central Peruvian cordilleras have been chosen as favourite places for the execution of stunts of all kinds known to Western civilization. *Ski-extreme* is another, with incredibly steep S faces of Peruvian peaks boldly descended by Italians and French. Finally, it could also be added that winter mountaineering by the South Americans themselves has been slowly developing, particularly in the central districts of Chile and Argentina.

The following are only the more noteworthy activities registered for 1988.

Colombia

A Colombian-Polish group successfully climbed the N face of Alto Ritacuba (5464m), highest point in the Cordillera Oriental, but the exploit ended in tragedy. A collapsing serac from the summit dragged the Pole M Danielek and the Colombian Jairo Guerrero to their deaths. The only survivor was the Pole R Gajewski (18 April).

Peru and Bolivia

The main ascents in the Peruvian season (June–August) belong to the Cordillera Blanca. The grandiose peak of Nevado Santa Cruz (6241m), believed by many to be finer than Alpamayo itself, was climbed by a variant of the W face by R Gocking and A Berliner (13 August). Norwegians J Maardalen and H Martens achieved the near first ascent of Nevado 5697m in the Huantsán group (July), although the pair did not win the last 20m of the summit ridge. A French military group led by A Estève realized several ascents, including the Barrard

route of Huascarán Norte (6654m) and a new variant on the SW face of
Taulliraju (5830m), 'a couloir on the great buttress on the right of the face'. The
leader, by the way, descended on to the summit of Huascarán Sur (6769m) by
parachute, jumping at 7200m from a Cessna, and continued his descent to the
lower valleys by paraglider.

(*H Adams Carter adds*: In Peru's Cordillera Blanca, Charlie Fowler soloed
on 4 June a new route to the right of the Italian ridge on the W face of Taulliraju
on icy slabs up to 80°. Among other climbs with Bill Mooz and John Arnow, he
made a two-day new route on Chacraraju Sur's S face between the American
and Italian lines. Arnow and Fowler did a new route on the W face of Cayesh in
two days. It was in the middle of the face, mostly on rock with only two pitches
of ice on the main face, but the final knife-edged snow ridge was scary.)

In the Cordillera Huayhuash, the Italian skiers T Valeruz and T Weiss
introduced a new variant to the left of the Ferrari route on the W face of Nevado
Sarapo (6143m). Valeruz then descended the face by ski.

In the Cordillera Vilcabamba the magnificent mountain Salcantay
(6271m) was climbed by a complicated and somewhat zigzagging route on the
N face by the well-known Peruvian guide Alberto Callupe and his German
client Hans Zebrowski (21 June). Ausangate (6372m), highest in the Cordillera
Vilcanota, was scaled by the E face and SE ridge by Poles M Karon and
A Makaran (27 June).

The only exploratory journey known for the 1988 Peruvian season was a
minor venture by a solo mountaineer. Evelio Echevarría entered the Cordillera
de la Viuda, in the Lima hinterland, and, besides some pleasant repeats, realized
the first ascent of three peaks 5150m high, situated S and SW of Rajuntay,
highest in the range. An attempt on Nevado Uco (5100m) failed because of the
bad quality of the rock, an unpleasant characteristic of this very accessible
Peruvian cordillera (June).

The only noteworthy enterprise for the Bolivian season fell to the five-
man scientific-sportive expedition of the Yorkshire Ramblers' Club that
operated in August on the western side of the Cordillera de Apolobamba.
Members D Hick and M Smith (leader) opened a new route, the N ridge of
Nevado Cololo (5916m), and ascended Nevado Nubi (5710m) by the 1957
German route.

Chile and Argentina

No new activities have been reported for the Chilean side of the Andean
frontier, although a number of important repeats take place there every season
(December to March). It should be mentioned that the ice cascade of the S face
of Cerro Negro (4975m), an imposing rock peak NE of Santiago, was at last
climbed. On 28 January 1987 C Buracchio and C Thiele overcame the 250m
high cascade whose steepness varies from 60 to 90°, a locally much coveted
goal.

On their side of the border, the Argentinians registered the following
important ascents:

Northern Andes or Puna: Cerro Pilar de las Pailas (5900m by altimeter), first ascent on 15 April, by eight climbers from Salta led by C Vitry.

Cerro Bonete Chico, 6395m, third ascent of this very remote mountain (end of March 1987), by G Planes and E Steenhus.

Central Andes: Aconcagua, 6960m. First ascent of W face, keeping close to the SE ridge, by Argentinians D Alessio and D Rodríguez (11 January); they placed three high camps, found rock-walls some 50m high alternating with ice and rock gullies, ice cascades and tongues of very hard snow. Attempt by a new variant of French route, keeping to the right of it; with some 1700m already climbed, the route had to be abandoned because of danger and bad weather (31 January–2 February); the participants were Yugoslavs M Romih and S Sveticic.

Andes Australes (southernmost Andes of Chile and Argentina): in late 1987 seven Italians trekked to Patagonia where some members climbed Cerro Torre and opened new routes on the left of the E buttress of El Mocho, on the SSE spur of El Ñato and on the W face and W spur of Aguja Saint-Exúpery. In the San Lorenzo massif, members also accomplished the first ascent of Cerro Dos Picos (2275m).

In the *Paine district* the following meritorious enterprises were also reported by Italians. Torre Sur: F Leoni, G Bagatoli, J Espen and Michele Cagol (11 November). Torre Norte: F Leoni, C Fruet and Paola Fanton-Leoni, Monzino route (November). The same climb was repeated afterwards by other Italians and, later, by Swiss. Torre Central: E Salvaterra, Ginella Paganini (5 November). The names listed indicate the remarkable participation of women in difficult climbs.

(*H Adams Carter adds*: In Patagonia, Jim Bidwell did two new routes, one on Cerro Stanhardt and the other on Desmachado. Alan Kearney also did some excellent routes, but details are missing.)

In Memoriam

Ecuadorian Ramiro Navarrete fell to his death when descending from Annapurna in the Nepal Himalaya. He had travelled widely, having climbed in the Pamir (Pik Kommunizma, by a difficult route), Xixabangma, invited by Jerzy Kukuczka, and he had a large number of important Andean ascents to his credit, in Peru, Bolivia, Colombia, and, of course, in his native Ecuador, where with a companion he made the entire traverse of Chimborazo. He was also an author and editor of Quito's *Campo Abierto*. He will be remembered as one of the most accomplished South American climbers.

Jordan and Oman 1988: More Rum Goings On

TONY HOWARD

(Plate 104)

In last year's Area Notes I left Miguel and Xavier Gallego suspended on the third day of their new route on the E face of Jebel Rum. I should therefore begin by belatedly announcing the completion of their route on the fifth day: The Red Sea, 400m ED, with pitches of VI+ and A2.

Since then (spring 1987), the area has continued to grow in popularity, with up to 100 climbers visiting the valley in both spring and autumn seasons as well as a few in midwinter. A large quota of new climbs has been added, in particular by Italian and Austrian climbers. Perhaps the best selection of first ascents in 1988 were a dozen climbs added by Wolfgang Hampolter and Albert Precht of Austria, in the spring, with grades varying from IV to VI on the massifs of Rum and Um Ishrin, lengths from 300 to 500m.

The English team of R M Austin and A D Erskine added a unique little climb out of the remote 'Pit' in the Great Siq which gashes the summit of Jebel Rum. They named it The Empty Quarter, 5B, and they also rediscovered a previously unknown Bedouin climb on Annafishiyyah.

Di Taylor and myself also called in *en route* to Sinai and Egypt's Eastern Desert and added a couple of pleasant climbs to Jebel Rum's rapidly growing 'tick list', as well as spending some days out in the desert sharing Ramadan and swopping yarns with our Bedu friends. Sinai proved less attractive than Rum but has many climbs to offer (going back to ascents by Comici), on granite walls and cracks unfortunately exfoliating because of the extremes of temperature. The area is nevertheless well worth visiting, and no doubt also has much to offer in the way of new routes as well as classics, many put up by Steve Read in the 1970s.

Wadi Rum, on the other hand, is now rapidly coming of age. Most of the classic lines in the main valley and within easy reach of the Rest House have been picked. Further afield, however, the place is still wide open for rock exploration. An updated 'New Routes Book' will be taken out to the Rest House in spring 1989. It describes about 50 new climbs, and for those seeking the best of the existing routes the following climbs are a few of the most popular (or should be!):

Jebel Rum

All the Bedouin Routes, in particular the Traverse of Rum, Althallamiyyah and Rijm Assaf. Mostly Grade 3 or 4. People who have done these routes are ecstatic about them.

Pillar of Wisdom. TD inf 350m. A real classic with a 5B (English grade) crux at the end. Beware of 'flashing' the route and getting lost on the summit domes!
Aquarius. TD sup 300m. The only route on the E Dome wall known to have had a number of repeats. Lots of variety!
Inshallah Factor and Towering Inferno. 450m. TD sup and ED inf respectively. Waiting for repeats. Both superb.
The Ziggurat-Aquarius-Atalla Connection. 450m ED (crux 6B English) has probably not yet been strung together as a single route and should be excellent.

Um Ishrin Massif

The Beauty and The Perverse Frog. TD and TD sup 200m. Justifiably popular crack and wall climbs respectively.
Autre Dimension. TD 500m. The only route to date to the top of N Nassrani. Unrepeated (crux 5C English).
Warriors of the Wastelands. ED inf 400m. The soaring corner of the E face of S Nassrani. Unrepeated (crux 6B English).

Further afield, the Barrah Canyon climbs are a must. Stay the night out there: it's magic. (Mostly routes of 100–200m at English 5A or above). Burdah E face slabs and Rock Bridge are on everyone's tick list and quite rightly so (Wadi Rum's Idwal Slabs), and down at the south end of the area Khazali is also a must with its rock carvings and climbs like Doug Scott's Crack of Cracks (English 5C, unrepeated).

For good deals on travel to Jordan from the UK, Jasmin Tours of Chalfont St Peter, Gerrards Cross, still seem to be the best contact.

The Mountains of Oman

During a four-week visit to Oman in December 1988/January 1989, Di Taylor and I travelled through most of the northern mountains, namely the massifs of the eastern and western Hajar, facilitated by expatriate rock-climber and adviser to the Sultan, Alec MacDonald.

The rock is limestone and rises to a height of 3009m at Arabia's highest summit, Jebel Shams, part of the Jebel Akhdar range in the western Hajar. Unfortunately, because of the nature of the rock and the extremes of temperature (freezing at high altitude in midwinter, and over 50°C out of the shade at midday, even in midwinter), the vast majority of the rock is either exfoliating or broken and not climbable with any feeling of great security!

Nevertheless, there is good rock to be found, and Alec MacDonald has collated details of about 60 routes on rock of varying degrees of solidity, some in the wadis of Aday and Mayh, near Muscat and others further afield. The biggest routes in the country are on Jebel Misht (2090m), on its six-kilometre long S/SE face which rises to a height of 1100m at the central 'Nose'. A route was climbed near the Nose by three French guides headed by Raymond Renaud, with extreme free climbing and 'some aid in the lower section'. In the western sector British climber Mike Searle and team added a difficult 1000m route and, at the western extremity, a 150m climb of a more amenable standard. Together with Alec MacDonald we added a 400m route, maximum difficulty 5B, up the SE pillar. We also climbed – and added some extra routes to – Alec's smaller cliffs, and did a lot of trekking into the many superb upper mountain valleys and canyons.

In the western Hajar, Jebel Akhdar (and Shams) have some superb treks in magnificent scenery in wild valleys where remote and beautifully terraced villages are situated. Here also are big walls of up to 1200m, but with loose rock despite their very attractive and challenging appearance. Some of the canyons, however, seem to have excellent walls of around 200–300m. The view from Jebel Shams down into the 1000m deep Saydran Canyon is reminiscent of the view into the Grand Canyon.

To the east there seem to be fewer opportunities for climbing, but the through-canyon of Wadi Dayqah is a particularly splendid 15-kilometre trek, with a 1000m cliff at its NE end and the journey through Wadi Bani Khaled, over the pass and down to Tiwi on the coast should be excellent. There is also considerable caving in both massifs, some very spectacular, and for bird-watchers both the mountains and coast offer an amazing variety, from vultures, eagles and ospreys to kingfishers and sun birds.

The best time of the year to visit the country is December–February, and for the climber or trekker looking for something new the possibilities are almost infinite. There are three main problems: first, a 'no objection certificate' is required, and is only obtainable from a resident in the country or an approved travel agent such as Jasmin Tours of Chalfont St Peter; second, a good robust vehicle (preferably four-wheeled drive) is essential for access to the mountains; finally, many of the best treks are through-treks (crossing the massifs from north to south, or vice-versa) and, to undertake these, arrangements have to be made to be met at the other end: it is best if there are two parties to take opposite routes and exchange vehicles.

Addendum: Note on Africa

EAST AFRICA: Andrew Wielochowski would be grateful for comments and information about recent developments and changes in East Africa to update guidebook information: A Wielochowski, 32 Seamill Park Crescent, Worthing BN11 2PN, or c/o the Alpine Club.

RUWENZORI: Henry Osmaston is updating his guide to this region and would appreciate new-route information: Dr H A Osmaston, Regil Farm, Winford, Bristol BS18 8BB, or c/o the Alpine Club.

Karakoram 1988

PAUL NUNN

(Plates 105, 106)

The summer seems to have been marked by relatively good early weather for high snow peaks, but conditions were poor for high-altitude climbing in July and early August, causing disappointment on K2 to all parties and some problems elsewhere. Nevertheless, there was a continued trend towards creative ascents of new routes, on peaks varying from just below 8000m to small technical and not-so-technical mountains.

The year began with the Polish-British-Canadian first attempt on K2 in winter. Bad weather caused immense difficulty in getting equipment to Base Camp, which delayed matters greatly. Andrzej Zawada, veteran of so many winter schemes, led the 22-member team. They faced high winds and temperatures down to −50°C. A high point of 7350m on the Abruzzi ridge was reached, but mostly the conditions seem to have been too bad to allow much progress. Roger Mear, Mike Woolridge and John Barry took part, though John did not go to Base Camp and Mike was ill.

The first winter ascent of Broad Peak was something of a consolation prize. Maciej Berbeka and Alek Lwow set out on 3 March on an alpine-style ascent of the ordinary route. On 6 March Lwow decided to stay at a camp at 7700m after the exhausting struggle to reach that point through deep snow. Berbeka reached the top that night at 6pm and got down to 7900m before being forced to stop. Next morning he rejoined Lwow in poor weather and they made the descent safely. Both suffered frostbite.

During the summer 57 expeditions took to the field. 38 went to the Skardu district, with 11 on Nanga Parbat and eight in the Gilgit area. Japanese climbers mounted 10 expeditions, West Germans and French six each, Britain five, Italy and the USA four each and Poland and South Korea three each. Austria, Spain, Switzerland and Canada had two each, and there were eight others, some bi-national in make-up. 26 expeditions claimed successes. Notably Czech, Yugoslav and Polish expeditions took along greater numbers of climbers, thereby enabling more people to participate in the activity than the typically very small British expedition.

K2 repulsed all comers, with some good weather early on, and bad from early July. A spirited attempt by 12 Yugoslavs led by Tomaz Jamnik sought to repeat the 1986 Polish route on the SSW pillar. Three camps were established, and 3300m of rope were in place when Andrzej Stremfelj and Filip Bence reached a high point of 8100m on 13 July. They had intended to set up a Camp 4 about 100m higher at the top of a big gully and try for the summit thereafter. Instead, bad weather forced them down and they were unable to try again seriously because of poor weather. Indeed, complete Camps 2 and 3 and the ropes had to be abandoned.

Americans Pete Athans, Steve Matous, Andrew Lapkass and the British Al and Adrian Burgess had the same basic problem on the Abruzzi. A June attempt reached 7500m, but five tries in spells between bad weather in July and early August had to be aborted. Similar problems defeated Catalans led by Jordi Guell, and Rob Hall's New Zealand group. It is little consolation to know that things were equally bad on the Xinjiang side N ridge. Pierre Beghin and five companions tried the route, but after the attainment of a high point of 7600m in July the weather was never good for more than three days at a time. Beghin went solo beyond 8000m, but only just managed to return in the subsequent storm.

On Broad Peak, by contrast, there were several successful ascents. The mountain was climbed by two Japanese teams, by South Koreans and by an Italo-Romanian party. Sadly, a porter, Hussain, was killed when he fell loaded into the Braldu River on 10 August. On the mountain there was another casualty when Jang Il Chung was avalanched from a steep slope at 8000m on 20 August. He was leader of a four-man South Korean expedition, three of whom reached the summit that day at 2.30pm.

Gasherbrum 1 was climbed via the SW face by Czechs led by Robert Galfy. Others had less luck. George Miranda's small Mexican expedition reached 7200m. Jorge Luis Brito then died of pulmonary oedema and the party retreated. Another party led by Ethan Van Matre tried the German route on the N face, but after early good conditions could make no progress in the subsequent bad weather. Nearby an American party led by Gary Speer wished to repeat the American route, but after long initial delays were prevented from going to the start of the American original route for military reasons.

In consequence they went on to Gasherbrum 2. Phil Boyer had altitude troubles and came down with Dr Chip Woodland. Gary Speer and Gary Silver went on. At Camp 2 Silver felt ill, and Speer continued alone, reaching 7950m before returning exhausted in deteriorating weather. While descending he met Silver going up with Dr Roland Willenbrock, a Swiss member of a Canadian expedition. They reached Camp 3, where they were trapped for some days in bad weather in which a metre of snow fell. On 9 July they started to come down, but at 7000m Silver collapsed and despite efforts to get him down he died. Altogether 10 parties tried Gasherbrum 2, making it the most popular peak after Nanga Parbat. Of course the variety of approaches is less, with almost all parties climbing on the Austrian standard route of 1956, as were the Americans above. Six parties succeeded, many of them in favourable June conditions. Bernard Muller's French commercial trip of 17 people allowed Georges Lozat, Jordi Pons, J P Renaud, B Vallet, Jacky Pèche and Muller to reach the top on 22 and 23 June. Next day Marc Buscail, Pascal Hittinger and Henri Albet also succeeded. A subsequent attempt at a mono-ski 'surf' descent by Henri Albet on 25 June ended in his death when he fell 1300m from the first turn. Later Belgians Jan Vanhees, Ingrid Baeyens and Lut Vivijs were held up by bad weather in late July. On 4 August they reached Camp 1 (6000m) and in the next two days climbed the Austrian Spur, finding Silver's body between Camps 2 and 3. On 7 August deep snow stopped them near 7600m, but next day they reached the top after an exhausting time with deep snow. Lut Vivijs thus succeeded on her third 8000m peak (Dhaulagiri 1 1982; Nanga Parbat 1986). All in all, Gasherbrum 2 was kind to women in 1988. Japan's womens' expedition was also successful by the normal route, with an 11-member team led by Ms Shiori Hashimoto. An attempt on the peak led by Jean Pierre Fidèle was less happy. Michael Basson died on 16 July from pulmonary oedema, though the party reached the top. Another ascent was by Max Eiselin's Swiss guided expedition of 12 people, and yet another by two Savoyards. Thus the standard route on Gasherbrum 2 remains overpopulated, with around 10 parties on one route at various times, five of them French, and several of them large commercial guided groups. It seems remarkable that five out of six French expeditions to the Karakoram went on the same mountain on the same route!

Of course invention is expensive in time and more uncertain of reward. Thus, despite it being a second try, Dai Lampard, Phil Thornhill and their party failed on the unclimbed and difficult SW ridge of Gasherbrum 4, stopping around 7000m at a steep rock barrier. This is a formidable possibility, with much more difficulty remaining between high point and summit.

Another innovative attempt was made by Mike Searle's group on the Baltoro peak of Biale (6730m) which is unclimbed. Between 1 and 6 July Searle, Mark Miller, Sean Smith, Simon Yates and Nick Groves found a route through the ice-fall at the head of the Biale glacier, across a wide snow basin and up ice and rock to the Cathedral Biale ridge around 6000m. Camp 3 was set up at 6000m, 200m north of the Cathedral. A point was reached under the summit headwall at about 6250m when storm forced retreat. Bad weather stopped subsequent July attempts around 6000m.

Elsewhere enterprise paid off. W Kurtyka and E Loretan made the first ascent of the E face of the Trango Tower (wrongly called 'nameless' ever since Galen Rowell). Two attempts on this very steep wall were stopped after their initial beginning on 24 June. Eventually they succeeded on 13 July, after eight days of effective climbing. The route is 29 rope-lengths, 1100m ED plus, with six A3 pitches and much other artificial climbing, though mostly using nuts and friends. They fixed 600m of rope, but completed another of the Tower's great test-pieces. Later in the summer 10 German climbers led by Hartmut Münchenbach followed their route for 220m, then traversed to the south on the big snow-ledge to the Yugoslav route and finished up that. On 3 September Wolfgang Kraus, Jörg Wilz, Thomas Lipinski and Jörg Schneider reached the top. On 6 September Kurt Albert, Bernt Arnold, Wolfgang Güllich, Martin Leinauer, Hartmut Münchenbach and Martin Schwiersch succeeded. Güllich and Albert made a free ascent, grading the route UIAA VIII or VIII+. Subsequently Arnold sustained pelvic and rib fractures after falling into a crevasse and had to be helicoptered out, an unfortunate culmination of a rare trip for the East German sandstone ace.

Nearby on Uli Biaho (6290m) an Italian party did a new route on the S pillar, and made the second ascent of this steep tower. Rosana Manfrini, Maurizio Giordani and Kurt Wald completed the climb in five days between 17 and 21 June, grading the climb VII A3. Two routes were also done on El Castillo (5844m). These climb a face to a lower summit (5300m) with sections of 6B, and were done between 19 and 28 May. The main summit remains virgin. After the Uli Biaho route Giordani soloed the Great Tower of Trango from the north side in nine hours, a 2000m route repeated by his friends afterwards.

Another Italian expedition climbed the far west peak of Masherbrum (7200m). It was led by Augusto Zanotti from Rome. In the Latoks Enrico Rosso, Marco Forcatura and Marco Marciani repeated the 1979 Japanese route on Latok 3 (6852m). They made the ascent alpine-style in near winter conditions in eight days, finishing on 15 June (VI and A2).

A West German party tried Baintha Brakk, the Ogre (7285m) but was not successful. Across the Biafo Glacier an Italian group climbed a fine pillar on Sosbun Spire 1, a peak of about 5500m. From Chokpiong they approached the west side of the range via the E branch of the Sosbun Glacier. An Advanced Base was made at 4350m on moraine in mid-August. They then climbed a steep pillar which had been tried by a Polish group led by Janusz Skorek in 1986. Their route was left of the Polish line. On 19–20 August 350m were climbed and fixed with rope, in unstable weather. Then the weather cleared and on 21 and 22 August the final ascent was made, starting with a bivouac on a snow-field half-way up the pillar. A blizzard began on the last pitches, but Paulo Vital, the 24-year-old leader, G Battista Gianola (25), Adriano Carnati (25) and Daniele Bosisio (25) reached the top at 3pm. The route was 1400m long with magnificent climbing, including 35 pitches of V, VI or VI+ and A1. The descent was made on 22 and 23 August. One member, Miss Sonja Brambati (27), missed the climb after being ill on the first attempt. The area, visited about a decade ago by Mick Coffey, has dozens of hard smaller peaks and can be reached in three or four days from Dusso. It is significant that an Austrian party, led by Heinz Zak, tried the route earlier in the season; it was defeated by bad weather.

On the Hispar climbing parties were few. The best British effort of the year hereabouts was the ascent of Kunyang Kish (7852m) by a new route up the N ridge. After setting up Base on 22 June, the five-man party set up Camps 1 (5400m) and 2 (5800m), then rested at Base in bad weather. On 1 July Keith Milne, Mark Lowe, Andrew Wingfield and Julian Fisher returned to the ridge and a camp was subsequently set up at 6700m. There they were caught in bad weather for three days, after which Fisher felt ill, so he and Wingfield descended. Milne and Lowe continued over the 7000m Sod's Law Peak, aptly named by its first explorers Dave Wilkinson, Steve Venables and Phil Bartlett in 1980. They continued, with low winds, reaching the top on 13 July. It was a bold effort, favoured by the weather, and only the second ascent of this formidable peak, following that of Zawada's strong Polish team via the S ridge in August 1971. Interestingly, that route too was originally reconnoitred by a Pakistan–British party in 1962, though an attempt was called off when Dick Jones and Jimmy Mills were killed in a fall down the E face (AJ68, 100–107, 1963).

Elsewhere on the Hispar the big peaks repulsed the climbers. Jacques Kelle from Marseille led an 11-member party to Pumari Chich (7350m), and Herbert Tschochner from West Germany again with 11 people tried Distaghil Sar (7885m). Like a British attempt upon Malubiting led by David Harries, these efforts failed. Herbert Streibel's West German group of 15 climbed

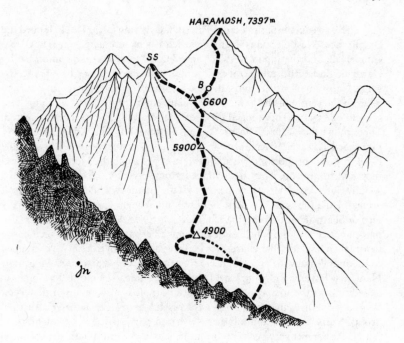

Spantik (7027m), and in a different vein Jamie Thin and a friend from Durham University did a route on the N face of one of the twin rock peaks at the eastern end of the Bal Chish massif, on the S wall of the Hispar. They climbed snow and ice runnels to a col and a rocky ridge to the top. How this relates to ascents of summits in this area by a Services expedition from the Kerolungma side is not known, but the route is almost certainly new despite these efforts, and climbs by the Poles in that region before their success on Kunyang Kish. Nearby too was the exploratory trek to the Gharesa Glacier, another cirque with many smaller unclimbed summits, led by Richard Hazko (UK).

Polish climbers led by Janusz Baranek made a major first, an ascent of the SW face of Haramosh from a base in the Ishkapal valley. This face, said to be 4000m high, had been reconnoitred by Polish climbers in 1984. Then two smaller peaks, Redam (5300m) and Godeli (5325m), were climbed. Base Camp was at 3200m, and higher camps were established at 4900m (29 June), 5900m (4 July) and 6600m (10 July). 3000m of rope was fixed up to this Camp 3. The lower part of the face was 50-degree ice, in a dangerous crevassed couloir. From Camp 1 to 2 was steep rock (V) and 70-degree ice in parts. From Camp 3, Jarosz Malczyk and Marek Pronobis crossed a dangerous hanging glacier and bivouacked at the foot of an ice-fall. Next day, after continuous climbing for 16 hours, they reached the top (7397m). This was the fourth ascent overall. On 30 July Baranek, Andrzej Mostek and Kazimiez Wszolek also reached the top, while other members Miroslaw Konewka and Jacek Wiltosinski reached one summit of Sari Sumari (c7000m), but were prevented by high wind and lack of time from going to the main summit.

The 10 expeditions to Nanga Parbat had varying fates. Three climbed the Diamir face: West Germans led by Heinrich Koch, another group led by Dr E Gundelach, and the Japan Research into High Mountains Expedition led by Haruyuki Endo. Efforts elsewhere were more innovative. On 25 June Francesco Mich, Constante Carpella and Angelo Giovannetti reached the top of a 2000m pillar in the centre of the N face. The pillar required four days' climbing, to a summit of 6550m. They judged the continuation too dangerous and retreated. Their pillar they called Pilastro Val di Fiemme. On the Rupal face Barry Blanchard, K Doyle, W Robinson and M Twight tried to repeat the Messner line of 1970. A storm appeared when they were at 7750m in the Merkl couloir, and they had to give up. They had climbed alpine-style over five days when the weather intervened on 13 July. Before that they made two fine new routes: the E arête of Laila (6095m) was done solo by Mark Twight (1800m TD) and the N face of Shgiri (c6400m), by Blanchard, K Doyle and W Robinson. They also made an ascent of the Schell route on Nanga Parbat to 7000m, to acclimatize before their final try (Blanchard, Doyle, Twight). A South Korean party climbed to Rakhiot Peak by the 1953 route. Three camps preceded a successful ascent by Nam Kyu Hwang and Jong Cheol Kim on 18 June. The aim is to mount an expedition to the main peak in a future year. It is also reported that Peter Worgotter's Austrian expedition was successful, but Robert Renzler's Austrian group, Swiss, Italians and another American party failed. Late attempts on Nanga Parbat met very poor conditions in September. An American expedition led by Tom Mereness from Boulder left Gilgit on 29 August, setting up Base at 3700m in the upper Rupal valley on 8 September. They attempted the Schell route, but on 4 October the weather worsened, with much snow. The resultant avalanche conditions stymied further progress, and a South Korean expedition on the Diamir Face led by Il Hwan Park also reached their high point of around 7000m in mid-September.

Relatively few parties tried higher peaks to the west of the Karakoram Highway. Poles led by Piotr Młotecki climbed the main summit of Batura Mustagh (7785m). From Base at 4000m on the Batokshi glacier moraines, three camps were established following the 1983 Koblmueller route. Attempts to climb Batura 1 West (7762m) failed. On 6 July Zygmund A Heinrich, Pawel Kubalski and Volker Stallbohm made a big push, sleeping at Camp 1 (4700m) and Camp 3 (6200m) and continuing alpine-style, using a tent for three bivouacs and a snow-hole for a last one. They reached the top on 13 July at 7.30am, staying two and a half hours. The weather deteriorated very fast and they failed to find their tent or equipment, so three snow-hole bivouacs were made without gear or food on the descent. Heinrich had a haemorrhage and Stallbohm frostbite. Eventually a party from Base helped them down the last stage, and Base Camp was reached after two weeks on the mountain. This was the third ascent of Batura 1 (previous ascents: German 1976; Austrian 1983). The first attempt was led by Mattias Rebitsch in 1951, and, despite ascents of many of the higher peaks, several of them and many smaller peaks remain unclimbed. Since this expedition Jerzy Wala of Krakow has produced a useful sketch map of this complex area, and there is also a very fine but rare Chinese map.

There were a good number of parties operating on peaks below 6000m. Many of the dozens of parties walking in the open zones tried some climbs and 300 people in 49 parties were given permission to trek in restricted areas. Among these were British climbers who tried Shani (5885m) by its unclimbed SE face, in June and early July (A Macnae, P Bale, R Spillett and S Thompson); their group ascended South Twin (5640m) by its N face, a 790m ice route, and the NW face of Mehrbani (5639m), also reported as TD inf. Elsewhere, Phil Bartlett and Lindsay Griffin tried Jur Jur Khona Sar (c6000m) near the KKH, but the excessive June temperatures made it too dangerous. Returning in late November, Mike Woolridge, Peter Cox and Griffin climbed the 2000m S face of Tapadan Sar (6100m). They set up Base at the snow-line of 3500m, in a shepherd's hut. There was winter snowfall – early, it is claimed, for the area. Daytime temperatures barely reached zero, but there was sun and night-time temperatures were no worse than alpine winter (−24°C). The party did the face in five days, with a summit day of 21 hours in crisp, clear and relatively calm conditions. Snow conditions were '. . . not unexpectedly abysmal, with much dry and unconsolidated powder'. This peak near Karun Koh was climbed by Andy Cave and John Stevenson in 1987. Another winter venture: Japanese intending to climb on Gasherbrum 2 were forced to abandon the idea at Urdukas around the same time.

The trekking parties who do climb have entered a new golden age of possibilities among the smaller peaks. In valleys like the Hushe there was a particularly extensive amount of activity. Most do little to record their activities, but modern technical abilities and equipment, and the relative ease of access to some areas, have broached a development which can provide new climbing for at least a generation. This makes the concentration upon *voies ordinaires* on the big peaks – hard unimaginative work as it is – look ever more myopic.

In the East Karakoram the ascent of Rimo 1 (7385m) by an Indo-Japanese expedition was the most significant event. Led by Hukam Singh, the expedition went from the Siachen glacier to Terong Topko. Floods ensured that four days were spent entering the valley, and a 'rope suspension traverse bridge' was used. After a traverse of the N Terong glacier and two camps, Climbing Camp 1 was made at the base of the Ibex Col (5960m). A couloir was then followed above and beyond the col, to a hanging glacier below the summit. Camp 2 was placed at 6800m on 19 July, and Camp 3 at 7000m on 27 July. There was then much bad weather, but on 28 August six members reached the top: Sumania of the India-Tibet Border Police, N D Sherpa of the Indian army, Yoshida and Ogata of Japan were on top at 2pm, and at 3.30 Kanhayalal and Ratan Singh also reached the summit.

A V Saunders adds:

Rimo 1, the Painted Mountain, was first attempted by Harish Kapadia's Indo-British Expedition of 1985, which climbed the W ridge in alpine style to a point near the Indo-Japanese Camp 3. During the same expedition Wilkinson and Fotheringham climbed Rimo 3 (7233m) in a single exploratory push from Base Camp on the Terong glacier. In 1986 Peter Hillary's Indo-New Zealand expedition made an attempt to climb the E ridge but suffered from delays.

It has been reported that Hukam Singh's expedition used some two kilometres of fixed rope between Camps 1 and 3, and a further five 'lengths' above Camp 3. I find this very disappointing. It must by now be obvious that a mountain of this size and difficulty should not be laced with fixed rope. Not only is this unnecessary, but it also contributes to mountain pollution. In addition, fixing ropes needs fixed camps and large, heavyweight expeditions with large numbers of porters. The resulting strain on the arid and fragile ecology of the Karakoram valleys can be irreversible. When we visited the beautiful and isolated Terong valley in 1985, there were several species of wildlife, hoof and paw prints covered the sands and copses of hardy conifers dotted the cliffs. Heavy expeditions would certainly destroy the beauty of the place, stripping the wood and ruining the habitats. A single evening meal for porters can mean the elimination of scores of the small (but sometimes centuries-old) trees.

This is not my view alone. The Mountain Wilderness conference at Biella, 1988, proposed that mountaineers could do their bit for the ecology by 'encouraging alpine-style mountaineering in the Himalaya and other remote ranges (light or ultra-light expeditions); recommending that host governments adopt and enforce measures to eliminate the negative behaviour and negative impacts of expeditions and trekking parties.' So it is particularly sad to see Hukam Singh's expedition being claimed as an important achievement. Let us hope its importance is as an end marker for this type of expedition.

Harish Kapadia adds:

Elsewhere in the Karakoram the second ascent of Mamostong Kangri was achieved by an Indian Army team led by Major A M Sethi. They crossed the Saser La and approached via the Thangman glacier from the east. The route of first ascent was then followed.

Apsarasas I (7245m) was climbed by the Indian Army in July, with six summiteers. A little to the south, Saser Kangri I and IV received an ascent by a Delhi team. This team came in from the Nubra valley to the Phuckpoche glacier. They set up three camps to follow the W ridge, first climbed in 1987 by the Indo-British army team. After several attempts foiled by bad weather, the summit of Saser Kangri I (7672m) was reached on 24 August by four climbers, including the leader Heera Lohia. On the same day Saser Kangri IV (7416m) was climbed by three others. There were injuries and, later, amputations.

This was an excellent achievement, more so for being the first civilian attempt on the peak.

Nepal 1988

(Plate 107)

Mount Everest (8848m)

The Sherpa who reached the summit of Everest on 22 December 1987 (see *AJ93*, 246, 1988/89) was Ang Rita. It was the fourth time Ang Rita had climbed Everest, and the third time without oxygen; at the time of his winter ascent, he was 48 years old.

The most significant ascent of the year was the 35th anniversary ascent by a small international team comprising Rob Anderson (leader, USA), Ed Webster (USA), Paul Teare (Canada), and Stephen Venables (UK). For a full account see the first article in this volume.

The least significant ought to have been the ridiculous international 'live television' effort. China, Nepal and Japan collaborated to put together a climbing team of 270 and a film crew of 35. They spent no less than £7 million. This sort of circus is not only unnecessary, but also environmentally extremely damaging. In the Himalaya, enough is already too much.

Two other British expeditions were active on Everest and are reported earlier in this volume.

Marc Batard followed up his solo of Makalu with a 22½-hour climb of Everest. He reached the summit on 26 September, via the South Col route. Eight other climbers reached the top the same day, including Marc Boivin (France) who parapented from the summit. Boivin was helped by two Sherpas, one to carry his 'chute and one to carry his skis. Unfortunately, these efforts were marred by yet another television extravaganza. The French had a media-dominated operation, with a budget of FF 32 million, 300 Sherpas, 6000 litres of fuel, 150 tents etc. How much money did the European sponsors allow for the environmental repairs?

Ngojumba Kang (7743m)

Yu Kwang Yeul and Chol Mi Ho made the first winter ascent via the S face on 11 February. The team had permission to traverse the connecting ridge to Cho Oyu, but gave up in bad weather.

Langtang Lirung (7234m)

On 3 January Kazimierz Kiszka and Adam Potoczek (Poland) made the first winter ascent via the Japanese SE ridge route.

Cho Oyu (8201m)

Pre-monsoon, six expeditions followed the Tichy (1953) route, or variations of it. Dave Walsh reached the summit alone on 30 April, the first British ascent of this peak (see the article in this volume). The other nations represented included

96. *The Last Bivouac.* (p 219)

97. *Vignemale N face.* (p 219)

98.   *Koshtantau 1889.* (p 219)

99. *View from the forepeak, or horn, towards the summit of Mount Bonney.* (p 227)

100. *The Reverend William Spotswood Green seated, flanked by two Swiss guides; taken on the Mount Cook expedition in 1882.* (p 227)

101. *Mount Bonney from the N in the morning light.* (p 227)

102.   N face of Brèche du Glacier Noir. (*Ailefroide Orientale L, Ailefroide Centrale R. The brèche is the gap to the R of the Ailefroide Orientale*). (p 229)

103. (Above) Sierra de Gredos: Riso Moreno and Ameal de Pablo. (p 231)

104. Jordan: Jebel Rum – East Dome – East Face. (p 250)

1 'I.B.M.' 400m TD
2 'Flight of Fancy' 5c
3 'Mad Frogs and Eng-
   lishmen' 5c
4 'Towering Inferno'
   300m ED inf
5 'Walk like an Egyptian'
   4c
6 'Troubadour' 5c
7 'Wall of Lace' 5a
8 'Goldfinger' 5a
9 'Inshallah Factor'
   450m TD sup
10 'Red Sea' 450m ED
11 'Atalla' 450m TD sup
12 'Aquarius' 300m TD
   sup
... through cave 'Eye of
   Allah'

105. *Karakoram: Gasherbrum 1.* (p 253)

106. *Karakoram: The Ogre's Thumb.* (p 253)

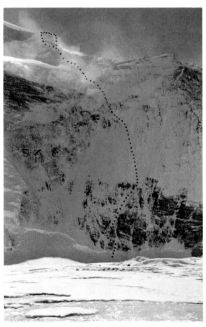

107. *The North Face of Cho Oyu.* (p 262)

108. *SE face of Pk 6292m on the S shoulder of Mana (7272m).* (p 267)

109. *Panchchuli III (L) and the upper snow-basin of the Meola ice-fall in the Darma valley. On R the E ridge of Panchchuli II (6904m). (p 267)*

110. *Gangotri: L Bhagirathi III with the Scottish pillar, R Bhagirathi I. (p 267)*

111. *Fritz Wiessner (1900–1988).* (p 311)

112. *Shawangunks: Fritz Wiessner on Rear Exposure (5.6) in 1986, aged 86.* (p 311)

113. *Michael John Cheney (1928–1988).* (p 311)

114. *James Joyce (1910–1988).* (p 311)

Italy, Germany, Switzerland, Austria and Holland. Stefan Woerner from the Swiss/German expedition began to suffer from AMS during the descent and, after spending the night at a camp at 7300m, he was unable to move the next day and died there during a spell of poor weather. Woerner was an experienced and popular figure on the Himalayan scene, with several 8000m peaks to his credit.

The French sent a large expedition to Cho Oyu during the post-monsoon season. They used Sherpas up to Camp 2. On 12 September six climbers reached the top, but only one walked down. Two summiteers ski'd down, one mono-ski'd, one surfed, and one parapented to Base Camp in 15 minutes. There have been four flights from 8000m peaks to date (January 1989); they are:

1985 Gevaux (France) from Gasherbrum 1;

1987 Japanese from Cho Oyu;

1988 Cormier (France) from Cho Oyu;

1988 Boivin (France) from Everest.

Cormier's flight was the only one not to use 'helpers' to get the canopy into the air.

The 2000m N face of Cho Oyu received its first ascent by an eight-man team from Yugoslavia; they established four camps on the face. On 2 November Dr Iztok Tomazin made a solo ascent from Camp 3 (Camp 4 was not established until the next day) and descended the Tichy route. Six more members reached the summit during the following days and descended by the route of ascent. This was an almost unknown face of the mountain, and the Yugoslavs had no prior knowledge of it.

Makalu (8463m)

Marc Batard made a controversial first solo ascent and first traverse of the mountain via the difficult W pillar, descending the normal NW face/ridge. In this remarkable effort Batard claimed a 'solo' even though he used Nepalese help to carry ropes to the bottom of the pillar, which he then fixed for 2000m before making his summit push on 26 April. During the descent he had the assistance of German and Italian route markers.

Doug Scott's expedition reached their high point when Rick Allen and Alan Hinkes climbed to 8100m, where Allen was carried away by a compact 'wind-slab' and fell some 400m over mixed ground. Hinkes was unbelayed, and unclipped the rope as Allen went by. Hinkes affirms that this action saved both their lives, as he was then in a position to climb down to the concussed and injured Allen, bringing him down to the Makalu La (7410m) where a Catalan team completed the rescue operation.

A Polish expedition led by Ms Anna Czerwinska followed the NW face/N ridge route and, on 14 October, placed two members on the summit, one of whom, Ryszard Kolakowski, failed to return. On the way to the summit the pair passed Carlos Carsolio who was having difficulty descending. It appears that they refused to help Carsolio, who would have perished had not the above-mentioned Catalan team sacrificed their summit chances to bring him down safely.

Chamlang (7319m)

A team of Dutch women led by Frederike Bloemers ascended the E peak via the N face/NE ridge. The summit was reached on 10 May by four members, followed by two more the following day.

Kangchenjunga (8586m)

A South Korean expedition led by Jung Sang Moo made an ascent of the SW face, reaching the summit on 2 January.

On 3 May, Peter Habeler (Austria), Carlos Buhler (USA) and Martin Zabelata (Spain) completed an alpine-style ascent of the N ridge, starting up the Messner route and finishing up the British route.

Manaslu (8163m)

On 1 May, a Swiss team reached the summit via the E ridge/NE face with three members, including the first Swiss woman to climb an 8000m peak (Ursula Huber).

Annapurna 1

On 10 May the Quota 8000 team, now renamed *Esprit d'Equipe*, completed an ascent of the S face via the British route. The team used fixed ropes but no oxygen.

In October Jerzy Kukuczka and Artur Hazjer (Poland) completed a new route on the S face. They were members of an international expedition with 11 climbers. The Ecuadorian Ramiro Navarrete reached the summit via the E ridge, but disappeared during the descent.

Józef Nyka adds:

Lhotse and Everest – Success and Tragedy

A Slovak-New Zealand Khumbu expedition 1988 had two objectives: to climb Lhotse by its normal route and Mount Everest by the still unrepeated British route on the SW face. The Slovak team was composed of Ivan Fiala (leader), Dušan Becík, Peter Božík, Jaroslav Jaško, Jozef Just, Jaroslav Oršula and Dr Milan Skladaný. They used the South Korean and French routes via the ice-fall and then established three camps and fixed ropes towards the South Col. After a period of bad weather the Slovaks left Base Camp on 21 September. On 27 September Becík and Just set out from Camp 3 (7250m) and after seven hours reached 8050m, where they bivouacked for four hours. Next morning the pair climbed for eight hours by moonlight, and at daybreak (6am) they reached the summit of Lhotse (8501m, according to the new American map). The ascent was completed without supplementary oxygen.

Now they turned to the Everest SW face, planning an alpine-style attack, including descent to the S Col. The first attempt was made on 7 October but failed at Camp 2 (6400m) because of bad weather. On 12 October Becík, Božík, Just and Jaško left Base Camp and reached Camp 2 again. Next day strong wind prevented the climb. On 14 October they started up the British route at 3am, making good progress and reaching 8100m at 6pm. On 15 October they had a nasty surprise: they took a whole day for the Rock Band Chimney, which was much more difficult that they had expected. The next night they spent above the Rock Band at 8400m. On 16 October the long rising snow traverse to the right was completed. Becík lost his strength and progress was slow. The last bivvy was beneath the South Summit at 8600m. The team was exhausted by the effort, and on 17 October Just went to the summit solo and reached it at 1.40pm. The other members separated and began the descent towards the South Col. At 4pm Just reported that he had joined Becík and Jaško, who 'is lethargic and does not want to descend'. At 5.30pm Just told Base Camp that they were all together but still at some 8300m. Although they felt bad, showing symptoms of high altitude sickness, they continued the descent. This was the last radio contact. The three-member American team (plus two Sherpas) watched the slope from the South Col, but unfortunately saw nobody. Visibility had been good, but the wind became stronger and stronger. At 11pm a storm of 120–150km/h set in, destroying four tents in Camp 2. The following day radio contact with the South Col at 10am brought bad news: the Slovak team had not reached the camp and had not been seen on the descent. In view of the exhaustion of the four and the terrible conditions during the night, there was no hope that they were still alive. On 19 October the last teams left Camp 2 and on 21 October the expedition began the walk down.

The speed ascent of Lhotse and the alpine-style conquest of the Everest SW face were splendid successes, unfortunately with a tragic epilogue: four men died, three of them being experienced Himalayan climbers with two eight-thousanders each. Their dramatic climb shows once again that oxygenless assaults on the five highest mountains of the world have their limits, demarcated by factors such as the height, the time of the operation, the difficulty of route-finding and, of course, the ability of the team. One extra unfavourable factor not included in the reckoning, and the enterprise changes into a catastrophe.

SW Buttress of Dhaulagiri, Alpine-Style

A Czechoslovak-Italian-Soviet expedition led by Peter Schnabl and Jiří Novak (climbing leader) hoped to make new routes on Annapurna and Dhaulagiri. One of its objectives was the first complete ascent of the SW buttress of Dhaulagiri (8167m), attempted in 1978 and 1980 by a French party (up to 7500m) and in 1985 by a Czechoslovak team (to 7250m). The buttress is 2200m high, and the snow-slopes above it 900m. The French reported great difficulties in three sections: from 5000 to 6000m a succession of rock towers; between 6000 and 6800m a fine snow ridge with steps up to 60° and enormous rock-and-ice towers; from 6800 to 7300m a vertical and partially overhanging step which is the crux section (on 400 vertical metres difficulties of VI–VI+, A2).

The ascent was completed by Zoltán Demján (33) from Bratislava, Juri

Moiseev (34) and Kazbek Valiev (36) from Alma Ata. Demján had climbed Everest and Lhotse Shar in 1984, Valiev had reached Everest by a new route, Moiseev had taken part in hard winter climbs in the Pamir (Pik Lenina, 1988).

Base Camp (3600m) was established on 16 September. The Advanced Base (5100m) of the trio was on the SW Col. They left Base Camp on 27 September, equipped for eight to ten days. They were lucky to have unusually good weather all the time. Because of climbing difficulties the team moved slowly, some 400m a day, carrying food, fuel and gear. The last bivvy was at 7350m, and they reached the top late in the evening on 6 October. The descent was by the same route and took four further days.

This 14-day climb was carried out by a strong team in pure alpine style, without camps, fixed ropes and other route protection. In view of the length and height of the route, its difficulty and the modern style of the climb, this ascent is undoubtedly the best accomplishment of the Himalayan year 1988.

India 1988

HARISH KAPADIA

(Plates 108–110*)*

The year began with celebrations. The Himalayan Club, born in 1928, celebrated its Diamond Jubilee in February at Bombay, Delhi and Calcutta. A series of talks, exhibitions and dinners was organized.

At Bombay, Stephen Venables was the main attraction with four talks on his climbing experiences. ('I filled in the gaps' was his understatement in a letter to a British magazine.) His presentations were highly appreciated and his presence symbolized the Club's British connection. Started by the British to look after visiting climbers, the Club flourished until the early 1960s when the last Britishers left. Then, for a decade, Soli Mehta ran the show single-handedly (he is still much involved in it). Since 1970 J C Nanavati as Hon Secretary holds the fort and has put the Club on a firm pedestal. The role of the Club was never to exercise bureaucratic control. Hence, with the arrival of other controlling bodies on the mountaineering scene, its importance, necessity and growth as a voluntary body did not diminish at all. It has always acted as the custodian of knowledge and it continues to do so through the annual publication of the *Himalayan Journal* and the *Newsletter*. For the *HJ* (started by the likes of Kenneth Mason) every tribute is due to R E Hawkins who reshaped the contents and presentation in recent years. In such as him and the many youngsters now joining in the labour of love lies the strength of the Himalayan Club.

All these memories were recalled and re-emphasized during this eventful year. The celebrations were formally inaugurated by Major General R V Kulkarni who commands the Indian troops on the heights of the Siachen glacier. He described the life of the soldiers staying at high altitudes for the entire winter. Observation of a large group of people staying above 6500m throughout the year has led to many theories about the high-altitude physiology of change. Many studies and mountaineering feats were carried out amidst the war. Amongst other speakers were Jean Mark Paris, a rock-climber from France, S N Dhar from Calcutta and Soli Mehta. At Delhi Charles Houston was the chief guest; he enchanted the audience with movie and slides of Nanda Devi (1936), K2 (1953–1983) and Everest (1950–1981). At Calcutta a series of talks was organized. During the entire year many functions were held. Finally, Pertemba Sherpa (the famous three-time Everester from Nepal, with the modesty of Everest) gave talks at each centre to round off the celebrations.

In Kishtwar, Brammah I (6416m) was ski'd down via a 1500m-high couloir with hard snow-cover and 55° steepness. The Swiss skier A N Dominique had established three camps with support from seven members before achieving this feat. A peak of 6322m ('Chomochior') opposite Kishtwar Shivling was climbed by Simon Richardson and Roger Everett on 9 September (see their articles in this volume). This was a sustained climb of 60 pitches on the 1400m high route. A group of British climbers climbed the Kalidahar Spire

(560om) in Kishtwar. This lies in a great rock-cirque on the south of the Darlang Nullah. Perhaps this climb ushers in a new era in Himalayan climbing: people prepared to travel such long distances to climb good rock-routes in the Himalaya which are not on high peaks. It is a most welcome trend away from the queues for the 8oooers.

In Himachal Pradesh, Dharmsura (6446m) was climbed by the Americans. Manirang (6543m) allowed a second ascent by a team of Indian paratroopers in the autumn. This peak was first climbed in 1952, and it is surprising that such a prominent mountain was not climbed again for so many years. Earlier in the summer it had beaten a young Indian team. Among other successful climbs in the Western Himalaya was a series of ascents of Nun Kun and a climb of Z3 by Italians in July.

An Indian team which climbed Kang Yissay II (61oom) brought back information and photographs to show that most parties climb this lower peak. The higher Kang Yissay (640om) has been treated with more respect. The record of climbs has been clarified.

Garhwal as usual saw a variety of activities. Earlier in the summer the Indo-Tibet Border Police made a magnificent route up the E face of Mana (7272m), from the Purvi Kamet glacier. This face had beaten two previous expeditions. It is a steep avalanche-prone route which leads to the final NE ridge and the summit: a new route. Later, in the autumn, the same peak was climbed from the south-west by an Indo-US army team. They approached from Badrinath to Gupt Khal and traversed over the W ridge to reach the summit. The route had been prepared earlier in the summer by a platoon of Jawans. Finally, it became 'a record climb within 16 days'. Talking of style, this was the route opened by Frank Smythe in 1937 for a quick three-day no-fuss first ascent.

Purbi Dunagiri was one of the last virgin peaks bordering the Nanda Devi sanctuary. Last year it was seriously attempted and this year finally climbed by two members of a team from Bengal. The summiteers slipped on their way back and were killed. This face is very steep and during last year's attempt, in a discharge of rocks and snow, the climbers had to run for their lives. This year's team has not given any further details yet.

A three-member team from Bombay covered much ground from Gupt Khal to Unta Dhura to Traill's pass. They followed Frank Smythe's route at first and then went across the Girthi Ganga by W H Murray's Scottish Himalayan route of 1950. Chalab (616om) was nearly climbed, while Kagbhusand was seriously attempted. Finally, in Kumaon they found an alternative to Traill's pass (Danu Dhura). Traill's pass, first discovered in 1830 by G W Traill, lies to the north of Nanda Kot. After a later crossing the porters were paid off and, to the surprise of the party, these lightly-clad porters returned by a different pass, from the south of Nanda Kot. This was recorded in a short note in the *Himalayan Journal* in 1929. This year the party followed the alternative pass; following local advice they discovered the old cairns leading to this pass. It was an amazing route and a real tribute to the prowess of navigation of the local Bhotias. The route needs to be completed.

Nearby Panchchuli II (6904m) received an attempt after many years. It was thwarted by atrocious weather.

In the Gangotri area the year began with a tragedy. Three engineering students were benighted on Gangotri III (6577m). The leader lost his life trying to rush down in a panic. Two other survivors had 10 fingers amputated. This was most tragic, as these novices were without the knowledge and ability to deal with such serious injuries. Later in the autumn an avalanche on Gangotri II killed four climbers and three HAPs, amongst them a most experienced and much-liked guide, Gopalsinh Gosain of Uttarkashi. Both these tragedies sent shock-waves through climbing circles and led to the Indian Mountaineering Foundation putting most stringent restrictions on the selection of Indian teams and their leaders. Some felt that this was bureaucratic and unreasonable, but surely something had to be done?

However, not everything was so grim. The Japanese climbed Sudarshan Parbat by the E ridge, while the SW buttress of Bhagirathi III (Bob Barton, Allen Fyffe 1982) was repeated by a New Zealand team. This was the finest route accomplished by New Zealanders in the Himalaya. Meru North was climbed by two different routes by the Yugoslavs, while Brigopanth was climbed by a Spanish team. They failed on Thalay Sagar.

Towards the east, in Sikkim, the central summit of Kokthang was climbed by a team from Doon School, Dehra Dun. Kokthang has a controversial history, due to its serrated summit ridge. The southern and central peaks are lower than the north peak. The team climbed the central summit, and the main summit remains still a virgin. Later in the year the southern peak was climbed by a team from Manipur.

In 1987 an ascent of Kabru Dome and Forked Peak I was claimed and recorded by an Indian army team. However, upon enquiry by Dorjee Lhatoo, the Hon Local Secretary (Darjeeling) of the Himalayan Club, and when confronted with the facts, the leader, Major K V Cherian, confessed to not having climbed these two peaks. The record stands corrected and the army has been asked to put its house in order.

Geoff Hornby joined an Indo-British team to peak Changuch in Kumaon. In later reports and articles first ascents of Nandbhannar, Laspa Dhura and Nandakhani were claimed. However, in their report to the authorities the leader, Hornby and the LO stated that Changuch, their allotted peak, was not climbed and 'no other peak was climbed'. Where do the poor editors go? No clarification is forthcoming at the time of writing.

The weather in the autumn unleashed sudden storms which trapped many trekkers. Six were killed on the Shigo La and one LO was missing on Nun, bringing the death toll to one of the highest in recent times. This provoked an article in *India Today*, a recognized fortnightly (an Indian equivalent of *Time*), and questions were asked in the Indian Parliament.

An Indian expedition was organized to Kangchenjunga from Nepal. This was the first such venture by an Indian private party to an 8000m peak. Unfortunately the means they adopted did not justify the end. Local provincial sentiments were aroused, political parties brashly involved and government ministers roped in to 'cut steps'. The otherwise brave effort was marred by this unabashed use of political contacts. Finally, the death of the deputy leader on the mountain led to the failure of the expedition. With Indian private parties

going for Everest and other high peaks in Nepal for the next five years in a big
way, it is hoped some decency will prevail.

On scholarly affairs, an Institute of Ladakh Studies has been established
by Henry Osmaston. A book, *Aksaichin and Sino-Indian Conflict* (J Lall), has
merit for serious students of Ladakh. It covers fully the history of the 1962
Chinese war and its origins; one can understand the geopolitics of the area well.
The author was Defence Secretary during those troubled times.

But the book *Rimo* by Peter Hillary recorded all the bickerings and sad
relations of the 1986 joint expedition. It was all that an expedition should not
be. The author claims to be the 'first westerner' (what is so special about that?)
in 40 years across the Saser La. But the knowledge of the area displayed is no
more than that of the last visitor. He gives a one-sided view of all the quarrels,
makes comments against the Indian army and ridicules the Indian members.
This book has infuriated the authorities and the climbing community alike. In
fact the grapevine was full of these 'Western misdeeds' in 1986, but the Indian
members were asked to be quiet (being mostly from the services). The writing,
like the climbing on this mountain, is not of high quality. This insensitive
behaviour should certainly make the authorities more careful and strict about
joint ventures.

Dr M L Biswas, Vice-President of the Himalayan Club (Calcutta) and a
committed communist, passed away during the year.

Stephen Venables, during his stay at Bombay, climbed a 15m-high
slippery palm tree on the sea-shore in his climbing shoes. As he swung in the air
we closed our eyes, expecting a thud and the end of a future Everester. But he
came down safely and went up the 1600m Kangshung face of Everest to the
summit. Moral of the story: you are welcome to start from the sea and the palms
in Bombay to reach the top. Any takers?

Józef Nyka adds:

Hagshu Once Again

The virgin Hagshu (6330m) in the Indian Kashmir belongs to the most
interesting objectives in this part of the Himalaya. Since 1983 it has been
attempted by British teams, without success. In 1986 a four-member party of
British mountaineering instructors disappeared there without trace.

In autumn 1988 a Polish expedition led by Tadeusz Słupski tried to climb
the mountain. It was composed of Paweł Józefowicz, Mieczysław Zaborniak,
Radosław Motrenko, Marek Głogoczowski, Paweł Szczepkowski, Dariusz
Załuski and as doctor Ms Katarzyna Piróg. Base Camp was established on 13
September at 4300m after a short approach (1½ days) from Agsho. Camp 1
was placed at the northern foot of the mountain at 5050m. Three days later a
temporary Camp 2 was made at 5200m, and on the S ridge of Hagshu a depot
was established at 5700m, in the right place for Camp 2. From 23 to 27
September continuous snowfall brought 2–2½m of fresh snow. When

conditions improved on 7–9 October they found their Camp 1 but could not trace Camp 2 nor the deposit where they lost much equipment. The expedition was abandoned.

Good Season in the Garhwal

Besides the Nun and Kun massif, the Gangotri area is the busiest part of the Indian Himalaya. Despite changing weather during 1988 dozens of expeditions and teams were in the field. The season – in the past limited to the summer – now became prolonged to nearly seven months. The Gangotri area, 'the famous Hindu shrine where the holy Ganga (Bhagirathi) originates', is now easy of access and abounds in beautiful mountains. There is much Indian activity each year, with youth groups and army expeditions. During spring strong army expeditions climbed in the Kedarnath massif. All trends of present-day 'Himalayism' are visible: exploration, new-route activity, modern rock-climbing.

A party from Bulgaria led by Vasil Gurev completed the ascent of the unnamed P6038m; it was probably the first ascent overall. On 13 October eight members reached the top, among them three women. Many ascents of popular peaks are reported. As usual, Satopanth (7075m) was ascended by the original route, but a Yugoslav team which planned a new route on its S face gave up because of dangerous conditions. Shivling (6543m) and Thalay Sagar (6904m) received a lot of attention, but some attempts were thwarted by bad weather and illness.

Good new routes are recorded too. One of the most notable was made by an Italian team which finally solved the problem of the S face of Kedarnath (6940m) which in 1981 and 1987 repulsed strong Japanese attempts. The Italian zigzag line is 3500m long and 2400m high; it was made by G B Villa, Lorenzo Salla and Domenico Chindamo who reached the summit on 6 September. Another Italian party made a new route on Vasuki Parbat South (6702m). On 4 September the summit was reached after three bivouacs by Ticiano Cantalamessa, Marcello Ceci and Massimo Marchegianni (denivellation 1500m, UIAA V). On 28 and 29 September a Polish party climbed the probably unascended NE ridge of Bhagirathi II (6512m).

Several hard routes were repeated. An American-New Zealand team consisting of Geoff and Mark Gabites, Bill King and Don Stevenson climbed the difficult SW ridge of Bhagirathi I (6856m), reaching the summit on 16 September. A New Zealand pair made in a seven-day effort the second ascent of the famous SW pillar of Bhagirathi III (6454m). The summit was gained on 20 September by Carol McDermott and Phil Castle. The New Zealand press suggests that this technical climb, made in good alpine style, will no doubt be the leading contender for the 1988 'climb of the year award' in New Zealand.

Combined ascents were completed in the area. On 17 April nine Indian skiers ascended Kedar Dome (6831m) and ski'd down to Base Camp. On 1 June the Italians Paolo Oliavo and Giorgio Daidola made a ski descent from the same peak. 'One of the world's most beautiful ski descents in high altitude,' they write. Ascents were combined with paraglide descents.

Also modern Himalayan big rock climbing continues to expand. In August and September a small team from Yugoslavia with the famous Franček Knez established two extreme routes on the E face of Meru North (6460m). The right-hand route is 1200m high and offers difficulties of UIAA grade VII, the left-hand route, 1000m high, is much harder: UIAA grade VIII with two short sections of AO. These are the technically most demanding big wall climbs made hitherto in the Indian Himalaya.

The huge activity resulted, as usual, in fatal accidents. More than 10 mountaineers and porters died during the 1988 season. The worst tragedy occurred on Gangotri II (6599m) where six Indian climbers and porters lost their lives in late September after the woeful snowfalls. Despite great activity, there is no serious problem with pollution. In the Gangotri area cleaning teams are often in the field and the expeditions made efforts to clean their own camping places. But there is an urgent need for the publication of a climbing guide to this beautiful area, where more and more important climbs escape notice.

Mount Everest Foundation Notes 1987–88

EDWARD PECK

The following notes summarize reports from expeditions which have received the approval of the Mount Everest Foundation, and this is in most cases accompanied by a grant. MEF approval is generally an essential first step to seeking assistance, financial or otherwise, from other organizations. It should be noted that the MEF only 'sponsors' expeditions in exceptional circumstances, e.g. the 1981 Mount Kongur Expedition.

Copies of the full reports of these expeditions are lodged, when available, with the Alpine Club Library and the Archives Section of the Royal Geographical Society, and may be consulted in these places. Some expeditions will already have been described in the *Alpine Journal* and other mountaineering periodicals.

The expeditions summarized in the following notes took place between July 1987 and August 1988. These notes are based on reports received up to 1 December 1988.

America, North and South, including Arctic

88/2 *Mexican Black Holes* (February–April 1988)

This successful caving expedition logged 40km of new caves in the Sierra de Zongolica, 500km ESE of Mexico City, the deepest being 390m and the longest 6–8km.

88/8 *British Andes: El Altar, Ecuador* (December 1987)

Poor weather and general alteration in snow conditions prevented this party from achieving their aim of climbing El Obispo. They were limited to an attempt on an ice route on the SE face of Monja Grande.

88/28 *UK-New Zealand, Mount Foraker, Alaska* (May–June 1988)

This two-member team reconnoitred Mt Foraker from the Kahiltna glacier side, abandoned attempts on both the NW ridge and Cassin ridge of Mt McKinley, but joined the standard W buttress route via Denali Pass to reach the summit of Mt McKinley. A manned medical station was visited at 4300m: it exists to collect data on high-altitude sickness and to provide a 'haemoglobin oxygen saturation' service to passers-by.

88/36 *British Siula Chico-Andes* (June–July 1988)

This three-man team, making their first expedition outside Europe, did well to succeed in a direct route up the W face of Jurac 'D', and in reaching within 500m of the summit of Trapecio (5500m) via the W face. They were frustrated on the W face of Siula Chico (6080m).

88/37 *Scottish Staunings Alps – NE Greenland* (August–September 1988)

This party's objective of a first complete ski traverse of the Staunings Alps from Nordvest Fjord in the S to Kap Petersen in the N along the central spine had to be abandoned half-way owing to weather conditions. Two hitherto uncrossed cols were crossed, but no peaks were climbed.

Central Asia: China and USSR

87/4 *China Caves: Guizhou Team* (October–November 1987)

This nine-man team explored underground sections of the Fala river in Guizhou Province, trained Chinese academics in modern caving techniques, instituted a programme of *karst* research with Guizhou University and reconnoitred other potential caving areas. (See also 88/12.)

87/40 *International Friendship Expedition to Muztagh Ata* (July–August 1987)

This well co-ordinated international team, with US, Venezuelan, Japanese, French and British members, failed in their first objective of reaching the N peak of Muztagh Ata (7427m) on skis, turning back at 6250m. Eight of the nine members successfully reached the summit of the main peak (7546m) and descended on ski.

88/7 *British Altai Expedition* (July–August 1988)

Unusually bad weather prevented this four-man team from achieving their objective of a first ascent of the NE face of 20th October Peak (4167m). Instead they climbed the N face of Ak-Ayuk (3770m), Bielukha (4506m) by the normal route and traversed Delone (4200m), up by Tomsk ridge, down by E ridge.

88/12 *China Caves: Guangxi Team* (January 1988)

16 British cavers working with 12 Chinese from the Institute of Karst Geology in Guilin split into three groups to explore the Tisu River, possibly the largest underground river in the world; also the complicated 7km long Jin Lun Cave, and Windy Cave with an underground shaft estimated at 330m deep. There is the prospect of much more cave exploration in Guangxi and neighbouring areas. (See also 87/4.)

88/17 *Eagle Ski Club: Tien Shan* (March–April 1988)

On this first recorded British visit to the Zailiyskiy Alatau range in the NW Tien Shan (Kazakhstan, USSR), this six-man team, based on the Alma Ata ski resort of Chimbulak, climbed, after approaches on ski, six summits between 3450m and 4230m, and made first ski descents of the Tuyuk Su and Bogdanovicha glaciers.

88/18 *Scottish Mountaineering Club Centenary Expedition to China* (July–August 1988)

This six-man team explored the interesting Shiwakte range to the E of Mt Kongur. Despite bureaucratic delays involving a roundabout approach, two members successfully climbed Shiwakte II (6200m), also two easier peaks in the Chimghan range, and attempted the more difficult Shiwakte IIIA.

Himalaya

87/17 *Ama Dablam S Ridge* (September–October 1987)

The team from this eight-member party attempting to make an alpine-style ascent of the SW ridge of Ama Dablam retreated at 6400m in face of exceptionally heavy snow.

87/23 *Kongde Ri (Kwangde)* (October–November 1987)

This five-man party abandoned the NE ridge of Kwangde Shar in face of bad snow conditions.

87/24 *Swachand Bamak* (September–October 1987)

Two members of this eight-man London Hospital team succeeded in the first recorded ascent of P6465m to the S of Swachand Bamak in the Gangotri area.

87/25 *'Jade Venture': Xixabangma* (September–October 1987)

This strong team succeeded in forcing the difficult route up the E side of Pungpa Ri (7486m) to make the second ascent of this peak, first by this route. After a retreat owing to severe storms, Venables and Hughes repeated this climb and pushed along the ridge towards the summit of Xixabangma (8027m), retreating after a night at 7700m. Further attempts were prevented by a Chinese ban on expeditions. Meanwhile, useful glaciological and other scientific work was being carried out by Henry Osmaston and his team of students in the Nyalam valley.

87/27 *Indo-British Mount Changuch* (August–September 1987)

These joint Indian-British teams abandoned plans to climb Changuch in the Kumaon Himalaya owing to a difficult approach route. Instead they succeeded in a first ascent of the N ridge of Laspa Dura (5913m) and they also climbed Nandabhanar (6236m).

87/31 *Exercise Karnali Quadrant – Nepal* (October–November 1987)

The object of the 15-member team from the 47th Field Regiment, Royal Artillery, was to explore the remoter parts of the upper Karnali valley in NE Nepal. In fact they walked from Pokhara by way of Jumla and the Rara Lake to Surkhet.

87/37 *Altos NE Ridge of Everest* (September–October 1987)

This fourth attempt, sponsored by Altos Computers, on the 'last great problem' failed to complete the NE ridge. Despite severe snowstorms and very high winds, Doug Scott and Rick Allen pushed as high as 8100m. Sherpa Nima Tamang was killed in an avalanche.

87/39 *British Hagshu-Kishtwar* (August–September 1987)

This six-man party failed to reach its first objective: the unclimbed summit of Hagshu (6330m): but two members succeeded in reaching one of the summits of Chiring.

88/5 *British Avon Nun Kun* (May–June 1988)

This four-man team aimed to traverse Nun Kun up the E ridge and down the W ridge, but high water on the Suru River prevented access to the E ridge. They joined up with an Indian party for the W ridge and reached 6850m when Jed Meyer fell to his death and the climb was abandoned.

88/6 *Cho Oyu SW Ridge* (April–May 1988)

Two members of this small alpine-style party reached the summit of Cho Oyu by the SW ridge, using skis to about 6000m on the Gyabrag glacier. The third member suffered frost-bitten feet.

88/10 *British East Kishtwar* (August–September 1988)

Two members made a successful first ascent of Peak c6300m between the Umasi La and the Muni La in East Kishtwar at the head of the Chomochior glacier. They have proposed the name of Chomochior for the mountain.

88/13 *Menlungtse and the Search for the Yeti* (April–May 1988)

From a camp at 6600m on the W ridge of Menlungtse, Bonington and two members of his team retreated from the foot of the headwall. After reconnoitring the E ridge, Fanshawe and Hinkes reverted to the W ridge route and after a difficult climb up the headwall reached the W summit of Menlungtse (7023m) at 10.30pm, too late for continuing to the main summit (7161m). A night descent was involved. Various observations of possible yeti activity in the area deepened the mystery and raised questions difficult to answer.

88/15 *Everest – Kangshung Face* (April–May 1988)

This US/Canadian/UK team tackled the difficult and spectacular ice of the 'Neverest' buttress on the E face of the South Col. Three members reached the S summit. Venables continued alone to the top of Everest, returning in whiteout conditions and spending the night at 8500m.

88/16 *Everest – NE Ridge* (June–August 1988)

This strong team succeeded in overcoming the 'last great challenge' of Everest: the pinnacles of the NE ridge were traversed by H Taylor and R Brice on 5 August. Bad weather brought the wise decision not to attempt to push along the N ridge to the summit but to descend by the traditional route via the North Col.

88/23 *British Kalidahar Spires* (August–September 1988)

This six-man team made a successful first ascent of Mt Kalidahar (5900m) by the W ridge from Darlang Nullah in Kishtwar. They also climbed the Kalidahar Spire (5600m) by the N spur, and attempted the NW face of the spire, described as big-wall climbing on good granite.

Karakoram

87/32 *Anglo-Scottish Karakoram* (August–September 1987)

This six-member team visited the Shimshal valley in Hunza and made successful first ascents of the N and S summits of Yazghil Sar (5933m), an isolated snow peak at the confluence of the Yukshin-Garden and Yazghil glaciers. A photographic record was made of the region.

87/36 *Anglo-US Expedition to the E side of K2* (June–July 1987)

Two Britons joined two Americans and two Australians for a film-making expedition to the E side of K2. Though the face discouraged any attempt on it, they made some excursions to P6812m and Broad Peak.

87/41 *'RE 200' Exercise Total Enigma: Upper Shaksgam* (August–September 1987)

This inter-service team of 10 (7RE, 2RA, 1RM), mounted by the Royal Engineers' Mountain and Exploration Club, made a photographic survey of the Upper Shaksgam valley. After several attempts on 'Mt Crown' (7295m), said to be the third-highest unclimbed mountain (?), from a camp at 6670m, they were obliged to retreat.

88/4 *Karakoram Challenge* (June–August 1988)

Having had their permit for Broad Peak withdrawn, and after being delayed by local trouble in Gilgit, this five-man team reached 7600m on K2 before retreating in bad weather.

88/9 *British Kunyang Kish* (June–July 1988)

Two members of this four-man team succeeded in climbing Kunyang Kish (7852m) in the Hispar region, by the NW spur and the N ridge.

88/20 *British Gasherbrum* (May–July 1988)

This five-man team admits to being too small, allowing for illness and other eventualities, to tackle their objective of the unclimbed S ridge of Gasherbrum IV (7980m). Nevertheless, a determined attempt reached 7700m.

88/22 Durham University Hispar Wall Expedition (July–August 1988)

This two-man team climbed 'Sphinx Peak' (5950m) at the E end of the Balchhish range which forms the S wall of the Hispar glacier. Another peak at the W end was attempted. Useful data on snow structures and avalanche mechanisms were brought back.

88/46 British Shani S Face Expedition (June–July 1988)

This seven-member party from University College, London, was foiled in two attempts on the unclimbed SE face of Shani (5885m) in the Naltar valley, but succeeded in what were probably new routes on the N face of South Twin (5640m), the N summit of Mehrbani (5450m) and the SE spur of Sentinel South (5260m).

88/48 British Hunza Expedition (May–June 1988)

Continuous snowfall defeated yet another attempt on the 6100m spire of Bubli-Mo-Tin in the Naltar valley.

88/49 British Biale, Karakoram (June–July 1988)

All three attempts made by members of this six-man team on their objective of Biale (6730m) in the Baltoro glacier area were foiled by bad weather at about 6000m.

Book Reviews 1988

COMPILED BY GEOFFREY TEMPLEMAN

Touching the Void
Joe Simpson
Jonathan Cape, 1988, pp174, £10.95

In 1985 Joe Simpson and Simon Yates set out to climb the W face of Siula Grande in the Peruvian Andes. They succeeded in their objective after three days and started on the descent of the N ridge in atrocious snow conditions. After a night on the ridge they continued their slow progress, breaking through cornices and having short falls, until one such fall resulted in Simpson breaking his leg. Yates started lowering Simpson down the W face, and they had almost reached the bottom when Simpson shot off over an overhanging cliff and was left hanging. After a considerable length of time in which nothing could be done, Yates cut the rope.

Giving Simpson up for dead, he made his way back to Base Camp and, during the next three days, sorted out Simpson's belongings, burnt his clothes and prepared to leave camp. It was then that Simpson arrived in a state of exhausted delirium, having escaped from the deep crevasse into which he had fallen and crawled and hopped over the long glacier and moraine.

The book recounts the story in a graphic and frank way. The psychological trauma following the decision to cut the rope; the thoughts engendered by being trapped in a deep crevasse with a broken leg; the embarrassment of the eventual meeting: these things are written about in depth and with a clarity that is only too well understood. You know Simpson will survive, but the tale is like a thriller – I almost said, a cliff-hanger – progressing from one dramatic situation to the next. Comparisons with other books obviously arise. The Scott/Bonington saga on the Ogre has similarities, but it is the terrible aloneness of Simpson that strikes home. The Taylor/Barber drama on Kilimanjaro is also similar, but whereas that ended in acrimony Simpson dedicates his book to his friend.

The book ends with a postscript written in the Hunza valley in 1987. Against all the odds, Simpson was back in the high mountains again. His experiences in 1985 are something he will never forget; it is the readers' gain that he has been able to describe them so well. The award of the Boardman-Tasker Prize was well deserved.

Geoffrey Templeman

All 14 Eight-thousanders
Reinhold Messner (transl. Audrey Salkeld)
Crowood Press, 1988, £19.95

This book is intended for the coffee table. Glossy pictures predominate, yet despite initial appearances *All 14 Eight-thousanders* is not really a picture-book at all. The book is a celebration of the completion of the Himalayan Munros. There are, quite naturally, 14 chapters, one for each mountain. The chapters are structured identically. A chapter starts with a short chronology of the peak in question. The chronology is followed by a diagram of the mountain, short pieces of text by Messner's companions and admirers, and an essay by Messner. Each chapter is rounded out with a selection of photographs.

The 'chronology' is a very brief history of the peak. In this respect Messner's book tempts comparison with Louis Baume's *Sivalaya*, published in 1976. Messner brings the chronology of the climbing forward to 1986, and forms an addition to Baume, but the chronology is little more than a pointer to the events. There are few details of the expeditions involved, no references and no bibliography. There is in fact no real comparison; *Sivalaya* is authoritative.

I was most irritated by the poorly painted diagrams of the mountains which show the Messner routes, but no other. These diagrams are the real letdown of the volume. They correspond, in eight chapters, to full frontal photos of the mountain, but always from a differing, and usually confusing, angle. In the six remaining chapters there is no corresponding photograph at all. It is obvious that the artist has no interest in the detail of his subject. If you compare a Ginger Cain or a Phil Gibson with the offerings in this book, you will see exactly what I mean.

The 'companion' pieces are quite extraordinary. Some of them even cross the border of acceptable sycophancy . . . Messner has the 'instinctive, practical and intellectual capability to distil life from death . . .' and '. . . total harmony of body and mind, that bedrock upon which his philosophy is founded'. The companion pieces also tend to have lurid titles such as 'Survived – fourteen times', or 'Survived – even though the tent ripped'. One can only conclude that the editor is utterly lacking in any sense of humour.

For me, Messner's essays are the meat of the volume. They tell the story of each climb, factual and often gripping stuff. At 8000m on Nanga Parbat:

> . . . no bivouac equipment; no down jackets, no oxygen, nothing to eat or drink. It was a night that undermined us totally, physically and psychologically. The next morning . . . we began in despera-
> tion to descend the Diamir side of Nanga Parbat. I was nearly out of my mind . . .

We are used to thinking of Messner as some kind of superman. The book does nothing to dissuade us from this image. Messner writes: 'Only if a climber keeps forcing himself to train, if he lets himself be driven by his own fanaticism to the outposts of his potential, can these limits be moved . . . only thus is a climber capable of dismantling the inner barriers . . .'

And, in an echo from *The 7th Grade*: 'Good fortune and benign providence are presents from the gods, as the Tibetans say; they are an extra. But the prerequisites for success the climber has to acquire for himself – they are never given freely, anywhere.'

When he leaves the factual account, Messner indulges his taste for philosophical homily: 'Personality alone is what counts . . . mountaineering is not measurable in points and seconds.'

And yet, 'points and seconds' is exactly what Munro-bagging is all about. What other fascination can this particular subset of Himalayan peaks offer over other, less explored, mountains?

I remember watching the Pole Voytek Kurtyka examining the Messner philosophy at Buxton this year. They both had pint glasses in their hands. Voytek said:

> I like you as a human being . . . no, I do not like you as a human. I like you as an animal. I like the things you are doing, but I don't understand the things you are saying . . . You say, 'I was never in competition with others . . . others are in competition with me . . .' But also you are saying 'I, Messner, did it first!'

Voytek has an uncanny way of hitting the nail on the head.

The most successful photographs could have been (and possibly were) taken by trekkers. Dhaulagiri S face is stupendous. The most boring shots are the 'climbing' photographs. We are treated to the famous Messner 'tilt'. On the S face of Manaslu the angles are so bewildering that the climbers appear to be dangling from helium-filled rucksacks. There are exceptions, such as the stunning jacket cover, with an ice-encrusted Messner showing just how cold Makalu can be in good weather, and the superb Kangshung face of Everest in the background. But wait, the tent in the mid-ground has a strong shadow on the left, and Messner in the foreground is shadowed on the right. Surely he would not need to paste up montage for the cover, would he? You might think Messner must have hundreds of stunning 'natural' photographs, yet delving between the covers produces very few scenes of the same standard as the cover.

Last weekend I showed the book to a non-mountaineering friend. He is the sort of person who might actually go out and buy a good coffee table book. What he said was: 'I don't go a bomb on the pictures, but I suppose you can't expect a professional mountaineer to be a professional photographer too.' During a recent interview, Messner formulated a similar opinion:

> The more a climb is a show, the less it is an adventure. More it is an adventure, less it is a show . . . at the extremes of adventure, when you really push yourself, you cannot make a film, you cannot make a show. At maximum you can record, maybe, one photograph on the summit.

Perhaps this goes some way to explaining the paucity of really fine photography. Messner, in completing the first collection of all 14 eight-thousanders, was pushing the limits of mountaineering. Success, survival even, was a matter of the slenderest margins. There was no room in his world for anything else. This is what the book is really about. Extreme adventure.

A V Saunders

The Making of a Mountaineer
George Ingle Finch (With a Memoir by Scott Russell)
Arrowsmith, 1988, pp viii + 456, £19.95

This book is much more than just a re-issue of George Finch's classic on mountaineering; surely one of the most readable on the subject ever written.

Originally presented to me in a first edition soon after I started climbing, it almost became my mountaineering bible for a time. How exciting were Finch's exploits in Corsica and the Alps at that time! The great Monte Rosa, Mont Blanc and Chamonix Aiguilles climbs, particularly the traverse of the Drus. But it was the chapters on Everest which really caught my imagination then in youth, before I went to Everest myself in charge of oxygen.

To my mind, Finch's oxygen attempt on Everest was more important than anything that had happened before on the mountain. It failed to get him and his gallant companion Geoffrey Bruce to the summit, but it proved beyond doubt that oxygen could do so; as was confirmed by Peter Lloyd in 1938 and Hunt's party in 1953.

The re-reading of this charming book brought back pleasant youthful memories. But what makes this new edition doubly interesting these days is Scott Russell's long 'memoir' of George Finch which includes a new account of his quarrels with the Mount Everest establishment in the 1920s. Russell's researches in the Everest archives at the RGS have added additional information to what was reported by Walt Unsworth in his splendid book on Everest.

This new edition of *The Making of a Mountaineer* is well worth while, not only in its own right as a classic of mountaineering literature, but because of Scott Russell's memoir of a great mountaineer who became one of the most distinguished Presidents of the Alpine Club.

Charles Warren

Feeding the Rat. Profile of a Climber
Al Alvarez
Bloomsbury, 1988, pp152, £11.95

This book is a biography of Mo Anthoine. Accounts of Mo's early alpine climbs and later expeditions to the Himalaya and Karakoram are interspersed with chapters describing the building of his home from a ruin in Nant Peris and the establishment of his successful business, Snowdon Mouldings, in Llanberis.

'Feeding the Rat' is Mo's expression for what drives him and most other climbers out regularly to, in his words, 'flush out your system and do a bit of suffering'. Much of Mo's climbing philosophy is discussed and it is clear that the suffering should be within the overall context of having a good time with one's mates. Mo again: 'Expeditions are supposed to be enjoyable ... Admittedly, they're bloody hard work and sometimes you get frightened, but primarily they should be fun.'

Following these principles, over the last 15 years Mo has made an enviable series of low-key, largely unsponsored expeditions with small groups of friends to the Himalaya, Karakoram and South America. An exception was his participation in the 1986 Everest expedition, but we learn that there were not a lot of laughs on Everest. At a time when climbing in general and expeditions in particular are becoming more and more dominated by professionals, it is refreshing to read of Mo's traditional, publicity-shunning approach to mountaineering.

The book is short, with only 129 pages of text, and the few black-and-white photographs are well below the standard found in most modern books on mountaineering. The writing is in a simple style which is delightful to read; this is well illustrated by the evocative description of Llanberis on the first three pages.

I found that the most memorable chapters were the two where the author describes his own climbs with Mo, on the Comici Route on the Cima Grande in the Dolomites and on the Old Man of Hoy.

Rupert Hoare

Cumbrian Rock
Trevor Jones and Geoff Milburn
Pic Publications, 1988, pp257, £14.95

A Century on the Crags. The Story of Rockclimbing in the Lake District
Alan Hankinson
J M Dent and Sons Ltd, 1988, £16

After a long period without a thoroughly researched, commercially produced history of Lake District climbing, suddenly two contenders sprang forth fully armed in 1988. The long history was due for re-rendering, at a time when some deny the past's relevance while others risk serious misrepresentation of it from inadequate methods, present-mindedness, plain lack of knowledge or parochialism.

Different qualifications are brought to the task. Trevor Jones and Geoff Milburn produced the rich mine of *Welsh Rock*; this is the companion in format and writing style. Their climbing experience and insider knowledge of the broad scene are impressive, as is the industry involved. Alan Hankinson also climbs, and has written before on the Lake District's Golden Age. Originally an historian, he salutes the fiery old revisionist A J P Taylor in his dedication, as historian, fell walker and Pillarite. Thus one can expect a critical approach to the sources, some weighing of the evidence and analytical sifting of wheat from chaff. Already he has succeeded in resurrecting the 'first tigers' from the black-and-white contrasts of the Abraham brothers' photographs, in a book and an associated film. Now aided by new-fangled interview and antique diary, he tries to bring the story up to date.

These histories had the advantage, not only of excellent FRCC guides and journals, but also of the 1986 special edition of the Fell and Rock Journal which celebrated *A Hundred Years of Climbing in the Lake District*. In its way, as with the *Helyg* book produced by Geoff Milburn for Wales, this did much to clarify the key items for any would-be writer. It was legitimized by its authors who include among others H M Kelly, John Wilkinson and Pete Whillance. Hankinson acknowledges these and other bibliographical debts. Despite more extensive quotations from a mass of sources, exact references are not given and there is no bibliography in *Cumbrian Rock*. That is a pity, for it will make the book a good deal less useful in the future. Nor is there a list of illustrations. Also helpful to these writers were Bill Birkett's biographical sketches of *Lakeland Pioneers*, and to some degree the colourful but wildly inaccurate booklet published by Border TV to accompany their *Lakeland Rock* series of films.

What are we to make of the results of their labour? On general design and book production *Cumbrian Rock* is richer fare. Its photography is lavish, in colour and black-and-white, integral to the text and strongly supporting clean pages of bold typefaces. Its glossy paper feels made to last, and heightens the effects of the muddiest of ancient snaps. It allows, too, the survival of some black-and-white from slides of modern parentage. Dent have been much more penny-pinching, with two bunches of black-and-white athwart a text printed on passable paper. The black-and-whites come out a little punchier on photographic paper, as many deserve, but generally their impact is vitiated by their consignment to two ghettos. They are a slightly eccentric collection, with the wonderful ageing hippy of Borrowdale, Millican Dalton, getting far more coverage than the rock stars of any era. He does look more interesting than some.

The two books have parallels in structure, particularly in their middling chapters. Each makes H M Kelly worth a chapter and follows with another on the Welsh influence from the late 1920s. Does the structure of events really determine this irrevocably, I wonder? They give fairly convincing accounts, for those of us far too young to remember, of long distant times. Their use of the relatively ample sources varies a little. Hankinson uses Sid Cross to recall his first encounter with Alf Bridge and A B Hargreaves on Gimmer in 1931, whilst *Cumbrian Rock* recalls Bridge's impressions of these able but technically untutored youths from Kendal, making more of his overhearing the lads' opinion of the experts as '. . . a pair of doddering old devils'. Does anything ever change?

Frankly, this story underlines a difference between the books throughout. The Hankinson text is smoother, less encrusted with material, flowing and shaping into manageable chapters. *Cumbrian Rock* seems to me closer to its subject, less tidy and even losing its thread at times, but humorous, vital, lively and rich to a degree pasteurized out in the other book.

However, by the 1960s life becomes more difficult for both, as too many folk were now in the thick of it and are still alive and kicking. On that ground few can hope to please. Hankinson gives little space to the whole post-Dolphin emporium. Perhaps he was less comfortable with it. He has little idea of the interconnections of people, so that climbs appear as *deus ex machina* without much reason for their invention. Nor does he seem aware of the widespread advance in technical aids from the early 1960s onwards, including perlon, drill nuts on wire, wired wedges and harnesses. Partly this is the product of looking at the district through the microscope, and losing sight of wider influences such as Welsh and Scottish sea cliff and eastern alpine and Chamonix climbing, in which many leading activists of the 1960s were steeped.

Trevor Jones knows all this and in general gives a more convincing account. Notables like Pat Fearnehough, bridging RAF mountain rescue, the Peak, two Great Gable Guides and much alpinism, are at least mentioned. Both books, however, fall into the parochial trap of taking the Paul Ross versus Allan Austin controversies at face value. Much of the Keswick presented as supportive of Paul was active in Llanberis, Chamonix and on limestone. Quite simply, the parish pumps of Langdale and Keswick hardly mattered in the 1960s, though some of the issues did (people did not misuse the word ethics then). In particular, there was a sustained attempt to keep aid down, and to reduce it where possible on repeat ascents. This was what the Niche controversy was about in the early 1960s, though Trevor's text misses that vital point, and so it was with many other routes on their second or subsequent ascents. Until the new protection became more generalized and versatile after 1966, new routes kept on acquiring a jot too many bits of aid or fixed protection, but much of it was soon whittled down, a tendency which generically developed into the early 1970s, with the Read and Adams routes and what came after. Meanwhile, the rock attempted got harder and harder, to the point where someone had to consider modifying bodies and performance as well as changing the rules. Livesey's approach made its impact four years after Henry Barber's blitz on Britain, and after the high point of more generalized going to Yosemite and coming back 'born again'. By September 1971 Rab Carrington had chalk in his baggy trouser pockets on our ascent of Woubits, Henry Barber had been over twice, with his first six weeks in Tony Riley's (Alpha Club) house in Sheffield, and Ed Drummond was teaching John Allen (at High Starrs school, but not his climbing).

My suggestion is a simple one. After the 1960s, internalist accounts of particular districts of Britain make even less sense than they did before 1900. In the Lake District what happened was that the 1960s performers walked on to other stages, with the exception of Allan Austin and other dedicated local (plus Peak or Yorkshire) oldies. Thus on 7 October 1971 Tut Braithwaite and myself did three short new routes on Number 5 Gully Buttress on Ben Nevis. It rained overnight. Next afternoon we tidied the Medlar on Raven Crag, Thirlmere (tried before its first ascent with Martin Boysen on the same weekend as our controversial first repeat of Hiraeth in September 1962). Ross had long been alive and well with Henry doing all sorts of climbing in New Hampshire. Everybody who was anybody was setting sights on the big faces, not merely on the Alps, in the 'run-in' which ended on Everest SW face in 1975 and with the great successes and tragedies of the ACG between 1970 (Ian Clough and Tom Patey) and 1986 (Al Rouse). The rock athletes were to perform better, on a stage bequeathed to them by abdication after more than a decade of hegemony. Perhaps that is why the only climbers on Creag an Dubh Lochain one June weekend of 1975 were Les Brown, Pete Turnbull and his mate from the old Wall End barn days, me, Pete Whillance and Jeff Lamb. Not that the Lakes were finished. In new route terms they had just entered a stage too blacksmithing for fun, requiring a new dedication.

These are very personal views, but the later stages of these books do not lead me to revise them. Both become guidebook-like, a catechism of rather ill-digested pieties about a world of which the authors can have experienced little. In Trevor's book the signal is an unwarranted put-down of Alan (Richard) MacHardy, whose Vikings in 1969 was the hardest route in the district at the time. It was not at all surprising that he led the route, as Trevor claims. Physically he was probably the strongest of the Alpha Club group, though technically others were more capable. Overall he was almost certainly the keenest, and, if his solo ascent of the Grooves and Overhanging Arête on Cyrn Las and of dozens of other Extreme climbs, as well as a notable alpine career and early repetition throughout the decade of many hard routes (Dinosaur on Gogarth, June 1968) did not put him in the first rank, I don't know what did – he certainly couldn't cheat as imaginatively as Drummond, Pete Crew or even the Baron Brown. Nor was it an accident that he did Vikings with rising star Paul (Tut) Braithwaite. 'Richard' MacHardy had shivered his apprenticeship on the E buttress of Scafell a decade before, holding the rope for his clubmate Les Brown, new-routing on Centaur. Paul Braithwaite was later involved in the *Cumbrian* controversy with Rod Valentine. For all the noise nobody did it much better for three years after their first ascent in 1974. Valentine did a free ascent in 1988.

These are the carpings of old men. We are better off for these books, and each has its advantages. Both suffer from occasional typos, mistakes and misinterpretations. Nevertheless, their weakness is more often lack of analysis rather than mistaken fact. Keen as Pete Livesey was to disconnect rock climbing from its moorings to enhance its status, and with it the significance of his major contribution, still in public profile it has proved essential in recent times to use Chris Bonington to make it interesting (the *Lakeland Rock* films). It would be better perhaps if it were not so, but the recent free rock-climbing ascent of the Trango Tower by Bernt Arnold and Wolfgang Gullich suggests that not all rock-climbers have signed the self-denying ordinance. At least that means that some will retain the breadth of vision to see how much real climbing remains to be done. As always the best know that, while lesser mortals muddle on in misconceptions, whatever their muscle power.

Paul Nunn

Aladağlar. An Introduction
Haldun Aydingün
Redhouse Press, Istanbul, 1988, pp74, npq

In view of the growing popularity of climbing in Turkey, Haldun Aydingün's English edition of his pocket-guide is a welcome 'introduction' (he hopes to produce a full survey of the range later) to the 3700–3400m summits of the Ala Dağ range in Central Anatolia. Seven sketch maps, 21 clearly drawn topos and 16 pages of coloured plates illustrate the access routes and a variety of climbs in this interesting range, now said to be within reach of a long weekend from Istanbul. Rather different from the two-day walk-in from the Pozanti road-

head by Robin Hodgkin and your reviewer in 1943, when they made the first
ascent by the couloir on the SW face of Demirkazik (second ascent) now known
as 'Peck's Couloir'. In fairness this should have been Hodgkin-Peck's Couloir,
were this name not harder to pronounce in Turkish.

Edward Peck

Nanda Devi. The Tragic Expedition
John Roskelley
Oxford Illustrated Press, 1988, pp240, £9.95

The American expedition which Willi Unsoeld led to Nanda Devi in 1976 has
had to wait for over 10 years for its activities to be chronicled by Roskelley, one
of the three members who reached the summit. It was, as the title states, a tragic
expedition, riddled with dissension and culminating in the death of Nanda Devi
Unsoeld. Maybe it was a story that could not easily be told until after Willi
Unsoeld himself had died, his being the leading hand in the organization and in
the effort to get his daughter to the summit of the mountain after which she was
named. The assembled group were so mixed in their views, their personal
relationships and their technical ability that dispute and argument were
inevitable.

The fact that the author was the strongest, and loudest, critic of the
enterprise makes a reader (this one, at least) long to hear an opposite point of
view during much of the book, although he seems to mellow a little in the later
stages. An interesting book, therefore, but an expedition that it was probably
better to read about than participate in.

Geoffrey Templeman

Byron's Travels
Allan Massie
Sidgwick & Jackson, 1988, pp224, £14.95

Byron's travels, as described in his incomparable letters, are quite fascinating.
This book should therefore be read to the end by those interested in Byron's
travels in general. But from the Alpine Club's point of view, it is really only the
second chapter which concerns us.

In 1816, self-exiled from home, Byron travelled to Geneva through
Germany, visiting the 'field of Waterloo' on the way, and lodged there at the
Hotel d'Angleterre where he met the Shelleys. Then here, near the town, a week
or two later he rented the Villa Diodati where he lived for some months near the
Shelleys in a house which had once been lived in by Milton.

It was probably those few months on the shores of Lac Leman which were
the happiest and most formative of his life, for it was here that he sailed up the
lake with Shelley, almost getting shipwrecked on the way, to visit Chillon and
write his famous poem about Bonivard – inaccurate historically, but good
poetry.

It was during this brief but highly important visit to Switzerland in 1816 that Byron visited the Oberland with his friend Hobhouse. From the Wengernalp and the Scheidegg he admired the Jungfrau, and it was this visit which inspired him to write *Manfred*; the inspiration for that great picture by John Martin of 'Manfred on the Jungfrau'.

It was during this visit to Switzerland that he visited Chamonix, of which he wrote somewhat disparagingly. No, it was the Oberland tour that appealed to him and led to *Manfred*.

Charles Warren

Flora of Bhutan, Volume I, parts 1, 2 & 3
A J C Grierson & D G Long
Royal Botanic Garden, Edinburgh, for the Overseas Development Administration, London, and the Royal Government of Bhutan, 1983, 1984 & 1987

In June 1975, in the days when visitors to Bhutan in one year could be counted on one hand, Thimphu was rife with speculation about two Scotsmen who were coming out to do an inventory of the flora of Bhutan. As the authors write in their foreword to Part 1:

> From 1914 onwards a small number of privileged botanists and horticulturists, mostly British, were able to travel extensively in Bhutan and bring back to Britain large plant collections. The greatest of these collectors were undoubtedly Frank Ludlow and George Sherriff who made seven visits to Bhutan between 1933 and 1950 and amassed over 6000 herbarium specimens as well as large numbers of living plants and seeds.
>
> In spite of the considerable collecting activity, almost none of the resulting information has been available to those in Bhutan, such as the forestry department, for whom (J D Hooker's) *Flora of British India* remains the only reference work. In contrast, neighbouring Sikkim has enjoyed much more intensive botanical exploration for many decades, and numerous publications bear witness to its extremely rich flora.
>
> The Royal Government of Bhutan not unreasonably felt that some of the information on their flora should be made available to them, and in 1974 they requested the Overseas Development Administration in London that a botanist be employed in Britain to prepare an inventory of the flora based on herbarium and living collections ...

From their initial visit, those in the Forestry Department and elsewhere had no doubt about the professionalism of Andrew Grierson and David Long, and the sight of the lanky red-haired Long and his keen young Bhutanese assistants wielding penknives and plastic bags up some ferocious hillside gully was a novel feature of the Thimphu region. But as they moved to distant parts and the size of their task became increasingly apparent, there must have been some heart-searching in ODA at the inexorable lengthening of the time-scale of the project.

As the work progressed, it transpired that the emphases of past collectors were on temperate, alpine and horticultural plants. So Grierson and Long's work has been directed towards tropical plants and to filling gaps in the database. Many new species have of course come to light – including a pine and two new rhododendrons, as well as many scores of species new to Bhutan. After several years' work, the need to include Sikkim became evident, in order to include many plants known from there but not yet found in Bhutan; and so, by 1979, a final format was adopted and a revised work-programme laid out. So far, in four field trips some 5700 specimens have been collected, and are now housed in Edinburgh. Many duplicates are deposited in Thimphu, where it is hoped a herbarium can soon be established. All this has been achieved by two botanists and a scientific assistant, but from this year the Royal Botanic Garden, Edinburgh, is increasing the research team to four, with a part-time scientific assistant, while ODA funds one botanist, all travel and subsistence, artist's fees and publishing costs.

Thus, the ideal 'developmental project' has been established, with the gradual production of a low-budget *Flora of Bhutan* which provides basic keys, short descriptions and some illustrations, while also serving as a check-list. The language has deliberately been kept as simple as possible, and unnecessary jargon and abbreviations have been reduced to the minimum. As the authors say:

> Many plant groups are, by their nature, difficult to classify and identify (often also because of inadequate herbarium material or lack of knowledge), and the flora will be hard to use without some experience. For some groups (eg *Rhododendrons*) the taxonomy is relatively well-defined, but others, like *Salix*, are so poorly known as to make future re-revision essential after further field study.

The first three parts, which are of a sensible size for a rucksack, are in distinctive yellow limp boards, with good quality paper and a most pleasing layout and type-face, while the 49 illustrations by Mary Bates and others have a linear clarity which would commend them to any collector, whether professional or amateur. The reference map is helpful, and it is a pleasure to find complete consistency in the spellings of place-names.

The bibliographies in each part are worth detailed study, as are the geographical outlines, the classification of vegetation, the local and medicinal uses of plants, and the authors' remarks on conservation policy – surely a lesson to Bhutan's neighbours. The hoped-for completion during the next few years of Volume II, comprising four more parts, will provide a *Flora of Bhutan* with a relevance from Nepal to Assam, particularly for botanists and foresters, and in other parts of the world where Himalayan plants are studied or grown in gardens; and it will no doubt prove to be the definitive work on the flora of this little-known part of the Himalayan region.

John Tyson

Seven Summits
Dick Bass & Frank Wells, with Rick Ridgeway
Aurum Press, 1987, pp10 + 336, £14.95 (Also in a Pan pb edition)

As Bass and Wells say in a personal note introducing the book, they didn't write it – the sole author is Rick Ridgeway, and an excellent job he has made of it. The seven summits of the title are the highest summits of each of the seven continents – McKinley and Aconcagua, Elbrus, Kilimanjaro, Kosciusko, Vinson (Antarctica) and, of course, Everest.

Dick Bass – an entrepreneur in oil, coal and ranching, and owner of the Snowbird Ski Resort in Utah – and Frank Wells, then president of Warner Bros Studios, independently had the idea of being the first person to climb the seven summits, originally in one year. Each was in his early fifties, and each had done a little climbing. Bass had climbed Fuji, the Matterhorn twice and McKinley, while Wells had done Mont Blanc, Kilimanjaro and some smaller fry. They decided to join forces and have a go, and they did it, Bass doing all seven and Wells six, his wife saying when it came to the final assault on Everest that it was either the mountain or her! Their first attempts on Elbrus, Aconcagua and Everest were unsuccessful, and they lost Marty Hoey – one of their guides and an inspiration to Bass – when she fell to her death on Everest. But they were successful on Aconcagua, in 1983. The next attempts on Everest in the same year resulted in some of the team reaching the top, but not Bass or Wells. However, McKinley, Kilimanjaro and Elbrus fell quickly after that. Vinson then became a logistical nightmare, the flight in and out being almost the most scary part of the expedition, but they got there. Kosciusko, of course, was a doddle, but it finally came to Everest again. Bass tried to attach himself to various expeditions, each time being rebuffed with either unfriendliness or bureaucratic intransigence, but finally he and David Breashears were accepted on a Norwegian expedition, the same one on which Chris Bonington attained the summit. Bass and Breashears made it, and the Seven Summits were a reality.

I had originally thought that the story of two men buying their way up mountains around the world wouldn't be for me. But, as I said, Ridgeway has written an excellent book. The characters of the participants come over well. Their brashness and typical 'entrepreneurial attitudes' are well shown, and so also are their devotion to the job in hand, their humour and, above all, their determination. It's a racy narrative, well worth reading. After all, you don't get many mountaineering books that quote not only Chris Bonington on the cover, but Clint Eastwood and Robert Redford as well!

Geoffrey Templeman

Le Grand Livre des Cabanes
Orell Füssli Zürich, 1988, pp240, 66 Swiss Francs

In 1892 the Swiss Alpine Club published its first list describing the 40 mountain refuges or *cabanes* which had by then been constructed. Three subsequent lists followed, the last one in 1946. To mark its 125th anniversary in 1988 the SAC, under the direction of Section Uto, one of the founder sections of the Club, has published a handsome new edition prepared by Willy Furter, describing the 154 huts and refuges belonging to the various sections of the Club, plus eight others owned by affiliated Academic Alpine Clubs. The cost of publication was guaranteed by an anonymous Club member, and a subsidy was provided by the Swiss Credit Bank.

The text – which appears in the three national languages, German, French and Italian – is concise and factual without frills or superfluities. The illustrations, as was to be expected, are of high quality and they form the major part of the book. The presentation is clear, as befits a good book of reference, and the information provided is about as complete as climbers and skiers could require.

The end-papers comprise a map of the whole Alpine region from Martigny to Scuol, on which each hut is positioned and numbered on an east to west system for quick identification, with corresponding numbers used throughout the book. An introductory alphabetical list provides the hut number, the section to which it belongs, and the pages on which it is described in the two main sections of the book – illustrated and descriptive which, for ease of reference, are printed respectively on white and on grey paper. The illustrated section devotes a full page to each hut, containing a colour photograph plus an orientation map and map reference numbers. This section is sub-divided into the six main Alpine regions Vaud/Valais, Bernese Oberland, Uri/Schwyz, Glarus, Grisons, Tessin, with the first two containing the largest number of huts, 46 and 36 respectively. The descriptive pages that follow include information about date of construction, size, access, base for climbs/excursions, and also provide useful SAC Guidebook references.

If a trifle bulky at $25.5 cm^2$ – not exactly pocket size! – this is a reference book of great merit and a magnificent volume for those who can afford its price.

Trevor Braham

Rimo. Mountain on the Silk Road
Peter Hillary
Hodder & Stoughton, 1988, pp176, £12.95

The expedition to climb Rimo was organized as a joint Indo-Australian effort but, as this account makes only too clear, it became 'joint' in name only. Most of the 'Australian' part of the group – which included a New Zealander, a Yorkshireman and an American – were what could be described as typical, independent climbing *aficionados*, while a number of the Indian party were military personnel. It could therefore be seen from the start that differences of opinion would arise.

The major factor, however, was that Rimo lies in that part of the Eastern Karakoram close to the border with Pakistan and China and actively occupied by the Indian Army. The team was kept under military surveillance the whole way and bureaucratic delays were frequent. When at last they reached the mountain, two attempts on the summit failed because of bad weather, technical problems and the expiry of their army permit. The retreat was quite an epic, with the relationships finally breaking down, their film being confiscated and Hillary himself ending up with a terrifying encounter with the wrong end of a Sten gun.

The book is interesting to read, even though written in rather a pedestrian way, because of the author's views on the attitudes of the various members; once again, it would be interesting to have an Indian account to read at the same time. (See Harish Kopiada's comment on p 270.)

Geoffrey Templeman

Pinnacle Club: A History of Women Climbing
Shirley Angell
The Pinnacle Club, 1988, pp xiv + 258, £14.95

The Pinnacle Club began in 1921 and is still flourishing. We have here an account of its founding and an admirably detailed record of everything that has happened since. Most office holders and many members are mentioned by name. Innumerable club meets throughout the years are recounted, with notes of routes climbed and who climbed them. More adventurous expeditions to the Alps and Himalaya are described in detail, and we are even told of mountaineering exploits by members outside the umbrella of the club.

Through this vast mass of fact percolates a marvellous feeling of the atmosphere of the club. Always warm, welcoming and supportive, it is friendly to spouses, offspring and newcomers. Especially in the early days, there were some eccentric characters, but we are left in no doubt that their hearts were in the right place. There are many references to the club hut at Cwm Dyli and its very special role in the life of the club is lovingly recounted, though we hear of some of its problems too. Alongside all this, very high standards of climbing are aspired to and achieved, with more capable members going to great trouble to help and encourage the less experienced. We also learn of the attitude of men to women climbers in the early days, and why even today there is a place for a women's club where women can climb together without men.

This book reflects an enormous amount of painstaking meticulous toil, extracting information from club records and members' diaries and recollections. It is brought alive by frequent verbatim quotes and the lively style of the author. Liberally illustrated with photographs spanning the whole period, all from the Pinnacle Club collection, it will be an absorbing read for all who know the people or the places or have even a passing interest in climbing.

Anne Andrews

Matterhorn
Beat H Perren
Stadler Verlag, Konstanz/Zürich, 1988

Essentially a book of pictures, containing about 250 colour photographs, mostly full-page with several double-page spreads, this is an impressive volume 35×27cm in size and weighing about 2½kg. The technical excellence of the photography and reproduction create an immediate and startling impact, with the eponymous mountain pictured on every page and seen from every angle. The author, one of the founders in 1968 of the Air Zermatt Rescue Service and now its President, was born in Zermatt, grew up there, and from the age of 14 when he first climbed the mountain became fascinated with the Matterhorn. Since his parents had a photographic shop in Zermatt, photography and the mountains must have exercised a strong influence from an early age; obviously the right credentials for the conception and production of this book. Added value, with international sales in mind, is the provision of six languages (including Japanese) for the photo captions. Apart from the author's introduction and a short biography, there is no other text.

Air photography has been used exclusively. Besides a tendency to create more dramatic effects, air views possess certain advantages when they reveal the configuration of the various ridges and faces of the Matterhorn, as well as the sense of perspective relative to some of its illustrious neighbours that only an air photograph can give. But the reality of the routes, from the climber's viewpoint, is lost; and, with a large majority of the route photographs featuring climbing figures, a recurrent 'flies on a wall' setting characterizes most of the photographs.

The general concept and layout are admirable. 12 dazzling pages of the peaks and glaciers that fill the arena are followed by 33 pages of the mountain 'in all its splendour'. (There is not a single photo caption for the first 64 pictures.) While some of these views are breathtaking, a few are included for their photogenic value. The six sections that follow provide a picture series of the main climbing routes: Hörnli, Zmutt, Italian, Amici, Furggen, N face. The composite ridge or face view with which each section begins would have been greatly enhanced by a caption and a route sketch. The subsequent stage-by-stage route sequences leave one in some cases with the impression of apparently desperate climbing situations – as vertical views tend to do.

The book's merits depend upon whom it is aimed at. For pictorial air coverage, it deserves full marks. But not a single map or map reference is to be found, and there are no complementary sketches of any sort. The photo captions, such as they are, are grouped together and placed at the start of each section, making the search for them occasionally tiresome. There is no index, but this might have been hard to provide in an exclusively pictorial book. The reader might be excused for being lulled into the belief that the Matterhorn is immune from bad weather and storms, with flawless weather prevailing from the first page to the last.

For a book of such proportions, at a price beyond the reach of many mountaineers, the merits need to outweigh the flaws. Depending upon one's point of view, perhaps they do. Just take a look at the pictures on pp23, 103, 207. There are several others!

Trevor Braham

High Altitude Studies in Man

A number of important studies on this subject have been published in recent years; below is a review of nine of them.

High altitude studies in man are important because they throw light on the oxygen transport system which is essential to life. The degree of adaptation to oxygen lack is truly remarkable, for a man acutely exposed to the height of Everest (8848m) in a decompression chamber will become comatose and probably die, yet a Sherpa has now climbed Everest four times without supplementary oxygen and two continental climbers have ascended and descended the mountain from 5800m in two days, also without bottled oxygen. Oxygen lack affects every system in the body, and man at altitude serves as a model for those at sea-level with the chronic oxygen lack associated with heart and lung disease; and these are among the commonest ills that afflict humans.

In the mid-19th century the way in which oxygen is transported in the human body began to be studied by physiologists, their work coinciding with the start of the exploration of the world's highest peaks and the formation of the Alpine Club; ever since there has been a close relationship between the mountaineer and the medical scientist. In the last few years, interest in these studies has greatly increased and medical textbooks carry sections on the disorders of altitude and cold.

Millions of people now enjoy trekking, climbing and skiing in the mountains, and it is common to be lifted to 3000m and above by ski-lift or helicopter, so mountain sickness and its complications have become familiar to many. Increasingly, too, expeditions to extreme altitude – particularly in winter – are exposing mountaineers to the limits of tolerable hypoxia and cold. Finally, there is an increasing interest in the high-altitude populations of the world – in South America, Central Asia and parts of the United States of America. For these reasons there is a continuing need to update information about cold and hypoxia and this is what these books provide.

Hypoxia and Cold
Ed John Sutton, Charles Houston & Geoffrey Coates
Praeger, New York, 1987, pp16 + 560

Hypoxia and Cold records the proceedings of a meeting held at Chateau Lake Louise in Canada in 1985; these meetings, started by the Alpine Club at Plas y Brenin in North Wales in 1975, are now held at regular intervals in North America, are attended by scientists worldwide and in many different disciplines, and provide a real stimulus for research. For non-scientific mountaineers, the chapter on 'Limiting Factors' emphasizes the biological knife-edge on which the climber at extreme altitude is functioning, while the section on the physiological and psychological make-up of élite mountaineers, who are world class athletes in this particular dimension, is also most interesting.

This volume, as its title suggests, covers both cold and altitude and it is right that it should; these two stresses must always be taken together in the mountain environment, for each modifies the effect of the other on man. In addition, the effects of exercise must always be taken into account. This point should be stressed, because in the laboratory each tends to be studied separately, whereas in the field (which is analogous to the clinical situation) all combine. This makes the interpretation of laboratory findings as difficult in the field as it is in the clinical dimension.

High Altitude Deterioration
Ed J Rivolier, P Cerretelli, J Foray & P Segantini
Karger, Basle, 1985, pp16 + 228

High Altitude Deterioration is the proceedings of a symposium organized by the Medical Commission of the UIAA which was held in Chamonix in 1984. Its flavour is European, and again it holds much of interest to the mountaineer and skier – in particular, the information that an avalanche victim dug out from the encompassing snow which prevents wind-chill may, if left unprotected from the wind, die rapidly from hypothermia. The crevasse victim, too, may lose heat very quickly to the walls of ice in which he is jammed. There is also a wide-ranging retrospective survey of accidents in the Greater Ranges of Asia. My criticism of this excellent book is the title, for 'High Altitude Deterioration' is a term used to describe a specific clinical entity brought about by long stay at altitude, and is associated with distinctive clinical features.

Seminars in Respiratory Medicine: Man at Altitude (Vol 5 No 2)
Ed John Sutton
Thieme-Stratton Inc, New York, 1983, pp103–216

Man at Altitude is one of a series in *Seminars in Respiratory Medicine*, and like the other volumes is mainly for the medical scientist and clinician. Of particular interest to the mountaineer is a series of short articles on the history of high-altitude medicine, and resumés of the Silver Hut Expedition 1960–61 in the Everest region, the American Medical Research Expedition to Everest in 1981, when measurements were made on the summit, and studies carried out on Mt Logan between 1967 and 1979.

Within the last few years there have been three important studies in high altitude medicine and physiology. Firstly, the successful scientific expedition to Everest in 1981, led by West, to which I have referred above; and, secondly, the successful completion of Operation Everest II. This was carried out in the decompression chamber at the US Army Department of Environmental Health at Natick, Massachusetts, under the direction of Cymerman, Houston, Reeves and Sutton. Volunteers spent 40 days and 40 nights (a suitably biblical span), being decompressed gradually to the 'summit' of Everest. Extensive studies were completed, including a number of invasive techniques to measure heart function which are too dangerous to be carried out in the field. Finally, the results of Chinese work, both in the laboratory and in the field in Tibet and elsewhere, are becoming available.

Hypothermia and Cold Stress
Evan L Lloyd
Croom Helm, London, 1986

This book is a veritable encyclopaedia about hypothermia and stress due to cold in all walks of life, but there is relatively little about local cold injury. The author, who is an anaesthetist, is well known for his method of central rewarming via a face mask or tube into the lungs which has been carried out successfully in field conditions, and the chapter on mountain hypothermia will be of particular interest to AC members. With over 1500 references, the book is also invaluable for the research worker in this subject and it should be in every library that deals with environmental hazard.

High Altitude and Man
Ed John B West and Sukhamay Lahiri
American Physiological Society, Bethesda, Maryland, 1984

This is the report of a symposium stimulated by research carried out on the American Medical Research Expedition to Everest 1981. This was led by Professor John West, who writes in the opening chapter about 'Man on the Summit of Everest'. Each chapter and section has important implications in the field of high altitude physiology and there is a considerable input from China. That one section has five chapters on sleep at altitude illustrates how important this subject has become, for man spends about one third of his life asleep. As all who go to altitude know, irregular breathing (and snoring) are a feature of sleep, and the implications for the normal control of breathing are important. Although called Cheyne-Stokes Respiration, the first (1781) clinical description of the phenomenon was made by John Hunter, the father of scientific surgery, and is contained in his clinical case-books. The first observation of this condition at altitude was made on the top of Mont Blanc and is reported in John Tyndall's book *Glaciers of the Alps*.

Hypoxia, Exercise and Altitude: Proceedings of the Third Banff International Hypoxia Symposium
Ed John R Sutton, Charles S Houston, Norman L Jones
A R Liss Inc, New York, 1983

This book has an immense breadth of interest, with papers on sleep, control of respiration in early life and Sudden Infant Death Syndrome, as well as chapters on fatigue and metabolism and nutrition at altitude. There are also two fascinating papers a little outside the mainstream of human physiology. One is by Hermann Rahn on altitude adaptation in organisms without lungs – that is, plants, insects, spiders and birds' eggs (at least 21 species of birds nest above 4000m). The other is on breath-holding in mammals, with considerable implications for the human swimmer.

Abstracts from UIAA Mountain Medicine Conference held at St Bartholomew's Hospital, London, 1987

Among the many and varied topics contained in these abstracts there are two of especial interest, the use of various climbing harnesses and the occurrence of brain damage due to residence at extreme altitude. Both are controversial.

The recommendation that both seat and chest harness should be worn seems reasonable enough, but ease of movement and fitting are important practical considerations and have to be taken into account before this type of harness becomes worn universally.

The question of brain damage after going to altitude will assume a greater importance as more people climb to extreme altitude without supplementary oxygen. It seems that, as the measurement of mental functions becomes more sophisticated, so more changes are found after long stay at altitude, and whether these are temporary or permanent is not yet known. In the long term, mountaineers may have to decide for themselves what level of damage they individually can accept, and it does seem that there is room for the manufacture of a very lightweight oxygen set which can be used at great altitude if only for medical purposes.

Hypoxia, Polycythemia and Chronic Mountain Sickness
Robert M Winslow, Carlos Monge
The John Hopkins University Press, Baltimore and London, pp255, 1987

In 1925, Carlos Monge gave the first description of a case of chronic mountain sickness which occurred in a Peruvian miner working at Cerro de Pasco (4300m).

Since then many cases have been reported at Leadville, Colorado and in South America, but so far none in the Himalayan villages. However, evidence is accumulating that this condition occurs in Tibet, and Hedin in 1903 may well have described a case in a gold-mining community in north-western Tibet.

The medical scientist is interested in this condition because it is not a disease, as no specific pathological process is described, but rather it appears to be a result of over-response to the normal physiological process of acclimatization to altitude.

There is an increasing regard too for the public health aspects of high-altitude populations, and this book gives an excellent account of the background to an expanding subject.

Hypoxia. The Tolerable Limits
Ed John R Sutton, Charles S Houston & Geoffrey Coates
Benchmark Press Inc, 1988, pp373

Every two years the Hypoxia Symposium is held in North America, and this book records articles written for the fifth symposium held at Chateau Lake Louise in Alberta in 1987.

A number of papers deal with the results obtained during Operation Everest II in which a group of medical scientists was decompressed gradually, in order to acclimatize, to the height of Mt Everest. This was a natural development from Operation Everest I, carried out over 40 years ago at Pensacola Air Base by Houston and his colleagues, and it was the natural follow-up to the American Medical Research Expedition to Everest in 1981, led by West, when alveolar gases were obtained on the summit. Experiments in the decompression chamber complement field work and, while field conditions cannot be entirely mimicked, more invasive and potentially dangerous procedures may be carried out safely. For example, a catheter may be passed, via a vein in the arm, right into the chambers of the heart to measure pressure during exercise and at rest.

For the general reader the most interesting section is that on 'The Tolerable Limits of Hypoxia'. For instance, it is astonishing to learn that the Painted Turtle can recover after three months of complete oxygen lack at 3°C; while the caretakers of the Aucanquilcha sulphur mine at 5950m in South America live at this altitude for two years or more, taking a day off each week to descend to lower levels to play football. Finally, the medical background to the K2 tragedy of 1986 is discussed; a topic of great interest to the modern mountaineer.

The mountaineer can learn much from these books which, if 'inwardly digested', will improve performance at extreme altitude, make climbing safer and, most importantly, make it more enjoyable. The need therefore for a comprehensive and up-to-date text for medical scientists and clinicians incorporating all this work and relating it to common diseases of oxygen transport is now very pressing.

                                                              Michael Ward

Wild Walks. Mountain, Moorland and Coastal Walks in Britain and Ireland
Compiled by Ken Wilson & Richard Gilbert
Diadem Books, 1988, pp224, £19.95

The big Diadem 'Walk' and 'Climb' books continue to get better. The present volume follows on from *The Big Walks* and *Classic Walks*, and is the mixture as before – just under half in Scotland, fewer in England, fewer still in Wales and half-a-dozen in Ireland. The differences are, firstly, that now every picture is in colour and, while all are good, many are superb – photos that really linger in the mind. Secondly, 40 out of the 59 route descriptions are written by Gilbert and, although he writes well, there is a sameness about some of them, the memorable ones turning out to be one or two by other hands. However, this is a marvellous book with an excellent selection of walks and, although some might say that the Manifold valley, for instance, hardly comes into the 'wild' category, there is plenty here for all tastes. You are not likely to find too many people on Abergwesyn Common at any time of year, for a start! One small quibble: the

Welsh word *mynydd* must be one of the most common in climbing literature about the Principality, yet it is spelt in three different ways in the article on the Lleyn Peninsula. Fortunately, one of them is right!

Mont Blanc, Chamonix, Courmayeur in the Old Prints
Gherardo Priuli & Efisio Noussan (transl. John Iliffe)
Cordee, 1987, pp476, boxed, £80

This magnificent volume was published in Italian to celebrate the bicentenary of the first ascent of Mont Blanc, and has now been translated (in separate volumes) into English, French and German. £80 is an awful lot of money for a book, but the contents and style of production make this one well worth the price. The reproduction of the 627 prints is superb, and I would think that every old print in existence showing Mont Blanc, Chamonix and Courmayeur is here. Well-known ones from Whymper's guide and *Scrambles* are alongside obscure views which have hardly ever seen the light of day, all arranged in approximate date order. All the variations of the prints of de Saussure's expeditions are here, including the original where he appears rather portly and its successor where he is shown to be slimmer and smarter. For anyone interested in alpine history, good book production, or both, this is a must.

Physiology of Man at High Altitude
Nauka, Moscow, 1987, pp520, in Russian

Our Honorary Member Eugene Gippenreiter has presented the Club with a copy of this recently-published Russian book on national and international experience in the field of high altitude physiology. Whilst covering the field in general, special chapters cover the selection of candidates for the Soviet Mount Everest Expedition 1982 and the choice of food, oxygen equipment, etc.

Avalanche Awareness for Skiers and Mountaineers
Martin Epp & Stephen Lee
The Wild Side, 1987, pp137, pb, £4.95

A very detailed guide to understanding snow conditions and the creation of avalanches, and what to do if you are unlucky enough to be caught out. Concisely presented, and a perfect size for the pocket.

Ancient Pathways in the Alps
Giovanni Caselli & Keith Sugden
George Philip, 1988, pp192, pb, £7.95

The authors detail six long-distance walks following ancient tracks and drove-roads through the Alps, from the high lands of Provence to Salzburg, concentrating on journeying with a 'theme from the past'. Well presented, with a map section and colour photos on each double page, it is just a pity that the tall, narrow format and tight binding make the centre of each map section difficult to read.

100 Best Routes on Scottish Mountains
Ralph Storer
David & Charles, 1987, pp224, £14.95

This book attempts to emulate the continental *100 Best* . . . volumes, but falls rather short of their standards in content and presentation. Each route is a circular walk with description, photo and map, and includes an attempt at grading and a guide to pronunciation which is very useful for the harder Gaelic names. It is also useful in that it includes not only Munros, but a number of lesser hills not covered in some recent publications.

Danziger's Travels. Beyond Forbidden Frontiers
Nick Danziger
Grafton Books, 1987, pp viii + 424, £14.95

Nick Danziger won an Open Category Fellowship awarded by the Winston Churchill Memorial Trust to travel to Central America. Various events caused him to abandon this project, and he turned to Asia, proposing to travel from Turkey to Peking via Iran, Afghanistan, Pakistan and Tibet. This book recounts his travels which, as you can imagine from the fact that he was often travelling in these countries without official authorization, were not without their adventurous side. Absorbingly written and well illustrated, this is a travel book which is hard to put down once started.

The Amundsen Photographs
Ed Roland Huntford
Hodder & Stoughton, 1987, pp200, £17.95

In the spring of 1986, the widow of Roald Amundsen's nephew found a packing case marked 'Horlick's Malted Milk' in the attic of her Oslo flat. Inside were more than 200 of the explorer's lantern slides – from the North-West Passage expedition of 1903, the South Pole expedition of 1911, and the journey along the Siberian coast in 1918, the majority being of the South Pole. This book collects together more than 150 of these slides, together with an introduction and description of each expedition by the editor. They are in remarkably good condition, many hand-tinted, and give a fascinating picture of polar travel in the early years of the century.

Bell's Scottish Climbs
Intro Hamish Brown
Gollancz, 1988, pp236, £12.95

J H B Bell's *A Progress in Mountaineering* has been a sought-after semi-classic for many years now, and Hamish Brown has had the excellent idea of collecting together all the Scottish chapters of that book for the modern reader, including the original photographs and delightful drawings. Bell was one of the great characters of British mountaineering. Hamish's introduction emphasizes this, and the articles themselves bring out the flavour of Scottish climbing of the time. It is good to have them in print again.

Mon Excursion Au Mont-Blanc
Henriette d'Angeville (Preface: Roger Frison-Roche)
Arthaud, 1987, pp200, pb, 85FF

In 1838, Henriette d'Angeville became the second woman to attempt the ascent of Mont Blanc. Her journal of the ascent was never published, remaining in the family, unread until recently. This paperback edition is therefore of some historical importance, giving her hour-by-hour thoughts and emotions.

The Great Outdoors Book of the Walking Year
Ed Roger Smith
Patrick Stephens, 1988, pp192, £14.95

The 12 chapters in this book correspond to the months of the year, each one written by a contributor to the magazine *The Great Outdoors*. They range from reminiscences of the Pyrenees and Himalaya to forgotten tramways in South Wales and, whilst the editor states that it was written by 'enthusiastic writers who were competent photographers (or better) as well', it is a pity that the many black-and-white photos are generally so poorly reproduced as to mar enjoyment of the book. It is even more of a pity as some of the photos can be seen to have been good in the original, and are shown up by the fact that care has been taken with the colour photographs. At this price, one expects better.

The Story of the Mount Everest National Park
Cobb/Horwood Publications, Auckland, no date, pp192, npq

This beautifully-produced book tells the story of the 1200km^2 that form the Sagarmatha National Park in Nepal. The various chapters cover the geology, weather, flora and fauna and the people, and then go on to describe various journeys through the Park, but the greatest delight is in the wealth of excellent colour photos which are on almost every page. An excellent introduction to the area.

The Tibet Guide
Stephen Batchelor
Wisdom Publications, 1987, pp xiv + 466, pb, £13.95

This superbly illustrated guide to Tibet is written by someone fluent in scriptural and colloquial Tibetan, who has been a Buddhist monk for the past ten years. It follows, therefore, that the main emphasis is on the monasteries, people and religion of the country, and the catastrophic events of the last few years. The general traveller is well catered for, however, with descriptions of routes to take and places to stay in the more 'popular' areas – Lhasa and the surrounding Central Area, the Tsang region centred on Shigatse and the Mt Kailas area in the west. General travel hints, an iconography, glossary and 'useful words and phrases' round off a book which will be indispensable to any traveller in Tibet.

Eddie McGee's Complete Book of Survival
Eddie McGee
Stanley Paul, 1988, pp192, pb, £9.95

'Complete' has to be the correct word for this book – survival at sea, in the mountains, deserts, jungles and the arctic; how to navigate, light fires, find water, trap animals, fish and cook; plus personal safety and basic medicine. Written by an acknowledged expert and well illustrated.

Mountain Days and Bothy Nights
Dave Brown & Ian Mitchell
Luath Press, 1987, pp 6 + 186, pb, £5.95

This very enjoyable and entertaining little book reminds one immediately of Alastair Borthwick's classic *Always a Little Further*. Hilarious tales of goings-on in all the well-known cottages, bothies and howffs of the Highlands are well told, complete with original dialect, and illustrated with line drawings.

Tales of a Cross-Country Skier
Guy Sheridan
Oxford Illustrated Press, 1987, pp185, £9.95

Exactly what the title says, tales of cross-country skiing in Norway, Iran, the Himalaya, Iceland, the States and places nearer home, by an acknowledged expert. Starting off with early experiences in the Royal Marine Commandos, the author recounts the stories in an interesting and amusing way, with a lot of information on technique tucked away in the text.

A Love of the Lakes
Geoffrey Berry & Brian Redhead
Constable, 1988, pp190, £14.95

Geoffrey Berry's name is the one that comes foremost to mind when matters relating to the preservation of Lakeland scenery are under discussion. The battles he fought as Secretary of the Friends of the Lake District are well known and, during his many years there, he took hundreds of photographs. Brian Redhead writes an introduction and also the captions to a selection of the photos which, while not all of high artistic merit, give a good overall picture of the Lakes and are a fitting memorial to Berry.

Hamish Brown's Scotland
Hamish Brown
Aberdeen University Press, 1988, pp xiv + 238, £12.50

This is a collection of short articles written by Hamish Brown over the years for publications as various as the *AJ*, *Rod and Line* and the *Glasgow Herald*. Not all pieces are on mountaineering, but the hills are in the background all through and, as the author says, it is 'a book to dip into while sitting in the garden, or reading in bed'. It has a slightly 'old-fashioned' feel, but is none the worse for that.

Personalbibliographie Historischer Persönlichkeiten des Alpinismus
Deutscher Alpenverein, 1988, pp412, DM160

This bibliography is an elaboration of an archive left by the late Toni Hiebeler. It lists data (mainly references to autobiography, newspaper articles, obituaries) on over 5000 persons connected with alpinism, from the beginnings to 1986; German and Austrian entries tend to be covered more thoroughly than others. Many of the references are to press cuttings and short notices kept in the library of the DAV.

The Alternative Guide to British Rock Climbing
Gill Fawcett
Unwin, 1988, pp viii + 232, pb, £6.95

This rather quirky guide gives you a brief 'insider's' view of each rock-climbing area, followed by a list of recommended pubs and cafés with appropriate comments. Fun, provided you appreciate the 'The Old Nag's Head is easy to find, it's on The Old Nag's Shoulders' type of comment, and have a vulgar sense of humour. Despite the description as 'British', Scotland and N Ireland are not included.

Further volumes this year in the series of paperback monographs published by
the *Museo Nazionale della Montagna 'Duca degli Abruzzi'*:

No. 56 – *Alle Origini Dell'Alpinismo Torinese.* Montanari e Villeggianti
     nelle Valli di Lanzo. Giuseppe Garimoldi/Bruno Guglielmotto-
     Ravet. A history of mountaineering in the Torino region.

No. 57 – *Fosco Maraini – Una Vita Per L'Asia.* A superb collection of
     photographs by Maraini, mostly from his visits to Japan, Tibet and
     the Greater Himalayan Range, but with a few Alpine and Sicilian
     subjects.

Wainwright in Scotland
A W Wainwright/Derry Brabbs
Michael Joseph/BBC, 1988, pp224, £14.95

Wainwright's fourth book in collaboration with the photographer Derry
Brabbs covers the Scottish mountains in similar format to the others, mixing
photographs, descriptions and drawings. It reached the best-seller lists and
stayed there for many weeks, and is obviously a very popular book with visitors
to Scotland. Wainwright's personality comes through in his reminiscences, but
some of the photographs do not seem to reach the standard that Brabbs has
shown in other publications. He obviously didn't manage to get any shots on
Skye: the only photo in this section, headed 'Skye from the mainland,' is a rather
unusual one that doesn't look like Skye at all!

Rocks Around the World
Stefan Glowacz & Uli Wiesmeier (transl. Martin Boysen)
Diadem, 1988, pp144, £16.95

With all due respect to the author and translator, this is the photographer Uli
Wiesmeier's book. The climbs featured are in France, Britain, USA, Japan,
Australia and Germany, and mostly feature Glowacz climbing. Needless to say,
the climbs are 'out of this world', but the photographer really shows them to
their greatest advantage. The contrast of vertical cliff and flat plain at Arapiles,
the towers at Teufelsturm, the hordes at Verdon, are all unforgettable images,
but so many of the pictures are excellent – and obviously obtained under very
difficult conditions – that this book must rank as one of the best in the genre.

My Scotland
Hamish MacInnes
Constable, 1988, pp182, £15.95

MacInnes's latest book is really a photograph album. Following a short
introduction there are 82 photos, one per page, mostly but not all of mountain

subjects. Some are good, some are poor, with various shades between, but no attempt is made at full descriptions.

John Cleare's Fifty Best Hill Walks of Britain
John Cleare
Webb & Bower, 1988, pp208, £14.95

There seems to be rather a surfeit of 'best walks' books at the moment, but this can be recommended as one of the better ones, principally because the author is an acknowledged expert mountain photographer – and his shots are well reproduced here – but also because he uses OS maps to illustrate the walks. All the hilly areas of England, Wales and Scotland are represented, with one or two less common routes included for good measure.

Climbing the Corbetts. Scotland's 2500ft Summits
Hamish M Brown
Gollancz, 1988, pp382, £14.95

Having very successfully written about the Munros, Hamish Brown has now done the same for the Corbetts, the 2500ft summits in Scotland. One has only to think of peaks such as Ben Loyal, Foinaven and Quinag in the far north, all of which are Corbetts, to realize that some of Scotland's finest and most interesting mountains come into this category. Each peak, or group of peaks, is described as the author climbed it, thus combining personal anecdote with accurate information.

Mountain Hazards
Kevin Walker
Constable, 1988, pp272, £8.95

Medical Handbook for Mountaineers
Peter Steele
Constable, 1988, pp248, £8.95

Two new guides from Constable. Walker's book is essentially for the beginner, and joins the numerous volumes in existence teaching 'mountaincraft'. Steele's book is a rewritten second edition and is a very different kettle of fish. Covering every type of affliction that can hit you in the mountains, there are facts here which can be learnt by everyone, no matter how skilled a mountaineer. For the layman it is a mine of useful information presented in detail, but with great clarity, with additional information in different type for those already possessing medical knowledge.

Honey Hunters of Nepal
Eric Valli & Diane Summers
Thames & Hudson, 1988, unpaginated, pb, £16.95

For centuries the Gurungs of Nepal have been collecting honey from the hives of the giant black bees in the area. The photographer Eric Valli accompanied 63-year-old Mani Lal and his assistants to hives high up on a cliff in the foothills in west central Nepal, and photographed him while he swayed about on a long bamboo ladder high above the ground, dislodging the hive and surrounded by swarms of angry bees. The result is a very large format picture book of stunning photographs illustrating what must be a dying profession.

The Pure Land. A Celebration of Wild Places
John Beatty
Thames & Hudson, 1988, pp112, pb, £12.95

John Beatty has become well known for his audio lecture shows on wild places, but this is his first one-man exhibition, so to speak. Although the book is in paperback, the publishers have done him proud, the reproduction being superb. The photos cover locations from the British Isles to the Grand Canyon, Greenland to Antarctica and the Alps, mostly landscapes but with a few action and 'nature' shots. One or two of the landscapes that include figures veer towards the romantic but, generally speaking, this is a fine collection by a master photographer.

The following guide books, instructional manuals and similar volumes have also been received:

Climbing Fit. Martyn Hurn & Pat Ingle. Crowood Press, 1988, pp96, pb, £6.95

The Adventure Alternative. Colin Mortlock. Cicerone Press, 1987, pp160, pb, £6.95

Climbing School. John Barry & Roger Mear. Stanley Paul, 1988, pp192, £14.95

Italian Rock. Selected Climbs in Northern Italy. Al Churcher. Cicerone Press, 1988, pp200, £7.95

White Peak Walks. The Southern Dales. Mark Richards. Cicerone Press, 1988, pp10 + 278, £7.25

Best Walks in North Wales. Richard Sale. Constable, 1988, pp294, £8.95

Escalades Sainte-Victoire. Saint-Ser. D Gorgeon, P Légier, A Lucchesi. Édisud, 1988, pp104, npq

Les Deux Aiguilles. Le Signal. P Bestagno, D Gorgeon, A Lucchesi. Édisud, 1988, pp120, npq

Randonnées Pédestres dans le Haut-Var Occidental. Alexis Lucchesi. Édisud, 1988, pp192, npq

Topo Guide des Voies d'Escalade du Verdon. Patrick Bestagno, Bernard Gorgeon, Alexis Lucchesi, Claude & Yves Rémy. Montagnes, 1988, pp384, npq

AMC Maine Mountain Guide. Appalachian Mountain Club, 6th Edition, 1988, pp xxx + 306, $12.95

Scotland. Central and Southern Highlands. 100 Classic Climbs. Ken Crocket & Steve Ashton. Crowood Press, 1988, pp224, £8.95

The Island of Rhum. A Guide for Walkers, Climbers and Visitors. Hamish M Brown. Cicerone Press, 1988, pp100, £4.95

The Peruvian Andes. Cordillera Blanca. Cordillera Huayhuash. Ph Beaud. Editions Glénat/Cordee/Cloudcap Press, 1988, pp288, £11.95

North Carolina Hiking Trails. Allen de Hart. Appalachian Mountain Club, 1988, pp xxiv + 510, $14.95

Best Walks in the Peak District. Frank Duerden. Constable, 1988, pp320, £8.95

Rock Climbs in the Verdon. An Introduction. Rick Newcombe. Cicerone Press, 1988, pp56, £5.50

Snow and Ice Climbing. John Barry. Crowood Press, 1987, pp144, £12.95

The Expedition Cookbook. Carolyn Gunn. Chockstone/Cordee, 1988, pp10 + 198, pb, £7.95

Classic Walks in Europe. Ed Walt Unsworth. Oxford Illustrated Press, 1987, pp168, £14.95

Sun Rock. Murcia Klettern & Monaco Mittelmeer. Panico Press, no date, pp364, pb, £12.95

The Avalanche Book. Betsy Armstrong & Knox Williams. Fulcrum, 1986, pp10 + 232, £9.95

Mountain High, Mountain Rescue. Peggy Parr. Fulcrum, 1987, pp10 + 192, £10.50.
(Both Fulcrum books obtainable from Cedar Tree House, Loughton, Essex, IG10 1QP)

Skiing Real Snow. The Handbook of Off-Piste Skiing. Martyn Hurn. Crowood Press, 1987, pp176, £12.95

Cairngorms. Winter Climbs. Allen Fyffe. Cicerone Press, 1987, pp120, £6.95 (3rd edition)

North York Moors. Walks in the National Park. Martin Collins. Cicerone Press, 1987, pp 240, £4.95

Walks in the Cairngorms. Ernest Cross. Luath Press, 1986, pp8 + 86, pb, £2.20 (Rev edition)

Jersey and Guernsey. Ian Smith & Alan Hill. Cordee, 1987, pp192, £5.95

Monte Viso. Alpi Cozie Meridionali. Michelangelo Bruno. CAI/TCT, 1987, pp600

Escalades dans le Massif de la Sainte-Baume. P Giffon & A Lucchesi. Édisud, 1988, pp168, 60FF

BMC New Climbs 1987. Gary Gibson. BMC, no date, pp236, £4.95

Kinder Log. T Nelthorpe. Cicerone, 1987, pp160, £4.95

Walks in the Engadine Switzerland. Kev Reynolds. Cicerone, 1988, pp186, £7.95

Walking Austria's Alps Hut to Hut. Jonathan Hurdle. Cordee, 1988, pp240, £7.95

Tour of Mont Blanc. Andrew Harper. Cicerone, 1988, pp136, £6.95 (3rd edition)

Yorkshire Limestone & Gritstone Supplement. Graham Desroy. Yorkshire MC, 1987, pp92, npq

Traversée Occidentale des Alpes. (Haute Randonnée Alpine II). Club Alpin Français. Édisud, 1988, pp168, 60FF

Guide des Refuges et Gîtes des Alpes. Association de la Grande Traversée des Alpes. Glénat, 1988, pp256 (Cordee, £7.95)

German and Belgian Rock Climbs. An Interim Guide Book. John Hart. Cordee, 1988, pp78, £4.95

Walk Snowdonia & North Wales. David Perrott & Laurence Main. Bartholomew, 1988, pp64, £3.95

North Wales. 100 Classic Climbs. Steve Ashton. Crowood Press, 1988, pp224, £8.95

The Peak & Pennines. W A Poucher. Constable, 1988, pp456, £7.95 (5th edition)

Scafell, Dow & Eskdale. A Phizacklea. F&RCC, 1988, pp324, £7.95

Escalades Calanques. Sormiou. L Denante & A Lucchesi. Édisud, 1988, pp120, 60FF

Descente Sportive de Gorges et Canyons. J-P Lucot & R Quintilla. Édisud, 1988, pp132, 80FF

Trekking Dei Pirenei. 1000km dal Mediterraneo all'Atlantico. Franco Michieli. Edizioni Mediteranee, 1987, pp114, L 15,000

Arrampicate nel Bresciano. Dalla Maddalena alla Val Salarno. S Zizioli & F Magri. Edizioni Mediteranee, 1988, pp112, L 15,000

Alte Vie delle Dolomiti. I grandi sentieri dei Monti Pallidi. Claudio Cima. Edizioni Mediteranee, 1988, pp216, L 20,000

Le Alpi a Piedi. 1950km dalla Liguria all Jugoslavia. Riccardo & Cristina Carnolvalini. Edizioni Mediterranee, 1988, pp140, L 20,000

The Hill Walker's Manual. Bill Birkett. Oxford Illustrated Press, 1988, pp128, £14.95

In Memoriam

COMPILED BY GEOFFREY TEMPLEMAN

(Plates 111–114)

The Alpine Club Obituary	Year of Election
Erwin Schneider	Hon 1970
Wilbur John Smith	1974
Michael John Cheney	1976
Donald Metford Clarke	1962
Maxwell Hector Vandermere Fleming	1949
Edwin Arthur Ling	1948
George Abercromby Mitchell	1933
Fritz Hermann Ernst Wiessner	1970
John William Howard	1945
Count Guido Monzino	1963
James Barclay Joyce	1942
Hon Sir John Ramsay Willis	1956
Kenneth Neville Irvine	1929
Alexander Harrison	1939

Michael John Cheney 1928–1988

One of Nepal's best-known expatriate Britons and a leader in its trekking and mountaineering scene, Michael John Cheney, known as Mike to all his acquaintances, died in his sleep at his home in Kathmandu in the early hours of the morning of 20 February 1988, apparently from heart failure. He had been ill for the previous week or two after having had what doctors suspected was a stroke. He had also broken his left arm close to the shoulder at about the same time while on a trip in one of the more remote areas of western Nepal.

Mike was only 59 years old, but had had several episodes of serious illness during the past two decades which had taken a severe toll on his strength. He actually should have died years before, but his fierce will to carry on the work he found all-absorbing kept him going against great odds. But finally his strength gave out. He was buried in the hillside cemetery maintained by the British Embassy in Kathmandu, with about 200 Nepalese and expatriate mourners at the graveside.

Although he kept his ties to his family back in England and considered Beckford Grange, Tewkesbury one of his homes, it was his wish to live and die in Nepal, where he spent the last 22 years of his life. He never married – women seemed to terrify him – but he was generous with his kindness to Nepalese children as well as to adults in distress.

After obtaining his School Certificate, Mike served in the British army from 1946 to 1957 in the Royal Armoured Corps and the 10th Gurkha Rifles. During these years he saw active service in Korea, Kenya and Malaya and rose to the rank of captain. He then became a tea-estate manager in the Darjeeling area of north-eastern India. In 1965 he moved to Nepal and spent two years in tea there before ill-health forced him to stop working for two years.

When he was able to resume work, Mike returned to Nepal and took a job in the fledgling trekking industry with the world's first trekking agency, Lieutenant-Colonel Jimmy Roberts's Mountain Travel, which had begun sending mountain-lovers on treks in the northern regions of Nepal just four years previously. He remained in trekking till the last day of his life, although he left Mountain Travel in 1976 and was an executive of three successive other agencies. His last post was as General Manager of Rover Treks & Expeditions (P) Ltd.

Mike was a champion of the poorly-paid porters who carry heavy loads under difficult conditions for expeditions and trekking groups, and he actively promoted the employment as trek leaders and mountain climbers of men who belong to tribes other than the Sherpa clan. He was certainly no desk-bound trekking organizer. He spent many weeks each year out in the hills scouting new trekking routes in central and eastern Nepal for clients who wanted to travel away from the paths which have become greatly overcrowded in the Everest and Annapurna areas. And he sometimes went with the mountaineering expeditions whose logistics he helped to arrange, most notably as a member of Chris Bonington's 1975 British South-west Face Everest Expedition, which he served as Base Camp manager. He was very proud of having been an actual member of that historically successful team.

Mike was an active member of the Trekking Agents Assocation of Nepal and of the Himalayan Rescue Association in Kathmandu, the Local Hon Secretary of the Bombay-based Himalayan Club, a fellow of the Royal Geographical Society and a member of the Alpine Club. He followed the mountaineering scene in Nepal closely and was correspondent for several alpine journals and mountaineering magazines in Europe and the United States.

Elizabeth Hawley

Donald M Clarke 1907–1988

With the passing of Donald Clarke the Club has lost a very unassuming but competent mountaineer. He became a member of the Club in 1962.

Donald walked and climbed widely in the British hills and was a steady leader on rock climbs up to mild severe. Prior to 1951 he had walked in the Maritime and Bavarian Alps and in that year he started climbing in the Valais. In subsequent years he made many ascents in various areas of the Alps, most of the climbs being guided. In 1957 he had a very successful season in the Oberland, with the Mönch (by the ordinary route but descending by the SW ridge) amongst his climbs.

Although he enjoyed climbing in the Alps, the less frequented mountain areas held a fascination for Donald. In the late 1950s and early 1960s, in company with Arnold Galloway, he visited Northern Norway, Swedish Lapland and Iceland. In Norwegian Lapland they spent three weeks exploring the then little known Lyngen peninsula. They spent a similar time in Swedish Lapland exploring the rather remote Sarek region and climbing (*inter alia*) Sarekjakko, the highest peak. In Iceland Donald and Arnold climbed Hekla and several peaks in the Akureyri area. On other occasions their fascination with volcanoes took them to Etna and Stromboli.

In 1962 Donald went to Greece and climbed on Olympus with Wynne Jeudwine and Wendell Jones. 1963 found him in the High Atlas with Wendell Jones and Peter Ledeboer, and they climbed many of the higher peaks in the area. Later the same year Donald and Wynne Jeudwine were climbing in the Picos de Europa in northern Spain.

Donald was again in Spain in 1967, this time in company with Fred Jenkins and Freddie Smith. They climbed first in the Sierra de Gredos and then revisited the Picos de Europa. In 1978 Donald visited Corsica with Hamish Brown, Ernst Sondheimer and Martin Waddell, but bad weather with a lot of snow severely restricted the climbing.

An unfortunate accident occurred to Donald when he was trekking in the Himalaya. He broke his back falling over an outcrop outside a Dak bungalow in the dark, but he made a remarkable recovery.

As he began to ease up in his later years, Donald became much taken with long-distance footpaths and walked many of them, including the Pennine Way and Offa's Dyke. With Arnold Galloway he tried to work out a 'Hebridean Way', in the course of which they climbed the other Hekla on South Uist.

Donald was born and lived all his life in the Caversham area of Reading. He took a great interest in local affairs and was an active member of St Andrews church, the Caversham Heights Society and the Chiltern Society. He frequently gave lectures to local groups on his travels and climbs and led parties of ramblers through the Berkshire countryside.

Donald's quiet and modest manner belied his considerable strength of character and physique. He was very determined but never foolhardy. He was supportive of and considerate to the other members of his party. Donald did not waste words, but what he said was to the point. He had a dry sense of humour. When I met him once he was limping and my enquiry as to his health brought forth the reply that he had fallen when climbing solo. I asked which rock climb had been involved and he replied 'It wasn't a rock climb – I was picking apples and I fell out of the tree!'

Donald was one of the older school who did not aspire to great technical heights but was very competent and safe in all that he did, and he loved his mountains. He will be much missed by all who climbed with him.

Maurice Bennett

Maxwell Hector Vandermere Fleming 1904–1988

Max Fleming started climbing in the Alps in the early 1930s when on leave from the Sudan Political Service. He later studied at the universities of Grenoble and Freiburg and was active with a very strong group of continental climbers, doing the first traverse of the airy Arête des Cornes on the Pic Bourcet in the Dauphiné. During the Second World War he was in Cyprus as chief inspector of schools; early on he explored ski-routes in the Troodos Range and rock climbing on the limestone of Pentedhaktilos, to which he introduced Arnold Lunn, John Hunt and Mike Banks.

He was elected to the Alpine Club in 1949 and shortly after was posted to Nigeria as an education administrator. Although unable to do much serious climbing because of a knee injury caused by a motor-cycle accident when serving in the Cyprus Defence Force during the war, he continued his lifelong interest in climbing and skiing; he also took to ocean racing and crewed in several Fastnet races. In his retirement he became an avid field archaeologist, a hobby which gave him the physical challenge he used to enjoy in the mountains.

Peter Steele

Fritz Hermann Ernst Wiessner 1900–1988

The climbing career of the German-American mountaineer Fritz Wiessner was one of the most pivotal of any 20th-century mountaineer. His new routes and mountain conquests are the stuff of climbing lore, but his boldness was not without cost. History remembers not only Fritz Wiessner's stunning successes, his first ascents of Mount Waddington and Devil's Tower, but one very notable controversy – the 1939 K2 tragedy. Other facets of Fritz's long life included a contented family and business life, but perhaps most visible to other climbers was his insatiable appetite for rock climbing which kept him following 5.6 (VS) until the age of 86. Fritz Wiessner was 'The Durable Champion'. He died at home in Stowe, Vermont on 3 July 1988.

What made Fritz Wiessner an important figure was his influence upon the evolution of climbing and mountaineering thought – in both Europe and America. After advancing rock-climbing standards on his hometown crags near Dresden and in the Dolomites in the 1920s, Fritz carried his strict free-climbing codes to America, emigrating in 1929 to New York City. In 1932 he participated in the German-American Nanga Parbat Expedition with, amongst others, Willy Merkl, Peter Aschenbrenner, Rand Herron and Elizabeth Knowlton. It was the second attempt ever made on this Karakoram giant. Ascending the Rakhiot Face, Fritz reached 7000m and Camp VII on the mountain's E ridge, but attempts on the summit were thwarted by deep snow and continuous storm.

In the mid-1930s, with another leading figure, Robert Underhill, Fritz brought American rock climbing out of its infancy, initially in New Hampshire's White Mountains. Then came a landmark event in American climbing: Fritz's discovery in 1935 of the immense potential of the Shawangunk cliffs in New York state. With his friend and partner Hans Kraus, he climbed the renowned High Exposure, a locally famous climb on the Trapps, in 1944. Fritz continued to climb regularly at the 'Gunks' until 1986.

Wiessner applied his mountaineering experience to North American peaks, beginning with the first ascent of Mount Waddington (4040m) in Canada's British Columbia Coast Range in 1936. The ascent of the 'unclimbable Mount Mystery' with Bill House was heralded as the hardest climb in North America. A year later Wiessner and House made the first technical ascent of Devil's Tower in Wyoming with Lawrence Coveney. Though thoroughly different in character, these two significant ascents signalled Fritz Wiessner's full maturation as a mountaineer.

Remembering Vittorio Sella's unsurpassed K2 photographs, Fritz's eyes returned to the lofty, snowy horizons of the Karakoram. His expedition proposal led to the first American attempt on the mountain. Sadly, when permission was finally granted, Fritz could not go. The eventual 1938 expedition, led by Charles Houston, determined that the Abruzzi Ridge was the most feasible route to the summit. That year a high point of 7925m was reached.

Fritz led the second American expedition to K2 in 1939. Above Camp IX, on the first summit attempt, climbing without oxygen and at a height of 8390m, Fritz urged an all-night climb to the summit, only 220m higher. Afraid of the mountain's spirits and not realizing the top was so close, Pasang Lama held the belay rope firmly and suggested they descend. Reluctantly Fritz gave in. During the descent their crampons, becoming tangled in the abseil ropes, were fatedly dropped. Without them the second summit bid also failed. Theirs was a brilliant effort nonetheless, accomplished with virtually no back-up, without radios or bottled oxygen. Had they succeeded, their first ascent of K2 would have radically changed the course and history of Himalayan mountaineering.

Only Dudley Wolfe, alone at Camp 13, was in support. During the trio's descent, they discovered the lower camps had been mysteriously destroyed, tents cut open and food scattered in the snow. More importantly, the extra sleeping-bags and mattresses had also vanished. The exact events remain baffling today. After Jack Durrance had ordered the evacuation of the lower camps (in the surmised belief that the mountain had been climbed), unsupervised Sherpas stripped two higher camps after witnessing a supposedly 'fatal' avalanche near the summit. When all the sleeping-bags were returned to Base Camp – with no corroborative evidence of the summit team's death besides the avalanche story – the gear was not immediately returned to the mountain. Instead, after two open bivouacs, Wiessner and Lama dragged themselves into Base.

Wolfe, who had volunteered to stay behind at Camp 7 for a third summit effort, was now stranded. Several rescue attempts were mounted; finally Pasang Kikuli, Pasang Kitar and Pintso disappeared without a trace in a gallant last-ditch effort. A ferocious storm broke, and none of the four men was ever seen again.

Upon returning home, Fritz as expedition leader was blamed for the tragedy. After an American Alpine Club inquiry 'whitewashed' the whole affair (to use Fritz's expression), he resigned from the AAC in 1940. In an effort to make amends, he was unanimously voted an Honorary Member of the Club in 1966. However, the K2 tragedy continued to haunt him, a troubled under-current to a contented old age. 'The mountains have given me my greatest joys and most profound sorrows,' Fritz once observed, 'but always it was men who failed me.'

Fritz married Muriel Schoonmaker on 10 January 1945. They had two children, Andrew and Polly, and there are now four Wiessner grandchildren: Mia, Angus, Silas, and Nicholas. A manufacturer of ski waxes and waterproof coatings, Fritz moved his chemical company to Burlington, Vermont in 1946. The Wiessners moved permanently to nearby Stowe in 1952.

While Fritz never returned to the high mountains, he travelled and climbed extensively. In 1960 he completed all the 4000m peaks in the Alps. His final snow climbs were Popocatepetl and Orizaba in 1968. He also continued to rock-climb at a phenomenally high level, in America, Mexico, England, France, Italy, and of course Saxon Switzerland near Dresden. As a roving ambassador for the American and Canadian Alpine Clubs, Fritz helped with UIAA relations.

Historically, Fritz Wiessner was one of the first climbers to fulfil the mountaineer's boldest dream: to progress from a rock-climbing background to the accomplished stature of a seasoned Himalayan mountaineer, climbing above 8000m alpine-style, on a new route and without oxygen. It is a path few men have followed in the intervening 50 years. For generations to come, Fritz Wiessner's exemplary life will be an inspiring example.

Ed Webster

James Barclay Joyce 1910–1988

James Joyce – Jim, as he was always known – had a distinguished career as a climber and as a pioneer obstetrician and gynaecologist in West Cumbria. He was elected to the Alpine Club in 1942.

The eldest son of Leonard Joyce, also a well-known surgeon, he was educated at Shrewsbury, where he was co-winner of the Ladies' Plate at Henley, and at Pembroke College, Cambridge where he did some night-climbing and also became for a time a keen racing motor-cyclist, until overtaken by a greater, life-long enthusiasm – mountains.

He seems to have stumbled almost accidentally upon the climbing scene when, with a friend in 1934, he ascended the Needle Ridge – 'unroped, in shoes, with mackintosh, carrying a 3¼ × 2¼ reflex camera', as his diary informs us. Thereafter, with Dr John Ryle as his first tutor, he rapidly developed his natural aptitude for rock-climbing until as a medical student at Barts he became, with Charles Warren, the prevailing force in the Hospital Alpine Club. That was when I first met and climbed with him, coming under the spell of his remarkable gift for encouraging the less expert, with whom he took endless pains to instil confidence and safe technique. In addition to Hospital meets in the Lake District and at Helyg there were also several new routes made at night on the Medical Block, then in course of construction, and on the tower above the Casualty Department in Giltspur Street!

Just before the war, on holiday at the Riffelalp, he met a beautiful girl to whom he was introduced by Michael Harmer, a close friend and fellow-climber. She was Hedy Seiler, granddaughter of Alexander Seiler who built the Monte Rosa hotel and was the first to encounter Edward Whymper on his return from the Matterhorn in 1865. Jim and Hedy were married soon afterwards.

During the Second World War his service record in the RAMC included Dunkirk, Sicily and North Africa where he became a Lieutenant-Colonel in command of a Field Ambulance and, later, Medical Officer and Instructor at the Army School of Mountain Warfare in Italy. The war over, he took up obstetrics and gynaecology, became a member of the Royal College in that speciality and was then appointed to set up a new department based on the West Cumberland Hospitals at Workington and Whitehaven, where previously all consultant work had had to be transferred to Carlisle. The family moved into Bank Farm at Eaglesfield, between Cockermouth and Buttermere – an old rambling house with a marvellous view of the fells, where they have lived ever since and where Jim died on 13 October 1988 at the age of 78.

Jim's climbing diary – a heavy, black, leather-bound tome, treasured from the beginning with loving care – tells the story of his earlier adventures with much wise, pithy but always kindly comment. His companions on Welsh and Lakeland rocks, in the Dolomites and in the Alps are too numerous to name in full, but members of the Club and others recorded include Charles Warren, Arnold Lunn, Colin Kirkus, John Barford, Ashley Greenwood, Rusty Westmorland, Claude Elliott, David Cox and Jack Longland. Michael Harmer, Jim's frequent climbing companion before the war, to whom I am much indebted for kind personal help with this memoir, tells of the many visits they made together to Gatesgarth, Buttermere, then the home of Professor Pigou of King's College, Cambridge, and later of Claude Elliott.

Jim did not take his diary to the war and left hardly any record of the days at the Mountain Warfare School; however, serving with him as a fellow-instructor was another member of the AC – Tom Peacocke, who has kindly offered to fill in this part of the story. Shortly after the war a distinguished paper was read to the Alpine Club with the title: 'In the Dolomites with an Orientalist' (AJ 55, 362–373, 1945–46). In this discourse Jim ranged far and wide over the implications for the future of mountaineering of developments during the war: the dangers of competition based on nationalist ambitions, and the grading of climbs. It was in several ways a prophetic message worth re-reading with the knowledge of all that has happened since.

A few brief extracts from the diary help to give some idea of his character and philosophy: 'There is no doubt boots teach a better standard of climbing than rubbers'; 'Borrowdale "difficults" are not at all the same as Scawfell "difficults".' After finishing 'Longlands', led by Kirkus: 'a life's desire satisfied and a new one takes its place – to lead Longlands' Climb'. On Army climbing: 'X (a fellow officer) does not understand mountains. They are not for assessing physical differences between individuals, but rather something to compete against. The whole party climbs as a whole, the weakest member as important as the strongest.' Of another friend (S H Badrock): 'Sandy has not yet quite got the idea of party climbing, with everyone looking after themselves and one other.' And of a severe climb on Tryfan, the Terrace Wall Variant: 'At every difficult pitch B (the leader) resorted to the bottle.' Sadly, his diary entries, though not his climbing, ceased altogether with the onset of a serious illness in 1955.

One other fellow-climber, and a tragic one, deserves special mention. Before the war, and also in 1940 and 1941 before being posted abroad, Jim did many climbs, including a number of new routes, with Menlove Edwards. The standard was nearly always VS or higher, so that inevitably a close-knit partnership lasting several years was forged between the two. Jim always insisted that no hint, or shadow of a hint, of the perversities attributed to Menlove by later writers ever entered or even crossed his mind in all their times together on and off the mountains. In fact he thoroughly distrusted and strongly deplored these aspersions – some by writers born long after Menlove's death – upon a superb climber and former friend, later to suffer the double calamity of mental breakdown and premature death.

As a companion in the hills Jim Joyce was unsurpassed, combining strength, confidence and graceful movement with an outstanding degree of patience, serenity and consideration for others on the rope. He was also humorous and the characteristic twinkle in his eye, familiar to all who knew him, was one of his most endearing features. In addition he was no mean mountain artist, proficient in both oils and water-colour. Especially he loved to paint the country near his home – the Buttermere, Crummock and Borrowdale fells, whose every ridge and wrinkle he knew so intimately that he might have said with Matthew Arnold 'I know these hills – Who knows them if not I?' Since his death some 300 of his pictures have been listed and catalogued by his family; one is already in the Club's collection, and there may be more to come.

He was on every count a true gentleman of the mountains. The Club and all of us who knew him mourn his loss and extend our deep sympathy to Hedy, to their son Tony, himself a mountaineer, and to their two daughters Tessa and Anna.

Edward Smyth

Ashley Greenwood writes:

I climbed regularly with Jim in the years immediately before the Second World War, and I also ski'd with him. In both sports Jim was the most fanatical enthusiast whom I ever met, and the quickest to improve his standards. He seemed oblivious of time and weather and, in skiing, even to injury. If it was a fine summer day in North Wales, he would climb till dark before eating and starting for home in his open GM, bivouacking by the roadside or in a barn and arriving in London at breakfast time on Monday ready to begin his week's work at the hospital. In a very short time he had progressed to leading routes of almost the greatest difficulty then climbed. If he thought a route beyond him he would enlist the aid of a top climber, as when he got Colin Kirkus to lead our party of 10 up Longlands. Incidentally, the tenth member had still not taken off when Colin had finished, descended to the bottom and was occupying himself soloing the Curving Crack. On his first skiing holiday in Grindelwald in 1938 Jim broke his leg, but the feats he performed on a luge with his leg in plaster became a legend among his friends. Except for a few days in 1939, I did not ski with him again till 1944 at Terminillo and on the Gran Sasso. By then Jim was an accomplished and graceful skier and, typically, he would persuade one – with an engaging smile – to prolong the day, however exhausted one was, until one could hardly see one's skis, let alone the slope.

We lost touch for a number of years while I was abroad after the war, but a chance encounter on the way home from the Alps in the late 1960s resulted in many happy visits to Bank Farm, and when heart trouble put an end to his own climbing he would use his fabulous knowledge of the Lake District to recommend climbs, scrambles and walks for others, and would listen to their accounts of their days with as much zest as if he had been with them himself. He took to his increasing disability without complaint and with his usual good humour, even when, as on the last time I saw him, he could only hobble a few steps without resting.

Tom Peacocke writes:

I first met James Joyce at the Mountain School, Terminillo in the winter of 1945–46. His enthusiasm for mountaineering knew no bounds and he was a great addition to our party. In January 1946 I was involved in an avalanche with seven soldiers. Luckily James was on some exercise nearby and he speedily came to the rescue, evacuating one casualty who had a broken leg. Then he tried artificial respiration on four others who had been buried deeply, but unfortunately to no effect; their lungs had been crushed by the weight of snow. I was somewhat shocked after being buried, and he kept me in bed for three days. He was a very careful doctor.

We were together in an ascent of the Corno Grande on which, owing to my impetuosity, we were overtaken by night and caught in a winter blizzard, being forced to make snow bivouacs. Towards the end of March 1946 we had a very fine climb together, doing the traverse of the three peaks of the Corno Grande with the ascent of the Camino Iannetta, a severe rock and ice chimney which James led with great skill.

When the Mountain School broke up we went our several ways, but I used to meet James regularly at AC dinners. He was a very good friend.

The Hon Sir John Willis 1908–1988

John Ramsay Willis, Jack to his countless friends, was a distinguished lawyer who completed a long much-respected career when he served as a Judge in the Queen's Bench Division of the High Court from 1966 to 1980. He was educated at Lancing College, where he was a scholar, and at Trinity College Dublin where he obtained his degree with first-class honours. Called to the Bar at Gray's Inn in 1932, he quickly built up a practice in planning, rating and local government law. His career was interrupted by the Second World War when he joined the Territorial Army and served in the Royal Corps of Signals, reaching the rank of Lieutenant-Colonel and serving on the staff of Mountbatten at SEAC and of General Slim in the 14th Army in Burma. After resuming his career, he became a Bencher of Gray's Inn while still a junior, in 1953, and took silk in 1956. In 1965 he was appointed Deputy Chairman of East Suffolk Quarter Sessions and Recorder of Southampton. He was knighted on his appointment to the High Court Bench in 1966, and in 1969 became Treasurer of Gray's Inn.

Jack's first introduction to the mountains came when, as a young man, he worked for a time as a travelling secretary for Sir Henry Lunn. Among other places, this took him to Maloja in the Engadine. It was there that he was taken on a mountain walk by a stranger – who, he later discovered, was a future President of the Alpine Club, Leo Amery. It was not until the 1950s, however, that he started more serious climbing. In 1953 he was in the Ötztal, and he completed some winter climbs in Austria in the following year. In 1955 he started in Arolla and went on to Zermatt, where he climbed the Matterhorn and traversed the Alphubel to Saas Fee.

Later he climbed the Blümlisalphorn with John Poole and R S Hargreaves, to whom I am indebted for most of these details. In 1956 he traversed the Lagginhorn with Hargreaves and his other regular Alpine companion, Dr F S Jackson – also the Allalinhorn, Rimpfischhorn and Monte Rosa. It was in that year that he was elected to the Club. In 1961 the same trio traversed the Rimpfischhorn and climbed the Zinalrothorn, but there were no major ascents recorded after that. He continued, however, to walk and climb in Britain, particularly in North Wales and in the Cuillins, and in 1977 he was walking in Nepal with his son Michael. In June 1988, a few weeks short of his 80th birthday and four months before his death, he spent a week in Borrowdale when his last expedition, completed in glorious sunny weather, was the ascent of Scafell Pike.

Jack Willis was a delightful companion. He has left behind a wide circle of friends with many happy memories, both on and off the hills. Our sympathy goes to his widow, Barbara, and to his two sons by his first marriage, Michael and Christopher.

J H Emlyn Jones

Alpine Club Notes

OFFICE BEARERS AND COMMITTEE FOR 1989

HONORARY SOLICITOR............................   S N Beare
AUDITORS ....   A M Dowler
                                                 Davey & Co

GENERAL MEETINGS OF THE ALPINE CLUB 1988

12 January   Sheila Cormack, *Shimshal to Skardu – in the steps of
                    Schomberg and Shipton*
9 February   Lt Col Henry Day, *Soldiers and Scientists on
                    Xixabangma*
15 March   Steven Berry, *Climbing in the Buddhist Kingdom of
                    Bhutan*
12 April   Roger Mear, *In the Footsteps of Scott*
10 May   Martin Boysen, *From Harrisons to the Himalaya*
20 September   Premises debate
11 October   Stephen Venables, *South Col Direct – the Neverest
                    Buttress*
25 October   Viktor Wyss, film show: *175 Years of Alpinism in
                    Switzerland* (extra meeting, jointly with ABMSAC,
                    to mark the 125th anniversary of the Swiss Alpine
                    Club)
15 November   Roger Everett, *Alpine Climbing in Europe and Asia*
2 December   Annual General Meeting: Julian Freeman-Attwood,
                    The Three Highest Peaks of Africa

CLIMBING MEETINGS 1988

20–21 February   ACG Winter Meet, Glencoe.
12–13 March   North Wales. Informal dinner.
17–19 June   Derbyshire. University of London hut, Fallcliffe
                    Cottage, Grindleford.
21 July–5 August   Cornwall. CC hut, Bosigran. Family meet held
                    jointly with Climbers' Club.
25 July–13 August   Zermatt valley. Joint meet with Climbers' Club and
                    ABMSAC.
24–25 September   Lake District. Informal dinner with lecture by Victor
                    Saunders, *Jitchu Drake.*

EXHIBITION

The Club arranged a small exhibition, opened on 25 October 1988, of relevant historical features, to mark both the 125th anniversary of the foundation of the Swiss Alpine Club and the centenary of the birth of Sir Arnold Lunn.

THE CAUCASUS CENTENARY MEMORIAL SERVICE

100 years ago, and 31 years after the Club's foundation, there occurred an accident to two of its members overshadowed only by that of the Matterhorn in 1865. Harry Fox and William Donkin, then Honorary Secretary, with the Swiss guides Kaspar Streich and Johann Fischer, all disappeared in an attempt on Koshtantau.

Their last bivouac, illustrated in a fine watercolour hanging in the Committee Room of the Club, was discovered by a relief expedition the following year, 1889 (see C A Russell's article, pp219–225 of this volume, for an account of the search). Captain C H Powell, a member of the expedition, made an immediate sketch of the bivouac site and it is from this that the painting, by H G Willink, was taken.

Amongst other effects, including knapsacks and clothing, they found Harry Fox's diary, its last entry dated Sunday, 26 August 1888, an entry concluding: '. . . climb Koshtantau . . . and descend to the Dyksu Glacier.'

On Sunday, 11 September 1988 a special exhibition and memorial service for those lost in 1888 was held in Wellington, Somerset, the home of the Fox family. The Alpine Club was represented by the President and the Honorary Archivist.

Tonedale House, where the exhibition was held and where Mr Richard Fox received the guests, has been the family home for generations, and it was from here that Harry Fox set out for the Caucasus in 1888. Mr Hubert Fox of Buckfastleigh, who played a major part in organizing the centenary celebration, was present, together with many other members of the family. The Foxes, it is worth recalling, were closely related to the Tucketts, and Francis Fox Tuckett, pioneer climber and Vice-President of the Alpine Club, was married to Alice, Harry's sister and herself a mountaineer.

The Donkin family, numbering five distinguished members of the Club elected between 1879 and 1936, was represented by Colonel T P T Donkin, Royal Marines.

The family of Johann Fischer was charmingly represented by two ladies, both now elderly, who gallantly came over from Switzerland especially for the occasion – Frau Doktor Riggenbach-Fischer, daughter of Johann's brother Andreas who took part in the relief expedition of 1889, and Mlle Dora Fischer, a cousin of Johann. These ladies very kindly brought with them a number of letters and manuscripts, formerly belonging to Johann and relating to the accident, which they wished to donate to the Club archives – a valuable addition for which we are most grateful.

After lunch a memorial service for the climbers was held in Wellington church, with an address by Mr J Kendall-Carpenter, headmaster of Wellington School and a former captain of the England Rugby fifteen. This was a fitting tribute to Harry Fox, himself a noted Rugby player in his day.

The exhibition comprised a notable collection of mountain memorabilia, including some remarkable sketch-books and paintings by Edna Fox and other members of the family, old and rare books and some of the famous photographs from the enormous camera of W F Donkin. Special mention must be given to two paintings – a portrait in pastel of Elisabeth Fox-Tuckett (F F Tuckett's sister) by Holman Hunt, and a dramatic picture by H G Willink of the guide Ulrich Almer holding single-handed the remainder of his party, under whom a cornice had collapsed, after having thrown himself backwards over the opposite side of the ridge. Eventually the rope froze into the ice firmly enough for Almer to release his hold, and the party was saved. An ice-axe of mammoth proportions with a beautifully polished shaft, belonging to a lady, Marion Fox, also commanded our respect and admiration for its owner.

We extend our warm thanks to the Fox family and to all contributors to this outstanding memorial of an important chapter of mountain history, and a most enjoyable occasion.

Edward Smyth

ALPINE CLUB SYMPOSIUM 1988:
ALPINE AND ARCTIC NORTH AMERICA

This important and regular event on the Club's calendar took place on 19 November 1988 and was held, as previously, at Plas y Brenin. The National Mountaineering Centre provided its usual friendly and informal atmosphere, although the large audience found acoustics and oxygen supply (especially after lunch-time refreshments!) to be somewhat deficient. The proceedings were efficiently chaired by our President George Band, and the speakers included Rob Collister, Simon Richardson, Roger Mear (all speaking on areas and topics in Alaska), Derek Fordham (Arctic Canada and Greenland), Robin Pearce (Cirque of Unclimbables), David Hopkins (Western Canada and Pacific NW USA), and Dr Simon Travis (cold injury specialist). The speakers gave enthusiastic accounts of their experiences which were all very well received. Particularly enjoyed were Simon Richardson's photographs of Mt Hunter's 'happy cowboy' pinnacles, Roger Mear's informative style, Simon Travis's horrifying pictures of frostbitten hands, and Robin Pearce's deadpan humour. Many salient questions came from the audience at the end of the day, and some felt that it might have been better to allow more time for questions after each contribution. The point was also made that general descriptions of climbing areas tended to convey more useful information than accounts of actual climbs.

The symposium happily coincided with an improvement in the strength of sterling against the US dollar; and, judging by the many conversations about routes, areas, peaks, etc during the dinner and social which followed, coming years should see more British parties visiting North America. My final task as organizer of the event is to thank everyone who contributed to the symposium, with special thanks to Sheila Harrison whose thoroughness made my job very straightforward.

Roger Payne

THE ALPINE CLUB LIBRARY

Use of the Library continues to increase steadily; there have been more visitors and a much greater number of postal or telephoned queries to be dealt with by Mrs Johnson. Following the part-time engagement of Mrs Anne Andrews to help with the Himalayan Index, and data contributions from a number of members, we look forward to opening it for use during 1989. This is expected to shorten the time needed for research, but will probably generate a further increase in enquiries.

Arrangements for the move from 74 South Audley Street in 1990 cast their shadows before them. Identification of unwanted duplicate books has mainly been carried out. There is also an accumulation of printed matter, photographs and slides, much of which has little relevance to mountains or mountaineering and which should be sold or otherwise disposed of; surplus items are being identified, with great care not to discard anything relevant to the rest of the collection. At the same time, plans are being drawn up for a 'working library', for use if and when the Club moves to temporary premises while a more permanent home is completed.

An important step towards the production of a new catalogue has been taken, in the machine reading of the existing printed 'Volume 1'. We are greatly indebted to Mike Esten for this. Further solid progress in the cataloguing of the 'tracts' has been made by Sonia Jacobs.

As usual, we owe a great debt to members who give freely of their time and energy to help with the Library. Peter Ledeboer adds numerous tasks to his job as Secretary. Jon Mellor, Honorary Treasurer, is kept very busy by the sales efforts of Bob Lawford, who continues to be the linchpin of the whole effort. Edward Smyth has been greatly helped in his work on the archives by Margaret Darvall – who better than Margaret to ensure that the Ladies' Alpine Club archives are in order? We are grateful to all of them, as well as to many other members who, by their covenants or gifts of books, give us financial and moral support.

Michael Westmacott

ERRATA

The following errors in *AJ93* have been noted:

pviii, lines 10 and 11. For 39 read 40; for 40 read 39.

p216. The temperatures in lines 10, 12 and 13 should be negative.

p227, first paragraph. The northernmost land in the world lies, not in Ellesmere Island, but in Peary Land in North Greenland, at latitude c83°40'N.

p228, line 17. For 'west' read 'east'.

p309, lines 16–17. The longest-surviving member of the 1924 Everest expedition was John Noel who died on 12 March 1989, aged 99.

Plate 1. The Sokha La is out of the picture, to the right. The rock buttress extreme right is part of Sosbun Brakh.

Plate 28. For 'Bodga' read 'Bogda'.

Plate 32. The picture should be turned through 90°, with the left-hand side at the bottom.
Plate 44. The height of Nyanang Ri is 7110m.
Plate 47. For 'exchange' read 'exchanges'.

The assignment of photos to articles is as follows (articles without photos are omitted):

	Page	Plates
The Golden Pillar. *A V Saunders*	1	2–7
Karakoram Lessons. *Roger Payne*	7	8–12, 41
Crossing the Kurdopin. *Philip Bartlett*	12	1, 13–15, 42
A Note on Kinnaur. *Harish Kapadia*	29	16, 17
Kharcha Kund North Ridge Expedition. *Robin Beadle*	35	18
Expedition Style–A Himalayan Perspective. *T Braham*	57	19
Xixabangma 1987. *Luke Hughes*	63	20–22, 24, 43
Sun, Snow and Science on Xixabangma. *Henry Osmaston*	71	23, 44–46
Amne Machin: A Closer Look. *John Town*	77	25–27
North Muztagh. *Michael Jardine*	84	47–50
Sojourn in Xinjiang. *Sandy Allan*	88	28–29
Over the Hill. *Edwin Drummond*	92	30
Pieniny. *J W Gajewski*	99	31–35
Damp Days on the Lalidererspitze. *Geoff Hornby*	102	36
The Romansch Way. *Walter Lorch*	105	37–40
Home from the Eiger. *Luke Hughes*	110	53
Mont Blanc. *John Hunt*	123	54–57
A First Look at the Dauphiné Alps. *Marian Elmes*	129	58, 59
The Picos de Europa. *J G R Harding*	137	60
The Gran Sasso d'Italia. *Johanna Merz*	146	61, 62
Sudan Saga. *Tony Howard*	152	63–66
A Pilgrim in the Atlas. *Kev Reynolds*	155	67
Northern Iceland. *G S Hamilton & H E Martin*	165	68
Wind Rivers. *Malcolm Sales*	168	52, 69–71
Alpine Club Peru Meet. *Robert Sneyd*	181	72–75
One Hundred Years Ago. *C A Russell*	207	76–79
Area Notes		
Jordan 1987. *Tony Howard*	222	80, 81
East Africa 1987. *Andrew Wielochowski*	224	51, 82, 83
Canadian Arctic 1987. *Ted Whalley*	227	84, 85
India 1987. *Harish Kapadia*	248	86–89
New Zealand 1987. *Bill King*	261	90
In Memoriam.	305	91–93

ACKNOWLEDGEMENTS

Again I owe thanks to many. My gratitude is undiminished to all those I listed last year, on whom I have again depended so heavily for help and advice. In addition, I thank Marian Elmes, who has undertaken the important task of compiling the annual index. The Club is much indebted to John Murray and his helpers in a major project: the compilation of a new Cumulative Index, covering the years 1969–1987. For practical reasons the journal's annual index cannot be as detailed as one might wish, and it is the Cumulative Index which constitutes the real work of reference to which the researcher into mountain history must turn.

Last year I could only hint at the changes under way in the arrangements for the production and distribution of the *Alpine Journal*. Under a new agreement with Century Hutchinson the journal is now published under their imprint Frederick Muller, in association with the Alpine Club. As a result the print-run has been doubled, the journal will be marketed by Century Hutchinson world-wide (though Cordee will deal with the mountaineering trade and members' requests), and the Club has benefited financially. I thank Alan Blackshaw, Richard Coatsworth and Steve Town, who patiently (in the midst of other Club preoccupations) negotiated the agreement and whose support and advice have been invaluable; and I must not forget our member and literary agent, Andrew Nurnberg. A warm word of valedictory thanks is due to Swindon Press who were our printers from 1981 to 1987 and who by general consent did an excellent job.

I also thank our new publishers, especially Paul Sidey and Rowena Webb, for taking on a project new to them and for their friendly interest, zeal and helpfulness. They will agree that *AJ1988/89* came into the world not without a few birth-pangs. But the journal in its handsome new style and format has been received by our members with feelings in which pleasure has preponderated over annoyance – and always with considerable interest. Let us hope that our journal will continue to thrive, profiting (as C A Russell reminded us last year) 'by the occasional use of stimulants in the form of adverse criticism'.

Ernst Sondheimer

Contributors

CHRIS BONINGTON, Britain's best-known mountaineer, crowned his distinguished career in 1985 by reaching the summit of Everest at the age of 50. His latest volume of autobiography was published in 1986. He continues climbing and writing at undiminished pace.

BILL BROOKER has been climbing in Scotland for over 40 years and made many new ascents in the 1950s. He is a former president of the Scottish Mountaineering Club and was editor of its *Journal* from 1976 to 1986.

HAMISH BROWN is a travel writer based in Scotland, when not wandering worldwide or making extended visits to Morocco. Recent books include *Climbing the Corbetts*, *Hamish Brown's Scotland* and *The Great Walking Adventure*, and the anthology *Speak to the Hills*.

BARRIE CHEETHAM is a British chartered engineer who lives in Cape Town. He has climbed extensively in Africa, and also in Britain and the European Alps. He is to be found most weekends climbing on the crags of Table Mountain.

JULIE-ANNE CLYMA grew up in New Zealand, but now lives in Great Britain. She has climbed in the Alps of New Zealand and Europe, and has led and participated in four expeditions to the Greater Ranges.

GEOFF COHEN lives in Scotland and lectures at Edinburgh University. He has been climbing for over 25 years and has made many trips to the Himalaya and Karakoram. He has a penchant for unvisited areas and long climbs.

KEN CROCKET is editor of the *Scottish Mountaineering Club Journal*. He has made over 60 first ascents in Scotland, and has climbed in the Alps and North America. His books include *Ben Nevis – Britain's Highest Mountain*, 1986.

EVELIO ECHEVARRÍA was born in Santiago, Chile, and teaches Hispanic Literature at Colorado State University. He has climbed in North and South America, and has contributed numerous articles to Andean, North American and European journals.

ROGER EVERETT is a molecular biologist at the Medical Research Council Virology Unit in Glasgow. He is hopelessly addicted to climbing objects of snow, rock, ice or concrete, ranging from the Glasgow climbing wall to medium-sized Himalayan peaks.

ANDY FANSHAWE is 26 years old and lives close to the Peak District, though you would not guess it if you watched him climb gritstone. In 1984 he climbed El Obispo West Ridge (Ecuador) and in 1986 he traversed Chogolisa.

PETER FLEMING, formerly a marine engineer, is now a businessman in the electrical trade. He has travelled widely in the Far East, has twice been to the Himalaya, and has climbed extensively throughout the Alps over a 30-year period.

NIGEL GATES is senior lecturer in geography at Hatfield Polytechnic and Lieutenant Commander in the Royal Naval Reserve. He enjoys mountaineering and skiing and visits the Alps frequently. He has climbed in other ranges and is now considering visiting Aconcagua.

STEPHEN GOODWIN is the parliamentary correspondent of *The Independent*. Over the last decade or so he has climbed somewhat eclectically throughout the Alps and has taken part in several long ski tours, including a descent of Mont Blanc.

LINDSAY GRIFFIN, after early climbing in the Alps, nowadays specializes in 'exploratory mountaineering'. His trips are lightweight, alpine-style, and he has made many first ascents and quite a number of solo ascents and excursions.

JOHN HARDING is a solicitor, but was formerly in the Colonial Service in South Arabia. He has climbed extensively in Europe, Asia, Africa and Australasia.

RUPERT HOARE works for the London & Scottish Marine Oil Company as a geophysicist and devotes nearly all his holidays to mountaineering or ski-touring. He is president of the London Mountaineering Club.

TONY HOWARD, a founding partner of Troll Safety Equipment, took part in the first ascent of the Troll Wall in 1965. His expeditions include Greenland, North Canada and desert mountains in Morocco, Algeria, the Sudan, Iran and Jordan.

LUKE HUGHES is a furniture designer. He has climbed many new routes on Old Wardour Castle, Eric Shipton's climbing nursery, and has also climbed in the grown-up playgrounds of Europe, America and the Himalaya.

HARISH KAPADIA is a cloth merchant by profession. He has climbed and trekked in the Himalaya since 1960, with ascents up to 6800m. He is at present honorary assistant editor of the *Himalayan Journal*, and compiler of the *HC Newsletter*.

JOHANNA MERZ is a photographer specializing in audio-visual presentations. She has climbed in the Pennine Alps, the Mont Blanc Chain, the Brenta Dolomites, Bernina, Ortler, Dauphiné and Apennines.

PAUL MOORES works as a professional mountain guide, lecturer and climbing consultant. His Himalayan expeditions include Annapurna II, Nanga Parbat, Lhotse, Lhotse Shar and Everest. He has been on numerous expeditions to Africa, Alaska, Mexico and the European Alps.

JOHN NIXON is a geography teacher in a comprehensive school in County Durham. He has climbed in the Alps and has led expeditions to the Himalaya, Karakoram, Peru and Central Africa.

LLOYD NORTHCOTT lives in Revelstoke, British Columbia. A former infantry officer, he is now the Anglican priest of a parish which includes Mount Bonney. He and his wife Grace enjoy the freedom of the hills all the year round.

PAUL NUNN PhD is principal lecturer in economic history at Sheffield City Polytechnic. His numerous climbs include first ascents of the British Route on Pik Shchurovsky and the SW Pillar of Asgard. He has been on nine Himalayan expeditions.

SIR EDWARD PECK was in the Diplomatic Service until 1975, when he retired to Tomintoul. He has climbed in the Alps, Turkey, Kulu, Borneo and East Africa. His object when serving abroad was generally to reach the highest point available.

SIMON RICHARDSON is a petroleum engineer. He has derived greatest pleasure from climbs where the outcome has been uncertain, such as a new route on Taulliraju in Peru and a storm-ridden ascent of the E face of the Grandes Jorasses.

C A RUSSELL, who works with a City bank, devotes much of his spare time to mountaineering and related activities. He has climbed in many regions of the Alps, in the Pyrenees and in East Africa.

DOUG SCOTT is one of the world's leading high-altitude and big-wall climbers, who has pioneered new routes on many of the world's most difficult mountains. He is firmly committed to the concept of lightweight, alpine-style expeditions.

KARL SMITH has climbed in Britain, the Alps, Yosemite, Canada, Norway, Spain and has trekked in several other countries. A trekking leader by profession, he lives near the Lake District.

EDWARD SMYTH is a retired orthopaedic surgeon. He was elected to the Alpine Club mainly on the strength of some climbs in the Canadian Rockies. He is the Club's honorary archivist.

JOHN TEMPLE is a Yorkshireman, scarred externally and internally from youthful struggles with gritstone. Later, brief periods of serious climbing punctuated longer family-focused intermezzos. He has been rusting since rustication to Kent, but skis a little as a displacement activity.

DUNCAN TUNSTALL, 26, is an executive with Shell International. He has been climbing for five years and is hoping to emulate George Band and Mike Westmacott in combining his mountaineering interests with a business career.

ANN VENABLES admits to a lifelong love of alliteration, a persistent yearning for adventurous pursuits at times rather beyond her capacity, and a firm belief that life begins at 50. The untried 60s should offer endless possibilities; any ideas?

STEPHEN VENABLES, besides enjoying several careers, all poorly paid, since leaving Oxford in 1975, has continued to ski and climb in the Alps, Andes and Africa, and has made 10 expeditions to the Himalaya, written two books and climbed Everest.

DAVE WALSH is an international mountain guide and chief instructor at Plas y Brenin. He has climbed extensively in the Alps since 1963, and his climbs in other ranges include first ascents in the Karakoram, Kashmir and Norway.

ERIC WARBURG spent 32 years in a subsidiary of British Airways and has travelled extensively. He has ski'd and ski-toured all his life in the Alps and has trekked in the Himalaya, including the Garhwal, Kulu, Nepal and the Karakoram.

MICHAEL WARD is a consultant surgeon who has combined exploration on Everest, the Bhutan Himal, Kun Lun and Tibet with high-altitude research – the mountaineer, *nolens volens*, being a model for sea-level patients with chronic heart and lung disease.

CHARLES WARREN is a consultant children's physician (retired). As a member of Marco Pallis's Gangotri expedition 1933, and of the Everest expeditions 1935–36–38, he made several first ascents, and he has climbed on Mt Kenya, Kilimanjaro and Table Mountain.

JOHN WEST is professor at the University of California. He took part in the 1960–61 Himalayan Scientific and Mountaineering Expedition, and he led the 1981 American Medical Research Expedition to Everest which obtained the first physiological measurements on the summit.

TED WHALLEY is a research chemist who works for the National Research Council of Canada. His extensive climbing experience includes many first ascents on Baffin Island and Ellesmere Island. He was president of the ACC, 1980–84.

ANDY WINGFIELD is a civil engineer. He has climbed in the Alps, Peru and the Karakoram, and is currently developing lightweight parapentes for mountain use.

GUIDANCE FOR CONTRIBUTORS

The *Alpine Journal* has been published regularly since 1863 as 'A Record of Mountain Adventure and Scientific Observation'. The *Journal* has always been a record of all aspects of mountains and mountaineering and, although its main function is to record mountain adventure, articles on mountain art, literature, anthropology, geology, medicine, equipment etc are all suitable. Articles should be informative, and a good literary style is important. Scientific or medical papers should be of the general style and technical level of *Scientific American*.

Articles   Articles for the *Journal* should normally not exceed 3000 words (longer articles can be considered in exceptional cases. Please indicate the number of words when submitting your article). Papers should normally be written in English. Translation is usually possible from French, German and Italian, but papers requiring translation should be submitted at least three months before the editorial deadline.

Articles submitted to the *Journal* should not have been published in substantially the same form by any other publication. Authors are not paid for articles published in the *Journal*, but they do receive a copy of the issue in which their article appears. Please send articles direct to the Editor at 51 Cholmeley Crescent, London N6 5EX.

Typescript   The complete typescript including the text of the paper, list of references and captions to illustrations should be typed on one side of A4 paper, at *double spacing* and with 20–30mm margins. Authors should keep a spare copy. Authors are asked, as far as possible, to adopt the *Journal*'s house style for proper names, abbreviations, mountain features, etc (for which recent copies of the *Journal* should be consulted). The Editor will advise if necessary, and he reserves the right to edit or shorten articles at his discretion.

Illustrations   The number of colour photographs which can be printed is very limited and only top-quality photographs will be accepted. Prints should preferably be black-and-white, between 150 × 200mm and 220 × 300mm in size, and printed on glossy paper. Colour transparencies should be at least 35mm format and should be originals (not copies). A portfolio of up to 10 photographs should be provided. Maps and line drawings should be of a similar size to the prints and be finished ready for printing. Place-names appearing in the text, where relevant, should be marked on the maps also.

Each photograph should be clearly labelled with title, author and any copyright. This information should be typed on a separate sheet of paper attached to the photograph and not written on the back of the photograph itself. Routes of climbs should be marked on separate sheets of transparent paper.

Always take special care in sending prints through the post. Do include adequate stiffening to prevent folding and clearly label the cover: 'Photographs: Please Do Not Bend'. Do not include paper-clips or pins which could damage prints.

References   Many articles do not require references. If other publications are referred to in the text, details should be given in a separate list at the end of the article (not as footnotes), and should be set out as in the following examples:

BOOKS   3 G B Schaller, *Mountain Monarchs*. Univ. Chicago Press, 1977, pp15–25 or: London (W S Orr), 1932.

JOURNAL ARTICLES   2 B C Osborne, 'Ladakh'. *Oryx17*, 182–189, 1983.
For *AJ* references, give volume number, first and last page of article, year: *AJ90*, 201–207, 1985.

Units   Metric (SI) units should be used throughout except when quoting original material which uses other units.

Biographies   For the 'Contributors' section of the *Journal* authors are asked to provide a 'potted biography', in not more than 40 words, and without using abbreviated style, listing what they consider to be the most noteworthy items in their career.

Deadline   Copy must be with the Editor by 1 January of the year of publication. Space in the *Journal* is strictly limited, and early submission improves the chances of acceptance. Articles for which there is no space may be considered for publication in a subsequent year.

Index